ENDLESS WAR

ENDLESS WAR

Fiction & Essays
by Wang Wen-hsing

Shu-ning Sciban and Fred Edwards

EDITORS

East Asia Program
Cornell University
Ithaca, New York 14853

The Cornell East Asia Series is published by the Cornell University East Asia Program (distinct from Cornell University Press). We publish reasonably priced books on a variety of scholarly topics relating to East Asia as a service to the academic community and the general public. Standing orders, which provide for automatic billing and shipping of each title in the series upon publication, are accepted.

If after review by internal and external readers a manuscript is accepted for publication, it is published on the basis of camera-ready copy provided by the volume author. Each author is thus responsible for any necessary copy editing and for manuscript formatting. Address submission inquiries to CEAS Editorial Board, East Asia Program, Cornell University, Ithaca, New York 14853-7601.

Calligraphy of title highlighted on cover by Ms. Li-yun Hsu; all other calligraphy by Mr. Wang Wen-hsing.

Number 158 in the Cornell East Asia Series.
© 2011 by Shu-ning Sciban and Fred Edwards. All rights reserved.
ISSN 1050-2955
ISBN 978-1-933947-28-0 hc
ISBN 978-1-933947-58-7 pb
Library of Congress Control Number: 2011921844

25 24 23 22 21 20 19 18 17 16 15 14 13 12 11   9 8 7 6 5 4 3 2 1

This book is dedicated to my professor,

Dr. Milena Doleželová-Verlingerová

for her fine teaching and inspiration to my study of Wang Wen-hsing's writing,

and to my parents,

Mr. and Mrs. Kuang-yean and Lin Horng Huang

for their love and never-fail support.

Shu-ning Sciban

Contents

❖

PART I SHORT FICTION *continued*

PART II NOVELLA and PLAY

PART III ESSAYS

Author's Preface

❖

This collection includes my earliest story, "The Lingering Night," a piece I wrote when I was eighteen, fifty-two years ago. During all of those fifty-two years, everything I have written has been directed toward specific goals that I established for myself at the time of writing each particular work. Throughout those fifty-two years, I rarely paid much attention to the differences between Chinese and Western art and literature. Recently, though, I have been giving this question more thought. I don't know how these reflections will influence my future writing but this is the question that preoccupies me now.

I feel deeply that the uniqueness of Chinese art and literature is represented by poetry—especially the *ci* poems of the Song dynasty[1]— and calligraphy—especially seal inscription. To Western scholars, both poetry and calligraphy are wrapped in mystery. Take the example of Song dynasty *ci*. It could be argued that the content of thousands of *ci* poems consists of nothing more than "the sorrow of separation." Yet in the *ci* genre this is developed and amplified to become truly soul-shaking: it represents "the void." Calligraphy, especially in inscription, can be impossible to decipher—not only the object being represented but even the words themselves. This represents calligraphy's "abstract" quality, and I once referred to it as a

---

1. According to Kang-I Sun Chang, *ci* (or *tz'u*) is defined as "lyrics" or "song-words," a poetic genre that emerged during the Tang dynasty (618–907) and reached its height during the Song dynasty (960–1297).

"departure from the real world." I have seen an even better description: "transcending the real world." From the "void" of Song *ci* to the "transcendence" of seal inscription, we can see that the dominant characteristic of Chinese art and literature has been to "extract spirit from body." Those four words are as far as my speculations have taken me. Perhaps this concept represents the main difference between Chinese and Western art and literature. Perhaps I will have to continue my search until I can find a more satisfying answer.

I hope, eventually, to find it. Then I would be able to solve the mystery of Chinese art and literature.

Wang Wen-hsing
Translated by Shu-ning Sciban

Editors' Preface

Wang Wen-hsing is one of Taiwan most celebrated writers. *Endless War: Fiction and Essays by Wang Wen-hsing* consists of translations of all his fictional works, with the exception of his two novels, plus five essays that illuminate Wang's ideas about creative writing. The translations are arranged chronologically, according to their date of publication. Among the twenty-nine translations, twenty-three are being published for the first time. Wang Wen-hsing has also written an Author's Preface for this anthology, revealing his thoughts on Chinese and Western art and literature, which reflect indirectly the principles he has employed in his writing. In addition, the anthology provides a brief chronology of the author and a bibliography of his publications. The editor's goals are to introduce Wang's short literary writings to Western readers, while also shedding light on the development of his writing, since most of these works were written before the publication of *Jia bian* (Family catastrophe), Wang's first novel and the work that is widely regarded as his masterpiece.

In terms of Romanization, this anthology generally uses the pinyin system to transliterate proper names. The few exceptions include the city of Taipei and the names of writers and scholars who do not use pinyin to transliterate their own names; they are Wang Wen-hsing, Ch'en Chu-yun, Wai-lim Yip, Ouyang Tzu, Pai Hsien-yung, and T.A. Hsia.

Acknowledgments

❖

The translation project of *Endless War: Fiction and Essays by Wang Wen-hsing* began several years ago. We wish to express our deepest gratitude, first of all, to Professor Wang Wen-hsing for his unfailing support, from granting copyright permission to translate these works, to providing all kinds of essential information, to even finding the text of "Jieshu" (Conclusion) and the long-lost story "Shou ye" (The lingering night). We are similarly grateful to Professor Ch'en Chu-yun (Mrs. Wang Wen-hsing), who not only contributed several translations to this project but has always given us her warm-hearted support and encouragement. It has been our privilege and honor to be able to work with Professors Wang and Ch'en on this project.

On the eve of publishing this anthology, our thoughts are also with the translators who worked so diligently to translate Wang's challenging prose and who have provided their moral support to the editors to this day. We have learned a great deal about professionalism from these dear colleagues and feel thankful to all of them from the bottom of our hearts.

We would like to express our special appreciation to the Taipei Chinese Center, International P.E.N. and the National Institute of Compilation and Translation in Taiwan for their support in granting us permission to reprint six translations that they had published previously. In addition, Dr. Joseph Lau (Liu Shaoming) also kindly gave us special assistance in obtaining permission to reprint "Flaw" (the translation of "Qianque"). We are sincerely grateful to him.

Many colleagues and friends assisted us in one way or another. We would like to thank Ms. Furong Hsieh of the Cheng Yu Tung East Asian Library at the University of Toronto, who provided valuable reference material. We also want to thank Anita Lin, Emily Wen and Roma Ilnyckyj for their assistance in compiling the bibliography of Wang Wen-hsing's publications.

We want to thank the Faculty of Humanities at the University of Calgary for providing grants to cover data collection and travel expenses. Mai Shaikhanuar-Cota, the Managing Editor of the Cornell East Asia Series, provided all sorts of support and advice on editing the manuscript. Mr. Xianming Zhao of the University of Calgary assisted us with computer technical support in our preparation of the final manuscript.

Finally, we want to thank our families for their love, and for their support for this project over several years. In preparing the final version of the manuscript, Lloyd Sciban (Shu-ning's husband) helped with bibliographical formatting; Donna Maloney (Fred's wife) read the manuscript and made valuable suggestions for improvement. Shu-ning's father planned to contribute his calligraphy to the publication, but was prevented by illness. His love is deeply appreciated.

Introduction
Wang Wen-hsing's Life and Narrative Art

❖

"If there ever comes a day when modern Chinese literature and art reach their ultimate success, it must be the time when the Eastern and Western cultures can merge harmoniously in the work."

—Yu Guangzhong[1]

In 1999, two lists of the best Chinese literary works of the twentieth century were published. One, organized by *Lianhe bao* (United daily) in Taipei, chose the best thirty literary works published in the second half of the twentieth century in Taiwan. The other, organized by *Yazhou zhoukan* (Chinese newsweekly) in Hong Kong, selected the best one hundred fictional works by writers from China, Taiwan and Hong Kong. Wang Wen-hsing's first novel, *Jia bian* (Family catastrophe), appeared on both lists. Among the Taiwan

---

1. This line is from Yu Guangzhong's "Ying Zhongguo de wenyifuxing—xingdao shuiqiong chu, zuokan yunqi shi" (Welcome to the Chinese renaissance—at the moment of reaching the end of the stream, and sitting down to watch the sun rise), published in 1961. I have quoted it from Ke Qingming's "Liushi niandai xiandai zhuyi wenxue?" (The 1960s modernist literature?), in *Sishi nianlai Zhongguo wenxue* (Chinese literature in the past forty years), eds. Zhang Baozin, Shao Yuming, Ya Xian (Taipei: Lianhe wenxue, 1994), 91.

intelligentsia, Wang has long been regarded as the conscience of literary aesthetics. His reputation rests on his devotion to an innovative literary language and writing style, demonstrated primarily in his two novels, *Family Catastrophe* and *Bei hai de ren* (*Backed against the sea*). His persistent application of this ideal has challenged standard aesthetic views about Chinese literary language and conventional reading strategies. He views writing much as he does painting, music or any other art form: while acknowledging the importance of content, he foregrounds the form. His fictional works, therefore, are not only pieces of creative writing but also creative artworks; each word and sign should be appreciated like a musical note in a song or a brush stroke in a painting. This ideal pushes him constantly to search out the precise method to describe a specific subject, and each new method he finds is added to the reservoir of Chinese rhetoric. In the overly eventful twentieth century, most Chinese writers focused on describing the blood and tears shed during the country's dark days. Wang, however, stands out brilliantly and uniquely among his contemporaries by his emphasis on "how to describe." In October 2009, Wang won Taiwan's National Award for Arts (literature category) in recognition of his contributions to contemporary Taiwan literature. Now in his seventies, he continues to wield an incisive pen while adhering to his strict code of literary aesthetics, which means that readers can continue to expect the unexpected from this unique writer.

WRITING AS A FAMILY TRADITION

Wang Wen-hsing was born in 1939 in Fuzhou, the capital of Fujian province in mainland China, to a literary family. His grandfather, Wang Shouchang (1864–1926), introduced the Alexandre Dumas novel *La Dame aux camellias* to his friend Lin Shu (1852–1924) and co-translated it with him. This marked the beginning of Lin Shu's busy career as a translator. Wang's uncle, Wang Qingji (1882–1941), also translated French literary works with Lin Shu, while Wang's two aunts, Wang Zhen (1904–1971) and Wang Xian (1906–2000), were published poets. Wang's father, Wang Qingding (1900–1982), was no exception in this literary family; he was adept at traditional poetry, had a university degree in French literature and studied in Belgium.[2] Wang Wen-hsing regarded writing as a family tradition and he never considered any other career.[3]

YOUTH

Wang Wen-hsing spent his childhood in the cities of Fuzhou and Xiamen before moving with his parents to Taiwan in 1946.[4] During the first year in Taiwan, they resided in Donggang but his father was transferred to Taipei the following year and the whole family moved with him to the capital city. After moving to Taipei, Wang was enrolled in the Taipei Mandarin Experimental Elementary School, a renowned public school with a fine Chinese language program. He went on to attend the junior high program at the middle school affiliated with National Taiwan Normal University. Upon graduation, he

2. For biographical information on Wang and his family background, see Huang Shu-ning (Shu-ning Sciban), "Xiandai jiaoxiang yue—Wang Wen-hsing fangtan" (Modern symphony—an interview with Wang Wen-hsing), *Lianhe bao* (United daily), April 28–May 1, 2000; Wang Wen-hsing and Ke Qingming, "Wang Wen-hsing dashi ji" (Record of major events in the life of Wang Wen-hsing), *Zhong wai wenxue* (Chung wai literary monthly) 30.6 (Nov. 2001): 396; Wang Wentong, "Wang Shouchang yu *Bali chahuanü yishi*" (Wang Shouchang and *La Dame aux camellias*), *Fujian wanbao* (Fujian evening edition), Oct. 20, 1999; Wang Yichun, "Wang Shouchang yu *Bali chahuanu yishi*" (Wang Shouchang and *La Dame aux camellias*), *Fujian ribao* (Fujian daily), March 26, 2002; Chen Songxi, "Lin Shu yu Wang Qingji" (Lin Shu and Wang Qingji), *Fujian wanbao* (Fujian evening edition), Dec. 21, 2004; Wang's letter to the author on Dec. 23, 2005.

3. Lin Xiuling, "Lin Xiuling zhuanfang Wang Wen-hsing: tan *Bei hai de ren* yu Nanfang'ao" (Lin Xiuling's interview with Wang Wen-hsing: On the relation between *Backed Against the Sea* and Nanfang'ao), *Zhong wai wenxue* (Chung wai literary monthly) 30.6 (Nov. 2001): 45. This is a special issue on Wang Wen-hsing, edited by Lin Xiuling.

4. Wang Wen-hsing and Ke Qingming, "Wang Wen-hsing's Record of Major Personal Events," 396.

was admitted to the senior high program without taking the entrance examination because of his excellent academic performance.

Wang's interest in art appeared early in his youth. In elementary school, he enjoyed music and was a member of the school choir.[5] From grade six to junior high, he had an opportunity to explore a broad range of art—modern and pre-modern, Chinese and Western—through the influence of a good friend. In high school, he buried himself in fiction, including May Fourth literature and English works, both in translation and the original English. Many of the books he read were hard to find in post-war Taiwan and were lent to him by teachers.[6] Wang was particularly close to three of them: Wu Xieman (?–1987), Jin Chengyi (1920?–1990?) and Guo Ren (1928–), who provided guidance in reading English literature, broader literary appreciation and creative writing. This was the environment in which Wang began to write.

THE RISE OF A WRITER

In 1957, Wang entered the Department of Foreign Languages and Literatures at National Taiwan University (NTU), the most prestigious humanities program in Taiwan. Wang, however, was more interested in the departmental library's rich collection than in the course offerings, so he devised his own study plan. Among the professors he encountered, there were two he particularly appreciated: Li Liewen, who taught him introductory French, and Jacob Korg, a visiting American scholar who provided special guidance in reading English poetry and the works of Franz Kafka and D.H. Lawrence.[7]

---

5. This was mentioned in Wang's letter, dated Nov. 30, 2009, to the author.

6. Wang's reading during his high school years is described in Xiaoqun'er's "Shu yu cheng de dieqi—ji Wang Wen-hsing" (The building of a book collection and a city—a portrait of Wang Wen-hsing), an article posted on January 25, 2007, at http://fsso227.pixnet.net/blog/post/3129142.

7. Wang Wen-hsing and Ke Qingming, "Wang Wen-hsing's Record of Major Personal Events," 397.

For Wang, the importance of his four years at NTU was more than just educational. Although he had started to write in high school, his first publication, "Shou ye" (The lingering night), appeared in 1958, during the second term of his first year at university. In addition, fifteen of the twenty-three short stories he has written were published during his university years. Wang has never been a prolific writer but this was his most prolific period. He had been writing fiction since high school so it was natural that he sought opportunities for publication, and he received encouragement from T.A. Hsia (1916–1965), a professor in the department, and like-minded students. Some of these classmates, such as Pai Hsien-yung, Ouyan Tzu, Chen Ruoxi, Wai-lim Yip, Liu Shaoming (also known as Joseph Lau), Congsu, Wang Zhenhe and Du Guoqing, became well-known writers themselves. They founded a literary society called "Nanbei she" (South and North Club), a name chosen to reflect the fact that its members were from all over China and Taiwan. Their talent was recognized by Hsia, who supported them by publishing their works in *Wenxue zazhi* (Literary review), a journal he founded in 1956. *Literary Review* played a significant role in contemporary Taiwanese literature in the second half of the 1950s, which generally was preoccupied with anti-Communist propaganda. Hsia's promotion of social realism encouraged non-propagandistic literature, and *Literary Review* nurtured many young talents, including Wang and his writer-classmates. During his first three years in university, Wang published five short stories in *Literary Review*, which got his writing career off to a strong start.

FOUNDING *MODERN LITERATURE*

Unfortunately, *Literary Review* was short-lived, and Hsia moved to the United States in March 1959. In June of that year, Wang and members of the South and North Club decided to found a student literary journal so they could continue to publish their writing. After overcoming financial difficulties, the journal was formally established in

March 1960 as *Xiandai wenxue* (Modern literature) and it survived until 1973. A reincarnation functioned between 1977 and 1984.[8] The appearance of *Modern Literature* has commonly been viewed as the inauguration of literary modernism in Taiwan.[9] Like *Literary Review*, it made a lasting contribution to the development of Taiwanese fiction. Not only did it introduce modern Western fiction through translation but, more significantly, it stimulated a spirit of experimentation.[10] This was apparent in the Western-inspired literary forms and techniques employed by many of its contributors. The legacy of this baptism into Western styles has been obvious in Taiwanese fiction ever since, including works by the best writers of *xiangtu wenxue* (nativist literature). Other editors remember Wang Wen-hsing as the brains of the editorial board during the journal's formative period.[11] He was influential in deciding what to print and helped set the journal's goals, making a significant contribution to the development of contemporary Taiwanese fiction in the process.

In the summer of 1961, Wang graduated from NTU and began his compulsory military service. As was the case with many young men from big cities in Taiwan, military life was eye-opening, par-

8. Historical accounts of the establishment of *Modern Literature* can be found in two articles: Pai Hsien-yung, *"Xiandai wenxue de huigu yu qianzhan"* (*Modern Literature* in the past and future), in *Xiandai wenxue xiaoshuo xuanji* (Selected fiction from *Modern Literature*) Vol. 1, ed. Ouyang Tzu (Taipei: Erya chubanshe, 1977), 5–18; and Ouyang Tzu, "Huiyi *Xiandai wenxue* chuangban dangnian" (Recalling the founding of *Modern Literature*), in *Xiandai wenxue xiaoshuo xuanji* (Selected fiction from *Modern Literature*) Vol. I, ed. Ouyang Tzu (Taipei: Erya chubanshe, 1977), 23–33.

9. Sung-sheng Chang gives a detailed description of the Taiwan modernist literary movement in her *Modernism and the Nativist Resistance* (Durham & London: Duke University Press, 1993).

10. Leo Ou-fan Lee, " 'Modernism' and 'Romanticism' in Taiwan Literature," in *Chinese Fiction from Taiwan: Critical Perspectives*, ed. Jeannette Faurot (Bloomington: Indiana University Press, 1980), 14–17; Lucy Chen (Chen Ruoxi), "Literary Formosa," in *Formosa Today*, ed. Mark Mancall (New York: Frederick A. Praeger, 1964), 135.

11. Pai Hsien-yung, *"Modern Literature* in the past and future," 7; Ouyang Tzu, "Recalling the founding of *Modern Literature,*" 28.

ticularly the opportunity to experience life in the remote areas where he was stationed. Some became settings for his stories, such as Zhuzikeng in Taizhong, the setting for "Caoyun di shengxia" (Midsummer on the prairie); and Nanfang'ao in Hualian, the setting for "Haibin shengmu jie" (The day of the sea-goddess) and *Backed Against the Sea.*[12]

In 1963, Wang received a scholarship and went to study creative writing at the University of Iowa in the United States. In 1965, after receiving his MFA and working for a short period at a Chinese restaurant in Washington, D.C., Wang decided to return to Taiwan because he considered it a better environment for his writing. That same year, he accepted a teaching position at his alma mater and resumed his editing duties at *Modern Literature*, which he continued until November 1968. Wang met his wife, Ch'en Chu-yun, at NTU during this period. They were married in the summer of 1969 in Los Angeles before going on to the State University of New York at Buffalo, where Wang was a research fellow for one year. Coming from a diplomat's family, Ch'en had grown up abroad and only returned to Taiwan in 1963. She is bilingual in English and Chinese and a scholar of English literature. She has given her full support to Wang's writing and has translated several of his stories. Wang and Ch'en both became professors of English literature at NTU and remained in their positions until retiring in January 2005.

DEVOTION TO THE NARRATIVE ART

In 1972, Wang published his first novel, *Family Catastrophe*, and became famous overnight. *Family Catastrophe*, a work of less than two

---

12. Lin Hsiuling has done extensive study on the connection of Nanfang'ao as the setting of Wang's *Backed Against the Sea* (Lin Xiuling, "Lin Xiuling zhuanfang Wang Wen-hsing: tan *Bei hai de ren* yu Nanfang'ao" [Lin Xiuling's interview with Wang Wen-hsing: a discussion on *Backed Against the Sea* and Nanfang'ao], *Zhong wai wenxue* (Chung wai literary monthly) 30.6 (Nov. 2001): 32–50; Lin Xiuling, "Nanfang'ao yu *Bei hai de ren* yu" [Nanfang'ao and *Backed Against the Sea*], *Zhong wai wenxue* (Chung wai literary monthly) 30.6 (Nov. 2001): 51–74.)

hundred pages that took seven years to complete, first appeared in
Zhong wai wenxue (Chung wai literary monthly) in serial form
from September 1972 to February 1973. The novel's plot describes
the downfall of a father-and-son relationship but the initial criticism focused on Wang's innovative language style as much as the
theme. As he explained in the preface to the 1978 edition, Wang felt
that the work's experimental nature made it an unlikely bestseller—
indeed, his original plan had been just to make a few mimeographed
copies to distribute among friends. In the first few years after publication, Taiwan scholars of Western literature such as Yan Yuanshu,
Zhang Hanliang and Li Youcheng praised Wang's experimental
style but readers among the general public found his language difficult. This divergence of opinion was evident at the *Family Catastrophe* Forum organized by *Chung Wai Literary Monthly* in 1973.[13]

Wang Wen-hsing published his second novel, *Backed Against
the Sea*, in two volumes, in 1981 and 1999, respectively. It consists of
the monologue of a social outcast uttered over the course of two
nights as he raves against his bad luck in all aspects of life. Despite
the mixed opinions that had greeted his first novel, Wang's second
was written in the same style, and its two volumes took him twenty-
four years to complete. During those years, Wang lived a simple,
quiet life, devoting himself completely to his writing, with the exception of teaching and taking care of his elderly parents. Wang is
known for his slow pace of writing. In order to find the most suit-
able words and symbols, he has evolved a unique method. According to his wife, he writes thirty characters a day, including punctuation, over the course of two hours. Why such a short time? Ch'en
Chu-yun explains:

> [W]riting for him has always been a most strenuous task, not only
> mentally, but physically as well. Not for him the quiet scribbling on
> paper or soundless tapping on a keyboard. He literally pounds out
> his words in the form of dashes on tiny scraps of used paper, using

13. Lin, Haiyin, et al. "*Jia bian* zuotanhui" (Family catastrophe forum), *Zhong
wai wenxue* (Chung wai literary monthly) 2.1 (1973): 164–77.

very short and worn-down pencil nubs in order to nail down *le mot juste*. These efforts are accompanied by grunts, growls and other vocal expressions. He is literally fighting a battle at such times. The exhausting physical labor involved makes any other form of exercise or workout unnecessary for him.[14]

Wang established the routine of writing for two hours a day while he was working on "Qianque" (Flaw), and the two-hour limit is understandable considering the physical exertion his method requires. He spent more than thirty years to write his first and second novels, both of which ended up being much shorter than he had originally planned. His original intention for *Backed Against the Sea* was to write four volumes but he finished it in two.[15] In recent years, he has given up his hobbies of listening to classical music and watching movies in order to create more time for writing, and has donated his music and movie collections to the library at NTU. His devotion to the narrative art has led others to compare him—with the utmost respect—to an ascetic.

If Wang has one regret during his long writing career, it would be his participation in the debate over *xiangtu wenxue* (nativist literature), which occurred from 1976 to 1979. The word "*xiangtu*" (native land) conveys a strong sense of national consciousness, and the term "*xiangtu wenxue*" first appeared in Taiwan in the 1930s

14. Ch'en Chu-yun, "A Quiet and Simple Life," a speech given at "Art of Chinese Narrative Language: An International Workshop on Wang Wen-hsing's Life and Works" (University of Calgary, Calgary, Canada, February 19–21, 2009). Shan Dexing (Shan Te-hsing) also describes the process of Wang's writing in his interview with him. See his "Chuilian wenzi de ren" (The wordsmith), in *Duihua yu jiaoliu* (Dialogues and interchanges) (Taipei: Miantian chubanshe, 2001), 46–47. This article was a reprint of his "Wang Wen-hsing tan Wang Wen-hsing" (Wang Wen-hsing on Wang Wen-hsing), *Lianhe wenxue* (Unitas) 3.8 (1987): 166–95.

15. Shan Dexing, "Ou kai tianyan qu hongchen—zai fang Wang Wenxing" (Heavenly glance at the mundane world—the second interview with Wang Wen-hsing). *Zhong wai wenxue* (Chung wai literary monthly) 28.12 (2000): 182–199. Reprinted in *Duihua yu jiaoliu* (Dialogues and interchanges) (Taipei: Miantian chubanshe, 2001), 80–104. The indirect quotation is at the beginning of the article, pages 85–86.

during the Japanese occupation. A rejection of literature written in Japanese and a protest against Japanese colonialism, *xiangtu wenxue* told stories in Taiwanese dialect about events and people on the island.[16] During the early seventies, Taiwan experienced several severe diplomatic defeats, including the Diaoyutai incident in 1970,[17] expulsion from United Nations in 1971, U.S. President Richard Nixon's visit to mainland China in 1972, and the establishment of formal diplomatic relations between Tokyo and Beijing in 1972. Public hostility arose against Japan and Western countries, especially the United States. Taiwan's politics, economy and culture were reevaluated and criticized because of their heavy dependence on or influence from foreign countries. In literary circles, *xiangtu wenxue* again became a trend, gradually supplanting the modernistic literature that had been popular in the sixties. One of the reasons for this, perhaps the most important one, was that its underlying ideology—the promotion of regionalism or nationalism—was compatible with the political climate.[18]

16. Ye Shitao, *Taiwan wenxue shigang* (An outline of Taiwanese literary history) (Gaoxiong: Wenxuejie zazhishe, 1987), 26.

17. A territorial dispute with Japan over the Diaoyu, or Senkaku, Islands in which the United States sided with Japan.

18. The word "*xiangtu*" means "native land" or "homeland," which can refer to the whole nation as well as a region. In the cultural context of Taiwan, it has been used to mean both "Taiwan" and "China" since 1930. Taiwanese during the Japanese occupation thought that writing in Chinese, not Japanese, was a way to express their patriotism and resistance to Japanese colonialism. The reason they chose to use Taiwanese dialect was that Taiwanese writers, who were influenced by the May Fourth literary movement during the twenties, agreed that they also should write in the vernacular. However, they were not familiar with Mandarin, the national standard language, and had to use the local dialect. In the seventies, "*xiangtu*" was used in the same way at the beginning but gradually developed into two exclusive interpretations. One followed the original meaning, including both "Taiwan" and "China"; the other meant only "Taiwan." The former usage is seen in Chen Yingzhen, the latter in Ye Shitao. Ye Shitao, "Taiwan xiangtu wenxueshi daolun" (Introduction to the history of Taiwan's *xiangtu wenxue*), *Xiangtu wenxue taolunji* (A collection of essays on *xiangtu wenxue*), ed. Yu Tiancong (Taipei: Yuanliu chubanshe and Changqiao chubanshe, 1978), 69–92; Xu Nancun (Chen Yingzhen), "*Xiangtu wenxue de mangdian*" (The blind spot of *xiangtu wenxue*), *Xiangtu wenxue taolunji* (A collection of essays

The debate over *xiangtu wenxue* began with some critics' concern over whether *xiangtu* should refer to Taiwan or China. Later, the central themes in *xiangtu* fiction, which revolved mainly around the plight of the poor, caused unease in other critics' minds. Some stories were suspected of being too closely related to "worker-peasant-soldier literature" and "proletarian literature," genres promoted by the Chinese Communist Party in mainland China. This suspicion irritated the promoters of *xiangtu* literature but also worried the party in power, the Guomindang. The government eventually intervened and put an end to the debate.

Some promoters of *xiangtu wenxue* also attacked writers who had been influenced by Western literature. Modernistic writers, with their interest in psychological fiction, were considered to be too detached from the land of Taiwan. This type of criticism was based on ideology, not artistic performance. In a speech delivered at Gengxin Wenjiao Yuan (Gengxin Art and Literature Institute) on January 1, 1978, Wang Wen-hsing openly objected to this line of criticism. His main point was that literature's function is aesthetic, not social. He criticized the formulaic theories of *xiangtu wenxue*, which rejected all works that depicted any aspect of life outside of the lower classes in Taiwan.[19] In the second half of the speech, Wang further commented on Taiwan's economic and cultural issues, concluding that, from a long-term point of view, Westernization could actually benefit the country.[20] His speech annoyed many people, including *xiangtu wenxue* supporters and nationalists among the general public.[21] The concept of "Westernization" has since become em-

on *xiangtu wenxue*), ed. Yu Tiancong (Taipei: Yuanliu chubanshe and Changqiao chubanshe, 1978), 93–99.

19. Wang Wen-hsing, "Xiangtu wenxue de gong yu guo " (The accomplishments and improprieties of *xiangtu wenxue*), *Xiangtu wenxue taolunji* (A collection of essays on *xiangtu wenxue*), ed. Yu Tiancong (Taipei: Yuanliu chubanshe and Changqiao chubanshe, 1978), 518–27. This article appeared first in *Xia chao* (Summer tide) 4.2 (1978): 64–74; this is a reprint.

20. Ibid., 529–41.

21. The reaction against Wang's criticism can be found in many writings; the following are just some of them: Hu Qiuyuan, "Lun Wang Wen-hsing de Nonsense

bedded in criticism of Wang and his work by local critics. In most cases, the term "Westernization" is cast in a negative light as critics lash out at "meaningless" and "decadent" modern Western literature and at ignorance of contemporary Chinese writing.[22] While many modernistic writers in Taiwan were criticized in this way, Wang Wen-hsing in particular was singled out for abuse. His Gengxin speech was the most important reason for this, but there were other contributing factors. His dissatisfaction with contemporary Chinese literature seemed to fit in with his wider support for Westernization. In two interviews in the 1970s before the debate flared, Wang said that most of his reading consisted of Western fiction because in form and technique it was superior to modern Chinese fiction.[23] He advised his fellow writers in Taiwan that the best way to improve their writing was to study Western thought

zhi sense" (On the sense of Wang Wen-hsing's nonsense), in *Xiangtu wenxue taolunji* (A collection of essays on *xiangtu wenxue*), ed. Yu Tiancong (Taipei: Yuanliu chubanshe and Changqiao chubanshe, 1978), 731–58; Li Qingrong, "Shi faxisihua, bushi xihua" (It is fascistization, not westernization), in *Xiangtu wenxue taolunji* (A collection of essays on *xiangtu wenxue*), ed. Yu Tiancong (Taipei: Yuanliu chubanshe and Changqiao chubanshe, 1978), 693–700; Hou Lichao, "Lianjing jituan sanbao yikan de wenxue budui" (The Lianjing group's literature army of three newspapers and one magazine), in *Xiangtu wenxue taolunji* (A collection of essays on *xiangtu wenxue*), ed. Yu Tiancong (Taipei: Yuanliu chubanshe and Changqiao chubanshe, 1978), 666–84.

22. Gao Tiansheng's and Lü Zhenghui's articles are the best examples. Gao Tiansheng, "Xiandai xiaoshuo de qitu—shilun Wang Wen-hsing de xiaoshuo" (The wrong path of modern fiction—discussion of Wang Wenxing's fiction), *Wenxue jie* (Literary circle) 1 (1982): 75–85; Lü Zhenghui, "Wang Wen-hsing de beiju—sheng cuole defang, haishi shou cuole jiaoyu" (Wang Wenxing's tragedy—was he born in the wrong place or educated in the wrong way?), in *Xiaoshuo yu shehui* (Fiction and society) (Taipei: Lianjing chubanshe, 1988), 19–35.

23. Li Ang, "Changpao xuanshou de guji—Wang Wen-hsing fangwen lu" (Loneliness of a long-distance runner—record of an interview with Wang Wen-hsing), *Zhong wai wenxue* (Chung wai literary monthly) 4.5 (1975): 39–40. Xia Zuli, "Mingyun de jixian—Wang Wen-hsing fangwen ji" (Line of Fate—an interview with Wang Wen-hsing). *Wobi de ren* (Holders of the pen) (Taipei: Chunwenxue chubanshe, 1976), 29–30.

and literary techniques.[24] His emphasis on Western literature gave the impression of a narrow mind, while his absolutist attitude was, if not offensive, then at least irritating to other Taiwanese writers. This was the first and also the last time that Wang participated in a political debate. Asked recently about his lack of involvement in political issues, he replied that while he counted music, art, cinema and politics among his interests, he could not afford to waste time on them.[25] He has committed himself completely to writing with only one exception—religion. In 1975, Wang told an interviewer that writing, as a form of creation, was one of the two meaningful aspects of his life, the other being reading.[26] In 1985, he converted to Catholicism after a long search for spiritual fulfillment. Now he places religion ahead of his artistic career, the impact of which is revealed in one of his more recent works, a one-act play (the only play he has written), titled "M he W" (M and W, 1988). Like *Backed Against the Sea*, "M and W" is a satiric comedy that mocks romantic love and materialism. Its central themes—illusion and reality, life and death—contain a strong religious flavor.

PERIODS OF DEVELOPMENT

Wang Wen-hsing's development as a writer can be divided into five periods: early influences, the search for a style, transition, maturity, and his return to classical Chinese literature. In the first period, from childhood to the publication of "Wanju shouqiang" (The toy revolver), family background, friendship, formal education and special guidance from teachers shaped his interest in and appreciation of art. The stories Wang published during this period reveal the

24. Wang Wen-hsing, "*Xin ke de shi xiang* xu" (Preface to *New Stone Statue*), *Xiandai wenxue* (Modern literature) 35 (1968): 218–19.

25. Wang's letter to the author on Nov. 30, 2009.

26. Li Ang, "The Loneliness of a Long-distance Runner," 33; Wang Wen-hsing, "Weihe xiezuo"(Why write?), in *Wang Wen-hsing de xinling shijie* (Wang Wen-hsing's spiritual world), ed. Kang Laixin (Taipei: Yage chubanshe, 1990), 48.

talent of a young writer and the fundamental themes of his writing. In the second period, from the publication of "Muqin" (Mother) to "Han liu" (Cold front), Wang became more aware of stylistic differences among writers and also more conscious of his own writing style. Dissatisfied with his own literary language, he looked for models in Western literature. After trying a number of different styles, he gradually evolved one consistent with his ideals. With renewed confidence, he wrote another three stories, "Qianque" (Flaw), "Hei yi" (The black gown) and "Longtian lou" (Dragon inn), his only novella, which served as preparation for novel writing. These three stories mark the transitional phase in his development. In the fourth period, he set himself free by using the style he had created, and wrote the two novels that established his reputation. During the fifth period, which continues to this day, Wang has displayed more and more admiration for classical Chinese literature, evident in the story "Mingyue ye" (Nights of the shining moon) and non-fiction works rich with classical Chinese language.

EARLY INFLUENCES (1939–1960)

During the first twenty-one years of his life, Wang took intellectual nourishment experiences from many sources without knowing which would have a decisive influence on the development of his writing. Growing up in wartime China, he recalls that his childhood was not enjoyable in the least. "I was not happy before entering school; I had neither toys nor playmates," he once said.[27] "It was like being imprisoned."[28] In an interview, however, Wang admitted that his solitary childhood was helpful in establishing his habit of meditation and was beneficial to his writing.[29] The benefit is imme-

---

27. Wang Wen-hsing, "Haishang huayuan" (Garden on the sea), in *Shu he ying* (Books and films) (Taipei: Lianhe wenxue chubanshe, 1988), 287.
28. Xia Zuli, "Line of Fate," 24.
29. Ibid.

diately apparent when the dominant theme of Wang's writing is examined; fourteen of the writer's twenty-three short stories and half of his first novel, *Family Catastrophe*, deal with child or adolescent psychology.

Wang once said that the goal of all of his work has been to convey a certain spiritual or mental state.[30] Take, for example, the seven stories Wang wrote at the beginning of his career. The very first one, "The Lingering Night," describes the thoughts and dreams of an amateur writer who tries unsuccessfully to write a story in the course of one night. His second, "Yitiao chuisi de gou" (A dying dog), depicts a student's observation of the cruel killing of a dog.[31] The protagonist's disturbed feelings and his sympathy for the dying animal are revealed through Wang's depiction of the indifference of the crowd that watches the dog die. "Yige gongwuyuande jiehun" (The marriage of a civil servant) is a farce about how a civil servant comes to marry a housemaid.[32] Told by a chatty woman in the neighborhood, this story is the first work in which Wang experimented with the use of monologue, a technique frequently seen in modern works of psychological realism. "Can ju" (Withered chrysanthemums) is about the fading love between a young professor and his wife.[33] The gradually cooling romantic relationship is subtly reflected through the professor's thoughts one chilly afternoon. His impatience, disinterest and even disapproval of whatever his wife is doing contrast sharply with his enthusiastic reaction to a visitor's comments about his relationship with his girlfriend. "Bi" (Paralysis) describes a university student's first experience at a dance party.[34]

30. Li Ang, "The Loneliness of a Long-Distance Runner," 35.

31. Wang Wen-hsing, "Yitiao chuiside gou" (A dying dog), *Wenxue zazhi* (Literary review) 4.6 (Aug. 1958): 58–60.

32. Wang Wen-hsing, "Yige gongwuyuande jiehun" (The marriage of a civil servant), *Wenxue zazhi* (Literary review) 5.6 (Feb. 1959): 41–51.

33. Wang Wen-hsing, "Can ju" (Withered chrysanthemums), *Wenxue zazhi* (Literary review) 6.2 (Apr. 1959): 56–67.

34. Tong Ma (Wang Wen-hsing), "Bi" (Paralysis), *Wenxue zazhi* (Literary review) 6.4 (Jun. 1959): 69–74. This is the only short story Wang has published under

All the excitement of young men dancing with women for the first time is described through the protagonist's eyes. "Xiawu" (Afternoon), an ambitious short story—considering the author was a nineteen-year-old university student at the time and unlikely to have had many experiences with small children—is a psychological portrait of a ten-year-old girl who has dropped out of school to work as a maid at a private home, where she entertains herself and the baby under her care.[35] In terms of attentiveness to detail, "Afternoon," the sixth short story Wang published, represents a remarkable advance in his ability to describe a character's mental state. In "Afternoon," Wang's unique technique of controlling the acoustic effects of language also appears. The rhythm of the story moves gradually from slow to fast, matching the changing mood of the little girl and reflecting Wang's sensitivity toward sound even at this early stage of his career.[36] "Wanju shouqiang" (The toy revolver) focuses on a conflict between two university students.[37] The action unfolds from a sensitive young man's point of view; the portrayal of the protagonist's feelings of embarrassment, frustration and anger marks a significant development in Wang's use of symbolism.

These first seven stories display the author's innate interest in psychology. Wang explores a wide range of characters—young and middle-aged, men and women, children and adults, single and mar-

a pen name, although it is possible he has published poetry under other names. Shan Dexing has quoted poet Dai Tian (a classmate and colleague of Wang Wen-hsing) as saying that Wang used Dai Tian's name to publish some poems in *Modern Literature*. Wang also confessed that he had used "Wu Liaozhai" as an earlier pen name. Shan Dexing (Shan Te-hsing), "Wang Wen-hsing tan Wang Wen-hsing" (Wang Wen-hsing talks about Wang Wen-hsing), *Lianhe wenxue* (United literature) 3.8 (Jun. 1987): 175.

35. Wang Wen-hsing, "Xiawu" (Afternoon), *Wenxue zazhi* (Literary review) 6.6 (Aug. 1959): 66–77.

36. Wai-lim Yip, "Wang Wen-hsing: Novelist as Lyric Sculptor" (keynote speech delivered at "Art of Chinese Narrative Language: An International Workshop on Wang Wen-hsing's Life and Works," University of Calgary, Calgary, Canada, February 19–21, 2009).

37. Wang Wen-hsing, "Wanju shouqiang" (The toy revolver), *Xiandai wenxue* (Modern literature) 1 (Mar. 1960): 55–71.

ried. Being the first few stories he wrote, these works could be the result of Wang experimenting with different techniques, although it is interesting to note that the narrative mode in all of them is subjective, a method that allows a writer to give his readers as close as possible a look into the inner world of the characters.

The use of the subjective narrative mode, a common technique in modernist Western fiction, would appear to stem from Wang's intimate acquaintance with Western literature. Yet his very first story, "The Lingering Night," a psychological tale that employs the subjective narrative mode, was written in grade twelve, predating his university years, which points toward sources other than Western literature.

In August 1993, Wang published "Huai Zhongyuan" (Zhongyuan: An appreciation),[38] a nostalgic recollection of an old friend who shaped Wang's interest in both Chinese and Western art. It begins: "If you asked me who had the greatest influence on my pursuit of literature, I would have to say it was Zhongyuan." "Zhongyuan," the pseudonym Wang created for Min Zongshu (1933?–2005?), was a close friend of Wang's for about four years, from grades six to ten, and later became a scholar of *ci* poetry (a genre that emerged during the Tang dynasty and was popular during the Song dynasty) and a professor of classical Chinese literature at Zhengzhi University.[39] In the essay, Wang says: "Zhongyuan had a very broad interest in literature and the arts. He liked Chinese poetry, Western fiction, Western painting, Chinese painting, inscriptions on metal and stone tablets, film and music. He tried his hand at classical poetry, fiction, Western-style painting, traditional Chinese painting and seal cutting. I, usually standing amazed in front of his desk, would listen as he talked with great excitement about these topics. Although I did not necessarily understand what he was saying, I be-

---

38. Wang Wen-hsing, "Huai Zhongyuan" (Zhongyuan: an appreciation), *Zhongguo shibao* (China times), August 22, 1993.

39. Wang Wen-hsing revealed the name of "Zhongyuan" during the author's interview with him on June 4, 1999 (Huang Shu-ning, "Modern symphony—an interview with Wang Wen-hsing").

lieve I was strongly influenced by him, especially in regards to reading."[40]

Like "The Lingering Night," "Zhongyuan: An Appreciation" is crucial to our understanding of the development of Wang's writing style. It describes his first contact with various forms of art, from the East and the West, classical and modern. Later in high school, these subjects were reintroduced to him by several teachers, particularly the three mentioned earlier, Wu Xieman, Jin Chengyi and Guo Ren. They were intellectuals who had moved to Taiwan along with the Nationalist government after 1949. In Taiwan, they started out teaching in high schools but pursued their academic interests and went on to become scholars of English literature, Chinese history and literature, and fine arts. It was Wang's good fortune to meet them during the formative period in his late teens. Like Min Zongshu, they introduced Wang to their personal interests in literature and art, unselfishly providing him with advanced knowledge in those fields and supporting his writing during his initial development as a writer.

THE SEARCH FOR A STYLE (1960–1963)

After studying Western literature at university and on his own for more than two years, Wang reflected on his writing and began to search for a personal writing style. Wang's 1987 essay "Wu xiuzhi de zhanzheng" (Endless war) describes this search:

> [W]hen I was about twenty, I suddenly discovered some problems had developed in the way I habitually expressed myself. First of all, my writing lacked originality. Second, it was just a jumble of words, without any steady rhythm. At that time, I was reading Flaubert, Maupassant and Tolstoy. In their language I could hear a really pleasant sound, low and gently flowing, just like a cello. I immediately vowed to abandon my original writing style because I felt that its immaturity and confusion were unforgivably shameful.

40. Wang Wen-hsing, "Huai Zhongyuan"; the translation is the author's.

When I was twenty-two, I read Hemingway. From then on, I became even more deeply engaged in the war over my writing. Since then, I have waged a bloody battle against my writing every day in a fight to the death. It's true: Hemingway was the one who dragged me into this war, who put me through hell and made me taste extreme bitterness, but it is a hardship I endure gladly. Hemingway sets such a shining example! He not only incorporates the same low, gentle flow of sounds as Flaubert, Maupassant and Tolstoy, but he goes one step further, concise to the point of vividness, full of the color and flavor of life. After reading him, in tribute I immediately set this as my goal in life.[41]

It was 1959, when Wang turned twenty, that stylistic innovation became noticeable in his work. After finishing "The Toy Revolver," he tried a new approach in "Mother," "Dadi zhi ge" (Song of the earth) and "Caoyuan di shengxia" (Midsummer on the prairie), which appeared between May 1960 and May 1961.[42] "Mother" is a story about a boy's sexual awakening. "Song of the Earth" describes a university student's frustration as well as his excitement while witnessing the intimate behavior of a pair of lovers in a quiet café. "Midsummer on the Prairie" depicts a group of soldiers on a one-day training exercise. These stories differ from his earlier efforts in their heavy use of symbolism and poetic syntax in the prose narrative. "Midsummer on the Prairie," for instance, can be read as a poem, with many paragraphs functioning like stanzas. The story also contains one of the first examples of Wang's use of an existing Chinese character to convey a new meaning. This is one of the most striking techniques in Wang's literary repertoire and is mistakenly believed to have first appeared in his first novel, *Family Catastrophe*. For instance, consider the use of "cao" 艸 (grass),

41. Wang Wen-hsing, "Wu xiuzhi de zhanzheng" (Endless war), *Wenxing* (Literary star) 103 (1987): 104–05; reprinted in Wang's *Books and Films*, 195–96.
42. Wang Wen-hsing, "Dadi zhi ge" (Song of the earth), *Xiandai wenxue* (Modern literature) 6 (Jan. 1961): 83–84; Wang Wen-hsing, "Caoyuan di shengxia" (Midsummer on the prairie), *Xiandai wenxue* (Modern literature) 8 (May 1961): 102–14.

which replaces the commonly used character "cao" 草 (grass) in the sentence: "但是，在鋼與火底下面，卻是那柔弱，艸綠色，如植物似底肉身" (but beneath that fire and steel there is only weak, grass-green, plant-like flesh). Wang uses the image of green blades of grass to represent the soldiers' bodies.[43] Through the innovative use of characters, Wang maximizes their visual and acoustic effects. This is an example of a visual effect, as 艸 looks more like blades of grass than 草. To this day, Wang still holds these stories dear. He says: "With my new understanding, I attempted a few stories, including 'Mother', 'Song of the Earth' and 'Midsummer on the Prairie.' Although I could see the direction I should be going, I realized that in these few stories I remained a vast distance from my goal. Each sentence still fell short of the desired effect."[44]

Wang wrote two other stories during this period: "Rili" (Calendar) and "Zui kuaile de shi" (The happiest thing).[45] In "Calendar," a boy suddenly realizes the span of a human lifetime is just a moment in the existence of the universe, while in "The Happiest Thing" a young man discovers there is no happiest thing, not even sex. Though these two stories employ standard language, the author's terse, direct and dramatic manner produces an extremely striking effect, comparable to the precision and power of poetry.

These five stories stand out as the gems of Wang's highly experimental early short works, which explains why he chose only these five to be published in a single volume in 1996.[46] Wai-lim Yip also sees this period as crucial in Wang's evolution as a writer, although he pushes its beginning back one year to August 1959 and the publication of "Afternoon," which he regards as a landmark in Wang's

43. Wang Wen-hsing, "Caoyuan di shengxia" (Midsummer on the prairie), in *Shiwu pian xiaoshuo* (Fifteen stories) (Taipei: Hongfan shudian, 1979), 38.

44. Wang Wen-hsing, "Endless War," 195.

45. Wang Wen-hsing, "Rili" (Calendar), *Xiandai wenxue* (Modern literature) 4 (Sept. 1960): 76–77; Wang Wen-hsing, "Zui kuaile de shi" (The happiest thing), *Xiandai wenxue* (Modern literature) 5 (Nov. 1960): 91.

46. Wang Wen-hsing, *Caoyuan de shengxia* (Midsummer on the prairie) (Taipei: Hongfan shudian, 1996).

development. Yip points to two fundamental narrative features: first, by quickening the rhythm of the language Wang establishes the central theme; and second, the meaning of the story is revealed through the main character's interior monologue.[47] Yip's first point is that by the time he wrote "Afternoon" Wang had learned how to express meaning through the structure of a story. His second point confirms what has been said above, that Wang's writing focuses on the psychology of the protagonist. While I agree with Yip's views about "Afternoon" and think "The Toy Revolver" also shows the same features, I feel the five stories, "Mother," "Calendar," "The Happiest Thing," "Song of the Earth" and "Midsummer on the Prairie," demonstrate a clear departure from Wang's previous style and a move away from conventional prose narrative toward a more poetic style. The change, which is confirmed by Wang's own words, was part of his deliberate search for a personal writing style. However, after these five stories, Wang worried that he had moved too far from the norm and would be rejected by readers, so he returned to his previous writing style, something he regretted many years later.[48]

After these five experimental stories, Wang went on to publish seven more short works: "Jieshu" (Conclusion), "Liang furen" (Two women), "Da feng" (Strong wind), "Jian yue" (Contract fulfilled), "The Day of the Sea-Goddess," "Mingyun de jixian" (Line of fate) and "Han liu" (Cold front).[49] In terms of language, "Strong Wind"

47. Wai-lim Yip, "Shuilü de nianling de mingxiang—lun Wang Wen-hsing 'Longtian lou' yiqian de zuopin" (Meditation at a young age—on Wang Wenxing's literary works before 'Dragon inn'), in *Zhongguo xiandai xiaoshuo de fengmao* (Style and features of Chinese modern fiction) (Taipei: Chenzhong chubanshe, 1970), 29–50. This article is reprinted in *Ye Weilian wenji* (Wai-lim Yip's collected essays), Vol. 1, (Hefei: Anhui jiaoyu chubanshe, 2002) and the quote is on page 248.

48. Wang Wen-hsing, "Xu" (Preface), in *Shiwu pian xiaoshuo* (Fifteen stories) (Taipei: Hongfan shudian, 1979), ii.

49. Wang Wen-hsing, "Jieshu" (Conclusion), in *Daxue shenghuo* (University life) (Hong Kong: Youlian chubanshe, 1961), 45–50; the other six stories were published in *Modern Literature* in the following issues and page numbers: 10 (Sept.

uses a pure colloquial style for the pedicab driver's monologue. The other six represent Wang's meditations on various problems in daily life. He shows particular interest in attempting to understand the workings of undefined cosmic forces upon humanity. "The Day of the Sea-Goddess," "Line of Fate" and "Cold Front" all reflect this concern. Wang has confessed that in his twenties he felt that humans stood helpless before their fate and wrote about this in many stories, including these three.[50] As for "Conclusion," it returns to university student life to describe a unique friendship; "Two Women" examines the theme of jealousy; "Contract Fulfilled" revisits the subject of sexual awakening and the appreciation of female beauty.

During this period of searching for a personal style, Wang also served as a member of the editorial board of *Modern Literature*, actively participating in the development of the journal by helping to set its goals. These were clearly expressed in the following three editor's messages to readers, all of which he wrote:

> In our last issue, we introduced Kafka and created a furor on the literary scene of Free China. Some readers wrote us in support; other readers complained that they didn't see Kafka's merits. Kafka's stature has long been confirmed. That our readers are not accustomed to him is due to their lack of exposure to modern Western literature. Accordingly, in this issue we have promoted Thomas Wolfe, an American author who will surely baffle even more readers. Moreover, we will from now on consistently bring out fiction written in brand-new styles. Whether you are stunned or want to curse us, we are determined to shock the literary world of Taiwan.[51]

The editors of *Modern Literature* share three common characteristics: (1) their "dissatisfaction with the declining state of contempo-

---

1961): 53–59; 11 (Nov. 1961): 66–72; 13 (Apr. 1962): 95–112; 16 (Mar. 1963): 22–35; 17 (Jun. 1963): 31–41; 17 (Jun. 1963): 64–80.

50. Shan Dexing, "Wang Wen-hsing Talks about Wang Wen-hsing," 176.

51. *Modern Literature* 2 (May 1960): 124. Translation by Leo Lee; see his "'Modernism' and 'Romanticism' in Taiwan Literature," 15.

rary art and literature" in Taiwan; (2) their desire "to assimilate modernism from Europe and America, while at the same time reassessing classical Chinese literature"; (3) their youthful age—"all between the ages of twenty and thirty."[52]

If someone were to say that this Chinese effort to experiment with modernism betrays a mentality of adulating foreign things, we would regard it as intolerable. Are Chinese not permitted to create new forms? . . . In the opinion of some people, Chinese cannot write psychological or symbolist fiction or novels of fantasy, nor should they experiment with surrealism or accept existentialism. These people are like fathers who forbid their children's activities— no ball-playing, no running, no singing, no riding bicycles, no listening to radios—all because of one reason: that they are foreign things. Dear reader, if you meet such a father, please give him some good advice.[53]

The goals of *Modern Literature* were to promote a spirit of artistic innovation in both form and theme and to introduce Taiwanese readers to modern Western literature. In the three passages quoted above, the objectives Wang set for contemporary Taiwanese writers can also be regarded as goals he set for himself.

Wang's opinion of the literary language employed by modern Chinese writers has been consistent ever since. In his preface to *Xin ke de shi xiang* (The new stone statue), a 1968 anthology of short stories that he edited, he criticized contemporary Taiwanese writers for being careless with language, exclaiming: "We do not know how we could have allowed our literary language to degenerate to the present state."[54] He labeled the language used by most contemporary writers as "colorless and flavorless" (wuse wuxiang wuwei).[55]

52. *Modern Literature* 7 (Mar. 1961): 4–5. Translation by Leo Lee; see his "'Modernism' and 'Romanticism' in Taiwan Literature," 15.

53. Ibid.,16.

54. Wang Wen-hsing, "Preface to *New Stone Statue*," 218.

55. Wang Wen-hsing, "Chuangzao wenyan, baihua, ouhua de lixiang wenti" (To create an ideal literary style by blending classical, vernacular and Europeanized Chinese), *Lianhe bao* (United daily), May 5, 1979: 12.

Wang's dissatisfaction was associated with his emphasis on individual creativity. He urged writers to develop language with a personal style and to study Western literary techniques.[56] According to Leo Lee, all of the four main editors of *Modern Literature*—Wang, Pai Hsien-yung, Chen Ruoxi and Ouyang Tzu—were inspired by modern Western fiction. As Wang's early short stories show, however, he was a particularly "conscientious . . . practitioner of style and form."[57] Indeed, in Wang's short stories, psychological portrayals and symbolist descriptions are frequently seen, while surrealism and existentialism can also be detected.[58] Western influence and his vigorous pursuit of style and form are the main reasons critics commonly regard him as the standard bearer of Taiwan modernism.[59]

TRANSITION PERIOD (1964–1966)

Wang began his vigorous search for an ideal language during the second half of his university career. In 1963, after finishing his two-year military service, he won a scholarship and entered the master's program in creative writing at the University of Iowa. Although he has made no public reference to what he learned in Iowa, by 1964 he finally felt confident about his writing. As he said in an interview with Shan Dexing (also known as Shan Te-hsing): "After the completion of 'Qianque' [Flaw, published in 1964], I no longer sent my

---

56. Ibid.

57. Leo Lee, "'Modernism' and 'Romanticism' in Taiwan Literature," 17.

58. Liu Shaoming (Joseph Lau) mentions existentialist color in some of Wang's stories; see his "Shi nian lai de Taiwan xiaoshuo (1965–1975)—jianlun Wang Wen-hsing de *Jia bian*" (Taiwanese fiction in the past decade [1965–1975]—also on Wang Wen-hsing's *Family Catastrophe*), in *Xiaoshuo yu xiju* (Fiction and drama) (Taipei: Hongfan shudian, 1977), 6–7.

59. Gao Tiansheng, "The Wrong Path of Modern Fiction," 110; Gu Jitang, *Taiwan xiaoshuo fazhan shi* (A history of Taiwanese fiction's development) (Taipei: Wenshizhe chubanshe, 1989), 333. Actually, most of the other Taiwan modernist writers, such as Pai Hsien-yung, Chen Ruoxi and Ouyang Tzu, have immigrated to the United States.

writing to others before publication, because I knew my strengths and weaknesses. I did not think other people's opinions were important anymore. I knew I had done my best in every single work. If I was not perfect, it was because it was beyond my ability. I could do nothing about it. I have been this way since 'Flaw.' "[60]

"Flaw" is a story that occupies a special position in Wang's career; it not only represents the maturing of his writing style, but also is one of his rare romantically sentimental stories (the French translation of the title is "Premier Amour"—"first love.")[61] It traces a teenager's first romantic attachment, subtly depicting his emotional rise and fall, while some passages describing the natural scenery are comparable to lyric poetry. Stylistic features common in his novels, such as the innovative use of characters, newly coined words and unusual syntax, can be found on many pages. For instance, "嫻嫻的" (lanlande), with the female radical on the left of the first two characters, replacing the more popular form "懶懶的," invokes the feminine aspect to describe the languid movement of a cat.[62] Unconventional syntax is evident in the underlined sentence below:

愛在一個早熟的孩子身上，髣髴一朵過重的花開在一枝太纖細的梗莖下，不勝其負荷。我纔體味到愛原來是一種燃燒，光亮的火光如果是愛的快樂，<u>造成這火光的卻是燃料牠自己的燒灼</u>。我實在不能相信這種用燒灼自己來換取快樂的自虐狀的倒錯是種快樂。

Love in a precocious child, like a heavy blossom atop a frail stem, is a burden too heavy to bear. Only then did I realize the consuming nature of love, <u>how the joyous blazing flames of love burn the very fuel that makes the flames possible</u>. I found it hard to believe that true happiness could be achieved by masochistically burning myself up.[63]

60. Shan Dexing, "Wang Wen-hsing Talks about Wang Wen-hsing," 170.
61. Camille Loivier, trans. "Premier amour," in *La Fête de la déesse Matsu* (Paris: Zulma, 1999), 5–25.
62. Wang Wen-hsing, "Qianque" (Flaw), in *Shiwu pian xiaoshuo* (Fifteen short stories) (Taipei: Hongfan shudian, 1981), 163.
63. Ibid., 165. English translation is by Ch'en Chu-yun, and the underlining is

This unique syntax foregrounds the pain of self-immolation, highlighting the torment that love has caused the young boy. Although this story can be read as an elegy for old Taipei before its modernization in the mid-1970s, it also represents the maturation of Wang's lyrical prose style.

After "Flaw," he wrote "The Black Gown," the darkest story in the author's oeuvre.[64] It depicts a dinner party where a five-year-old girl is confronted by a Mr. Jin, an attention-hungry intellectual. "The Black Gown" is a very different story than "Flaw" thematically, but it also demonstrates the mature Wang's ability to control the tone of his language—calm but forceful. Once again he employs rarely used forms of characters and creates new characters to convey special meanings, techniques he began in "Midsummer on the Prairie."

In these two stories we can sense the formation of the style he would use in his novels. However, the most important work of this transitional period was "Dragon Inn," written between May 1964 and November 1965.[65] "Dragon Inn" is a novella about several Guomindang officers, their dangerous journeys into exile from Shanxi province in mainland China to Taiwan, and their reunion there. Because of the historical background and the particular status of the protagonists, the language is permeated with colorful expressions in the style of popular (*tongsu*) novels, which is unusual in the work of this sophisticated writer. However, the most significant aspect of the novella is that Wang decided to return to the language style he used in "Midsummer on the Prairie" for a longer work in preparation for writing novels.[66]

In his article on *Family Catastrophe*, Zhang Hanliang states that Wang rejuvenated the Chinese language by fully exploiting the potential of Chinese characters.[67] This practice actually began with

the author's.

64. Wang Wen-hsing, "Hei yi" (The Black gown), *Xiandai wenxue* (Modern literature) 20 (Mar. 1964): 58–66.

65. Wang Wen-hsing, "Longtian lou" (Dragon inn), *Xiandai wenxue* (Modern Literature) 27 (Feb. 1966): 177–232.

66. Shan Dexing, "Wang Wen-hsing Talks about Wang Wen-hsing," 180.

67. Zhang Hanliang, "Qiantan *Jia bian* de wenzi" (A brief discussion of the

"Midsummer on the Prairie," not *Family Catastrophe*. Wang returned to this style in "Dragon Inn" with deep confidence. Wang's innovative use of Chinese characters aims to evoke or restore their visual and acoustic effects in order to enrich the semantics of the words he uses and to project a lively, picturesque description of his fictional world, regardless of current conventional usage. This is what he means by "writing freely."[68]

An example of Wang's bold and unconventional use of characters is "擭." This character has two pronunciations: when pronounced "hù," it means "to protect"; pronounced "shū," it means "to stretch out relaxingly."[69] It has a completely different meaning, though, in the following segment from the story:

我在受搥擊後，一個匪幹軍幹部走我跟前經過，忽然又返轉身來，瞪住我問："你是將官嗎？立正！"　然後刷的一聲，他擭下我的肩章，接着連出手幾下，擭下我的勳章，領章，青天白日帽徽。

"After I was beaten, a Communist army officer walked past me, quickly turned and asked, 'Are you an officer? Stand at attention!' I remember the ripping sound as first he pulled off my epaulets, then in quick succession he tore off the decorations on my chest, my collar insignia, and then grabbed my cap with its white sun badge."[70]

In the context of the text, the word means "to tear or grab something quickly and forcefully," which is not the definition given in dictionaries. Wang, though, makes a subtle arrangement that allows

language of *Family catastrophe*), *Zhong wai wenxue* (Chung wai literary monthly) 5.7 (Dec. 1976): 125.

68. Shan Te-hsing (Shan Dexing), "Wang Wen-hsing on Wang Wen-hsing," *Modern Chinese Literature* 1.1 (Sept. 1984): 61.

69. Xu Qingti, ed. *Ci yuan* (A comprehensive Chinese dictionary) (Taipei: Daxin shuju, 1978), 685.

70. Wang Wen-hsing, "Longtian lou" (Dragon inn), in *Shiwu pian xiaoshuo* (Fifteen stories) (Taipei: Hongfan shudian, 1979), 201. The translation is Steven L. Riep's. The underlining is the author's to indicate the neologism.

the newly invented meaning to be understood without a dictionary. This new meaning can be inferred from the visual appearance of the character. First of all, "摅" has the "hand" radical on the left, which signals it is related to something done with the hands. The component on the right consists of two parts; on the top is a sign for tiger, and on the bottom is a grammatical particle that in classical Chinese indicates a question or exclamation. Both of these components are pronounced "hū," suggesting the probable pronunciation of the word. In addition, the top component also contributes the image of a fierce tiger, while the bottom provides the sound the tiger would make when the beast uses its claws.

This interpretation comes not only from the character's form, but also arises from the context. We understand the word is meant to describe a violent action because it has been anticipated in the preceding words, such as "beaten," "enemy," "suddenly" and "staring," as well as in the tone of the officer's words. When we come to the character "摅" we can almost visualize the officer being transformed into an attacking tiger, waving his hands to tear off all the badges on the prisoner's uniform that irritate him. Because he moves so fast and forcefully, we also seem to hear the rush of air made by his hands. The way Wang Wen-hsing uses the character "摅" provides the reader with an almost cinematic description of this scene by presenting visual and acoustic effects simultaneously. These effects, in turn, provide a precise description of the action implied by the word. In other words, the semantics are revealed through these effects.

When "Dragon Inn" was completed, Wang was ready to write novels in his fully developed personal style, one of the most innovative literary styles in the whole of twentieth-century Chinese literature.

ACHIEVING MATURITY (1966–1999)

Using his new stylistic language, Wang began writing *Family Catastrophe* in 1966. He intended to achieve acoustic, visual and semantic effects by exploring all sources of twentieth-century Chinese, including classical and vernacular, spoken and written, foreign and native; his every single character, word, phrase, sentence, non-verbal sign, punctuation mark and layout arrangement is used with a specific consideration in mind. All elements on the pages of the novel are contextualized. This reminds us of his "Preface to *New Stone Statue*," where he explained his ideas about literary language, saying: "[w]ords control tone, atmosphere and viewpoint," and "[w]ords have to be like mathematical symbols, each one having its own function."[71] In comparing the functional principle of literary language with that of mathematical signs, Wang echoes Edgar Allan Poe's and Ezra Pound's advocacy of the poetic principle.[72] In our separate research work, Wai-lim Yip and I have found that Wang's works are like poetry; Yip calls Wang "a lyric sculptor" and I have described Wang's language as "poetic."[73] While Wang has never openly admitted that he has modeled poetry in his fiction, we are not surprised when we read his description of modern literature:

> What precisely is the unique quality of "modern literature" produced by this generation of ours? That is, what aesthetic experiment constitutes the "modern literature" of our generation? (Below, we'll simply call it "modern literature" and eliminate the overly burdensome "our generation.") I believe the most concise answer is this: prose written in the form of poetry and poetry written in the form of prose. ... There have always been certain preferences for one thing over another in lyric poetry: structure (such as repetition, neat divisions) is preferred over character development, the repetition of language (density, multiple images, syntactic innovation) is preferred over plot development. The poeticization of fiction has followed from the appropriation of these lyrical qualities.[74]

71. Wang Wen-hsing, "Preface to *New Stone Statue*," 218.

72. In "Wang Wen-hsing: Novelist as Lyric Sculptor," Wai-lim Yip calls Wang "a lyric sculptor" and compares Wang's writing to that of a modernist poet by quoting Poe's and Pound's description of the writing process of lyric poems.

73. Yip, ibid.; Shu-ning Sciban, "Wang Wenxing's Poetic Language" (Ph.D. diss., University of Toronto, 1995).

74. "Qian lun xiandai wenxue" (A brief discussion of modern literature), in *Lianfu san shi nian wenxue daxi: pinglun juan 3* (Literary supplement of United daily thirty years of literature series: criticism Vol. 3) (Taipei: Lianhe bao chubanshe, 1981).

Since the publication of *Family Catastrophe*, there have been numerous discussions about Wang's style. In addition to his language, the overall structure of the novel—which is inseparable from his language—raised eyebrows among readers. As Wang says in his description of modern art in "Xiandai zhuyi de zhiyi he yuanshi" (The challenge and primitiveness of modernism): "The new spirit of modern art naturally brought about a transformation in form as dissatisfaction with traditional forms gave rise to 'fragmentation,'" and he points out that breaking down the traditional sequence of time and space is a feature of modern literature.[75] *Family Catastrophe* is a manifesto of "fragmentation." The story has two timelines, one in the past and one in the present. The past is fragmented into 157 sections marked by Arabic numerals, while the present is divided into 14 sections designated by letters of the English alphabet from A to O. The two timelines are further interwoven so they merge into a coherent four-part structure typical of traditional Chinese literature, especially classical poetry. This structure allows the story to unfold in the sequence of *qi* (exposition), *cheng* (development of the theme), *zhuan* (transition) and *he* (conclusion).[76]

Wang's second novel, *Backed Against the Sea*, a satiric comedy—a genre of interest to Wang in the past two decades—is a critique of contemporary society delivered via the drunken protagonist's two monologues uttered over the course of two nights. The writing style is the same as in Wang's first novel. In addition to common language usage, the two novels also share a similarity in structure. Their plots are not event-oriented; time and space are fragmented so they change freely according to the flow of the drunken man's thoughts.

Reprinted in *Shu he ying* (Books and films) (Taipei: Lianhe wenxue, 1988), 187–93. This article is translated by Christopher Lupke.

75. "Xiandai zhuyi de zhiyi he yuanshi" (The challenge and primitiveness of modernism), *Zhongguo shibao* (China times daily) August 15, 1986: 8.

76. For an analysis of the plot structure of *Family Catastrophe*, see Shu-ning Sciban's "The Structure of *Jia bian*: A Reflection on the Studies of Twentieth-Century Chinese Fiction," *East Asia Forum*, Vol. 2 (Toronto: The Department of East Asian Studies, University of Toronto, 1993), 36–49.

By the time *Backed Against the Sea* was published, Wang had traveled a great distance in his search for a personal writing style, a journey that began forty years earlier when he was only twenty. Throughout, he has followed the aesthetic principles of high modernism and done so sincerely. However, as indicated by the traditional nature of *Family Catastrophe*'s plot structure, Wang's artistic achievement in his novels can be appreciated only through an understanding of both Western and classical Chinese literature. This suggests that his journey has doubled back to Chinese literature.

RETURN TO CLASSICAL CHINESE LITERATURE (1999–PRESENT)

In June of 2006, Wang published his most recent short story, "Ming yue ye" (Nights of the shining moon). This story demonstrates a clearer connection with classical Chinese literature than any of his previous fiction. It opens with a quotation from Qian Yong's (1759–1844) "Bayue shiwu bu" (The night after eight months and fifteen days), an anecdote in a chapter titled "Xiangyi" (Miraculous and extraordinary) in Qian's *Lüyuan conghua* (Lüyuan anecdotes).[77] *Lüyuan Anecdotes* is an example of *biji xiaoshuo* (note-form fiction), which consists of brief prose fragments about extraordinary people and events.[78] In addition to the citation from Qian Yong, the story's theme of prophecy and its plot development reflect Wang's familiarity with the *biji* tradition. While the language in "Nights of the Shining Moon" contains some of Wang's typical stylistic innovations, it is much closer to standard written Chinese, with a stronger classical flavor.

---

77. Qian Yong's *Lüyuan conghua* (Lüyuan anecdotes) was first printed in 1838. The edition the author has seen was published by Wenhai chubanshe in Taipei, 1981, two volumes; "The Night after Eight Months and Fifteen Days" is on page 285 in volume 2.

78. William H. Nienhauser, Jr., ed., *The Indiana Companion to Traditional Chinese Literature* (Bloomington: Indiana University Press, 1986), 280.

Sun Yuanxiang, a friend of Qian Yong's, explained the meaning of each chapter's title in the preface to *Lüyuan Anecdotes*: "The chapter called 'Miraculous and Extraordinary' portrays the vastness of the universe."[79] "Nights of the Shining Moon" also calls our attention to the vast, unknown universe and a power beyond human comprehension, a motif with profound religious overtones that appears repeatedly in Wang's stories. The significance of "Nights of the Shining Moon" is that Wang has remodeled a religious theme common in traditional Chinese *zhiguai* and *biji* literature.

To many readers of Wang Wen-hsing, the suggestion of an affinity between his writing and classical Chinese literature would come as a shock. However, pioneering research has been carried out on this relationship: Wai-lim Yip delineated the classical poetic structure adopted in "Mother";[80] Ke Qingming connected Taiwan's modernist literature of the 1960s—using many of Wang's stories as evidence—to traditional Chinese literature;[81] and I have analyzed the influence of classical poetry on the overall structure of *Family Catastrophe*.[82] Sung-sheng Chang says Wang has made a "roundabout journey from an absolute embrace of Western artistic models to the deep contemplation of elements from traditional Chinese culture."[83]

In addition, from early in his writing career, Wang's concept of a literary language has included classical Chinese literature and classical Chinese language. The first sign of his strong interest in classical Chinese literature came in 1968, in his "Preface to *New Stone Statue*." In it, Wang spoke about the importance of precision in literary language, advocating the concept of "no wasted words." He took

79. Sun Yuanxiang, "*Lüyuan conghua* xu" (Preface to *Lüyuan anecdotes*), in *Lüyuan conghua* (Lüyuan anecdotes), Vol. 1 (Taipei: Wenhai chubanshe, 1981), 1.

80. Ye Weilian (Wai-lim Yip), "Xiandai Zhongguo xiaoshuo de jiegou"(The structure of modern Chinese fiction), in *Zhongguo xiandai xiaoshuo de fengmao* (Style and features of Chinese modern fiction) (Taipei: Chenzhong chubanshe, 1970), 1–28.

81. Ke Qingming, "The 1960s Modernist Literature?"

82. Shu-ning Sciban, "The Structure of *Jia bian*: A Reflection on the Studies of Twentieth-Century Chinese Fiction."

83. Sung-sheng Chang, *Modernism and Nativist Resistance*, 79.

the language of classical poetry as a model and urged modern writers to do the same. In an interview with Li Ang in 1975, only two years after the publication of *Family Catastrophe*, he admitted that although he was influenced more by Western literature, he considered his lack of knowledge of Chinese fiction (possibly he meant classical Chinese fiction) as a shortcoming. Furthermore, he said that when he had learned enough from the West, he would return to study Chinese fiction.[84] He expressed his fondness for and desire to read more classical essays written during the Tang (618–907), Song (960–1279), Ming (1368–1644) and Qing (1644–1911) dynasties.[85] Most significantly, he said: "I always feel classical language is better [than the vernacular language]. . . . Maybe any change in my style is the mark of my struggle between vernacular and classical languages; I want to find a way out."[86] What Wang revealed here seems to confirm our hypothesis that classical literature has been a strong influence. In 1979, Wang Wen-hsing wrote his reflections on the May Fourth Movement concerning literary language, saying that since the movement advocated literary freedom, writers should not limit themselves to only one language. He criticized modern young people in Taiwan for being completely disengaged from classical language and traditional poetry. This problem, plus ignorance of Western literature, hindered the progress of Chinese literature after the May Fourth era, he said.[87]

In the 1980s, Wang began to publish his thoughts on Chinese prose and paid considerable attention to Pu Songling's (1640–1715) *Liaozhai zhi yi* (Strange stories from a Chinese studio). Since then, Wang's interest in classical Chinese literature has continued to grow, as can be seen clearly in four books: *Shu he ying* (Books and films);[88] *Wang Wen-hsing de xinling shijie* (Wang Wen-hsing's spiritual world,

84. Li Ang, "The Loneliness of a Long-distance Runner," 39–40.

85. Ibid., 40–41.

86. Ibid., 37.

87. Wang Wen-hsing, "To Create an Ideal Literary Style by Blending Classical, Vernacular and Europeanized Chinese."

88. Wang Wen-hsing, *Shu he ying* (Books and films) (Taipei: Lianhe wenxue, 1988).

1990); *Xiaoshuo mo yu* (Beyond fiction, 2002) and *Xing yu lou sui xiang* (Random thoughts from Star-rain Tower, 2003). *Books and Films* is a collection of forty-three articles and reviews written by Wang during the previous two decades. *Wang Wen-hsing's Spiritual World* also is an essay collection, including works by Wang and other writers, which portrays his religious life but also includes some important information about the development of his writing career. *Beyond Fiction* and *Random Thoughts from Star-rain Tower* are two more essay collections, mostly written in 1990s or later, revealing the continuous development of Wang's appreciation of classical Chinese literature and other arts, such as calligraphy.

Recently, Wang has been invited to give public speeches on classical literature. Judged by the works he discusses, we realize our modernist author has turned into a scholar of traditional Chinese literature. Take the six speeches he delivered at Jinshitang ("Kingstone" in English), one of the biggest bookstores in Taipei, from August 21 to September 25, 2008. The topics covered *Shiji* (Records of the grand historian), *Zhuangzi* and works in the genre of *zhiguai xiaoshuo* (fiction of the supernatural and the fantastic), *biji xiaoshuo* (note-form fiction), Tang *chuanqi* (classical language fiction that arose during the Tang dynasty), five-syllable *lüshi* (eight-sentence regulated verse) from the Tang and Song dynasties and *ci* poems from the Song, Ming and Qing dynasties.[89] It is obvious that classical Chinese literature has occupied a central position in his intellectual life. In his opening remarks on "Reading and Writing" at a symposium on his work at the University of Calgary, Wang said:

> Looking back, I always felt that it was better to say that I am a reader rather than to say that I am a writer. This is not only because, considering things over time, I spent much more time reading than I did writing (it is like that now, but it has even been more so my whole life)—but also because reading basically cannot be

---

89. The literary works discussed in Wang's speeches are in the blog of Maitian chubanshe: http://ryefield.pixnet.net/blog/post/19740408, last accessed on April 2, 2009.

separated from writing—reading indeed is the source of writing; even more so, before one can judge what kind of writer he is, one must first examine what kind of reader he is—thus to say I am a writer is not as good as saying that I am a reader.[90]

This explains why Wang's recent works have reflected the rich influence of classical Chinese. And, significantly, this influence probably has been present in his writing from the very beginning of his career.

Because Wang Wen-hsing is still writing, it is hard to make conclusive statements about many aspects of his work. Nevertheless, he certainly is one of the most creative and devoted writers of fiction in the world. His devotion to literary artistry is evident in the effort he puts into the slow and painstaking process of writing,[91] and his determination to maintain his ideals and principles regardless of the difficulties and pressure from society. His writing is a genuine artistic achievement in narrative language, one that harmoniously merges the Western and Chinese literary traditions.

This anthology consists of all of Wang's fictional works with the exception of his two novels, as well as five of his essays that contain his essential ideas about modernist literature, literary language and his own writing. I hope it will provide English readers with an opportunity to appreciate Wang's literary artistry and to understand his development as one of the most prominent contemporary writers in Taiwan.

Shu-ning Sciban
March 2010

90. Wang's keynote speech at the "Art of Chinese Narrative Language: An International Workshop on Wang Wen-hsing's Life and Works" (University of Calgary, Calgary, Canada, February 19–21, 2009).

91. Wang said that he uses his imagination only when writing his first draft. When he writes the final draft there is no fun anymore, just hard work. This is why he can write only about one hundred and twenty words a day. Shan Dexing, "Wang Wen-hsing Talks about Wang Wen-hsing," 170–73.

PART I

SHORT FICTION

The Lingering Night

April 1958. This is Wang Wen-hsing's first published story, a psychological tale that employs the subjective narrative mode. Written when Wang was in grade twelve, it reveals his innate interest in human psychology.

Midnight. A distant temple bell, absolute silence in its wake. Black sky, not a flicker of stars or moon.

Fan Ruofu's head rests on his hands, arms exhausted from supporting the weight, eyelids heavy, closing ever so slowly. All feeling slowly drains from his limbs as if he is drifting into another world, gradually, softly. Suddenly, a fleeting sense of responsibility ferociously shakes all weariness from him. He rubs his eyes purposefully.

The light above his head emits a weak glow. Previously, it sat in the middle of the room but now hangs from a string above the table. Lying in front of him is a sheet of paper containing two lines of words, the beginnings of his novel:

"Li Ya had seemed upset these past few days, hunched over, his head perpetually bent, eyes trained on the ground."

Fan Ruofu scans the lines, chewing on his pen, puzzling over how to proceed. Behind him, a bed is pushed against the wall, his wife and seven-year-old son breathing evenly, already fast asleep. Beside the bed is a nightstand with a hot-water bottle, its enamel chipped. Two crude porcelain teacups and an old clock sit in the dark. The clock makes a steady ticking sound, "tick-tock, tick-tock, tick-tock . . ."

"Li Ya looked as if he had been very upset these past few days." He changes the sentence a little; this way there are a few more words on the page. The number of words is extremely important. A thousand words would bring in fifty yuan while two thousand words would mean one hundred yuan; more words naturally mean more money. It just so happens that he needs money, and he needs it urgently. After deductions, his paycheck this month was a hundred yuan, and all that's left now is a measly twenty. And it is only the fifteenth, a long way from payday. What can he do with twenty yuan? It's not even enough to buy four days' worth of food. On top of that, his son needs a summer shirt, his wife a dress, and he needs a new pair of leather shoes for work. His old shoes are worn beyond recognition; an old man's grin decorates the toes, the heels are missing, and the stitching in the front is torn. He has become very careful while walking. His colleagues ask him: "What happened to your feet?" He can only hang his flushed face in embarrassment, mumbling that he has sprained his ankle. He must buy a new pair of shoes but, no, it would be better to get his wife's and child's clothing first. He will wait and see about the shoes.

"One linen shirt," Ruofu says. Outside on the street, florescent lights flash, illuminating the shop's goods in the window.

"What type would you like?" the salesclerk asks.

"The best, of course," he answers.

The salesclerk gleefully brings out a stack. Ruofu pulls out the finest and whitest shirt, puts the money on top of the cool glass counter, and leaves. The street is very busy with everyone pushing everyone else. A moment later and he is in another shop, its light so bright that he has to squint against the glare.

"I need a bolt of cloth, three yards long," he says.

"What type would you like? What color?"

"I want the best material and most beautiful colors."

He is dazzled by a flurry of colorful cloth; so many colors and so many patterns strike him all at once that he cannot begin to decide which one to choose. He wants the one with a red flower but the next moment he's looking at a blue flower.

"I don't want a blue one."

The blue flower disappears instantly and in its place is a yellow flower. "No, I don't want a yellow one." The yellow flower then changes to a white one; the colors are changing endlessly. The salesclerk's mouth spreads to reveal white teeth in a sly grin, as if performing a magic trick. "What? That's not possible!" Suddenly it comes to him that this salesclerk is the same one who sold him the shirt! The salesclerk begins laughing louder and harder causing Ruofu's ears to ring painfully, shaking him so intensely it seems the floor is quaking as well. "Stop it! Stop!" he screams. With a start, he snaps awake, his heart racing.

Behind the building a train roars by, the sound diminishing as the train moves further away. His wife and child lie undisturbed, still breathing evenly.

Everything returns to its peaceful state as he refocuses his mind, reading yet again the words he has written. Ever since dinner he has been thinking hard about what type of story to write but still has no ideas. What type of person is Li Ya? He only knows that he wants him to be melancholy—someone treated roughly by life—because he is most familiar with this type of person. Most of the people he knows are like that; moreover, he is like that himself.

Ruofu knows he does not have time to write a moving story. He can only write something that normal people will want to read. It's just for the money anyway. He doesn't need to write a grand piece of literature. As long as he meets the word-count requirements, it will be fine. Thinking of this, he cannot resist a grim smile. It's not that he hasn't read the classics; he has read Tolstoy, Dickens and Flaubert. He once even dared to dream that he would be compared with them one day, but that's in the past, when he was still a young man. Now he can only stiffen his lips and laugh it off. His writing is strictly to make money and raise his family. Yet it's strange how he cannot come up with any story ideas now, even a story for the simple purpose of making money.

Fan Ruofu rereads the lines once more and is suddenly struck by their lack of flow. The sentence structure is much too disorderly.

The publishing company's editors have little love for long-winded works. Very likely they will reject the draft. He has already experienced many painful disappointments and is far from confident that his work will be selected this time.

Tick-tock, tick-tock, tick-tock . . . the clock murmurs from the darkness. He is very anxious, uncertain if his work will be selected, very anxious.

"Is this your story?" the man holding a stack of papers asks.

"Yes, yes." He recognizes that it is his.

"You know that one thousand words is fifty yuan, two thousand words is one hundred yuan, three thousand words is one hundred fifty, so four thousand words then is two hundred yuan." The man adjusts his overlarge glasses, muttering at first, then suddenly raises his voice: "That much money! It could last for a whole month without difficulty. A shirt, three yards of cloth, and even a pair of leather shoes could be bought with no problem."

"Huh? How did you know that?" he asks amazed.

"Ha ha! How could I not know?" the man laughs loudly. Throwing up his hands "Here, look!"

Ruofu is shocked; it is a check with many numbers written on it. Overjoyed, he leaps up. "Give it to me quick! How much? A hundred? Two hundred? Ah, three hundred? Four hundred? Come on!" He is just about to grab it when the man nimbly places the slip back in his pocket, laughing loudly.

"Ha ha! This isn't for you. Not only does your story stink, it is much too long. We don't want it!"

Ruofu goes mad with rage! "Give it to me! Give it to me! It's mine!" He chases the man around, yelling and fighting. He feels something strike him on the back and a familiar voice calls, "Wake up, wake up . . ."

Raising his head, he sees his wife standing before him. "It's almost light outside! Why haven't you come to bed?"

Dawn breaks across the sky, the meat vendor's cart rolls by the front door, its wheels creating a clack-clack-clacking noise.

"The sun's almost up?" He feels as though he has just jumped out of his skin.

"It's already four; go and get some rest."

"No, I need to finish this story," he says, looking at the two lines on the page. "Why don't you go back to sleep for a bit?"

He anxiously chews on his pen; there isn't much time left. He needs to write something with two thousand words, but he has written only how many?

His wife lies down and soon is breathing evenly again.

"Li Ya looked as if he had been very upset these past few days."

He looks at it once and quickly scratches it out, changing it back to the original version. "Li Ya had seemed upset these past few days." Then he stares blankly at these words, the ink not yet dry on the page, glistening under the lamplight. He anxiously chews on his pen: if only Li Ya could lend him a hand! If he could only make all his own actions and conversations appear on the page, how wonderful that would be!

His wife and child's breathing is a very soothing sound to him, rising and falling together evenly with his own.

Suddenly he sees Li Ya! Standing right in front of him! That's odd, how did he recognize me?

"Li Ya! Li Ya!" he frantically calls. Li Ya's face is not very clear, hidden by the darkness. "Quickly! Tell me your story! Li Ya, why do you always seem upset? Why are you always hunched over with your head bowed and eyes trained on the ground?" he desperately calls out. But, unexpectedly, Li Ya howls with a thundering shout, "Why did you write only two lines about me and then give up? Why didn't you finish writing about me? Why do you say I'm unhappy, why do you say I'm always hunched over, why do you say I bow my head, why do you say my eyes only look at the ground? You only want to use me to make money. You don't really want to write anything properly. Fine, let's see what you can come up with about me!" Li Ya's expression is frightening. His face is as white as parchment, his eye sockets red, cheeks hollow, eyes glazed and dull, jaw covered with stubble. With that, he turns and leaves.

"Li Ya, wait a moment!" Ruofu chases after him, unwilling to let him leave. But Li Ya pays him no mind and walks off, singing to himself. The song he sings is very strange and high-pitched. "Ah! Li Ya, Li Ya!" Ruofu chases, shouting. Li Ya's song sounds oddly like a rooster crowing.

"Cock-a-doodle-do . . ." Fan Ruofu actually hears the roosters calling, all of them crowing in succession. It is already morning. A ray of sunlight touches the windowpane and the sparrows chirp from a nearby tree. Li Ya has escaped with the dark.

Chopping sounds come from outside; his wife already is splitting wood for a fire. The shop next door is preparing to open. "Ah Tong, sweep the floor and wipe down the cupboards," orders a hoarse, drowsy voice.

"Okay, okay," a child's voice answers just as sleepily.

Momentarily, the street will slip back into its regular hustle and bustle. He needs to wash up, brush his teeth, grab something to eat, and rush off to the office. It is the beginning of another bothersome day.

The paper, which lies on the table before him, alas, has only two lines scrawled on it. All he can do is stare at it stupidly.

Translated by Rowan Sciban

A Dying Dog

August, 1958. This story, written during Wang Wen-hsing's first year of university, depicts a student's observation of the cruel killing of a dog. He expresses his sympathy for the animal while criticizing the bystanders' indifference.

At three o'clock in the afternoon on August 13, I was riding my bicycle north along Xinsheng South Road, Section 2. The dazzling white sun scorched the pavement. The dragon cypresses on the left side of the road seemed to be withering in the intense heat. There was no place along the roadside to provide cyclists with even the smallest patch of shade where they could escape the heat. Thinking that I could outrun the sun, I was riding my bike as fast as I could, but the sun always seemed to be waiting for me up ahead. My eyes began feeling a little dry and my head began to hurt—I was afraid I was getting sunstroke. I quickly dismounted to rest for a while and took refuge in one of the few patches of shade on the left side of the road.

When I saw a group of people gathered under the third tree further down the road, I figured something must have happened. Probably a car had run over someone. On Ren'ai Road a couple of months ago, I saw a young girl who had been run over by a truck. Her body was curled up like a small bundle of clothing and a small pool of fresh blood had emerged from her mouth, which was pressed against the road. At first I didn't want to see what these people ahead of me were looking at, but my curiosity got the better of me and I pushed my bike over to where they were standing.

This time it was a muscular foreign dog the size of a tiger, not the corpse of a girl, which lay at the foot of the tree. Its two front legs rested against the tree trunk while its two hind legs, which were bound with steel wire, stuck straight out behind. The gray skin on its belly was rising and falling like a leaking rubber ball. The dog turned its head and bit at the steel chain that restrained it. Because its leather collar had embedded itself in the flesh of the dog's neck, several pieces of loose skin moved back and forth as it turned its head. Its soft, pointed muzzle moved constantly and all of its muscles trembled.

Suddenly it turned its head—a head the size of a dinner plate— and the people who had gathered round took several steps back. Several of them softly murmured, "Blood!"

Its face looked like it had been washed in a basin of blood. Blood stains coated its mouth and dried blood plugged its black nose. Blood also stained the areas around its eyes. Its long tongue hung from its mouth like an old rag. Grainy patches of red vomit the color of wine dregs clung to the hairs of its neck. At the thought of wine dregs, I seemed to catch a whiff of their unpleasant stench. The dog's dark, muddy brown eyes had deep black pupils. I noticed a light suddenly appear in these eyes, an anxious, pleading, hopeless look like that of someone trapped in a burning building who wants to break down a locked door to escape. I found it was staring at me, but I did not dare look into its eyes so I stared at its hind legs instead. The hind legs were thicker than those of most dogs, and its paws were large as well, probably because of swelling. The dog chewed on the chain several times, but it was slippery and the dog could not grasp it in its mouth. It turned its head to the other side and bit at the chain a few more times.

"What happened to this dog?" a steamed-bun vendor who carried a wooden box on his back asked the group without looking at anyone in particular.

"He bit his owner," a man wearing a vest and sandals replied without looking at the vendor.

"Oh? He bit his master! And what happened to his master?" The vendor seemed pleased that someone had responded.

"He was taken to the hospital," said the man in the vest, casting a sidelong glance at the steamed-bun vendor with the wooden box on his back.

"Why is the dog bleeding?"

"The owner beat it."

"Why?"

"It bit him, so naturally the owner wanted to beat it." The man in the vest smiled slightly, as if he looked down on the person who had asked the question.

"Why did it bite its master?"

"The dog was sick, and the owner took it to the veterinary clinic across the street. The veterinarian told him there was nothing he could do, and as soon as they stepped out of the clinic, the dog attacked its master." Everyone looked at the man in the vest as he spoke.

Across the street from where they stood was a veterinary clinic with a sign in front featuring a picture of a dog's head.

"Oh, so its master took it to the vet's, and the vet wouldn't examine it, so then the dog bit its master and the master became angry. Ha ha!" The steamed-bun vendor seemed delighted, and as he glanced over at the dog on the ground, his smile revealed a row of yellow teeth.

At this point, the dog's front paws clawed at the bark of the tree. Its head turned back and forth as it continued to struggle to breathe and bite at the chain. This was to no avail, however—the exhausted dog seemed to be doing little more than closing its mouth on the chain. Every once in a while, it would get hold of a link, chew on it and then let it go. A short while later it stopped, panted and looked mournfully and anxiously at the people who surrounded it.

The sun continued to burn brightly without any sign of dimming. The group stood quietly under the tree watching the dog's futile struggle.

Not long after, several people left, leaving a few idlers to stay with the dog until its final moment. They were just killing time watching the dog chew here or there. Its chin was rubbed raw and the flesh under the skin was exposed. The white part looked like tofu and the red looked like fish gills.

"I'm afraid it won't live much longer," the vendor said as he waited impatiently. He ran back and forth and looked at the dog from every angle.

Several puddles of blood and yellow liquid lay on the ground. All of a sudden, the dog leapt up, and the onlookers could not prevent themselves from taking a step back as they forgot the animal was bound tight by the chain. Its two front legs, which had supported it against the tree, now came down but were not long enough to reach the ground, leaving it to swing back and forth. Once its front legs had dropped, it hung only by its neck. It raised its head, its pointed mouth opened wide facing skyward, as if it were tremendously thirsty. The leather collar slipped tighter around its neck. It panted and then began to shake as if it had fallen into water and was trying to shake itself dry. It trembled like this for quite a while. Then blood began to trickle from the corner of its mouth. It shook again for a time and another small trickle of blood flowed from its mouth. The blood soaked into the dog's matted hair, which looked like strands of red ribbon hanging from its neck.

"It won't be much longer. Look at its belly!" said the man in the vest.

Its belly was rising and falling faster, but not rising as high as it had just a few minutes before. When it opened its eyes, they were dull and lifeless, just like those of a putrid, day-old fish. I hoped it would close its eyes and mouth and hide those long, sparkling, white teeth.

But its eyes stared blankly without any trace of movement. Just then it lost its balance and shifted to one side. Its whole body turned upside down, all four legs pointing skyward, its two front legs sticking up stiff and straight like a couple of sticks. Because the dog's neck was held in place by its leather collar, its head could not turn so the head and neck were bent at a terrifyingly strange angle. Then, like a motor, it started a steady trembling. Only now did its tail, which had been stuck under its body, pop out. It was pink and hairless, swollen from ant bites—each of the large pores stood out clearly.

I pushed my way out of the group of bystanders, jumped on my bicycle and headed north as fast as I could with the dazzling sun shining down on me.

Translated by Steven L. Riep

The Marriage of a Civil Servant

February 1959. Written when Wang was in his second year of university, this story is a farce, describing how a civil servant comes to marry the maid who works in his rooming house. It marks the first time Wang experimented with monologue and a variety of individual speaking styles.

Ah! Haven't started dinner yet, Mrs. Wang? I'm bored to tears at home all alone, it's nice to have someone to talk to. No tea, please don't make tea. I'm not your guest, or anything, so if you go to the trouble of making tea, I'll have to leave. Yes, please sit down with me. Ah, have you heard that Ah Li, that girl in our hostel, is about to have her baby? What a disgrace! How could a lowly maidservant become a wife? Ha ha. I tell you, it's enough to make you laugh, that's right, a real mess. As far back as last year, I knew this day would come. That was when Ah Li first showed up to work in the dining room. I could see she was an innocent girl, with her plain face and dark skin, straight hair and simple clothes. Not much to look at, but a good worker. And it didn't take long to see that Mr. Liu was up to no good. Don't be fooled by that false front, with his genteel face and proper lifestyle. That's only because he doesn't have any money. He was on the lookout for a wife, since he wasn't getting any younger, but who'd have someone like him? Girls who hadn't even been to high school kept their distance. And that limited his choice to maidservants. You know why the previous maid, Ah Yun, left? Because Mr. Liu was hounding her. Ah Yun was a pretty girl who'd set her sights on someone a lot better than the likes of Mr. Liu!

I saw what was happening the first day Ah Li showed up—she couldn't keep her eyes off of Mr. Liu, but he just frowned. And when he spoke to her, he refused to make eye contact, which shows how cunning he was. A week later, Ah Li and I got to know each other better, and I often asked her to help with my grocery shopping. She told me she'd been adopted, which had made growing up a tough experience. This was her first job. I asked how she was getting along, and she said she liked the place, that all the men treated her well, ha ha, so I asked, "What do you think of Mr. Liu?" Her eyes widening, she said, "Mr. Liu is a wonderful man." "Yes," I said, "a college graduate, not much more than thirty, lives a decent life, frugal, might even have some money tucked away."

From then on, Ah Li often came to ask what sort of mainland specials she should prepare for the men, so I gave her several lessons—now she can fry shredded pork, make noodles with bean sauce and many other dishes. She also showed how thrifty she could be at the market, and never held back a cent from her purchases. Naturally, that was all part of her plan to impress Mr. Liu. He was fond of spicy food, which she managed to serve at every meal. Naturally, that didn't sit well with everybody, since they all pooled their food money. How come Mr. Liu got preferential treatment?

Mr. Liu remained aloof, neither chatty nor overly witty, but he often found an excuse to go into the kitchen for a glass of water. Even there he kept the small talk to a minimum, but the minute Ah Li saw him walk into the kitchen, she seemed out of sorts, not sure what to look at, suddenly all thumbs, a deep blush rising on her dark face. If she happened to be talking to me at the time, she stopped in mid-sentence. Mr. Liu would walk over to the stove, a frown on his face, all nice and proper, staring at the kettle for a full minute or two before taking off the lid to see if the water had boiled. Ah Li would go over to join him, also craning her neck. The way he'd remove the lid and replace it, over and over again, you'd think the two of them had nothing on their minds but whether the water in the kettle had started to boil. That would go on for five or six minutes until Mr. Liu would appear to have reached an important decision. He'd turn and walk off, looking very unhappy. Before long, radio sounds would emerge from his room in fits and starts as he moved up and down the dial, not stopping until he found a female singer. Then he'd turn the radio up good and loud, so he could sing along in his less than melodious voice. Even I can sing one of those songs: "Taiwan . . . a wonderful place . . . let's all sing a Taiwanese song!"

One day Ah Li said excitedly that Mr. Liu had told people it would be a shame if we let the large yard go to pot, instead of raising some ducks and chickens. The very next day, Ah Li was out in a corner of the yard feeding some yellow baby chicks that she'd bought with her own money. I don't have to tell you how happy that made Mr. Liu, though he hadn't been serious when he made the suggestion. A smile appeared on his face for the very first time.

Ah Li looked after those chicks like a mother hen, spending all her spare time out in the yard with them. She'd hastily finish her chores in the kitchen, then rush outside to see how her chicks were doing. And the first thing Mr. Liu did after work was go out into the yard, where he'd join Ah Li, the two of them on their haunches as they fed the chicks raw rice from a can. The blank look on Mr. Liu's face seemed to have disappeared, often replaced by a faint smile. And when he was in a particularly good mood, he'd affectionately pick up the chicks, one at a time, and set them on his arm, from his shoulder all the way down to his hand. One week passed like that, then a second, feeding time for the chicks getting longer and longer. On Sundays they'd stay out there till dark. Fortunately, few of the men came back for dinner on Sundays, and old Mr. Wang and the others would never raise a stink.

Those chicks grew like weeds, and their yellow fuzz turned into hard feathers in no time. They were ferocious eaters. Ah Li looked after them even more diligently. In order to stretch Mr. Liu's rice (they didn't dare take any from the kitchen), she fed them from the palm of her hand instead of tossing it on the ground. One day one of the brood sort of wobbled when it walked, its head nodding with each step, like it was sleepy. Ah Li was so worried she looked after that one chick for most of the morning, even forgot to go inside to prepare lunch. When Mr. Liu came over in the afternoon, he ran out to buy some poultry medicine, which they stirred with a little spoon and then poured down the chick's gullet. But the chick didn't snap out of it. In fact, it seemed sleepier than ever, which just about had Ah Li in tears. Sadly, she kept stroking the poor thing, trying to comfort it, I guess. As she watched it stretched out on the ground, not making a sound, she wondered if it was dead. She nudged it, and was happy to see it wake up. It was getting dark, and the men would give her hell if they missed another meal, so she carried the sick chick into the kitchen. She had no appetite at all that night. Mr. Liu joined her several times as she looked on helplessly. From time to time he glanced over at her, and seemed touched by what he saw. Finally, he said gently, "Go get something to eat. Starving yourself won't help. I'll stay out here."

By eleven o'clock that night, Ah Li was the only person awake. She took the ailing chick into her room with her. She didn't care if it did its business all over the tatami. When she heard a scraping sound on the straw mat, she sat up and turned on the lamp. The chick was all better, eyes shining as it looked around the strange place it found itself in, clucking nervously. She was so happy she picked it up and rushed out to tell Mr. Liu. Standing outside his door, she shouted, "Mr. Liu! Mr. Liu!" No answer. The room was dark. He was fast asleep. Feeling sheepish standing out there all alone, she decided to try again, which she did after a moment. A light went on in the room, the paper door slid open, and it was too late for her to leave. "What's wrong?" Dressed only in shorts and a sleeveless undershirt, Mr. Liu was standing there in front of her. A blast of stale air emerged from behind him. Having just awakened from a deep sleep, he looked pale. Ah Li held the chick out for him to see. "It's all better." Mr. Liu looked at her and paid no attention to the chick at all. The dark skin of her bare arm glistened coldly in the dim light. He seemed to have a little trouble breathing, and I'll bet his face was bright red. The way he looked scared her, of course. She started to back up, mouth open, but he grabbed her and dragged her into the room. The door was closed, the lamp turned off. I'll bet you're wondering how I know all the details. Sorry, I can't tell you.

The next morning, the little chick clucked its way up and down the hallway, then suddenly started to crow, and woke everybody up.

The group of men decided not to keep Ah Li on, partly because she was acting less and less like someone who worked for them, and more and more like Mr. Liu's personal maid, and partly because they were tired of eating pickled cabbage. That was about all they'd had for the past two weeks, it seemed, and they couldn't figure out why. Once her employment was terminated, Ah Li moved in with Mr. Liu. He dropped out of the food dining group, and the two of them took care of their own meals. This was more than the other hostel residents could take, and Mr. Liu's fellow workers all but stopped saying hello to him. No more joking around, and some of the old bachelors were openly envious. I even had to stop asking Ah Li to help me shop.

But then Mr. Liu started making himself scarce, unable to face people, avoiding everyone as much as possible. He walked with his head down, like he had something on his mind. And he didn't seem as fond of Ah Li as before. She'd started using his comb, and his mirror, and his radio, to his displeasure. But most of the time there was a faraway look in his eyes, no way to tell what he was thinking. One day Ah Li got a perm, but when Mr. Liu saw her, he closed his eyes and waved her away, telling her to go buy him a pack of smokes.

Talk was on the increase, and Mr. Liu, who valued pride, had a very short fuse. Mrs. Zheng was the worst gossiper of the bunch, and whenever she saw Ah Li or Mr. Liu, once they were past her, she made all sorts of gestures and sarcastic comments. Mr. Liu kept his anger bottled up inside. Then one day, not long before New Year's, it happened. Mrs. Zheng's son, Xiaomao, killed one of Mr. Liu's chickens with a rock. It was the little rooster they'd fed the medicine to. Mrs. Zheng said it was an accident, but don't buy it. You think a little boy can't be that mean? That's where you're wrong! Especially with a mother like that teaching him. Ah Li picked up the dead rooster and stared at it, so sad she was about to cry. After standing there stunned for a minute, she went looking for Mrs. Zheng, to talk, not to get her to pay. With her face set tight, Mrs. Zheng wouldn't even look at her. "My Xiaomao wouldn't hit your chicken even if you asked him to!" she said venomously. That made Ah Li angry, because that rooster had been her matchmaker. The matchmaker's dead, do you know what that means? Ah Li, whose face had turned ashen, didn't know how to tell off the woman in Mandarin, and all she could say was, "Listen to me, listen to me . . . you can't talk like that, you can't." It was late afternoon, and Mr. Liu was in his room when he heard sounds of an argument. He stayed put. Meanwhile, Mrs. Zheng was just hitting her stride. In the shrillest voice she could manage, she shrieked, "Ha ha ha, you shameless, wicked woman, we know what you two have been up to . . ." Mr. Liu's door flew open, and he stormed out so fast that Mrs. Zheng didn't have time even to think about running away. She stood there trembling. "Don't you dare! Don't you dare!" She'd barely gotten the words out when—pa! pa!—two slaps across her face. "That's to teach you people to hold your tongues." His lips were twitching. With a cry of pain, Mrs. Zheng threw herself on him like a madwoman. A wrestling match followed, and even though Mr. Liu was stronger, he couldn't shake her loose. Just about everyone who lived in the hostel had come running, but before they could make peace, Mrs. Zheng reached out and swiped her hand across Mr. Liu's face, leaving five bloody scratches. "Shameless, wicked adulterers, sleeping together at night like a pair of mutts," Mrs. Zheng said with gusto, just before Mr. Liu reached out and shoved her to the ground. He spun around and ran into the kitchen, returning with a cleaver that glinted in the light. That raised a howl from the onlookers. The women looked away, the men rushed up and wrapped their arms around him, wrenching the cleaver out of his hand. His face darkened and he was panting. The men pinned his arms to keep him from rushing Mrs. Zheng again. She was wailing and shouting, as if the cleaver had done its work already. She ran and dared him to finish the job. Mr. Zheng grabbed his wife; his face was ashen, his lips quivered. "How dare you try to kill her," he said. "How dare you try to . . . kill her." Xiaomao was clutching the hem of his mother's shirt and bawling like a baby, and when she noticed him, for some unknown reason, she scooped him up and began to wail piteously. But then she put him down just as quickly and ran up to Mr. Liu to goad him into trying to finish the job. Of course, a bunch of people blocked her way, while Mr. Zheng was so distraught he just ran around in circles. Even passersby out on the street heard the uproar and stopped, curious to know what was going on. That's when it dawned on the hostel manager that someone had to restore order. Trying his hardest to sound like someone in authority, he ordered the vendors and pedicab drivers to clear out. Mr. Liu's lips were purple. He took a step, turned back, and growled at Mrs. Zheng, "You come any closer, and it'll be a miracle if I don't kill you." Seeing him turn back like that, the onlookers circled him again. "What's the big idea, standing in my way? Can't I even go get my slippers?"

"Slippers! Slippers! Bring his slippers!" someone holding him shouted. But by then Ah Li was standing beside Mr. Liu holding his slippers. White patches showed on her dark face, her eyes were glazed. She held her ground beside Mr. Liu, but no one seemed to notice her. When Mr. Liu finally did, he glared at her. It took Mr. Liu several attempts to put his slippers on. Even after he'd walked off, Mrs. Zheng, runny nose, tear-streaked face and all, was still cursing him. She yelled herself hoarse. Once Mr. Liu was back in his room, the crowd finally dispersed. Mr. Liu sat in his chair, as always, leaning against the wall with his legs crossed, and stared straight ahead, seeming to forget that another person was in the room. Ah Li poured him a glass of boiled water, which he didn't drink. Then she handed him a wet towel to wipe the blood from his face, but he screamed at her to get away from him. Ah Li stood transfixed in front of him. When he finally stood up, she asked where he was going. He ignored her. But he'd only taken a couple of steps before his legs began to shake, and he stopped. Anxious, Ah Li fell in behind him. "Wherever you go, I go." Where he went was to see the janitor, Ah Hua. Ever since the "incident," Ah Hua was the only person in the hostel willing to talk to him, and that's because he was the person who had recommended Ah Li for the job.

Ah Hua was sitting on a window sill massaging his feet. Mr. Liu stood at the window with his head bowed. Ah Hua's son, Doggie, suddenly squirmed out from behind his dad's legs and ran laughing up to Mr. Liu, like this was the most fun he'd ever had.

All of a sudden, people from the hostel ran up shouting, just like the time there was an electrical outage. Ah Hua jumped down from the window sill, and Mr. Liu froze, expecting the worst, like maybe Mrs. Zheng had died or something. "Mr. Liu, Mr. Liu, come quick!" Mrs. Wu shouted breathlessly. "The police are here, they're asking for you."

Mrs. Zheng had cajoled her husband into calling the police. At first, he'd hesitated, but then he wilted under his wife's recriminations, turning to the crowd and announcing somberly, "That's intolerable, trying to kill my wife. Don't you think I ought to call the police to determine who's right in this?" "Why don't you just drop dead? You're half dead anyway! After what he did, you won't even get off your ass and call the police for me." Mrs. Zheng had a wicked tongue, and poor Mr. Zheng had no choice but to go inside, willingly or not, and change his shoes to stall for time. But in the end, he went and called the police.

The moment Mrs. Zheng saw the police coming, you just knew she was going to start wailing again, embarrassing her husband. He's a well-mannered man, but he went into far more detail than necessary in relating the incident to the police. When Ah Hua dragged Mr. Liu up, Mr. Zheng instinctively took a step backward. "Is he the one?" the policeman asked, pointing at Mr. Liu. "Is that him?" Mr. Liu had his own complaint, as he pointed to the scratches on his face, showing that he was the injured party, not the Zhengs. At that moment, the look on Ah Li's face was one of near reverence for her man. Not letting her clean his bloody face had been a wise move. Mr. Zheng glanced at Mr. Liu, but quickly looked away bashfully. "Let's see the cleaver!" the policeman said. Several people ran to the kitchen. The seriousness of the situation was impressed upon Mr. Liu when he saw the cleaver in the hand of the policeman, who rested his other hand on Mr. Liu's shoulder and said, "We can talk at the station." Mr. Liu shrugged off the hand, like it had given him an electric shock, and said softly: "For a minor incident like this, how come?" The policeman smiled. "What are you afraid of? You're not being arrested. It's just easier to get to the bottom of things at the station. You folks come along." Mr. Zheng muttered an OK, and they all set out, police in front with the cleaver, followed by Mr. and Mrs. Zheng. She was still cursing a blue streak, embarrassing her husband, who tried to get her to stop. A bunch of kids brought up the rear. People on the street stopped to ask what was going on. Mr. Liu moved like a sleepwalker, sort of like those traitors who were paraded on the street after the victory over Japan. Ah Li walked with her head down, stepping as lightly as she could, and that made the two of them look like a pair of adulterers being dragged into court. A bystander said with a laugh, "One man, one woman . . ."

While they were rehashing the details of the incident, the police officer sitting behind the desk looked over at Ah Li, paying particular attention to her belly. Then he rubbed a mole on his chin. "What's this woman to you?" he asked Mr. Liu, whose eyes grew wide. In a loud, firm voice he said, "At first she was my servant, but, but, I plan to marry her. Any reason I can't marry a servant?" I think he felt he said the wrong thing, and wanted to gloss over it, but didn't know how. Ah Li, whose face was bright red, kept her head down. But now she looked up, like she sought something from him. All of a sudden, Mr. Liu burst into tears, like a little boy. At first, he tried to stop himself because it was a loss of face. But then, he figured it was too late to do anything about it, and when he saw the smiles on the people around him, he really let loose. This struck the policeman as so funny he had to force a scowl onto his face to keep from laughing out loud. "You folks patch things up yourselves or it will be out of our hands. This isn't what you'd call a minor incident, threatening to use a cleaver on someone. It could be attempted murder, and that's a matter for the courts to decide. So now what?"

Mr. Liu didn't say a word. Just as when he'd seen the cleaver in the policeman's hand, hearing that the case could go to court reminded him of the seriousness of the situation. Mrs. Zheng surprised everyone by shouting: "No, no way!" Mr. Liu cast a pleading look her way. "All right," the policeman said, "we'll send this to court."

Mrs. Zheng couldn't have been happier, and crowed about how she'd won the day. She also made sure everyone heard how Mr. Liu had made a fool of himself at the station.

You know how things turned out. Mr. Liu sent someone to talk to Mr. and Mrs. Zheng, asking them to drop the charges. Mrs. Zheng was adamant, but fortunately the wives of some of the men joined Mr. Zheng in getting her to accept an apology from Mr. Liu, who spent twenty yuan on sweets and biscuits, which he left at old Mr. Wang's to await the arrival of the Zhengs. They dressed up for the occasion. While they were taking off their shoes, Mr. Liu rushed up and said, "Mrs. Zheng, I treated you badly the other day." He bowed. Then he turned to Mr. Zheng. "Mr. Zheng, I treated your wife badly the other day," he said. Obviously embarrassed, Mr. Zheng stammered something and, it appeared, halfway returned the bow. He even looked like he wanted to shake the man's hand, but he held back. Old Mr. Wang and some of the other peacemakers smiled, trying to look happy, and said, "All right, then, let bygones be bygones. A misunderstanding, now it's over. Remember the old saying about turning a spear into a precious gift, so from now on, let's greet each other when we meet, like we used to. We all live here, you know!" Rather than overstay their welcome, Mr. and Mrs. Zheng said their goodbyes. "Don't leave yet, sit a while," old Mr. Wang said. "Try these snacks." But Mr. Liu, who was standing toward the rear and trying hard to smile, said, "No thanks, I have things to do at home." Mrs. Zheng later told everyone that the snacks wound up being eaten by the kids in the Wang family. As soon as the Zhengs left, Mr. Liu followed, thanking old Mr. Wang on the way out for all his help. "Don't mention it," old Mr. Wang said. "That's what colleagues are for." Then, with great sincerity, he added that it was wrong for people to laugh about his relationship with Ah Li, and that modern society shouldn't tolerate old, bankrupt concepts. Mr. Liu gazed at him as he spoke, then said in his own defense, "Ah Li started it with me. I'm a college graduate, I wouldn't have done it." He said this loudly, his head high, as if he wanted everyone in the hostel to hear him.

Ah Li's belly swelled and swelled, and it would be quite a disgrace if they didn't get married soon. But Mr. Liu kept putting it off. One day I spotted Ah Li in the toilet in tears. When I asked why she was crying, she said Mr. Liu wanted her to have an abortion. I was furious. I told her to report him to the Women's Association, but she shook her head and said no. When the others found out, they warned Mr. Liu, saying he couldn't do whatever he felt like with women, and if he kept it up, they'd file charges against him as a result of public indignation. Even Ah Li's adoptive parents came from the south—naturally, that forced him to pick a wedding date. So Mr. Liu chose a date, but it rained that day as the couple rode to the courthouse in a pedicab. Old Mr. Wang and a few others were the only witnesses, and no party was planned. An hour later, they returned in their pedicab, but they were not met with a round of firecrackers.

I wonder if they'll be handing out red eggs one of these days to announce the blessed event. It'll be easy for them, since those chicks have all become laying hens. "They've been feeding them with rice stolen from the kitchen, which is why they're so fat." Mrs. Zheng was angry when she said this. Now, I think that's an unfair accusation, since face is so important to Mr. Liu.

Ah, it's past five o'clock! I can't believe we've been talking for an hour and a half. I'll be on my way, Mrs. Wang. Don't get up, I can see myself out. If you insist on being so polite, I won't be coming back.

Translated by Howard Goldblatt

Withered Chrysanthemums

April 1959. This story describes the fading love between a young professor and his wife. The relationship, symbolized by withered chrysanthemums, is subtly reflected through the professor's thoughts one chilly afternoon. This story is one of the four works that Wang wrote during his second year of university, a comparatively prolific period during his writing career.

I

Like the other teachers, Guo Muxian and Lin Xuan lived in the staff dorm just a block from the school. The dorm consisted of a row of green, one-storey wooden buildings with tile roofs that housed ten families, each provided with an identical apartment. You entered the living room with a smallish bedroom on the left side and a kitchen and bathroom in the rear. Behind each apartment was a small yard with a cinder-block wall separating it from the neighboring yard. This space could be used as a place to raise chickens or hang clothes to dry.

Originally, all ten families shared a large, flat expanse of lawn in front of the building. A straight white cement path extended from the doorway of each home, dividing the grass into a series of squares. At some point, a family living at one end of the building had erected a bamboo fence to enclose the patch of grass in front of their door. When the other families saw this, they followed the example and bamboo fences appeared in front of each home, enclosing the lawns with a series of nine fences that marked off each neighbor's territory from the others. As a result, not only did each family have a backyard, they also gained front yards three times as deep. Those with business sense could raise more Leghorn chickens; on sunny days you could see several white Leghorns strutting on the green lawn. Those not interested in raising chickens could plant flowers, while those with children could fence them inside their own yards, preventing them from getting into fights with the neighbors' children and causing more problems for their mothers.

Only Guo Muxian's family had failed to make good use of their front yard: they raised no chickens, planted no flowers and had no children. Neither husband nor wife took care of the grass, which had grown quite long and now encroached on the pathway. On the left side of the yard near the fence sat a bamboo stool. No one could remember when the stool had first been put there, but someone had forgotten to take it in. The yard's untidy state could be blamed in part on the fact that both husband and wife were too busy. Both were teachers, Guo Muxian taught English while his wife taught history at a girls' secondary school. Another reason was that Guo Muxian was lazy. It would not be completely correct to say that the idea of raising chickens began with the wives, though it would not be wrong to say that the idea of raising flowers had been suggested by the husbands. In any case, Guo Muxian had no interest in gardening. He cared only about reading his books and studying literature.

On a certain afternoon during winter vacation, the sky was overcast and everything had turned a uniform gray color. It had rained continuously for several days and had only stopped that morning, though it looked like it might rain again. Guo Muxian's bicycle was parked under the eaves of the building. A black rubber raincoat was draped over it and the kickstand straddled a sewage channel. No matter what the weather was like, the bicycle remained in the same place and was only wheeled into the living room just before bedtime each evening. Besides the raincoat-covered bicycle, there also was a rusted iron dustpan next to the front door. Although the bottom section had rusted out, it still held pieces of tangerine peel. Guo Muxian sat in the living room reading a book. The living room doubled as his study. Beneath the window was a desk. When the curtain covering the window was pulled back, you could see the front yard, but now the curtain happened to be pulled shut. Against the right wall sat a bamboo bookcase. Against each of the other two walls, pairs of rattan chairs were placed with tea tables between them. Together, these items represented all of the furniture in the living room. On the rattan chairs were several old seat cushions decorated with a purplish red floral pattern and on each of the tea tables sat a leaf-shaped rubber coaster. In one corner of the room was a large table that was used at mealtimes. On it were placed a thermos bottle for hot water, some upside down glasses and a vase of flowers containing some withered yellow chrysanthemums with drooping buds, curling leaves and blackened stems. The water in the vase had long since evaporated and the narrow petals looked like a mass of tangled hair. The only decoration on the walls was a Northwest Airlines calendar of scenic places—the month of February revealed a picture of the Golden Gate Bridge in San Francisco. Two or three days had passed since the last blasts of New Year's firecrackers had been heard. The room was quiet. The room was more than just quiet. The cold seemed to seep into it through the concrete floor.

Since getting up that morning at nine o'clock, Guo Muxian had been reading. Feeling he had wasted too much time during the winter break, he had taken the opportunity of the last few days of vacation to get busy, which helped him feel a bit more relaxed about the start of the new term. Since the weather was cloudy, the lamp on the table was turned on; otherwise, Guo Muxian would not have been able to see well enough to read. The lampshade was made of pleated green cloth while the ceramic base was shaped like a wolfhound with its head raised and tongue sticking out. Compared with the living room, which was relatively tidy, the desk was a frightful mess. Dictionaries, writing paper, magazines and paperback English novels were stacked one on top of the other, and an empty box that had once held a bottle of Parker fountain pen ink lay crushed underneath everything. On the window sill, a pile of students' English workbooks had yet to be graded. Guo Muxian intended to return them to the students next term—he would just have to tell them he hadn't had time to look at them. He refused to let Lin Xuan tidy up because even though he had made such a mess, he still could find what he needed with little effort. Had she tidied up, it would have been much harder for him to find things.

Guo Muxian had a rather long face with clean, pale skin. His mouth, which was small to begin with, looked even smaller when he pressed his lips together as he read. He had a narrow, pointed nose—the small, finely crafted kind. In spite of these features, he did not appear either disgusting or unhealthy. On the contrary, people thought of him as intelligent and meticulous, if also a bit proud, especially when his dark, thoughtful eyes looked out from behind his glasses, their frames bordered in red. With his glasses perched at the end of his nose, he looked just like a member of the registration office staff when they examined a student's photograph to verify his identity. As he read, his eyes moved slowly up and down and his lips opened slightly. In sum, Guo Muxian gave the impression of someone disposed to precision and deep thought. His V-neck pullover, cut narrow in the shoulders and made of a coarsely woven fabric, was a unique blend of violet and pale red, most likely the result of fading. The collar of a none-too-clean white shirt emerged from the sweater.

With his spine pressed against the back of the wooden chair, Guo Muxian sat upright and looked as serious as a judge in court. Whatever book he was reading always remained precisely the same distance from his eyes; he held this volume in one hand that was propped against the edge of the table. He sat in this position with hardly any movement, except to use a finger to reposition the glasses when they slid to the tip of his nose. Sometimes as he read he would feel with his hand for the teacup that sat on the table, remove its lid and take a sip of tea. At other times his hand would feel for the handkerchief that also lay on the table, which he would then use to wipe his nose because he had caught a cold, probably due to the fact that he had not dressed warmly enough after getting out of bed.

He read slowly. Sometimes when he came to unfamiliar words he was too lazy to look up in the dictionary, he would rack his brains to guess their meaning. This wasted a great deal of time, of course. Sometimes he could not focus his attention and his mind would wander to other things. As a result, he found he could not make sense of entire paragraphs of text. When he discovered he had missed the meaning of a particular paragraph, his stubborn nature would compel him to focus his attention and read it again and again until he understood it. When he came to a particularly well-written passage, he could not bear to move on and would read it over again and again. When he turned pages he used the greatest care—his long, clean, white finger dexterously brushed the top edge of a page, pulled it back and only then did he insert his finger into the space behind the page and turn it without leaving the slightest crease or fold. He took such great care because the book was new and he had borrowed it from a friend. Had it been one of his own older books, he would have been nowhere near as careful and would have made notes in the margins.

Someone pushed open the gate in the front yard and headed up the cement path toward the house, casting a dark shadow on the frosted glass door as they approached. Guo Muxian raised his head and recognized the shadow as belonging to his wife. As she turned the doorknob and pushed the door open, a gust of cold wind surged in from outside. Guo Muxian felt chilled, drew in his shoulders and knit his brows. Through the open door he could see the gray sky, the wet, dark fence and the morning glories climbing up it as well as the weeds that dotted the ground. He nervously awaited the bang that signaled the door was closed. Lin Xuan shut the door behind her, making the anticipated slamming sound.

Lin Xuan had just returned from getting a permanent at the hairdresser's. They had cut her hair so short that you could see her earlobes, which made it look like a round cake had been stuck on the back of her head. The tight, oily curls reminded Guo Muxian of a negro's curly hair. Guo Muxian disliked such short hair, preferring longer, shoulder length hair with large, soft, loose-hanging curls. She wore a black wool jacket and a pair of black wool pants, neither of them new. A flowery nylon scarf was knotted around her neck and stuffed into the collar of her coat. She carried a dark raincoat over her left arm. She had an oval face devoid of powder or lipstick, leaving a yellowish complexion that highlighted several pimples. The corners of her forehead were shiny with hair oil. She had rather attractive eyes. When she looked at something, she would lower her head ever so slightly and stare at the object for some time as if it had somehow aroused her sympathy. Just by looking into those eyes one could tell that she was too trusting of others, a weakness in Lin Xuan's character. At this moment, this was how she was staring at Guo Muxian. Neither spoke. Guo Muxian abruptly lowered his head and continued reading, in part because he did not want his wife to stand there bothering him. So Lin Xuan headed into the bedroom.

She emerged a moment later holding a mirror on a wire stand. She looked at herself in the mirror, turning her head this way and that, using her fingers to tease the hair behind her ears. She held the mirror first to her left and then, a few minutes later, shifted it to her right. Guo Muxian could tell that she was standing next to him, but he did not dare look at her. He wished he could shrink so small that he could escape her attention. He was taking in nothing that he was reading because he was upset, having had a premonition that at any moment Lin Xuan might speak to him. As soon as that happened, he would have to stop his reading. The longer this sense of anxiety continued, the more nervous he became.

Finally, with her back to her husband, Lin Xuan said, "I never expected that so many people would be getting their hair done so long after the holiday. Wasn't I gone for quite a while?"

Guo Muxian was annoyed. He made his answer as short as possible and spoke without raising his head, "No. Not too long."

"Not too long? Just about drove me crazy waiting. I was afraid I wouldn't get home in time to make dinner. Fortunately, they worked really fast. What do you think—how does it look?" Lin Xuan took a couple of steps toward her husband, and Guo Muxian had to force himself to look up. So his wife would not notice his indifference, he replied warmly: "Not bad, they did a good job."

"I don't like how short they cut it. Brother! It really looks hideous—isn't it too short?"

"No, it's just right, not too short at all." Guo Muxian was afraid of saying anything more so he lowered his head. Now Lin Xuan felt better. She noticed the oil on her forehead and went into the bedroom to wipe it off.

Guo Muxian could not immediately find where he had stopped reading. First he started reading a paragraph beyond where he had left off, and then ended up rereading a section he had already read. Only after a long period of searching did he find the right spot. "Katherine shouted loudly at Frank, and said tearfully, 'Get out! Get out! I don't want to see you. All your talk of love was nothing but lies—a pack of lies! . . .'"

Lin Xuan reemerged. She had put on a pair of green plastic sandals with pink plastic straps across them. They made a clip-clopping sound as they struck the concrete floor. Guo Muxian felt his wife was disturbing him again. As before, he braced himself for her to reenter the room. He fixed his eyes on the last word he had read so as not to lose his place. Lin Xuan did not go back into the bedroom but opened the door and went outside. Cold wind, the dark fence, the grass—he shrugged his shoulders and prepared himself for the slamming sound of the door, but this time she closed it gently and with great care. She clip-clopped along the cement path. Not long after, he heard the piercing voice of their neighbor, Mrs. Chen, saying: "Oh, Mrs. Guo, you just got your hair permed. It looks great!"

Guo Muxian was delighted, for now she would not come back and disturb him. He wiped his nose with a handkerchief and then felt around for the teacup. The tea had gone cold; as soon as the cold liquid touched his lips he put the cup back down. He was too lazy to get up and refill it with hot water. There was a single tea leaf stuck to his lips and, as he continued to read, he used the tip of his tongue to locate it. He was not sure how long it took to find the leaf and spit it out.

About half an hour later, he heard someone open the front gate and enter the front yard. He frowned, thinking Lin Xuan had returned but the sound of the footsteps wasn't right. The person approaching cast an unfamiliar shadow on the glass door. From the outside, the shadow called out: "Madam, please open the door."

Guo Muxian stood up and pulled the door open. A Taiwanese woman in her forties stood before him. She had a dark, thin face, had her hair in a bun and wore a cloth skirt. At first she seemed a bit surprised to see him. Then she seemed a little uneasy. Finally, she closed her eyes and spread her lips into a smile that revealed a full mouth of gold teeth that had turned black. "Oh, it's you, sir. Your wife isn't home? The laundry's done."

Guo Muxian nodded without a trace of a smile on his face as he took the stack of neatly ironed clothes and then shut the door right away.

After putting the clothes on the bed in the bedroom, he sat down again and continued reading, but the image of the Taiwanese woman remained in his mind. He suddenly recalled an article he had read in the morning paper about a laundry woman who had left two children behind when she committed suicide by jumping into the Danshui River. At that moment he felt sorry for the fate of laundry women in general, not just the woman mentioned in the newspaper, but for all laundry women, including the one who had just dropped off the clothes. Suddenly he thought, why not write a story about a laundry woman? He could use the woman he had just met as the main character and use the details from the newspaper article for the plot. This idea excited him for a while and he thought of all kinds of things he could write. After about ten minutes, though, his enthusiasm waned as he realized that none of his ideas was any good and the story didn't seem to make much sense. Dejected, he went back to reading his book.

Not long after, Lin Xuan returned. She and Mrs. Chen must have talked up a storm—she'd forgotten it was time to fix dinner, but Guo Muxian never paid much attention to what time his wife cooked or served for dinner. It was dark now. Li Xuan tied on her apron and went into the kitchen to take care of things. Guo Muxian seemed only half aware of the sounds of her washing rice, chopping vegetables and removing the lid of the wok. Regardless, it did not disturb him. When his eyes became dry and scratchy, he knew he had been reading too long. He took off his glasses and rubbed his slightly swollen eyes. With his glasses removed, his eyes looked lifeless and artificial. Beneath each eye was a white semicircle, caused by pressure from the frames. Guo Muxian decided to take a break so he put his book down on the table and inserted a fountain pen between the pages to mark his place. He stretched his tired back, extended his arms and yawned silently. Afterward, he felt like having a cigarette—he hadn't had a smoke all day. He headed into the bedroom to get them. A few minutes later, he came out and called into the kitchen: "Hey, what happened to my cigarettes? And what about my khaki pants?"

Lin Xuan was in the middle of chopping vegetables. She stopped and replied: "I put the cigarettes in the drawer for you. Matches are there, too. Your khaki pants were sent out to be washed this morning. Good thing I went through the pockets or a perfectly good pack of cigarettes would have been wasted."

He remembered that last night Lin Xuan had told him to empty his pockets before he went to bed because his khaki pants were to be washed the next day, but he had forgotten. When he heard what she said, an unhappy Guo Muxian replied: "You make it so hard to find things when you put them in the drawer. Why not put them on the table?"

As he was smoking, he realized that she was not in the wrong and that his complaint was unwarranted. Though he felt somewhat ashamed, he did not want to let her see any sign of regret on his part.

After smoking the cigarette, his desire to read had diminished significantly. He pressed together the pages he had already read and, to his surprise, found that he had completed quite a thick stack. He thought to himself that if he just read another ten pages or so, he would have finished about half the book. This vain ambition caused him to marshal his courage to keep reading, and he decided he would not take a break until he had finished half the book.

II

Guo Muxian had felt his cold take a turn for the worse that afternoon. Not only did he have a runny nose, but the bridge of his nose ached so much that his eyes watered. Lin Xuan was just about to serve dinner so she came in and stood on tiptoe to turn on the light. The lamp hung from the center of the ceiling and was covered with a hexagonal green shade with yellow tassels dangling from each corner. Guo Muxian did not much care for the shade but Lin Xuan had seen it while she was out one day—she liked it and bought it. The lamp swung back and forth, casting shadows that floated on the wall, making the small room look a bit like the cabin of a ship being tossed to and fro on the ocean. Guo Muxian was still four pages away from meeting the goal he had set for himself. He knew he could not finish them before dinner but he was caught up in the story. These particular pages described a pair of lovers discussing their feelings for each other.

Lin Xuan removed her apron and called him to the table. Guo Muxian gave a vague response but failed to move. Lin Xuan prodded him: "Hurry up. The food's getting cold."

Only at this point did Guo Muxian get up. The table that sat in the corner with the teacups and thermos bottle on it also served as their dinner table. At meal times, two round stools that normally were placed beneath the table were pulled out. The teacups and thermos were pushed to the back of the table, leaving about half of the surface clear for putting out plates and bowls and a blackened rice pot. Steam rose from the plates and bowls on the table. Guo Muxian sat down and Lin Xuan sat down after him. Guo Muxian again felt that he did not like her hair and lowered his eyes to look at the plates of food on the table. As he ate, he kept thinking about the pages he had yet to finish in his book. Lin Xuan informed him that three of Mrs. Chen's chickens had frozen to death, which had caused her husband, one of Guo Muxian's colleagues, much heartache. Mr. Chen had won one hundred yuan playing cards at New Year's. He had hoped to use the money to order a copy of *Webster's*

Dictionary but—who would have thought it?—Mrs. Chen wanted to use the money to buy their child, Little Mao, a winter coat. Mr. Chen had no choice but to go along with his wife. Guo Muxian took in none of this as his mind was still worrying about the pages he had left to read. In order to convince his wife that he was paying attention to her, he took his chopsticks, pointed to the pan-fried fish and said: "That dish is too bland, next time you should use more salt."

Lin Xuan explained that she had planned to add more salt, but the last time she had made it he had told her it was too salty so this time she was afraid to repeat the same mistake and had used less. With that, she took the half of the fish that remained and put it in her husband's bowl. Guo Muxian politely resisted out of courtesy but then accepted the fish. At this point, he felt that his wife had treated him much better than he deserved—he felt ashamed by her kindness but also grateful. His outward expression revealed no trace of these emotions.

Although Guo Muxian wanted to get back to reading as soon as he finished dinner, he did not rush his meal. Nevertheless, he left the table before Lin Xuan.

After dinner, in hardly any time at all, Guo Muxian finished the remaining pages by reading much faster than normal. He could not say why this was the case, but by the time he had inserted a piece of blotting paper to mark his place and closed the book, he felt bored again. It was still early and how was he to fill so much time? He thought of going out to have a chat with another teacher, Mr. Wu, but at that moment he could hear rain falling outside the window. Even though Mr. Wu lived nearby, Guo Muxian was too lazy to put on his raincoat and head out into the storm. Lin Xuan, who had finished washing the dishes, brought out the white flower tablecloth she had been knitting and sat down in one of the rattan chairs. She had intended to make two tablecloths over the holiday but winter vacation was almost over and she had yet to finish the first one. Guo Muxian shifted in his seat and turned on the radio that sat on the bookshelf. There were no classical music programs at this hour so he spun the tuning knob and the radio emitted a series of sharp, mouselike squeals.

"Let's listen to that one, that program sounds nice," Lin Xuan raised her head and said.

"Which one? This one?" Against his will, Guo Muxian forced the dial back to the previous station. He did not care much for popular American music but if Lin Xuan wanted to listen to it, he had no choice. He disdained the kind of music Lin Xuan liked so he turned down the volume in order to listen to it without offending his musical sensibilities.

Suddenly there was a soft tap on the glass panel of the front door. With rain falling and the weather outside so cold, who could it be?

"Who is it?" Lin Xuan called out.

"Uh, it's me," someone answered without identifying himself.

The voice sounded unfamiliar, and they had no idea who it was. Guo Muxian walked over and opened the door. "Oh, come in, come in. When did you arrive in Taipei?" Guo Muxian said to the person standing outside the door. Lin Xuan put down the tablecloth and stood up.

"I've been here a week," the guest answered.

In order to close the door, Guo Muxian stood to one side so the guest could step in. He wore a yellow canvas raincoat that had been soaked by the rain. His rain hat covered the upper half of his face, making him look rather mysterious. After he came in, he removed the hat and revealed a youthful white face with red cheeks covered with drops of water. His extremely broad smile made him look like a big, honest boy. His bright red lips were dry and cracked. He nodded to Lin Xuan and then removed his raincoat, revealing the leather jacket he wore beneath it. He was tall, quite large in stature. Unsure of what to do with his dripping raincoat, he just held it in his hand. Guo Muxian took it from him, careful to grasp it with just the tips of his fingers, and hung it on a nail protruding from the back of the door.

"Sit down, sit down," Lin Xuan said with a smile as she poured him a cup of hot tea. The guest took the teacup and sat down. He extended his long legs—the cuffs of his pants had been soaked by the rain. Guo Muxian returned to the chair he had been sitting in and adjusted it so that he faced the guest. Then, with a click, he turned off the radio without even a glance at Lin Xuan.

"How long have you been in town?" Guo Muxian asked as soon as he got himself settled. He had forgotten he had already asked this question.

"A week," the guest replied with another smile. He always smiled when he spoke. He had come to Taipei from Tainan.

"Are you staying at your older brother's place?" Lin Xuan asked.

"Yes," he replied as he used a handkerchief to wipe the raindrops from his face. His older brother was a university classmate of Guo Muxian's, and because they were all about the same age, the guest also was a friend of Guo Muxian's, though there was a certain reserve behind his politeness.

Guo Muxian was now in a happier mood—with the prospect of a visitor, the evening would not be boring. He reached over to pick up the pack of cigarettes on the table, removed one and leaned forward to hand it to the guest, but the guest smiled and said that he had yet to take up smoking. Guo Muxian smiled slightly, put the cigarette in his own lips, lit it and started to smoke. He sat up straight and raised his brow, smoke surging through his nostrils. He asked his guest with a smile: "What have you been up to?" When Guo Muxian smiled, his upper lip turned upward as if with contempt.

Thus their conversation began. Guo Muxian, however, was by no means a brilliant conversationalist, nor was his guest, so their discussion moved forward at a slow pace. Lin Xuan took the opportunity to resume working on the tablecloth while the men conversed.

III

Half an hour later both men were silent. Guo Muxian could think of nothing to say. Neither could his guest, who fidgeted with his teacup. Guo Muxian was getting tired and losing interest in what the guest was talking about. The guest loved to go on about what was happening at the company he worked for but Guo Muxian found this boring—he liked to talk about the latest books and what he had been reading. What's more, he felt the guest had no insights to offer—with each word he uttered, the visitor revealed how poorly thought out his ideas were.

Having finally thought of a new topic, the guest raised his head, smiled a childish smile and said: "What did you do during the New Year's holiday?"

"I played cards all evening," Lin Xuan responded as she knitted.

"Did you win or lose?"

"I lost," Lin Xuan replied with some hesitation. "But not very much, we played for the fun of it. Win or lose, it was only twenty or thirty yuan."

Guo Muxian glanced at Lin Xuan.

"He doesn't play," Lin Xuan added with a laugh, referring to Guo Muxian.

The guest looked at Guo Muxian and laughed but Guo Muxian did not smile and said nothing.

"As far as pastimes go, card-playing is wonderful fun, and as long as you don't overdo it there's no harm in it. What's more, it has benefits . . ." the guest added. Guo Muxian thought this was rubbish and felt disgusted so he averted his glance. There was another lull in the conversation. Guo Muxian crossed his legs and folded his arms in front of his chest, staring at the guest. The guest avoided Guo Muxian's gaze. Lin Xuan spoke up: "Your tea is cold. Let me pour some hot tea for you."

"Please, there's no need. I've already had plenty and I don't want any more, thank you," he responded. Lin Xuan still poured hot tea for him. Steam rose from his cup. Guo Muxian's eyes followed the movement of the steam as it rose.

"I heard that your sister-in-law has had another boy, right?" Lin Xuan asked as she returned to her seat and took up her knitting.

The guest blushed, smiled and nodded, saying that this was the case.

"He must be three months old by now."

"He's just two months old, at least I think that's how old he is. I'm not quite certain."

Guo Muxian continued to stare at the steam curling up from his guest's teacup. His mind was blank. Then he heard Lin Xuan say: "What about you? When will you invite us to your wedding banquet?"

Guo Muxian raised his eyes and looked at the guest. He wanted to hear how he was going to answer this question—his eyes now revealed a trace of interest. But the guest blushed, shook his head and stammered out a denial: "No . . . no . . . I still . . . still . . . still haven't started to look."

"Nonsense. I heard your brother say that you have a very attractive girlfriend in Tainan. You can't deny that!" Guo Muxian began to laugh as he spoke. The guest didn't know how to respond but sat squirming in his chair as the blood rushed to his head. He could only look at Guo Muxian and smile. Guo Muxian quickly forged ahead and asked: "Hey, tell us about your girlfriend! I want to hear about her." It seemed as if Guo Muxian had just awakened from a dream and was full of energy. He shifted his sitting position and crossed his legs, with the leg that had been on top now on the bottom. Strange, but at that moment, through his formerly congested nose, he now suddenly got a whiff of the withered chrysanthemums in the vase.

IV

The guest did not know where to begin, so Guo Muxian simply began asking him questions.

"Are you coworkers?" Guo Muxian queried as he lit another cigarette, his face illuminated by the glowing match. "She isn't a classmate, so how did you get to know each other?" he added right after exhaling a cloud of smoke.

A year earlier, the guest began, he had frequently visited the home of a friend. This friend's younger sister also happened to invite over a girl from her class, so that was how they had got acquainted.

"She's only in high school?" Guo Muxian asked, taken aback. The guest said she had graduated but did not pass the university admissions exam and did not plan to take it again.

As their conversation continued, Guo Muxian enjoyed interjecting a comment every now and then to tease the guest. For example, when the guest mentioned how he had first met the girl, Guo Muxian waved his hand and said: "So it was love at first sight, right?" This was so out of character for Guo Muxian that Lin Xuan wondered what had come over him. She soon forgot about it, though, and stopped paying much attention to their conversation—she'd made a mistake in her knitting and was anxiously counting her lines.

The guest had been reluctant at first to tell Guo Muxian how he had met his girlfriend, but as the conversation continued, he became more relaxed and talkative, and willingly divulged the smallest details as he remembered them. As he spoke, his face revealed a sense of happiness. Nevertheless, he intentionally brought up some of his girlfriend's idiosyncrasies, the usual picky criticisms that arise when you grow close to someone. He liked to shake his head and say with a sigh: "A bother. A real bother."

Guo Muxian laughed and said: "Nothing of the sort. How can love be a bother!"

After about half an hour, the guest sighed and said: "Well, actually she is still a child. Her mood is pretty unstable and changes from moment to moment so you can't predict how she'll behave. Sometimes in the morning she'll agree to go to a movie with me in the afternoon, but by the time afternoon rolls around, she'll cancel at the last minute. When I ask her why she can't go, she'll just say she suddenly decided she doesn't want to go. Sometimes I send her a whole series of letters but she doesn't answer a single one. When I see her later, I ask her why she didn't answer my letters. She becomes a real smart aleck and says: 'Well, aren't I talking with you now? Since we can talk face to face, what's the point of answering your letters?' How do you respond to that?"

Guo Muxian nodded and smiled.

The guest then described a disagreement they'd had. After the spat, she had refused to talk to him.

"Really, and what did you do? You must have lost some sleep over that. I bet you wrote and asked her to forgive you, right?" Guo Muxian quickly replied with a chuckle.

"It didn't go quite that way. I was sad, to be sure, but didn't lose any sleep," the guest said with a grin. "Of course, I did send a letter of apology, but as before she failed to respond. I sent one letter after another and got no reply. Fortunately, I'm reasonably patient, so after I sent a third letter and received no reply, I mailed a fourth letter. Still no reply, so I sent a fifth letter, gradually wearing down her anger and working out our differences. In the seventh letter, I mentioned that *A Farewell to Arms* was showing the next night. I would wait for her at the entrance to the theater. I didn't go to pick her up because she had forbidden me to go and see her. I figured she would come, but I waited until the movie was about to start and there was still no sign of her. I got nervous and thought she might not come. I decided to leave—I'd lost interest in seeing the movie. Just as I was about to go, she showed up. As soon as she saw me, she frowned and said: 'What are you doing standing out here? Why didn't you go in?' I replied: 'I was waiting for you!' She responded: 'Why wait for me? Am I worth waiting for?' "

"Oh, is that what she said? Did she really say that?" Guo Muxian said with amazement as he leaned forward, the light flashing off his glasses.

Later, Guo asked: "What does she look like? Describe her to me."

"My girlfriend? She's rather hard for me to describe. Well, you can't really say she's beautiful." (Guo Muxian interrupted with a laugh, "Of course you would say she's not attractive, but then I can't believe what you say, can I?") "She has long, shoulder-length hair, big eyes, long eyelashes, that's about all I can put into words."

"So she's not attractive, eh? Long, shoulder-length hair, big eyes, long eyelashes, sounds like she's really beautiful," Guo Muxian said, shaking his head as he praised her. He discarded the cigarette butt he was holding and stamped it out with his foot. He did not notice that he had dropped a significant amount of ash on his clothes.

The guest reached into the back pocket of his pants to get something. Guo Muxian quickly asked: "Do you have a picture of her? It would be wonderful if you do."

"Let me see if I brought it with me," he replied. Guo Muxian looked expectantly at the guest's slow, casual movements. Lin Xuan scratched her head as she watched the guest struggle to pull out his wallet. Finally, the black leather wallet was extricated. The guest opened it, flipped through it and said: "Nope. I forgot to bring it."

"Oh, how could you forget to bring it!" complained an extremely disappointed Guo Muxian. To Lin Xuan, Guo's reaction was quite strange.

V

Just before ten o'clock, the guest glanced at his watch, stood up anxiously and said: "Oh, it's quite late, I should be going."

Lin Xuan felt it was late as well. Perhaps because the weather was so bad, she felt tired and wanted to get to bed early. She had yawned several times while knitting the tablecloth. Since she had no interest in detaining the guest any longer, she stood up when he did, concealing another yawn with her hand. Guo Muxian, however, felt a tinge of regret. The guest's imminent departure disappointed him somehow. He knew he had little hope of delaying the departure of his guest, yet still he remained seated and said: "Stay a little longer. Why leave so early? You certainly don't go to bed this early."

Lin Xuan wondered if she should sit back down or remain standing. A real predicament.

"I usually stay up late, but my elder brother and his family retire early, and I don't want to have them waiting up for me."

Guo Muxian could do nothing but stand up to see off his guest. The man put on his raincoat and hat, which again made him look mysterious.

Lin Xuan said: "Please give your brother and sister-in-law our regards."

"I will," the guest replied with a smile.

"When you come to Taipei again, be sure to drop by and see us," Lin Xuan added. The man agreed, said goodbye and told Guo Muxian that he didn't have to see him off.

"He's just going out to shut the gate," Lin Xuan explained.

Guo Muxian opened the front door and followed his guest outside.

Although the rain had stopped, it was so cold that Guo Muxian began to shiver. He thought of putting on a coat, but it was too late. He could only grit his teeth and follow his guest. They walked along the cement path, which in the darkness appeared to be an especially vivid shade of gray. Guo Muxian opened the icy cold gate. The guest said: "See you later" and extended his hand. Guo Muxian hesitated for a moment, fearing his hand was too cold and shaking it would make his guest uncomfortable, but he finally decided to extend his hand and shake the warm, strong hand of the guest. Both men bowed to each other and the guest turned and headed off. Guo Muxian couldn't stand the cold so he hurriedly closed the gate, latched it, turned and headed back to the house. When he saw the bicycle sitting under the eaves, he remembered he should take it inside. He removed the black raincoat, shook off the water, rolled it up into a bundle and tied it to the rack on the back of the bike. He opened the front door, pushed the bicycle inside and put down the kickstand. The addition of the bicycle made the living room seem crowded.

Lin Xuan had already left the living room, having gone into the bedroom to make the bed and get ready to sleep. Guo Muxian felt the soreness in his nose and tears began to well up in his eyes. He knew his cold was getting worse. He inhaled through his nostrils to test whether he could still smell the withered chrysanthemums. Now that he couldn't, he was certain his cold really had gotten worse.

Translated by Steven L. Riep

Paralysis

June 1959. This is one of the rare works Wang Wen-hsing published under a penname—Tong Ma. The story describes a university student's first experience of dancing with women.

Shen Qingwen could not open his eyes. The light inside the house was too bright. His mother, wrapped in an old brown coat, had just crawled out of bed to open the door for him. Following him in, she said: "It's very late, probably already midnight." "It's 12:30," Shen Qingwen replied, opening his eyes slightly to look at his watch. Taking off his raincoat and tossing it onto the chair, he continued: "There wasn't even one bus and the pedicabs wanted to soak me for ten yuan, plus an extra yuan when I got off—Ma, please wake me a little later tomorrow. You should go to bed now." He went into his bedroom. "Walk a little softly, your father is sleeping," his mother ordered. He turned on the light to discover that his mother had already made the bed and lowered the mosquito netting. Even though his eyelids were heavy he was not sleepy but felt he could sit up until daybreak. He took off his suit jacket and hung it on the clothes rack. Then, lifting his head, he undid his tie and carefully pulled it off. He had borrowed this red tie from his father. He noticed that many of his classmates had tied a Windsor knot in theirs, which looked much better than his. If they held another dance, he would have to get them to teach him beforehand. After taking off his tie, he undid the shirt button at his throat and sat down to massage his right leg. It was the sore one. The left one actually did not seem tired. While Shen Qingwen was massaging his leg, he hummed the tune to *The Tennessee Waltz*. After humming a few bars, he stopped as his mind slipped into deep thought, then started humming again.

He stood up, slid forward into a three-step and, twirling his body, backed into another three-step. He just missed knocking over a chair, fell out of his slippers and tripped between two tatami mats. Shen Qingwen leaned against the wall and smiled. He realized how late it was and that he needed to sleep—he wasn't used to going to bed so late. He took off his clothes, shoes and socks, turned out the light and, in the pitch dark, opened the netting and crawled under the quilt.

"What is this? I can't make out the beat!" he asked.

"Jitterbug! Jitterbug! Quick, invite somebody to dance!" Chen Daming answered impatiently. He was standing beside the record player wearing a bright red pullover with two white deer woven into the front. It was only three days since the group had asked Chen Daming to teach them to dance—nobody knew how before—so Chen Daming couldn't avoid assuming a certain bossiness.

A row of girls sat behind the record player but Shen Qingwen did not go over to invite any of them. He was looking for Li Yaqin. She was sitting by the window but the crowd blocked his view of her. Worried that someone else would invite her to dance first, he squeezed his way through and even pushed aside a chair. He heard someone say, "It's really too crowded. This room should be bigger!" She was still there—that was real luck because she was the only one left. The two seats beside her were already empty—if he had been a step slower, she definitely would not have been there. He called her from a distance, fearful the boys standing closer to her would grab the opportunity first. Li Yaqin did not hear his first call so he called a second time. This time she heard him and, somewhat startled, lifted her head to look at him. He bowed vaguely, feeling it would be embarrassing and vulgar if he made a big deal out of bowing. Bending forward slightly and extending one hand substituted for the sentence: "May I please have this dance?" Although these gestures were no more elegant, overall they certainly were far more refined than a formal bow! Why was Li Yaqin startled? Was this the usual way she expressed herself? Could she really be surprised? He had invited her to dance a number of times already. Lowering her head, a slight smile on her lips, she got up slowly. She turned her back and put a small purse—it had been nestled in the folds of her skirt—on the chair. She did all this without looking at him. Her manner was composed, smooth, not as if someone was waiting for her. He, though, could not wait—he pushed right through the crowd and walked out onto the terrazzo floor of the large hall. It was only when he turned to look that he saw her pushing her way through the crowd with difficulty, her downcast eyes smiling slightly. They rose once to look at him as if to say: "It's so crowded I almost can't squeeze through." She was wearing a sweater—he was unsure if it was white or soft yellow. Beneath the red cellophane of the lampshade, the color was indistinct. The sweater wrapped her slim body—it was rather beautiful, the sleeves pushed up near the bend in her arms. A pair of slip-on gold bracelets rode her thin, round wrist—he could almost hear the metal clinking. She was half a head shorter than him, now standing so close as if she expected something but a little hesitant. He was such a fool—she was waiting for him to begin dancing! So he took her hand, perhaps too quickly, too rashly. Was that why she was a little startled again? Her small hand was soft and lustrous, her fingers thin and long with a coolness in them. As before, she did not say much. There was a steady, warm, light smile on her face, her eyes constantly lowered. Whenever she backed into someone else, her mouth opened round and the skin between her eyebrows rose slightly. But her smile remained unchanged even when her left hand rubbed the sore spot where her head had been bumped. He turned her, turned, turned . . .

"Even if you don't dance much, teaching me isn't a problem, is it? Just ignore my mistakes!" Zhou Xinfang's smile revealed a mouth of sparkling white teeth as she sprang to the floor from her chair. "If you make the wrong step, I'll take the blame!" he responded smartly, making them both laugh. Zhou Xinfang was wearing a tight, black wool sweater complemented with a silver butterfly brooch, her hair brushed back into a ponytail. She wore glasses over a pair of mischievous eyes and a small nose. If you came close enough, you would discover a few inconspicuous freckles. He led her to a corner bathed in the dim light of a string of small red and blue lights. There was not much room and they were bumped on all three sides. "Are my steps wrong?" he asked. Zhou Xinfang looked at him and laughed, "Step through it again." He paced out the dance again for her to see. "Was that right?" he asked. Zhou Xinfang's eyes had never left the floor and there was a hint of distress in her laughingly uttered "Uhhh." So they were wrong. This was a disaster! Everybody else was dancing. Only they were standing still. Should he lead her back? How to suggest it? He blushed. Fortunately, Zhang Bingxin offered a way out. Zhang Bingxin had wanted to tell him earlier but was afraid of embarrassing him so he waited until now to say: "You're wrong! This is still the jitterbug, not the cha-cha." Shen Qingwen took advantage of the situation to fake a loud laugh and say: "Oh, no wonder! I thought it was the cha-cha!" Although it was a tricky situation, in the end it seemed to turn out all right. He took her hand. Her fingernails were very long and sank into the center of his palm. "You said you danced poorly but you dance well!" she said. "Really?" He was elated. "We've only been practicing for three days in all. Last night we burned the midnight oil at a friend's place—practicing!" he proclaimed triumphantly. "To reach this level after only three days, that's remarkable! Genius! Why did you boys want to hold this dance, anyway? Is it someone's birthday?" "No, it's not that. We did it for the fun of it. None of us could dance so we thought we should use the occasion to learn, keep up with the times," he said, sidestepping any embarrassment. Both of them laughed. Then he said: "We're not as brave as you think. All we've done is make you girls suffer and prevent you from having a good time." He had not expected these words to come out so smoothly. Before the dance, everybody agreed to utter a few courtesies to the girls but he felt that stock phrases like "we have entertained you poorly" and "awfully sorry" were far too common. In fact, his statement had been the perfect response. Zhou Xinfang said with a laugh: "Not at all! We've had a good time! We thank you so very much!" She danced very well. Once he led her through at least four or five turns, maybe more. Her ponytail was flying and her large green patterned skirt flared out, as alive as a giant lily pad. She carried herself in an interesting way, legs slightly bent and turned at an angle to her upper body, a vision of dance . . .

"The girl in the black sweater dances with confidence. Is she in your class? What's her name?" Zhang Bingxin asked him. "Zhou Xinfang," he answered. "I'm going to ask her to dance! Hey, you all heard me! She's mine! I'm claiming the one wearing a black sweater!" Zhang Bingxin said with a laugh. Everybody laughed and said, "Sssh! Keep your voice down! Go! Go! No one is going to rob you." Zhang Bingxin was the exception among his classmates. He actually knew some of the steps, and dancing well had real advantages— girls like to dance with boys who dance well. Even so, hearing Zhang Bingxin's words made him strangely uncomfortable. Why doesn't he find someone else to dance with, why does he only want to dance with Zhou Xinfang? . . .

Hu Ancheng carried over a tea tray with seven or eight glasses sitting on it, steam rising from the purplish-red liquid. Looking at Hu Ancheng's bearing—he was the image of a servant—almost made him laugh out loud. Without waiting for Hu Ancheng to begin, he went ahead and picked up two glasses. One glass he politely passed to Li Yaqin, the second he passed to Zhou Xinfang, but Li Yaqin did not drink hers. Instead, she looked around for a place to put it down, so he took the glass back from her and put it on the window sill. . .

The crowing of a rooster drifted inside. It was very late, definitely after one o'clock. He rolled over onto his other side, closed his eyes and tried to sleep.

"Aren't you tired? I had four dances and I was beat," Wu Guojun said. Everyone was so warm they had taken off their suit jackets and wore just their white shirts and ties. They looked quite genteel, just like the Forsyth shirt advertisement. When he had first come in, everyone was in a suit, which made them look just like young adults and created an unusual gentlemanly ambience. He found this amusing. Now there was a break between songs: the records were being switched too slowly. They had not arranged them well the night before so the breaks between records were too long. His classmates leaned against the wall, wanting to express their opinions about the girls but dared not. Nobody dared even a smile among themselves, as if that also was against the rules. Even Wu Guojun's question had embarrassed him. He hurried to say: "With so many girls around, how can you give them the cold shoulder? Quick, go ask someone to dance! What's a little fatigue? Tonight we have to bend over backward!" Too bad Wu Guojun didn't get the joke, not one iota. Didn't everybody have to bend slightly when bowing to invite someone to dance? So wasn't it funny to say "bend over backward"? "Before you were opposed to dancing, now we should like it?" Wu Guojun asked. He was startled for an instant before saying with an awkward laugh: "What I said before doesn't count. Ha, ha, ha! . . ."

This was another four-step. He didn't care about Zhang Bingxin so he invited Zhou Xinfang to dance again. "When do you register for school?" he asked. "The twenty-fifth, there are still four more days. The winter holidays have gone by very fast and I haven't done a bit of studying." "The winter holidays are for us to have fun. You're too serious. Why do you have to study!" "I haven't had much fun yet!" "Do you mean this evening!" he said slyly. Zhou Xinfang gave a hurried laugh. She pointed her finger straight at him and said, "You, you love pointing out other people's flaws!" He laughed loudly. "I didn't know until today that Li Yaqin and you were both in foreign languages. I thought Li Yaqin was enrolled in history and geography." "Originally she was, but she transferred last semester." "That explains it. My memory isn't that bad if I do say so myself." "Of course, your memory isn't bad. You just needed half an hour to memorize an English lesson. Li Yaqin and I memorized for a whole day and we still couldn't do it." "Do you still remember that? I'd forgotten completely. See, your memory is better than mine." "You're just being modest again, just being modest!" she was pointing at him again. His repartee was deft tonight. He saw Li Yaqin dance by with someone else and that uncomfortable feeling arose again. He decided that as quickly as possible he would invite her to dance during the next number . . .

"I don't know how!" Li Yaqin shook her head and looked at him with a slight smile. Her voice was very faint but the next sentence surprised him, "Why don't you teach me?" Wow! Say that again! Say that again! "Alright, I'll teach you. It's really easy." After saying that, he felt ridiculous. He was a novice at everything—he couldn't do any of them better than her. Yet, incredibly, here he was flaunting his experience in teaching her. He said, "Look, extend the left foot twice, extend the right foot twice, then jump ahead one step, jump back one step, then again jump ahead three steps." He did it once for her to watch, then said: "Let's try!" At that point the two of them stood shoulder to shoulder. He put his arm around her waist and, somewhat hesitantly, she put her arm around his. After only one try, they had done it. "Did you already know how? You learned very fast. Quick, let's join the others!" he said. Li Yaqin laughed, a little out of breath, and followed him to join the group. He let her stand in front because in this type of dance the dancers lined up one after the other, the person behind holding the person in front steady. He placed his hands ever so lightly on her waist. For the first time he realized just how slender a girl's waist was—it could almost be circled with two hands. Chen Daming, wearing his bright red pullover, took the lead and called out: "Three! Begin!" Like a centipede they began to move. In unison, the centipede extended its left foot, together extended its right foot, then jumped, making dust fly. The girls' long hair flew in disarray as they rocked and swayed this way and that, like they were crazy. One by one the girls laughed to the point of breathlessness. At the same time the song on the record player sounded bizarre, almost like someone was being tickled, making everybody laugh. Because the hall was too small, the centipede found itself holding its tail in its own mouth. Everyone was really tired. Someone yelled: "I'm dead tired—I can't dance another step." At this point, the centipede's feet lost coordination and stopped in disarray, then its body fragmented. He had been watching Li Yaqin carefully but it was only then that he noticed she was holding a crumpled silk handkerchief pressed to her nose. She could barely breathe and her face was a little pale. As he escorted her back to her seat, without thinking he supported her around the waist. . .

He felt uneasy and, because he was standing in front of Li Yaqin again, he bowed slightly to her. Obviously, Li Yaqin was tired and was still using the handkerchief to wipe the perspiration from her face. This was a four-step and when they were halfway through, he said: "It's too crowded here, shall we go into the smaller room?" She nodded with a light smile. There were fewer people in the smaller room, which could only hold four couples. The lights were covered in blue cellophane. He realized he was holding her too close but did not want to move away. He knew Li Yaqin would be annoyed and an inner voice told him: "Move back! You're depraved!" But he didn't pay attention. They moved back and forth together. He could smell the fragrance of her hair and fine curls brushed his face several times . . .

Zhang Bingxin was behind Zhou Xinfang. Shen Qingwen had forgotten about Zhou Xinfang for a while. No doubt Zhang Bingxin had been at her side continually. In fact, he was speaking to her at that moment as if pleading with her. "I really have to go. I need to go home and get some sleep!" she said, putting on a wool overcoat. "Have a little more fun. I am bowing to you. Please stay a little longer," Zhang Bingxin bowed with a happy laugh. Already, dancing together had made them quite familiar with each other. Zhou Xinfang laughed as she bowed to him in return. "Thank you, thank you, thank you. Nevertheless, I really can't stay any longer. Next time I will definitely, most definitely, stay a little longer. I'm afraid, though, that you won't invite us next time." After this Zhang Bingxin said something to Zhou Xinfang that he did not try to hear. He saw that Li Yaqin was picking up a green wool overcoat and preparing to put it on. "Are you going too?" he asked her. "Yes, we'll go together!" Zhou Xinfang had turned her head, clasped Li Yaqin's arm under hers, and answered for her. She clasped it so tight that she looked childish. "Eleven-thirty already, if I don't go home now, my mother will kill me," Li Yaqin said to him softly as she tied her nylon scarf. "It isn't eleven-thirty! There's ten minutes to go according to my watch!" he joked as he looked at his watch. "My watch says twenty minutes to go," Zhang Bingxin responded with a laugh. "Liars, liars!" Zhou Xinfang put up two small fists pretending she was going to hit them. It was clear to him that she had waved her fists in his direction, not Zhang Bingxin's. They all laughed heartily. After that there was nothing to do except let them go, escort them outside the glass doors, and help them put on their raincoats. Zhou Xinfang raised her head and said: "Oh! Oh! I'm so tired. I can't even lift my eyelids!" He went out to call a pedicab. He had not expected that once he stepped outside the main doors he would see a sea of black pedicabs crowded around the doorway. After negotiating and paying the fare, he went back in to ask the girls to come out and get in the pedicab. Chen Daming was standing on the stairs and asked him: "Did you pay the fare yet?" "It's taken care of!" he answered. The girls squirmed into the vehicle and the pedicab driver buttoned down the curtain. Suddenly he wanted to see Li Yaqin again, so he lifted a corner of the curtain, put his head to the opening and said: "The fare has already been paid. Don't pay him a second time." But the interior was utterly black and he couldn't see anyone's face. He only heard Zhou Xinfang say: "Oh! Thank you, thank you! Good bye!" The pedicab pedalled away . . .

"Ladies and gentlemen, it is already twelve o'clock. Our dance is over. Thanks to all of you for attending!" Chen Daming announced standing in the middle of the hall. Then he turned to his friends and said: "Quick, escort our guests out! Quick, escort our guests out! Don't just stand there, get moving!" The glass doors were wide open and the girls were leaving. The boys were busy outside the main door negotiating fares with the pedicab drivers. It was not long before all the girls were gone.

Then everybody tidied up and put things away, turned out the lights, locked the glass doors and went home. "Quick, give me the keys! How could you forget! I have to return them to Mr. Liu tomorrow morning," Chen Daming continued his shouting. He was the one who had borrowed the place from Mr. Liu. Chen Daming kept muttering: "Tonight's dance was awful. Everyone danced terribly. We played mostly three- and four-step songs. There were no more than five or six fast ones. What an embarrassment!" "The dance wasn't up to your standards but we had a great time. Hell, the rain has gotten heavier!" He didn't recall who said it but it was something he had wanted to say . . .

The next morning—it was nearly ten o'clock—Shen Qingwen's mother gingerly entered his bedroom. She placed a couple of buns and the newspaper on his desk, then softly crept out. She went straight to the market to buy groceries. Shen Qingwen continued to sleep soundly for about half an hour before he finally woke. He heard the rain outside the window and opened his eyes. The first thing he saw was the top of the mosquito netting. Through the white blur of the netting, he looked vacantly at the black shadow of his desk. This was his usual routine after waking. In this state, no thoughts flickered through his mind. Suddenly, he remembered that he should think about one thing, and that was the dance last night. He became agitated because it seemed he had forgotten everything. He struggled to remember. Finally, the events of the previous night, one after another, slowly came back. He wanted to lie there longer under the warm quilt but knew that eventually he had to get up. Look at the time—it wasn't early. He made up his mind, pushed away the quilt, lifted the mosquito netting, and roused himself to sit up. Stepping onto the floor, his feet felt unusually cold. He dressed hurriedly, putting on a sweater, which he had not done yesterday. The weather was much colder today. He picked up his shirt when he rose but saw that the collar was black and its points had curled up. He had put it on yesterday afternoon to wear to the dance. It had not occurred to him it could get this dirty. There were large yellow stains in the armpits. He slipped into a dreamy state. The strains of *The Tennessee Waltz* still floated in his ears. Hugging his dirty shirt, he sat back lazily on the bed, lifted the netting, and lay down. Shen Qingwen lay in the foglike white blur of the netting, going over last night's dance: Li Yaqin's lightly smiling face, her long, delicate, cool fingers, Zhou Xinfang pointing her finger at him, also Li Yaqin's slender waist and Li Yaqin's fragrant hair . . . Both were embodiments of beauty. Oh! So pure, like poetry. He felt a sudden surge of emotion. He liked it. He wished he could linger in this state. He closed his eyes and dared not open them, fearful that the moment he opened them this exquisite melancholy would drift away.

Shen Qingwen just lay there like that, his pale face, a faint layer of shadow beneath his closed eyelids, that dirty shirt gripped tight to his chest, the stinging smell of sweat rushing to his nose.

Translated by Lloyd Sciban

Afternoon

August 1959. This ambitious story—considering the author was only a nineteen-year-old university student at the time and unlikely to have had many experiences with small children—is a psychological portrait of a ten-year-old girl. She has been forced by economic circumstances to drop out of school and work as a maid in a private home, where she entertains herself and the baby under her care. In terms of attention to detail, "Afternoon" marks a remarkable advance in Wang Wen-hsing's ability to describe a character's mental process and to control the rhythm of the story's action.

A cold, dark afternoon, still and silent. Ten-year-old Ah Yin kneels on a tatami mat and leans against the window. There is a small bamboo stool but she does not sit on it as she stares into the distance at the gate behind the clump of blood-red azaleas. The gate is shut tight. At New Year's, it received a new coat of paint as red as fresh pig's blood. She wants to go over to Mrs. Liu's house to play with Ah Yue. Ah Yue probably is scrubbing the floor right now and Ah Yin could help her draw water. But she remembers how Madame scolded her just last night. She hesitates, dares not rush over right away. Madame had never been so harsh. She warned her that, just because she was at work, Ah Yin shouldn't think she didn't know what was going on—Mrs. Liu told her everything. And if Ah Yin left the gate open when she ran out to play, well, it wouldn't matter so much if things went missing, but what if Little Mao were kidnapped? Then what would we do? "Starting tomorrow, you have to look after the house really well for me and take good care of Little Mao. If you disobey me again and sneak away, then the next time your mother comes I'll tell her to take you back. I don't want children like that working for me!"

It's only been a month since she came to Taipei from Taoyuan. One day her father went out to the field to work and was caught in a big thunderstorm. All of a sudden, he was struck dead by lightning. After that, mother and daughter had no one to support them and they had no choice but to come to Taipei to seek a living. Ah Yin had already finished three years of elementary school but had to drop out. After they got to Taipei, her mother went to work as a maid in a house on Ren'ai Road. Ah Yin, thanks to an introduction by Ah Yue, came to Mrs. Wang's house on Heping West Road to be a servant, but because she's so young and can't do much, she has a paltry salary, only one hundred and fifty yuan a month. Mrs. Wang said: "Try it out. If you work hard, I'll give you more." In truth, Mrs. Wang wasn't very comfortable leaving her in charge of the house and Little Mao, but it's not easy to find a reliable female servant in Taipei. None of them last long. You're always looking for a new one every four or five days—it's a big headache. For the most part, young girls will work a little longer, and they are a lot cheaper. The lower cost is the main reason Mrs. Wang hired her. In principle, considering Ah Yin had run off before without telling her, Mrs. Wang already should have dismissed her but, for some unknown reason, she kept her on. Today when Mrs. Wang went out, she was much more anxious than usual, instructing her over and over again before she left.

Ah Yin has long hair that falls over her shoulders. Although she washed it just this morning, it doesn't look too clean. It is black and glossy, like so many sleek, shiny, little black snakes. Her chubby cheeks are chilled blue and white. Her wide-set eyes are large, but a gauzy layer of mist seems to hang over them—regardless of what she looks at, she always seems to be dreaming. The whites of her eyes are much larger than normal. A jumble of long, thick, black eyelashes circle, her eyes and fine hair grows from the pores above her eyelids and cheekbones. Her lips have grown ever so round but are not blood red—rather, they form a grayish-white circle.

Since she can't go over to see Ah Yue, maybe Ah Yue can come over to see her. She wants her to come quickly, but she's been waiting so long now and Ah Yue still hasn't come, so her hopes have faded. Ah Yue likely can't get away. Mrs. Liu probably is making her finish scrubbing the floor before she can go. Little Mao is sleeping and she's alone in the house. What can she do? In a single motion, she turns and lies down. She looks up and strains to see the clock hanging on the wall. The clock's case is shaped like an owl. Its sharp, red beak is like a hook, and it has a pair of stony white eyes that shift back and forth. Hanging beneath it is a long chain with a large brass ball on the end—a mechanical clack comes from the owl's belly. Suddenly it whirs, and a long section of the chain with the ball on it slips down. What time is it? There are no numbers on the face of the clock, only some black stripes to indicate the hour. She looks at it for a long time before she is able to determine it is a quarter after two.

A crucifix hanging on the opposite wall and the owl gaze at each other from a distance. It's a very interesting crucifix because it has a silver-plated Jesus nailed to it. It's extremely realistic, just like a living person. Every time she looks at it, she is more and more amazed and it seems more and more realistic. But she doesn't understand why this Jesus has such a sad expression on his face, or why his feet and hands are nailed to the cross. Madame and Sir are both Catholics and every time they eat they say grace and genuflect. When she sees that, she can't help giggling.

The bedroom is small, just six tatami mats cover the entire floor. The ceiling is low as well, and it's stuffy. After they put in a big bed, a table and chair and a large clothes closet, they left hardly any room to move around. But there's no shortage of interesting things in the room. For example, besides the clock and crucifix, there is a landscape painting hanging on the wall, and a red balloon that's always trying to break its string and fly away. The balloon has already been hanging there for two days, shrinking each day. But the most amusing thing is a small sailboat on the paper transom. It's made out of polished black bones, even the sails. Now she looks at the boat and imagines it sailing. It sails along the wooden trim on top of the walls. There are people in the boat—really, really, tiny people, and she is one of them. Where is the boat going? It is sailing over to the owl! Okay, so it sails along, bobbing and tossing. Then suddenly, in the middle of the voyage, a great wind springs up. The boat heaves madly, and then it capsizes. All the people fall into the water, one after the other. Some call for help, some sink under the waves—she falls into the water, too! What can she do? She can't swim. So, like the others, she floats there with her head above the water, her hand raised, shouting for help. What to do? For a while as she lies there on the floor, she can't think of any way to rescue the Ah Yin who has fallen into the water; she's so anxious that she pounds her hands on the tatami. Think fast! If she can't think of something soon, it will be too late. She's already swallowed two mouthfuls of water! Her mind ticks over—Ah Yin decides suddenly that she can swim. That's right, contrary to her own expectations, her hands begin to move lightly, and somehow or other she's able to float.

Having resolved that difficulty with ease, a smile comes to her face and she imagines swimming confidently in the ocean. First she swims to the left, then to the right. She dives down to the bottom of the sea, then floats up to the surface again. She swims forward and backward, swimming for a long time without really knowing where she is swimming. Before she knows it, the sky is getting dark and she is the only person out on that big empty ocean. She looks in all directions and can't see anything anywhere. She begins to be afraid. It gets darker, until it is as black as ink. Besides that, there isn't even the hint of a sound . . .

Ah Yin curls up on the floor, trying to make herself as small and tight as possible. Her hands are pulled up to her chest and her face is pressed to the tatami. She starts to be truly afraid of the darkness and silence rising in her imagination. These thoughts are interrupted by her sudden awareness that only she and Little Mao are in the empty room. Little Mao is asleep, so it feels like she is alone. She pricks up her ears and listens carefully, and it feels like the whole house also pricks up its ears to listen carefully. Instantly, the silence around her seems to multiply from what it was just moments before. Two sides of the bedroom are walls, the other two are sliding paper doors. There are countless purple bats printed on the paper doors. The doors are half closed, one leads to the hallway at the far end of the house, the other to the living room. Ah Yin sits up. Those two half-open doors worry her. Her eyes turn from one opening to the other, searching back and forth. She thinks, maybe there is something there, maybe it's a person, maybe it isn't. It's hiding in the living room, or else it's hiding in the hallway. Maybe just now, when she wasn't paying attention, that thing sneaked in. Perhaps it's been lurking where nobody could find it for a long time now. Its form is very indistinct. It feels like its mouth is open and its tense eyes wide open. It squats as it walks along with its hands touching the floor, but its hands and feet don't make any noise. Just now, when it was walking, it seemed like it was getting closer to her. Now it knows she is paying attention, so it stops all of a sudden. Where is it? It seems to be in the hallway, just behind the door with its ear pressed to the paper, listening to her movements. Her hands freeze and she doesn't dare move. Listen! "Creak!" The sound of the floor straining under its weight! Her only chance is to risk running over and closing those two doors. She struggles with herself but eventually summons up her courage. Slowly, she stands up and narrows her eyes. Without blinking even once, she almost flies over to the living room door. With her head down, without ever daring to look through it, she slams the door shut. Then she rushes over to the other door and slams it shut. But just at that moment a huge, heart-stopping metallic crash suddenly explodes in the frozen atmosphere. She covers her head with her hands and screams in fear as she runs for all she's worth to the alcove in the wall. Little Mao is sleeping in the alcove, so her subconscious impulse is to flee there. She crouches and buries her whole face in the pram's mosquito netting. Fortunately, just then she realizes that the sound was the wok cover falling onto the concrete kitchen floor. A rat must have knocked it off—the same thing has happened before. Even so, despite this realization, her heart still pounds violently. She gasps for breath and pats herself on the chest. Shaking her head, she says: "Oh my, that scared me to death!" The sound of an awakened infant's crying comes from the stroller. It rises from a faint, indistinct murmur to a full-throated howl. The wok cover has woken up Little Mao.

Usually, Little Mao's afternoon naps last two hours, from two o'clock to four. It's too early for him to wake up now. But Ah Yin doesn't try to lull him back to sleep. She can't stand being alone and wants him to keep her company. After he cries a little more it looks like he is settling down to sleep again. But Ah Yin tries to wake him up. From outside the netting she smiles and in a loud voice says:

"Hey, Little Mao, you little devil, do you want to get up? Eh? Do you want to get up?"

As she speaks, she swishes the netting open. A mosquito buzzes out from inside the net. Probably she wasn't paying attention when she drew the netting closed and left that mosquito inside. Mosquitoes like to hide in the alcove because it's dark, like a mountain cave, except that the walls are covered with lime, not fine, dark green earth. Little Mao has not slept long enough. Naturally he does not want to be woken up, so he starts to bawl again. But Ah Yin doesn't care what he wants, and immediately picks him up, puts him on the chair and dresses him.

Little Mao is an ugly baby. His head is huge, and flat on the back. He's almost bald except for some soft, sparse, pale yellow hair that grows at the back of his head. Nothing grows on the front, which is round and completely bare. Below his left eye there is some swelling where the mosquito bit him. He also has a lump in the middle of his forehead where a black ointment has been applied. His face is very skinny and his skin is as white as soap. Because he was born prematurely, he is very frail—weak and prone to crying. Every two or three days he is stricken with some minor ailment. Ah Yin holds him with his face too close to hers, so she can smell the foul odor coming from his hair.

Little Mao throws his head back and lets out a long wail, his eyes closed and his mouth agape. Ah Yin gets a sweater and starts to put it on him. She scolds him: "You're going to die, you nasty little brat. Put on your clothes and stop crying!"

She gets one arm in its sleeve but she can't get the other in for the longest time. Every time she gets it halfway it gets stuck. Finally, Ah Yin grabs his arm and gives it a good hard twist. Only then does she manage to get it in. Once the sleeves are on, she starts to button it up for him, but she puts the collar button in the wrong hole. It should go in the first hole, but she puts it in the second one. After that, the whole sweater is tight, stretched so much beneath his left armpit that the fabric is bunched and wrinkled. Having dressed him, Ah Yin reaches out and feels his bottom.

"Wet again!"

She takes Little Mao's hand and gives it a couple of slaps. He's crying anyway, so giving him a couple of slaps to make him cry a little more doesn't really matter. But after she hits him he actually stops crying. He opens his mouth as if he is going to sneeze. He stays that way for three or four seconds, startling Ah Yin a little.

"Ahhh!" Little Mao finally inhales some air and starts to cry even harder than he was just a moment ago.

He really is a hateful little child. Sometimes he makes a big fuss in the middle of the night and even Sir, who doesn't usually have much to say, gets angry. He gets up, coughs to clear his throat, then shouts:

"Stop it! Stop it!"

At times like that, only Madame has patience. Calmly and soothingly she pats him lightly and says, "Ah, there, there, don't cry, don't be afraid. Daddy's bad!—you shouldn't frighten him, he must be feeling sick somehow or other. Tomorrow morning you should take him to the doctor!"

After Ah Yin changes his diaper she gazes at his ugly little face, now swollen red and covered with tears. In her heart of hearts, she hates him with a vengeance. She thinks, if I wasn't afraid of making him sick, I'd love to give him a good thrashing.

"Shame, shame, shame! You have no shame! Na na na na!" But Madame said that if Little Mao cries she has to pacify him right away, otherwise, if he cries too much, he might catch a cold! She has no choice but to use a gentler voice to try to console him and pat him like Madame does. She says, "Ah, there, there, don't cry, don't. I'm sorry—I said I'm sorry, isn't that enough for you?—Sorry, sorry, make a bow, kiss a sow, oh, it stinks and how!" Ah Yin starts to laugh, holding her nose with one hand and fanning the air with the other.

Little Mao brightens up a little, fascinated by her words, her laughter, her odd twisting movements. He does not understand, but he senses the strangeness, so he stares blankly at her as she thrashes about.

"That's good! Don't cry!"

How could she know that as soon as she stopped performing Little Mao's eyebrows would knit together and the corners of his mouth turn down again?

"You're such a crybaby!" Ah Yin says. "Have some milk! I'll give you some milk! You greedy little thing! I'll give you some milk and see if you still cry!"

She walks over to the table, takes the milk bottle and pours some hot water over it. He is supposed to get his milk at four o'clock, so this is very early.

> "Little yellow oriole,
> How do you ever know,
> Is it a dragon's head or a phoenix tail
> Embroidered on your shoe . . .?"

Ah Yin sits on the floor with one hand around Little Mao's neck, the milk bottle in the other and she sticks the rubber nipple into Little Mao's mouth. Little Mao doesn't fuss at all now. She can sing as she pleases. Her voice, deliberately suppressed, sounds sharp. The song is one she learned at school. She's already forgotten half of the words, and she doesn't have the melody quite right, but she sings it all the same, repeating it over and over again. People who hear her voice detect a tinge of sadness in it. She often sings, just as she is today. Her songs always make old Mrs. Wu next door shed tears of sadness because they remind her of her husband and eldest son, lost on the mainland. Old Mrs. Wu has complained many times to Mrs. Wang:

"Ah, that little girl of yours sure likes to sing! She sings until all my old troubles get dredged up again."

Mrs. Wang can only smile helplessly and say, "Ah, she's just a child!" Indeed, she can't do anything about it.

Little Mao gulps his milk noisily. After drinking half the bottle he is full. But Ah Yin just keeps singing her songs and doesn't notice. When Little Mao can't drink any more, he starts to squirm and shake his head, trying to escape the nipple. Ah Yin, thinking Little Mao wants to cry again, forces the nipple in tighter without even looking at him. She sings and thinks back to the time when they sang that song in the music room. The pretty music teacher wore a clean white blouse and a black skirt as she sat on a round stool and played the organ. Just then, a little bird really had stopped outside the window pane. It probably was a "little yellow oriole," she thinks. It's just that its feathers weren't yellow—they were brown. When the little bird heard them sing, it flew off with a flutter of its wings.

With the nipple jammed in his mouth, Little Mao cannot cry even if he wants to. At the same time, milk keeps flowing down his throat. He shuts his eyes and frowns, waves his arms, kicks his feet. Milk starts to run out the side of his mouth.

Ah Yin becomes aware that Little Mao is struggling, and as soon as she looks at him she knows what the problem is.

"You're not drinking any more? Look! There's still so much left! First you wanted it, now you don't!"

Finally she takes the bottle away and wipes his mouth with her sleeve. Little Mao suddenly opens his mouth wide and throws up a huge mouthful of milk.

"Damn!" Ah Yin says to herself. She rushes over to the alcove to get a towel to wipe his face. She knows she caused this disaster herself by giving him too much to drink, but just as soon as she finishes wiping up the mess he unexpectedly throws up another mouthful. Ah Yin's heart flutters and she immediately starts patting his back. She pats him for a long time, as if lost in a fog. Her eyes are half closed but never blink. Only after a long time, when she sees he hasn't spit up again, does she finally feel enormous relief.

After calming down, Ah Yin crawls along the floor and up to Little Mao's face. "Let's play dolly, Little Mao, come and play dolly, okay?" she asks him cheerfully. "I'll go and get her." Little Mao still can't talk and doesn't understand what she is saying, so he just stares at her silently.

Ah Yin goes to get the doll. She thinks it's on the big bed, but it's not. Then she goes to look on the table, but it's not there. She looks in the alcove. Not there. Not in the stroller, either.

"Huh, that's strange! Where's the doll?" she asks. She seems to be asking Little Mao and herself at the same time. Little Mao sucks his thumb and gazes at her. He yawns.

"Strange, strange, really strange! Hey, doll! Where are you?" she asks. She bends over and checks under the bed.

"Ah, so you were hiding here all the time! You made me look so long! Why do you want to hide? You bad girl!"

She burrows under the bed. The plastic doll lies there stiff, all by itself, face up. It has a big smile on its face and its hands are clenched into fists. Ah Yin grabs the doll and pulls it out.

"Little Mao! I found it. Here, it's for you," she says.

With great suspicion, Little Mao gazes at the doll now thrust in his face. He timidly reaches out to touch it.

Ah Yin abruptly raises her high-pitched voice to sing a song that has just come into her head:

> "A dolly, a dolly, I've got a dolly.
> All day long she smiles like that,
> It's just too bad she cannot chat."

For some reason or other, Little Mao lets go and the doll falls to the floor head first. Ah Yin picks up the doll again and gives it to him. She takes his two arms and wraps them around the doll to make sure he holds it tight. With a trace of terror in his eyes, Little Mao gazes at the doll's face. The doll has a mysterious fixed smile. Its eyes peer upward and its cheeks are crimson.

"A dolly, a dolly, I've got a dolly.
All day long she smiles like that,
It's just too bad she cannot chat."

Ah Yin sings again and then remembers there is a dance that goes with this song. So she dances over to the front of the dressing mirror on the clothes closet, where she can watch herself dance.

This mirror is very long and covered with a layer of dust, so reflections are a little fuzzy and indistinct. When she first looks at herself in the mirror, she's startled, but then an enchanted, intoxicated smile comes to her face and she whirls around in front of the mirror with one hand on her waist and the other raised above her head. She smiles as she sings and dances, now raising both hands above her head to flutter like a flag in the wind, now spreading her arms straight out to wave them like a bird flapping its wings in flight. Then she loses the gentle rhythm completely and shakes her arms wildly toward the sky, shouting madly at the top of her lungs, as if a miraculous light had appeared in the heavens. Now she throws her arms up at an angle and raises one foot like she wants to fly to heaven. She has forgotten the dance she learned in school and just dances and sings the way she wants. She doesn't stop until she is exhausted and out of breath. When she stops, she spits on her palm and wipes some of the dust from a section of the mirror. This allows her to see her own face clearly. She is shocked. The hair that used to fall neatly down her back now is a big mess covering her face, and her pale white face is really scary. She can't stop herself from flinching back behind the dusty part. After a time, she makes a face at the patch she rubbed, sticking out her tongue and putting her hand to her forehead to make cow horns. She turns around and calls Little Mao:

"Woooo—here comes a ghost!"

She moves closer to Little Mao. Little Mao stares blankly at her for a long time and then starts to cry from fright. Ah Yin quickly lowers her hand, brushes the hair from her face and says with a smile:

"It isn't real, it isn't real—ah! You're going to kill yourself! What are you doing? Put it down, put it down!"

Little Mao is holding the doll by one leg and licking its head. It tastes so bitter that it makes him screw up his face. Thinking about what's under the bed, Ah Yin reaches out and takes it from him. She scolds him:

"Aren't you afraid of being poisoned to death?"

After she snatches the doll away, and Little Mao sees it hanging in midair, dangling from her hand, he looks down and blinks slowly, as if pondering what is going on. Then he wrinkles his brow, twists his mouth into a frown and prepares to cry again.

"Oh, don't cry, don't cry!" Ah Yin spreads her arms, rushes over to him and picks him up. She hugs him very tight, so tight that Little Mao cannot breathe or cry. Ah Yin's face and head are covered with sweat. She holds him tight and rocks him for all she's worth. But because she is squeezing a certain part of his body so hard that it hurts, Little Mao only cries harder.

"I've had enough of you!" Ah Yin says angrily, putting him down to let him cry. Little Mao cries with his head thrown back and his eyes closed until his whole face is red. Ah Yin feels a wave of hatred surge in her heart and pushes him. She never imagined he would not be able to withstand her push, but he flops right over. For a long time he does not make any noise. Ah Yin is frightened, terrified by her own loss of control. Hurriedly, she props him up again and carefully examines his face as she calls his name. At first Little Mao is stunned, only later does he gradually start to whimper again.

"Phew!" She finally relaxes.

Thinking of a new way to make him stop crying is hard work. Ah Yin tired of it long ago and does not have the patience to humor him anymore. She just sits beside him and impassively imitates his crying, as if she were singing. When he cries, she cries the same way. She did not expect this would intrigue Little Mao or that when he heard her cry he would stop crying. Ah Yin smiles and thinks she might as well pretend to cry really hard for him, so she buries her face in her hands and makes sobbing noises, calling out "Daddy!

Mommy!" She covers her face, cries for a moment, laughs for moment, acting really crazy.

"Oh, right! Let's play selling things!" She has suddenly remembered that game. "Let's pretend we're selling bananas. I'll be the seller and you be the buyer. Ah, here's a chair, let me turn it over and it can be a cart with bananas on it."

She takes the bamboo stool and turns it over, placing the seat on the floor, then pushes it along like a wheelbarrow.

"Little Mao! I'm coming! Bananas for sale! Hey! Such heavy bananas. Little Mao, do you want to buy some? They're the best bananas, the sweetest. If they aren't sweet you can have them for free. Little Mao, you say you'd like some! You can't talk, so you can just nod your head." She holds Little Mao's head and nods it for him. Then she says: "Okay, you want to buy some. How many catties do you want to buy? Ten catties? That's not enough, not enough, buy some more. How about buying a hundred catties! Ah, ha ha, I forgot to tell you how much one catty is. One catty is ten yuan, so one hundred catties is—it's—never mind, you don't need to pay, I'll give them all to you. Wait a minute, I have to weigh them first. There, I weighed them, here you go. Wait a minute, I'll go and get some mandarin oranges to sell. Then later I'll have watermelon to sell, and pineapples."

Little Mao sucks his thumb and gazes at her, ignorant of what she is saying. She pushes the bamboo stool once around the room and then stops in front of him again. "Ah, right! Get in and we can play riding in a car, riding in a beep-beep." She picks up Little Mao and sticks him between the stool legs. Little Mao slides down inside with his arms and legs hanging out so he can't move. He draws in his neck and looks up. In that position, he can only look up.

Ah Yin waves her hands and shouts happily:

"Beep! Beep! We're driving the car! The car's coming! Get out of the way! If we run over anyone it's not our problem!"

She pushes Little Mao here and there, bouncing him up and down as she pushes.

"Child for sale!—Child for sale!—Does anyone want to buy a child?" she calls out excitedly.

She pushes him around until she is out of breath. Then she lies on the floor panting hard, her face drained white. She smiles weakly. Little Mao is still stuck in the stool unable to move a muscle. He cannot even turn his face and just makes a low whimpering sound. But the sound is weak and Ah Yin is light-headed from her playing. She pays no attention to him.

Ah Yin turns over and looks at the owl on the wall rolling his white eyeballs. It looks like he is worried something will happen. Is there someone hiding behind his back who wants to hurt him? She laughs and points at him, saying:

"Hey, hey, do you want to buy a little boy? I'll sell Little Mao to you, okay?"

"Clackity clack!" The owl rolls its eyes.

"Do you want one, too?" she turns to ask the Jesus on the crucifix. "Do you really want one, too? Fine, both of you can take him. No, Little Mao can't be split into two. If you split him in two, he'll die. So only one of you can buy him. It doesn't matter which one of you buys him, but not both of you can buy him—so, I'll sell him to you," she tells the owl and points to him again, saying: "Hey, hey, hey! Look how weird your eyes are!"

Little Mao sneezes. He's catching a chill. That's because Ah Yin has forgotten to put on his socks—his feet are as cold as stones. The way he's sitting is so uncomfortable that he starts to cry.

"Don't cry, don't cry! We'll play some more!" Ah Yin sits up. "What should we play now? Play—Play—Right! Come and play hide 'n seek! Ha! Hide 'n seek! Hide 'n seek!" Ah Yin has revived. "See if you can find me. You just sit here. Don't move! Ha ha ha, right. Just like that, sit here! You can't look, eh! You can't look until after I yell one, two, three! If you peek, then I won't play with you anymore!"

When she finishes speaking, she dashes off to look for a place to hide. She thinks the room is too small and there's just no place to hide. That is, unless she runs out of the bedroom. But she doesn't dare do that. Perhaps that thing is still out there.

She thinks of something. She can hide in the alcove.

"One—you can't peek!"

She climbs in.

"Two—I'm calling two—three!"

She squats by the netting with half her face showing so she can peek at Little Mao. She tries to stifle a laugh. Still stuck in the stool, Little Mao looks sideways toward her with his face pointed upward. It really is very uncomfortable, so he cries again.

"Ooh—ooh—ooh—Little Mao, where am I?" She laughs and speaks in a strange voice. After hiding for a while, she comes out of the alcove and crouches down to sneak up on him. Her mouth and eyes are wide open as she crawls along the floor, careful not to make a sound.

"Boo!" She suddenly appears in front of Little Mao with a loud shout, giving him a hell of a fright. She laughs uproariously. "I scared you to death, ha ha ha ha. Let's do it again! Little Mao! Let's do it again! That was so much fun!"

She thinks and thinks about how she should hide this time. In the end she comes up with a brilliant plan. She contains her excitement but her eyes gleam and she pants through her mouth. Then she sets to work, lifting Little Mao out of the stool. By this time, Little Mao's legs have gone numb. She lifts him with both arms, his back up and his face down. She carries him like this and puts him on the big bed.

Once she gets Little Mao settled, she says: "One—" and climbs under the bed, wriggling in on her belly like a snake.

"Two—three! Okay!"

It looks really interesting under the bed. It's dim, with only a tiny bit of faint blue light. The ceiling is the very low bed frame and there's a curtain separating her from the outside, the blue-checked bed sheet that's hanging down. She feels very cozy lying under there. It really is a great place to play hide 'n seek.

"Ooh, ooh, Little Mao, where do you think I am?" she laughs.

She waits a while, then thinks she should climb out. She gathers up her legs, but there's a squishing sound. She's stepped on something. She looks and sees that it's the doll. It's definitely broken.

Stunned, she reaches out to pick it up and see if it really has been flattened. Sure enough, half of the doll's smiling face has been squashed, its smile now the grimace of someone enduring great pain. What can she do? Madame will scold her! Just say Little Mao stepped on it. That's right, just say that. Madame definitely will believe that. She crawls out carrying the doll.

"Little Mao, here I am! You found me! Ha ha ha ha!" She says with a laugh.

She throws the doll on the bed, but worries that Little Mao will squash it more, so she tosses it to the foot of the bed. Then she turns its flattened face over so it is face-down on the bed.

"Little Mao, here I am! You found me! Ha ha ha ha!" She laughs again and says, "Let's play one more time! Once again!" She is flushed from playing and uses her sleeve to wipe away some of the sweat on her face. Although already completely exhausted, she still wants to play some more. When she spots the big, blood red, silk quilt at the foot of the bed, it prompts her to think of a new variation. With a gleam in her eye and a smile on her face, she starts to breathe faster in anticipation, like someone in ecstasy over having discovered a buried treasure. Any time she thinks up some bright new plan, she is like this. She gets busy spreading out the quilt. It is an extremely large quilt that covers the whole bed with its blood red color. Once it is spread out, she takes hold of one corner and gives it a pull so she can throw it over Little Mao. With the heavy quilt over his head, Little Mao bulges out of the bed like a little hillock. Ah Yin is so happy she claps her hands and laughs. The little hillock can move, too! It is Little Mao thrashing his hands and feet around inside. Oh! He's come out of the quilt.

"You can't come out! You can't come out!" Ah Yin says as she grabs hold of the quilt and covers up the place that had opened. She tucks the quilt again, this time a long way under Little Mao's feet and bottom. It is tucked so tight that it does not let in any air. This way, Little Mao will have a hard time getting out. It looks like a big chicken egg. Inside the big egg is a little chick. It is moving and the little chick is going to be born soon. She shakes with laughter, clapping her hands and singing:

"A dolly, a dolly, I've got a dolly.
All day long she smiles like that,
It's just too bad she cannot chat."

When she finishes singing, she crawls under the bed again. She likes lying under the bed in that half-dark, half-light bluish glow. It makes her feel very comfortable.

"One—two—three—Ooh—ooh—ooh—Little Mao!" She calls out in a strange voice, then starts to sing that song again. This time she can hide for a little longer because she has wrapped him up very tight and Little Mao will not be able to get out so easily. It will be more fun if she waits until he gets out and cannot find her before she reappears. She presses her hands to her face, covers her eyes and pretends to be sound asleep. Then she opens her eyes and calls:

"Little Mao, are you out yet? Faster!"

She sticks her head out to take a peek. The big egg is still sitting there and Little Mao still hasn't come out.

"Faster! I've already been waiting for such a long time!"

She waits under the bed for a while longer before sticking her head out to look, but Little Mao still hasn't come out.

"Little Mao, how about if I come and look for you?" She crawls out. "Oh, where did you hide? I can't find you!" She pretends to look all over for him.

"Oh, you naughty little thing, you little devil! Huh, let me think. Probably you're in here, probably you're inside the egg here! Aha! You little devil, you thought that I wouldn't find you. No matter where you hide I'm still going to find you. All I have to do is shout one, two, three, and I can find you right away! You're still not going to come out? Okay, then I'll come and get you. I'm going to catch you. I'm going to call one, two, three!"

She laughs as she stands in front of the piled up quilt. Pressing her hands together she slowly says:

"One—

"Two—

"Three!"

Ah Yin takes the quilt and opens it up. She freezes. Then she gives a frightened scream: Little Mao's eyes are closed and he has already stopped breathing. There is blood coming from his nose and his face is like a shiny, pale blue whetstone.

Translated by Terence Russell

The Toy Revolver

March 1960. This story depicting a conflict between two university students marks a significant development in Wang's use of symbolism and characterization. It also might be the first that met Wang's own literary standards, as he did not include the previous six in Shiwu pian xiaoshuo (Fifteen stories), *his short story collection.*

... for destruction ice
Is also great
And would suffice.

—**Robert Frost**, "Fire and Ice"

At six o'clock, boundless darkness engulfed the whole of Taipei like a tidal wave. The weather was raw, its touch on the skin like grazing against steel, as if the cold had the destructive power to pierce to the bone and corrode the flesh—like a powerful acidic solution in a chemistry lab.

A shadow darted into a quiet lane at the end of Ren'ai Road, Section Two, and slipped into a large compound enclosed by a high wall. Because the gate was unlocked, no one was disturbed. The shadow continued his assault, opening the screen door to the house, taking off his shoes, stepping onto the floor. He headed straight down a long, narrow hall, halting at last at the door to the living room at the end. He stood there, dazed, without advancing a step farther.

At first, the current of warm air inside the house surging over him made him giddy, as if he were slightly drunk. Once recovered, he discovered the hall opened abruptly into a spacious, high-ceilinged living room. Several dim lights encased in white glass globes hung from the ceiling. Under the faint yellowish glow, the living room appeared a fiery red. The floor was lacquered red, the ceiling a deep maroon; even the full-length drapes pulled across the windows were a scarlet red. The room appeared chaotic, the hum of voices audible above the wild rock music. There were people everywhere, crowded together on the sofa, slouched against the walls, leaning on the backs of chairs, even sitting or sprawling on the floor. Tables and chairs were askew. It looked like a railway station full of people fleeing a calamity, yet the people here did not seem anxious. On the contrary, they appeared peaceful, serene, as if only this state of confusion could calm their souls.

The intruder was a youth, short in stature, thin and frail, his body swaddled in clothing from head to toe: red-and-black checked scarf wrapped around his neck; black leather jacket zipped all the way up to his collar; a pair of black wool dress pants. "I'm late!" he thought to himself, his hands stuffed in his pockets. He stood in the doorway trying to catch his breath, his pale face lowered as he cast a melancholy look inside.

After a while, they noticed him and greeted him in unison with a strange wordless grunt, the mocking fashion current among this generation. Next, one of them walked up to him to shake hands. This was the host, Ma Rulin. Others followed, stretching their hands out to him, but he appeared uneasy and smiled unnaturally as he passively took their hands. A tall, strapping youth with broad shoulders appeared. He wore a white shirt and a print tie with red roses and looked like an athlete. He welcomed the small thin youth differently than the others, grabbing his shoulders and shaking him brusquely back and forth. "Hey! How come you look flimsier than ever?" he asked. Everyone laughed. The frail youth looked displeased. The host led him to a chair in the corner, and he sat down.

This was a birthday party for Ma Rulin. He had invited his middle-school classmates home for dinner. The youth who had just arrived was Hu Zhaosheng, a diligent liberal arts student. The tall husky youth who had tossed him around was Zhong Xueyuan. He was a basketball player, not much of a student and crude of speech, but the center of attention no matter where he went.

No one at that moment knew that Hu Zhaosheng, sitting off in the corner, was unhappy. He was sitting there feeling uncomfortable because of what Zhong Xueyuan had said, although no one else thought the remark had been sharp enough to puncture Hu Zhaosheng's self-esteem. Hu Zhaosheng deeply resented other people making fun of his shortcomings. When they mocked his slight physique especially, a hot flush filled his entire body. What Zhong Xueyuan had said not only made him flush, but it was embarrassing to be grabbed and shaken roughly. He felt it was demeaning, an insult. He had wanted to push Zhong Xueyuan away but was afraid the others would notice, so he just slipped out of Zhong Xueyuan's grasp. He did not know if the others had seen him do it or not. He hoped not. He hoped the others had not taken Zhong Xueyuan's remark as an insult, but he recalled he had clearly heard them roar with laughter. So they did know he had been insulted. Feeling anxious, he drew himself up rigidly in his chair.

Mortified and angered, Hu Zhaosheng sat there lost in thought. He stared straight ahead without blinking. He did not seem to notice the people weaving back and forth in front of him. He began to bite his nails. The nails on all ten fingers had already been bitten to a stub, but he began gnawing on them just the same.

Five minutes later, he withdrew his moist fingers from his mouth and stuffed them into his jacket pockets. Emitting a long sigh, he looked around the room from his corner for the first time. Nearby were two tables of people playing bridge. Fruit candy was scattered all over the floor, and even teacups were sitting on the floor. He remembered just then that Ma Rulin had not offered him a cup of tea, but then, seeing there were only a few teacups on the floor, he reasoned that perhaps those who wanted tea were supposed to get their own. Beyond the card tables, centered on a long sofa, a group was talking and laughing loudly. He recalled now that they had been laughing continuously since he entered the room. Six of them, one sitting in another's lap, were squeezed together on the sofa. Two others were sitting in overstuffed chairs. Others were sitting on the floor or standing. Behind them, the scarlet drapes hung like a theater curtain. Those who were not playing cards or talking crowded together around the stereo, selecting records or examining the stereo's construction and cabinet in detail. A few were not listening to records, but merely pacing back and forth in front of the scarlet drapes. Hu Zhaosheng felt the scene in front of him was like a dream he had stumbled into, and he noted the dreamscape's special characteristics in order to set them down in his journal when he went home.

He suddenly wanted to leave. Staying here simply was a waste of time. He glanced at his watch: six-fifteen. If he were at home, he would have eaten dinner by now and at seven o'clock he would shut his door, sit at his desk, open his book and begin his daily chore of reading thirty pages. Sometimes he would take up his pen to write in his journal. This would continue until eleven o'clock. These four whole hours were his alone. He had written off tonight as a waste of time. An anthology of Eliot's poetry was lying on his desk at home waiting for him! He really wished he could leave at this very moment and begin reading it. These people had too much time on their hands. When vacation began, they complained all day long: "What a bore! How can we pass the time?" But he did not—he felt he was in a race against time. He wished he could wrestle time to a halt and stop the days from passing so quickly, but now he could only stand by passively, watching the time slip away. He had not wanted to come in the first place, but since Ma Rulin had written on the card, "Haven't seen you for ages. Have you really forgotten all about your old classmates?" he felt he had to come. Now that he was here, there was no way he could get away. "Well, if it's wasted, it's wasted, and that's all there is to it," he told himself with resignation.

He felt that sitting all alone in the corner made it look like the others had banished him there. No one even noticed he was in the room. There was the large clique over there that formed one group, and then he, off by himself, a solitary unit. He was separated from them by a large distance, as if someone had punished him by making him sit in the corner. Furthermore, the chair did not have armrests, which made it seem even more like he was being held for questioning in a police station. If the chair had armrests, his position would not appear so unnatural. Hu Zhaosheng decided to leave the corner.

He walked over to one of the card tables to watch the card game. He stood there, watching. They sat with their bodies leaning forward, heads almost touching. He could not see their faces and lost interest. Strangely, he could not concentrate on the cards. Having watched for a while, he still did not know what was going on. He looked on absently, trying to make himself pay attention. He stared hard, but still without success. He thought: This is probably because I'm usually not interested in bridge. Just then, one of the players leaned back in his chair so Hu Zhaosheng could see his face. But the card player continued talking to the others, ignoring him. Hu Zhaosheng felt slighted, thinking the player should look up and acknowledge him. So he moved over behind someone else to see what would happen. When this one leaned back, he did not speak to Hu Zhaosheng either. Hu Zhaosheng felt certain that this person knew he was standing behind him and was ignoring him deliberately. Suddenly, one of them got angry. "No cheating, all right? How can you take it back once you've played it?" The person speaking was fat, his face a blur of white flesh, with a nose so short there was no bridge to speak of. He spoke angrily, arrogantly, and glared at the one who had taken back his card. Hu Zhaosheng suddenly felt an inexplicable anger surging over him, as if he were the one who had been yelled at. He turned and left.

He moved forward uncertainly toward the group of people talking together. At first, he stood in a conspicuous spot. Aware of this, he edged closer to two other people standing nearby. Everyone was laughing, mouths agape, slapping thighs and patting each other's shoulders. The people crowded together on the sofa could not budge. One was so squashed between the others that only his head stuck out, but no one heard his protests. Seeing them laugh so hard, Hu Zhaosheng broke into a stiff smile. Even so, he still had no idea what they were laughing about. He did not like the way they were sitting so crowded together. If it were him, he would rather stand. Someone called out to him from one of the overstuffed chairs, and made room for Hu Zhaosheng on the seat. Hu Zhaosheng refused the invitation, shaking his head in reply, but the one who had called out left the space open. Hu Zhaosheng hoped he would quickly move back over the empty part of the cushion because the bright red space made him uneasy. When they finished laughing, Zhong Xueyuan raised his deep, hoarse voice (his voice was obviously hoarse from laughing too much) and said something. Everyone burst out laughing once again. Hu Zhaosheng did not understand what he meant. He had said: "Only that broad of his could do that." What was a broad? And what could it do? He did not understand. If he had come over a little earlier, he might know what it was that could be done. But what was a broad? Later, someone said, "I saw him yesterday taking that broad of his to Mount Yangming." Hu Zhaosheng finally understood what a broad was. He wrinkled his brow. What a crude expression! Since he did not understand what they were talking and laughing about with all these strange names and secret expressions, he could only walk away.

He went back to the card tables to watch. This time, he watched the other table, but the cool reception they gave him was no different than the first table's. Still, he stood riveted to one place as if hypnotized. After a while, when he could no longer stand the feeling of monotony and emptiness that overwhelmed him, he turned and left.

He carefully avoided the cups on the floor. Without realizing it, he had walked toward the corner. There, he halted and thought to himself: "No, I don't want to return to that corner, but I'm like a ghost pacing back and forth. I should have brought a book to read. That's it. I'll go find a book to while away the time!" This sudden thought rescued him.

Hu Zhaosheng found an old pictorial magazine under the glass top on a card table. He picked it up and crept back into the corner. He spread it open. The others could not see him now, only the radiantly smiling face of some female movie star with sparkling eyes and bright teeth.

Before long, he forgot he was in Ma Rulin's living room. He did not hear the rock 'n roll music or the hum of voices and sound of laughter.

After leafing through the magazine, his eyes felt dry and he was breathing heavily. He put the magazine down to take a break. Just as he did so, he saw Zhong Xueyuan coming into the living room. Zhong Xueyuan had to pass in front of him but Hu Zhaosheng did not want to speak to him. He hurriedly looked down, pretending not to see Zhong Xueyuan. He felt him walk up to him, draw near and pass in front—he did not continue but seemed to stand in front, looking him over with a smirk. It was as if Zhong Xueyuan could guess his innermost thoughts and wanted to wait for him to look up so he could embarrass him. If that were so, then he ought to raise his head fearlessly and take him on. Hu Zhaosheng composed his face and jerked up his head. No one was there. Zhong Xueyuan was sitting far away with a group of people, arguing about something, gesturing vigorously as he spoke. He obviously had been sitting there for some time.

He picked up the magazine again and began rereading it from the beginning. This time, it did not interest him at all, and after flipping through several pages, he felt bored. But he did not have the willpower to put it down.

"*Pow! Pow! Pow! Pow!*" He suddenly heard the sound of a gun firing. He looked up to see a little kid wearing an off-white parka shooting at the circle of people with his toy revolver. He was Ma Rulin's younger brother. The group called him Little Ma and wanted him to let them see his revolver. He refused. Zhong Xueyuan grabbed him by the waist and lifted him up. Little Ma screeched, his little legs clothed in jeans thrashing wildly in the air.

"Let me go! Let me go! It's not yours!"

"I'm not going to take it away. I just want to look at it, okay? You still want my postage stamps, don't you, you little squirt?"

Hearing about stamps, Little Ma agreed delightedly. He passed the revolver to Zhong Xueyuan and said: "I have real bullets, too!" He reached into his pocket to bring out a bright red firecracker.

"It can shoot these?" Zhong Xueyuan asked.

"Yeah!"

"How do they go in?"

"You don't know how. I'll show you." Little Ma proudly took back the revolver and pulled it apart. Snapping the barrel open, he put the firecracker into one of the slots. "It can take six bullets. Six shots in a row. Really powerful!" he said.

He passed the revolver to Zhong Xueyuan, who raised it even with his right shoulder and readied his aim. Everyone circled around to watch the fun, even the bridge players who were engrossed in their game stopped when they were called to come and watch. Little Ma covered his ears with his hands, darting back and forth around Zhong Xueyuan.

Zhong Xueyuan pulled the trigger and "*pow!*" Something flew out of the barrel and exploded three feet away. Little Ma leapt for joy. The others shouted and screamed, falling over each other to grab at the revolver like little children. Wisps of blue smoke curled up under the light. The air was filled with the acrid smell of gunpowder.

Hu Zhaosheng watched in fascination. His interest, too, had been aroused. He also wanted to get hold of the revolver and shoot a few times for the fun of it. "The toy industry has really progressed. A toy so true to life that even adults want to play with it," he thought to himself scornfully. But he repressed the thought of joining in to grab at the revolver because it would surprise the others.

He went back to his magazine but the sound of the revolver going off kept startling him. "These people are such bores," he thought. "It's all right to play for a minute but to keep on is really childish! How immature!" He tossed the magazine aside angrily. "I'm not going to read anymore!" Actually, he had forgotten he had already lost interest. "Why haven't we started to eat?" he thought to himself again. Thinking about dinner calmed him down. When dinner was ready, things would be different. He wouldn't have to sit around being bored. Moreover, once he had finished, he could think up some excuse and leave early. He looked at his watch again. It was five minutes to seven. If they started eating at seven, then at the most he would be finished in half an hour and could take his leave of Ma Rulin. It would be only seven-thirty then and, once he got home, probably just eight o'clock. Then from eight to nine, to ten, to eleven—three full hours, only one less than usual. His spirits re-

THE TOY REVOLVER ❖ 83

vived so much at the thought of the book on his desk, that large anthology of Eliot's poetry, flat and squat like a bookend, that he almost started laughing. But what excuse could he give to Ma Rulin? That was easy. For example, just like saying, "I'm sorry. I have to go home to finish up an article that's due early tomorrow . . ."

"Hu Zhaosheng! Stick 'em up!" Just as he was daydreaming, his thoughts were suddenly interrupted by a curt shout. He looked up, panic-stricken. The magazine fell to his knees. The group had surrounded him silently. They burst into laughter.

"He's hiding here studying," someone said.

"The writer's probably meditating on something!"

Standing in the middle was the husky Zhong Xueyuan, the one who had just shouted at him, a wily smile, half playful, half malicious, on his lips. He gripped the revolver with his right hand, its shiny aluminum barrel aimed straight at Hu Zhaosheng's face.

He began to feel uneasy because so many people were laughing at him. It made him feel like he had done something shameful and been caught in the act, like a thief caught with the goods. He curled the corners of his mouth into a slight smile and tilted forward, thinking a perfunctory response was the best way to deal with them. But Zhong Xueyuan, thinking he was trying to slip away, said: "Stay right where you are! Don't move!"

Two people immediately came forward, one on each side, to hold his arms back like they were in a vice. He could not move. His magazine fell to the floor. He had not put up any resistance because he knew it was useless. But his arms were stiff with anger, making it difficult for them to control him. The people on either side of him then yanked his arms away from his body so he looked like the crucified Christ. Hu Zhaosheng felt ashamed of this martyred posture.

Zhong Xueyuan puffed out his chest and straightened his tie. This affectation made Hu Zhaosheng want to throw up. Zhong Xueyuan cleared his throat, chuckling loudly. "Eh-hem. The Chief Justice calls the court to order to bring you, this little rebel, to trial. Yes, you, this little rebel Hu Zhaosheng, nicknamed the Little Rat. Your natural disposition is cowardly, like a rat. You're frail of body, ill of health, but arrogant of manner, solitary and aloof. All you do is lock yourself in your room to study and ignore social intercourse with your classmates. The court hereby formally indicts you for treason. In the unanimous opinion of the jury of our whole class, you are found guilty. I, the Chief Justice, pronounce the sentence of death for the defendant. Death by firing squad will now be carried out. However, as I, the Chief Justice, am merciful and humane, I have seen fit to take into consideration the fact that you, the defendant, are a mere ignorant youth who has committed his first offence. Eh-hem. This, this, ah, therefore, if the defendant is willing to cooperate with the court in one certain respect, his sentence will be commuted and his life spared. We order you to immediately relate, publicly, your romantic history. Obey immediately and tell us, or else, needless to say, you shall have a taste of this weapon. And an imprint will be left on that handsome face of yours as a memento of the occasion. That probably won't be very pleasant, will it?"

Hu Zhaosheng did not dare look at Zhong Xueyuan while he was speaking. He kept his head down, staring at a piece of fruit candy on the floor. Zhong Xueyuan's words were like a pair of red-hot tongs searing him over and over. At several points he had not been able to stand it, and looked up anxiously at Zhong Xueyuan to see whether he was just joking or really serious. He could not tell, because Zhong Xueyuan's manner of speaking seemed to include both possibilities. "You thug!" he thought to himself.

When Zhong Xueyuan finished talking, everyone laughed again. There were so many people—all of them were here, even the ones who had been playing bridge. The fat card player had squeezed into the front row and was laughing derisively, his hand on his hips like a butcher. His classmates closed in on him, not leaving him any breathing room. One circle enclosed another, hemming him in. Zhong Xueyuan was only a step away from him. Someone from the row behind stuck his head into the circle. Others could not find a place to stand, so they stood on chairs and pressed against the shoulders of those in front, peering down at the circle from above. They all stared, eyes shining with excitement, mouths agape, revealing white teeth. Their eyes were riveted on him like a pack of hungry wolves preparing to tear him to pieces and devour him. Hu

Zhaosheng felt a shiver go through his body. At the same time, hatred of the whole group surged through him.

He felt his immediate response should be to express indifference toward this practical joke, showing firmness in the face of this travesty, so they would lose interest and disband on their own. So he lowered his head again and stared at that piece of fruit candy. He looked as if he were near death, not a breath of life left in his body. They could work their will upon him.

Suddenly something soft, padded and warm lifted his chin up. It was the hand of the fat boy. "Look up here!" he commanded. Hu Zhaosheng jerked his head free. He wanted to hit him but couldn't move his hands. He glared back at the fat boy, nearly coming out with a "____ your mother." Now he had no choice but to look up and face them. He raised his head in disdain, looking Zhong Xueyuan right in the eye as if to challenge him. This time he saw Zhong Xueyuan's expression clearly. What a despicable face! He refused to let himself look away. A pair of deep creases ran down along the nose of that haughty face. His upper lip was curled into a sneer, partially revealing his snowy white front teeth. What Hu Zhaosheng hated most was the purple birthmark on his left cheek. Because the weather was cold, blood had congealed there, making it look like the scar from a burn. Zhong Xueyuan's glare turned cold when he met Hu Zhaosheng's direct stare, which projected overwhelming hostility. Hu Zhaosheng relented and looked away. Zhong Xueyuan, probably realizing the inappropriateness of his change in manner, hurriedly curved his lips into a smile. All he achieved was an ugly smirk, the most malicious Hu Zhaosheng had ever seen. He returned it with an equally ugly sneer of his own. Zhong Xueyuan waved the revolver menacingly and shouted.

"Hu Zhaosheng, you rascal. We'll be nice to you at first but you'd better watch out. We won't be so polite later on. 'Fess up!"

"If I had any 'romantic history,' of course I'd tell you. Too bad, but I don't. So what do you want me to say?" Hu Zhaosheng strained to speak naturally, but when he had finished, he felt he had spoken too softly. His voice had trembled as well. The group's silence made him flounder. The only sound was his feeble voice, his last sentence was especially weak, as if he were pleading for mercy. His face remained flushed.

"If you don't 'fess up, I'll shoot!"

"Go ahead," Hu Zhaosheng said. He did not think Zhong Xueyuan would dare.

"Well, are you going to tell or aren't you?" Zhong Xueyuan suddenly shouted, lunging toward him like a lion going for his throat. This sudden violent movement startled Hu Zhaosheng.

"No!" Hu Zhaosheng glared at Zhong Xueyuan.

Everyone laughed. Hu Zhaosheng did not understand why they were laughing. Then he realized he had misspoken. By answering "no," did that mean he had a secret but would not tell?

"Well, everybody, you heard that, didn't you?" Zhong Xueyuan said, beaming broadly. He looked around happily. "Hu Zhaosheng's not willing to tell, so I'll have to tell it for him. Alright everybody, please listen while yours truly, the Chief Justice, relates one of Hu Zhaosheng's top secrets, his romantic history. Eh-hem. It was on a certain day in a certain month in a certain year, when spring was in full bloom. Eh-hem. It was in the morning, when birds were chirping away amidst the fragrant flowers, that Hu Zhaosheng gave a love letter—probably his first one—to one of his female classmates. I am not rumor-mongering; this female classmate's name was Yang Yumei, in the same department as Hu Zhaosheng. You can go look it up if you want. Hu Zhaosheng had been trying to make it with her for a whole year. He followed her home every day after school but never spoke to her. Then why did he suddenly write her a letter? According to my authoritative analysis, it's probably because he was influenced by the season. (Everybody roared with laughter.) Really, I mean it. Why are you all laughing? In this situation, when one is overwhelmed by certain feelings and the pen is all ready, a great love letter will be created. This has been true of poets throughout the ages. Isn't it 'natural' then? ('Ha! Ha!' Everybody roared with laughter.)

"I'll come to the point. It is said that on this particular afternoon, upon getting out of class, Hu Zhaosheng was already as jittery as an ant in a hot frying pan. When he saw Yang Yumei leaving, he immediately followed her all the way to the school gate. Then he raced up to her and idiotically shoved the letter at her. Yang Yumei didn't know what was going on. When she figured it out, she fled. Our little rat here then began a hundred-meter dash to catch up with her. He blocked her way and made her take the letter. He begged her, saying, 'Yang Yumei, if you don't take it, I won't be able to sleep tonight.' (Everybody laughed again.) This time, Yang Yumei was really angry and threw the letter on the ground. But this great poet of ours was undaunted. He picked it right up and gave it to her again. (Everybody laughed even harder. Some even leaned over to cheer him.) In the end, Yang Yumei flew into a rage, her eyebrows arched and eyes glaring. She stood her ground and slapped him mercilessly, screaming: 'Are you going to get out of here or not? You shameless brute! If you don't leave me alone, I'll get even with you!' ('Ah!' Everybody gasped.) In truth, Yang Yumei treated our poet here much too cruelly. It's enough to make one angry. Having taken a slap in the face, he could only let her go. Thus ended the tragedy of Hu Zhaosheng's first love!"

Hu Zhaosheng blushed furiously. But his shame and anger were second only to his surprise. He was dumbfounded. He asked himself: "Am I dreaming? Is this a dream? How could he know my secret? Is he some kind of a sorcerer? This isn't a dream. It isn't. I've got to get hold of myself. I'm, for sure, sitting right here in Ma Rulin's living room. And the person standing in front of me is actually Zhong Xueyuan . . ."

He stared woodenly at the delirious group. They were laughing and shouting, shoving and pushing around him like a tribe of Africans performing some ritual dance for the gods. But he did not hear what they were yelling at him. These savages had already killed their sacrificial offering and were going to eat him raw. They were ranting and raving so ecstatically.

He felt it was all over for him. This most shameful of his private secrets had suddenly been broadcast to everyone in the room. A feeling of futility swept over him. He finally remembered he had not denied it, so quickly blurted out: "Don't make up gossip. Who said so?" Hu Zhaosheng felt his denial was too weak. He had already given up.

"Oh? You deny it? Alright then, the Chief Justice will now announce how the sentence of death by firing squad of the poet Hu Zhaosheng will be carried out. This revolver in my hand can shoot six bullets in a row. Just a moment ago, I put a firecracker in. But, alas, I've forgotten which slot it's in. So now, Hu Zhaosheng, the court orders you to admit what I just said is true. If you don't, I'll shoot and keep on shooting until you admit it. You should know that the first shot might be the one with the firecracker so I advise you to hurry up and admit it. You can avoid a lot of pain that way. If you have any guts, though, you'll hold out to the end. It's up to you. I'll give you one last chance. Do you admit it or not?"

He hesitated. He no longer believed Zhong Xueyuan was afraid to shoot, but his self-esteem would not allow him to waver. Hu Zhaosheng shot back: "No!"

"*Pow!*" The gun sounded. Hu Zhaosheng shut his eyes and ducked, his whole body recoiled as if someone had knifed him in the buttocks. But because his two arms were held by the others, he did not fall off the chair. He felt blood rushing to his temples, throbbing as if pricked by thousands of tiny pins. Having recovered, he realized the chamber had not contained the firecracker because he felt no burning sensation on his face, and no hard pellet had struck his body. Besides, he had heard only a crisp "*pow*," not a second deeper "*bang*." He raised his head and saw everyone laughing uproariously at his terrified expression. Hating himself, he bit his lip deeply.

"Admit it?" Zhong Xueyuan repeated, his eyes sparkling.

"No!"

"*Pow!*"

Hu Zhaosheng shut his eyes and bent over again. His body lurched to one side. But there was no firecracker this time, either. He heard another roar of laughter. "This time, no matter what, I won't let myself move," he swore clenching his teeth.

"The first two shots didn't have the firecracker. You were lucky. Admit it?"

"No!"

"*Pow!*"

Hu Zhaosheng betrayed himself again. There was still no fire-cracker. A wave of laughter followed, like the cheering of the crowd at the high-jump finals.

"No! I'll never admit it!" Hu Zhaosheng suddenly screamed deliriously.

"*Pow! Pow!*"

Hu Zhaosheng cringed twice but the shots were crisp single sounds. Amid the laughter, he stole a glance at Zhong Xueyuan's face—cold, cruel and inhuman. His lips were parted to show a row of white teeth, but it was not a smile. He just opened his mouth as if smiling. Hu Zhaosheng felt that he hated him, but in his heart he shivered, fearing him.

"There's only one shot left, so it's got to be this one. Now I remember. I put it in the sixth slot!" Zhong Xueyuan waved the revolver around, spread his legs into a steady crouch and winked at the people around him. The blue smoke from the revolver, unable to disperse in the densely packed crowd, remained trapped in the circle, snaking its way through the air. The acrid smell of nitrate was so thick everyone choked. Hu Zhaosheng felt suffocated, his throat burning. He could see their faces through the blue smoke, at first distinct, then blurred. His own face was as white as a sheet and dripping with sweat, the muscles on his forehead bulging.

"That's enough. This is no longer a joke!" someone admonished Zhong Xueyuan.

"You'd better go ahead and admit it," someone said to Hu Zhaosheng.

"Well, Hu Zhaosheng, how about it?" Zhong Xueyuan said.

Hu Zhaosheng did not answer. He believed this shot would include the firecracker.

"I'd better step back a bit or else it'll fire too hard," Zhong Xueyuan said, retreating a step. The people behind him moved back with him.

"Zhong Xueyuan! Aim for his nose. Knock off that little nose of his!" Little Ma screeched from the front row and made everyone laugh. Hu Zhaosheng glared at him.

"Hurry up and make up your mind, Hu Zhaosheng! I'll give you two more seconds!" Zhong Xueyuan ordered him impatiently.

" . . . "

"Hurry up!"

"All right, have it your own way. Just say I admit it then," Hu Zhaosheng said, immediately feeling intense regret. He wished he could disappear into the ground.

The gun suddenly fired. Zhong Xueyuan had gone against his word and shot the sixth bullet at him anyway. He was not prepared and could not help yelping in surprise. The group exploded in laughter. Unlike the times before, this was the sound of happy, re- laxed, satisfied laughter, washing over him in gigantic waves. Zhong Xueyuan laughed the loudest. They released his arms. This act in the live drama had come to its happy ending. He then realized the sixth slot had not contained a firecracker, either. He had been de- ceived! Deceived! It was all a hoax. They had played a joke on him, making him look foolish for nothing! Punishing him for no reason! He leapt up from the chair, his fists clenched, breathing rapidly, staring in turn at each face as if trying to pick out an acquaintance in the midst of a crowd of strangers. Zhong Xueyuan returned the revolver to Little Ma. Then, spreading his arms out like the wings of a giant eagle coming to rest on the ground, he reached over and embraced Hu Zhaosheng, laughing and saying: "Sorry! Sorry![3] It was just a joke. You're not angry, are you?"

Hu Zhaosheng's face was crushed against Zhong Xueyuan's chest so he could not breathe, his mouth pressed into Zhong Xueyuan's shirt. He looked like a baby smothered in a quilt. He struggled to free himself, but he could not wrench himself out of Zhong Xue- yuan's grasp. As the others saw it, Hu Zhaosheng was submis- sively curled in Zhong Xueyuan's embrace, like a child who tried to act cute by snuggling up to his mother. Zhong Xueyuan then released his hold, continuing to repeat, "Sorry. Sorry." Just then Ma Rulin announced in a loud voice that dinner was ready and asked everyone to go into the dining room. The people around

---

3. In the original text, "Sorry! Sorry!" is in English here and below.

him dispersed. This happy affair had no sooner concluded than another exciting one commenced. Naturally, everyone was pleased. Smiling in satisfaction, they crowded noisily into the dining room.

"What is it, Zhong Xueyuan? Have you been fighting? Don't you dare break anything!" Ma Rulin's mother, a plump middle-aged woman, stood smiling in the doorway. She knew Zhong Xueyuan well, so she smiled at him as she spoke.

"If I break anything, I'll pay you back double for it, Auntie," Zhong Xueyuan said, returning her smile. He went into the dining room with the others. The dining room was off a side room separated by a door. Ma Rulin held the screen door open with his back so it would not snap shut. Hu Zhaosheng stood in the corner, taking out a handkerchief to mop away his sweat.

"Pumpkin, now listen to me. I'm going to take you to see a movie!" Ma Rulin's mother held Little Ma back because he wanted to go into the dining room with the others. Little Ma put up a struggle.

"You don't want to see a Western? Riding horses and shooting guns? All right then, I'll go by myself."

Little Ma hesitated.

"Hurry up or we'll be late. Oh! Just look at you. You've got that revolver in your hands again. You want to scare someone? What's all this bulging in your pockets? Firecrackers? Who bought them for you? Was it that big brother of yours? Hurry up and empty them out. You're not to play with guns again, you hear? What if you put out someone's eye?" She put the revolver and firecrackers on the table, smiling at Hu Zhaosheng as she spoke. Hu Zhaosheng watched her without speaking.

"We've got to hurry. Rulin! Take good care of your classmates. I can't stay to keep you company!"

Hu Zhaosheng was the last to go in. He opened the screen door himself and stepped inside. "Coward!" he cursed himself. His lips trembled and he repressed a sob. He was distraught, like a young child who might burst into tears at any moment.

The dining room was as large as the living room, lit with a blinding white fluorescent light that reflected off the white walls, white refrigerator, white tablecloth and china cabinet stocked with glass-ware. The dinner table was laden with large platters of cold food, two towering piles of dinner plates and a pile of shiny silver forks. The only sound was the clinking of dishes and silverware as the guests went up one by one to pick up the dishes and forks and circle the table helping themselves to the food. Having completed the circuit, each one found a seat and sat down. A few returned to the living room to eat. Hu Zhaosheng was the last in line. He unwrapped the paper around the fork, crumpled it into a ball and tossed it on the table, forgetting to wipe the silverware with it first. As he helped himself to the food, Ma Rulin urged him to take more. He nodded, but did not hear him clearly. After completing the circle around the table, he sat down in a corner. He speared a piece of duck neck with his fork, but did not raise it to his mouth. His ears suddenly reddened as he recalled the scene of Zhong Xueyuan revealing his secret.

"How could he have known about it? Was I careless and told somebody? No. Maybe there's something wrong with my nerves, and I really told somebody but can't remember now. There was no one around that day. And even if someone had been watching far away, he couldn't have known all the details. Only heaven, earth, Yang Yumei and I knew about it. It has to be Yang Yumei then. But how did she get to know Zhong Xueyuan? He was not in our school. Ah, I know. Zhong Xueyuan has a girlfriend who went to the First Girls High School in Taipei like Yang Yumei. That's it then. Yang Yumei told her, and she told Zhong Xueyuan. This means Yang told all her classmates about it. Then all the girls in our department who are her friends know about it. When they see me, they're probably laughing at me behind my back. Oh, God! People I don't even know. I don't know them, but they already know about me. When they see me, they're thinking 'so that's the one.' God! Everyone in the world knew except me!"

He despised Yang Yumei as well as all his female classmates. He despised the whole world. It seemed the whole world was against him.

He picked up his fork and took a bite. He did not taste anything.

He put his fork down and impatiently chewed on the bit he had taken.

"What am I doing here? Ma Rulin invited me for dinner but everyone's made me the butt of some joke, deliberately insulted me and made me look foolish. So now I don't even have an appetite. I can't even enjoy a good meal . . ." His eyes welled with tears, but his tears were from anger, not heartbreak. He was angry that he would even think of such a banal thing as his appetite at this moment. He felt nauseous. He hated these strange thoughts that mocked his self-esteem. He shook his head vigorously to try to banish them. Then he took two bites of food so he would quit daydreaming.

"No matter what, I shouldn't look wounded in front of everyone else. I ought to act more natural. I ought to pretend like nothing happened. As if what just happened was an insignificant little joke—wasn't it really an insignificant joke?—No! No!" He would not admit it was just a joke, because if he did, then Zhong Xueyuan would be blameless, and he was not going to let him get away with it. He felt Zhong Xueyuan had committed a grave offence that he could not forgive. So he listened to the side of his mind that accused Zhong Xueyuan and automatically suppressed the side that defended him.

"Relax, relax. Smile a little," he told himself, attempting to relax his facial muscles and look up, like someone who had been working hard and needed to stop and catch his breath. But he was dissatisfied with his performance. He felt his face would not loosen up.

It was stuffy inside. His eyes felt dry and his eyesight blurred. Although the bright fluorescent light shone on everything in the room, to him everything seemed to be clouded in mist. This happened to his sight whenever he had a high fever. He did feel feverish, but his hands and feet were as cold as ice.

He decided not to eat anymore. The act of chewing had become an unbearable task. He returned the plate he had hardly touched to the table, and retreated to the more dimly lit red living room. There were fewer people in there and he needed to find a quiet spot. The corner where he had first sat down was a welcome sight. His mind was in turmoil. The shame, anger and hurt he felt made it imperative that he think this whole thing through, or else he would be haunted by a sense of incompleteness. He sat with his head down, one hand planted on his abdomen, the other cupping his chin, as if he had a toothache, letting what just occurred buffet him over and over. Just thinking of his meek submission made his whole body smolder as if an electrical current were coursing through it.

"I've been bewitched. Why else would I have admitted it? He said, if I had any guts I'd hold out to the end. I took it for five shots. How come I didn't have the courage to take the sixth shot? Coward! I really don't know why I weakened all of a sudden. If I'd known the sixth shot didn't have the firecracker, would I have acted so shamefully? They deceived me! Deceived me! Deceived me!" He clenched his fist at the thought, as if their deception was more serious than their other insults.

The living room refilled with people. He had not noticed when they finished their dinner and came back in. He had not even noticed when the stereo had been turned off. His ears still buzzed with the sound of voices and music. Their faces were sweaty and jovial. Ma Rulin took out a box of his father's foreign cigarettes. The guests crowded around and made off with more than half of them. Lighting up with a cigarette lighter, they began to puff away.

"How shallow! Boring! Vulgar!" Hu Zhaosheng scoffed silently. The fat boy tried clumsily to make smoke rings but did not succeed in making even one. Just look at that imbecile, Hu Zhaosheng thought. He also felt a hatred for the two who had held his arms down, now slouched on the sofa, smoking, with legs outstretched. Naturally, the one he most despised was Zhong Xueyuan. Zhong Xueyuan puffed away dramatically as he chatted with the others, his head tilted back, eyes squinting merrily. He exhaled the smoke through his large nose, trying to show off. He even exhaled a puff out of his mouth to show that he was experienced. "Clown!" Hu Zhaosheng cursed. He took in Zhong Xueyuan's every move. There was not one that he did not find reprehensible and disgusting, but he kept his eyes trained on him anyway.

Suddenly, the fat boy appeared before him and asked: "Hey, great poet. How come you're sitting all alone here looking so unhappy?"

Hu Zhaosheng looked away in silence. After a while he looked over at him and smiled. "I'm just as happy as can be. Just watching you make smoke rings overjoys me!"

The fat boy moved away without hearing the sarcasm in Hu Zhaosheng's reply. He continued trying to make smoke rings.

Zhong Xueyuan was talking animatedly with the others about films. Hu Zhaosheng hated movies, considered them shallow and immature. He listened to their discussion with disdain.

"A great picture! A really wonderful, artistic film. It's adapted from a well-known novel by a French literary giant," Zhong Xueyuan said, exhaling a puff of smoke.

"Which literary giant? And what's the name of the well-known novel?" Hu Zhaosheng suddenly asked from across the room. He was separated from the others by the two card tables. Startled, everyone turned to look at him. They had not thought he would interrupt, had almost forgotten he was in the room. Hu Zhaosheng leaned back in his chair, the enigmatic smile gracing his lips his reply to their perplexed expressions, as if to say: "That's right. It was me who asked. So what?"

"I can't remember who wrote it. Something like Stahl. I've forgotten the name of the book, too. But the story is wonderful. Really moving."

"Stahl? Ha! Ha! Mmm. Wonderful. Really moving! What's wonderful about it? How is it moving?" His eyes and smile seemed to say, "Hurry up and answer."

"I don't know how to describe it. Go see for yourself."

"You don't know how to describe it!" Hu Zhaosheng exclaimed, nodding several times and smiling broadly. He then looked down, as if forgetting what he had just said, and kept his head down. There was silence in the room. Finally someone suggested they play cards and the chaotic hum of voices resumed.

Hu Zhaosheng sat with his head bowed for a long time, not daring to look up because his remark had been greeted with silence. He felt his sarcasm had not been very effective. Perhaps Zhong Xueyuan did not even know he was being sarcastic. But even if he had, his sarcasm had not been biting enough. It still did not satisfy his thirst for revenge. Moreover, he felt especially embarrassed, disappointed and angered by everyone's cold reception.

Bridge playing started up again at the two tables. Zhong Xueyuan was at the further table. Hu Zhaosheng stood up and walked slowly over to that one. At first, he watched silently behind someone else, then circled around to be behind Zhong Xueyuan. Zhong Xueyuan had won several hands already. Hu Zhaosheng watched for a while, then went over behind the person to Zhong Xueyuan's left. That player picked out a card and was preparing to play it when Hu Zhaosheng advised him, "Don't play that. He has the king."

"Don't tell," Zhong Xueyuan said, laughing.

Hu Zhaosheng smiled at him without replying.

The second time around the person pulled out the ace of Hearts. Hu Zhaosheng spoke up again. "Don't play that. He doesn't have a Heart[3] left. He'll play trump."

The player sitting across from Zhong Xueyuan stood up in anger. "Will you keep your mouth shut?"

"Who are you yelling at?" Hu Zhaosheng turned toward him. They stared at each other for about three seconds.

"Come on, Old Wang, let's play cards," Zhong Xueyuan said. The boy sat down. Hu Zhaosheng glared at him, then turned and left.

Hu Zhaosheng's hatred for that boy was as great as his hatred for Zhong Xueyuan himself. He returned to the corner and once again held his chin in his hand as if he had a toothache.

"Is tonight all a bad dream? I've been insulted, my secrets publicly exposed, made fun of, forced into submission and cursed at. Why am I so unpopular? When Zhong Xueyuan made fun of me, they all went along with him. But when I made fun of him, they didn't. Why? Because I acted like a coward? Is that why they don't respect me? That's probably it. But am I the only coward? Are they all heroes? If someone else had been in my place and been asked that at gunpoint, wouldn't he have given in too?" It suddenly dawned on him. He saw the light. "They're not any braver than I am. And neither is Zhong Xueyuan! They've never tested him. Well, then, let

1. The word "Heart" is in English in the original.

me be the one to do that. I'll expose this paper tiger! He might give in before I even shoot the first shot. Then they'll find out who's the hero and who's the coward! Zhong Xueyuan, your time has come! I'll get even with you!" He was aroused like an avenging poisonous snake hurtling out of its hole.

The others were arranging an empty coffee table for the birthday cake so Ma Rulin could cut it. The large frosted cake was decorated with burning red candles. "But will they side with him again and not help me test him? Then they'll look down on me even more! So what! Am I afraid of them? If it's just me, then it's just me. Lord! Just watch me take on the whole bunch of them then! I'm going to challenge them all!" He jumped up. They were all crowded around the cake and did not see him. He tiptoed over to the table where the revolver and firecrackers lay. That pretty revolver with its gleaming ivory-inlaid handle carved with the image of a longhorn steer lay on the table beside a pile of firecrackers that looked like a bouquet of flowers. Hu Zhaosheng grabbed it with one hand and the firecrackers with the other.

Zhong Xueyuan was leading them in singing *Happy Birthday*:

> Happy Birthday to you
> Happy Birthday to you
> Happy Birthday to Rulin
> Happy Birthday to you.[3]

They finished the song with a cheer, the kind of strange, wordless shout this generation of youth was partial to. Then, amid a gale of laughter, Ma Rulin blew out the candles.

"Take a deep breath and blow them all out in one breath!"

"He did it!" They clapped.

"Here's the knife. The birthday boy can cut his own cake!"

Hu Zhaosheng circled around the group, his hands thrust in his jacket pockets. He pushed someone aside and squeezed into the

---

2. The song is written in English in the original, except for Rulin's name, which appears in characters.

circle. He saw Zhong Xueyuan standing in the center by Ma's side. He leaped in front of them and pulled out the revolver screaming hysterically as if awakened from a nightmare: "Zhong Xueyuan, your time has come!"

Everyone was thunderstruck. Ma's first stroke had cut only part way into the cake. Zhong Xueyuan was holding an empty plate in his hand. At first he just stared dumbly at Hu Zhaosheng. Then, smiling slightly, he put the plate down.

"Don't move! One move and I'll shoot!" Seeing Zhong Xueyuan put the plate down, Hu Zhaosheng thought he was going to try to grab the revolver away from him, so hurriedly ordered him to stand still.

"I'll tell you right off... There aren't any firecrackers inside—but do you believe me?... I know you're beginning to doubt it. Ha! Ha! I'll let you guess... Zhong Xueyuan! Answer me immediately!... Did you ever kiss[3] your broad?"

The color went out of Zhong Xueyuan's face. They had never seen him look so ghastly before. No one knew what to do. Ma Rulin wanted to break in and stop it, but was afraid he would just make things worse, so he stood by watching helplessly. The two stood face to face, Zhong Xueyuan towering above and Hu Zhaosheng holding the revolver, the barrel shaking and tilted down.

"I'll give you three seconds to answer!"

Time seemed to stand still.

"You really want to know?" Zhong Xueyuan asked.

"Of course!"

"I've given Yang Yumei a kiss. Do you believe it?"

"..."

Hu Zhaosheng forced a smile. He raised the revolver, pointing it directly in Zhong Xueyuan's face. They were only two feet apart. Then, suddenly hesitating, he threw it to the floor and shoved his way out of the circle. He raced out of the living room and down the hall. Ma Rulin followed. Not knowing what to say, Ma Rulin stood

---

3. The word "kiss" appears in English in the original text, both here and in Zhong Xueyuan's reply.

there silently as Hu Zhaosheng put on his shoes. Finally he said, "Why don't you eat a piece of cake before you go?"

"No . . . thanks. I have to go home . . . I'm finishing up an article . . . tonight . . . sorry," Hu Zhaosheng said, feeling dizzy as if he were drunk.

Ma Rulin stepped into a pair of slippers and accompanied him to the main gate. It was only five or six degrees outside and as quiet as a deserted city. There was no moon or stars in the sky. Ma Rulin opened the door for him, and watched him disappear into the vast enfolding darkness, which swallowed him in a single gulp.

Ma Rulin scowled and returned to the living room. It was as quiet as it was outside. Zhong Xueyuan picked up the revolver, opened the barrel and emptied the red firecrackers. He counted them. Six altogether.

Ma Rulin went over to the stereo, put the needle down, flicked on the switch and turned the volume up as loud as he could. Out burst the din of drums, cymbals, trumpets and guitars, along with the frantic wild shout of a black singer, flooding the living room like a gigantic tidal wave.

Ma Rulin smiled and invited the others to share in eating the cake.

Translated by Jane Parish Yang

Mother

*May 1960. This story about a boy's sexual awakening was writ-
ten at the age of twenty, when Wang began his search for a
personal writing style. He employed the stream of consciousness technique combined with a rhythmic and thematic structure, and also experimented with punctuation by inserting extra space between sentences.*

The July sun, like the steady hum of silent music, sings from morning to evening.   After mid-day, the suburb's rice fields, the dense
clusters of newly built bungalows, the eucalyptus trees and the sandy beach all lie prostrate, quiet, patient, wrapped in thin gray fog,
waiting for still distant dusk.   In a blue sky filled with white smoke,
a lolling mass of white cloud fearlessly stretches its fat body like a
pregnant mother lying on a bed, resting.   A black sandbar has
emerged in the middle of the riverbed where the water has evaporated.   In a shallow pool, in a hollow in the sand, naked boys roll
around, slapping the water and shouting.

There is a stone-crushing plant on the opposite bank.   In the
morning, workmen use poles to push boats toward the middle of
the river and half fill them with gravel.   When the boats reach the
shore, the men's wives and children gather to shovel the gravel onto
trolleys, then the women and children push the trolleys along rails
that creep toward the plant.   Now, though, there is no one on the
beach, and the trolleys have been pushed together to one side; some
boats are gathered on the bank, the poles stuck in the water.   The
workmen have to wait until dusk to resume their work.   The

plant's motor makes a throbbing sound like the beat of a feeble heart.

She wakes up.   Pale and worried, she reveals the beauty of a woman over thirty.

"Mao'er,[1] come—," she says.   The room outside the bedroom, still empty, is quiet.

He sneaked out while I was sleeping.   Outside the sun is beating down.   What if he gets heatstroke?   You always make Mama worry.   I don't know where he went.   I don't have a clue where he went.   Could it be—the ten-wheeled truck, it is dark, oh, no, it is not permitted, it cannot, it won't.   Calm down, calm down.   The doctor said you have to stay calm.   Think about something else when you are agitated.   Sometimes I can't help feeling anxious. Gufang also tells me not to worry.   The boy is old enough.   He says the doctor was right, that I have a nervous temperament. Alone in the afternoon I suddenly get worried about him.   It's like when I saw his classmates bully him and beat him up.   Right away, I dashed to the school.   When I entered the school my heart was racing, like it would leap out of my throat.   Now my heart is beating fiercely.   I didn't dare go in to see.   Oh, thank heavens he was sitting in the classroom, unharmed.   My heart is beating fiercely. Calm down, calm down.   They tell me not to let my imagination run wild.   But I'm not well.   If they want to cure me, they have to tell Mao'er not to leave me.   Mao'er always must be at my side, every single moment.   Always at my side.   Now I will follow the doctor's orders.   I will follow his orders and be an obedient child. I can be a very obedient child.   Doctor, am I your obedient child? Oh, no no no no.   That's ridiculous.   He looks young enough to be a schoolboy.   When Mao'er was born, it was an old foreign doctor.   He spoke strange and amusing Chinese.   I liked that old doctor.   I preferred that old doctor, compared to the young one. Through his thick beard he said, "Madame, don't be afraid."   I really wasn't afraid anymore.   I liked him.   Madame, don't be afraid, and I really wasn't afraid anymore.   Mao'er.   Mao'er, come find

1. The name Mao'er literally means "cat's ear."

Mama, come.   She bent over laughing.   Her eyes were full of
tears.   She hid behind a thicket of shrubs.   He staggered forward
with his eyes wide open.   He was wearing a new, light blue child's
outfit, clean and fresh.   The collar was bordered with white lace.
A pair of round bare legs emerged below his shorts.   He was wearing a new pair of little white leather shoes.   He looked clean and
fresh.   Suddenly he started to cry.   Her face turned pale, she
rushed out from behind the shrubs.   Oh, honey, Mama is right
here.   Don't be afraid.   She held his cheeks close to her.   A small
crystal teardrop rolled down his cheek.   He was pouting, his lips
trembling.   He buried his face in her shoulder.   She kissed his
chest where it emerged from his collar.   He twisted around in the
curve of her arm and just giggled.   He was as tall as my shoulder.
......?...... He is completely different from when he was younger..
Oh, you are Mama's little darling, your pouting little mouth when
you're angry really makes you adorable, let Mama kiss you again
and again.   Now he can talk, and read and write like us.   ......?.
..... He seems to have his own ideas.   It is getting so that Mama
can't guess what you are thinking.   You have built up a wall and
you are keeping Mama out.   Really really really.   Sometimes
when Mama shows she cares for you, you are rude to her.   She says
it might rain and she folds up your raincoat and gives it to you but
you wave your hands and stamp your feet, accuse her of being fussy.
Look at that fierce glare.   You are hurting Mama's feelings.   Oh,
I'm really dumb really dumb.   How can I lie in bed crying?   It
really is a nervous condition.   It really is ridiculous.   Fool, fool.
Shedding more tears won't make you an obedient child.   You will
not be the doctor's obedient child.   Doctor, am I your obedient
child?   Oh my, you are talking such nonsense.   What a state I'm
in what a state I'm in.   I can't help feeling bad.   I just have one
child, Mao'er.   I hide my face on the pillow crying.   Gufang comes
over.   He wraps his arms around me and talks.   You really are
being silly.   What do you have to feel bad about?   It doesn't matter.   Don't we have Mao'er now?   Isn't having such a handsome
boy enough?   Then in my heart I'm really comforted.   I really am
a little fool.   Even Gufang is always telling me.   Mao'er is the most

handsome most handsome boy.   At school he is second in his class. That makes me feel wonderful.   Think about lighter things again. Mrs. Zhang came over to borrow the iron.   She's so fat she can't button up the collar of that dress from last year.   She said if she gets any fatter she won't know what to do.   She asked me if I knew that Miss Wu who moved into number fifteen or not.   She said she's divorced.   She won't lower herself to say hello to her.   I know that she worries about Mr. Zhang.   I won't lower myself to say hello to that kind of woman either.   You may say my way of thinking is old-fashioned but I don't care.   I look down on divorced women. She said she's lazy.   She only leaves for work at nine a.m.   At three p.m. she comes back.   She worries about Xiao San and she doesn't know if he'll pass his exams to get into middle school.   At the beginning of August they will announce the results of the examinations.   It is too early for Mao'er to go to middle school . . . . . . She falls asleep again.   The sound of the stone-crushing machine ceases momentarily, then continues to pound away.

On a slightly elevated patch of ground there is a big, thick banyan tree with rich green foliage that shades a large area.   A child stands in the shade of the tree, one hand on his waist, his posture mimicking that of a proud grown-up.   His eyes are big and clear, his arms and legs delicate, but his skin tanned a golden cheese-like yellow by the sun.   When a warm breeze wafts by, the leaves on the treetop sway with a rustling sound.   Here you can't hear the sound of the stone-crushing machine.   The child gazes at a row of houses below. A small powdery cement path borders the houses.   A row of eucalyptus trees stands by the path.   The child smells the cool refreshing scent of the leaves.   Once he took off his wooden sandals and clambered up the banyan tree.   He sat in the hollow between the two branches of the tree trunk flashing a heroic smile.   He picks up a bamboo pole from the ground, sits on the exposed twisting roots, his back against the solid tree trunk.   A flock of sparrows flies in from a field and also stops in the shade.   Startled, turning their heads, interrogating each other, suddenly they all ascend the

tree together.   The child looks up but he can't find them.   They
are hidden deep in the green shade.

A pink umbrella appears at the end of the white road.   The
child throws away the bamboo pole in his hand.   The umbrella
goes to the front door of a house near the middle of the row.   Slightly tilted, the umbrella folds up.   The child scrambles up, runs to the
white road and keeps running along the road.

"Oh!" The woman is startled.   Smiling, she shows a mouth full
of glittering white teeth.   Her face is flushed.   She wears a tight
black satin top that exposes her snowy white neck and perfect,
round, slender white arms.   Her upper body, wrapped in black
clothing, is like a cup-shaped flower bud.

"Where did you come from?" she asks.

"Over there."

The woman turns around.   She sees the big banyan tree on the
raised patch of ground.   The key turns in the lock.   Inside is a
messy little living room.   On the sofa are several rolled-up slips.
On the wall pictures of movie stars are pinned up.   On the table is
a plaster bust.   It's an angel with its head drooping, lost in thought,
but it's wrapped in cellophane.   She draws back the curtains and
pulls open the window.

"What were you doing under the big tree?"

He doesn't reply.   He doesn't dare tell her he has been waiting
for her for a long time.

"Mao'er, Mao'er, Mao'er," she suddenly begins to laugh, clear and
melodious.   "Oh, why did your Mama name you Mao'er?   Do
your ears really look like a cat's?"

His little ears redden.   His eyes look like an angry little tiger's.
He hates his mother.

"Such hot weather.   Do you want Auntie Wu to pour you a glass
of water to drink?"   He shakes his head.

Miss Wu pours herself a cup of cold water.   She turns on the
electric fan on the table.   Her two elbows prop up her flushed face,
her body bent close over the table.   The breeze blows her hair.
The thick black hair flutters behind her neck.   When she turns

around she finds his eyes meeting hers.   She smiles at him.   He is happy again.

"What is your Mama doing at home on such a hot day?"   Her buttocks press against the edge of the table; she is holding a tumbler of water in her hand.   Her fingernails are pointed and long, covered with bright red nail polish, glossy and round like coral earrings.   Her toes, peering out from her open-toed sandals, are also painted bright red.

"She's sleeping," he says lowering his voice.   She nods drowsily, smiling.   After she finishes the water she picks up a photo album and gives it to him.   Yesterday he hadn't finished looking at the photo album.   He curls up on the sofa with his head down, flipping through the album.   When he raises his head, Miss Wu is no longer there.   The electric fan blows open the green floral cloth curtain across the bedroom doorway.   Miss Wu is in the bedroom. She is standing in front of the bed.   She stretches out her hands, peels off her top and slips out of her skirt.   Soon her whole body is exposed, standing there in the middle of the bedroom.   She stands there flawless, perfect.   He thinks he has never seen anyone as pale as her.   After a minute she changes her clothes.   Using a brush that looks like a hedgehog she walks out, combing her hair.   On her feet she wears a pair of embroidered gold phoenix slippers. Miss Wu opens a box of chocolate candies and offers them to him.

Translated by Michael Cody

Calendar

September 1960. This is the second of five experimented stories Wang wrote when he was twenty. It is about a boy who suddenly realizes the span of a human lifetime is just a moment in the existence of the universe, a subject that reflects the author's concern for the human condition and an underlying theme in Wang's writing.

Huang Kaihua, a happy, carefree young man, is only seventeen. He has a round, ruddy face and sparkling black eyes. He often moves around the house in a running posture. Even when walking from the study to his bedroom at night he tightens his fists, lowers his body and mumbles "one-two, one-two" to keep his strong legs fit.

It is May. A Sunday afternoon. He has just finished his algebra exercises. His study is bright. A big window opens onto a courtyard filled with sunlight; the fragrance of coconut blossoms floats into the room. He rests his head on the desk, looking through the window like a curious puppy. Ah, who knows what happy thoughts he is having? Who could possibly count his thoughts?

He is dreaming about the summer break. His dream is all about green water, red watermelon and the basketball just going through the hoop. He takes a small notebook out of his pocket and turns to a page with a tiny calendar. Starting with the previous week, he crosses out each day and calculates how long it will be until the summer break. How slowly time passes. The crossed-out days, compared with those still left, take up only a small part of the page. This very day is less than halfway through, yet he crosses it off impatiently. After the summer, it will be September. He thinks. October, November, December, the semester will be over in the blink of an eye. In this case, time seems to pass quickly. After this December, it will be the year 1961. The page after 1961—it's the address page. No calendar. He wants to make one himself to continue. Huang Kaihua finds a large sheet of blank paper in his drawer. He begins to write:

1961

January

SMTWTFS

1. . .

Using the small calendar as a model, he prints the numbers on his version the same size. The more he writes, the more excited he becomes. Calculating the days of the future brings him an inexplicable and mysterious sense of pleasure, as if he suddenly possesses supernatural powers of prediction. Having finished copying the calendar for 1961, he continues on to 1962, then 1963. One year after another, he feels not even a hint of fatigue as he writes on. He murmurs excitedly: "Now I am thirty! . . . Now I am forty! . . . Now I am fifty! . . ." Finally, when he reaches September 2015, the whole paper is filled. There is no empty space to continue. Something that Huang Kaihua has never thought about comes into his mind. Will this be the end of life? He wonders. In 2015, he will be seventy-two. He has no idea if he can live that long. But this sheet of paper right in front of him, nothing but a paper, is filled with his future, all of it, all the days of his life.

Suddenly, this happy boy bends over and sobs.

Translated by Shu-ning Sciban

The Happiest Thing

November 1960. This story, Wang's shortest, is similar to "Calendar" in both theme and style. Its focus on one theme condenses the semantics of the narration to a level comparable to poetry. This is the third of five experimental works among Wang's early short stories.

The chilly morning has been creeping onto the street outside the building for hours. The young man opens his eyes and stares at the ceiling for a while, then puts on a sweater, leaves the woman in the bed and walks toward a half-closed window. He looks down at the street, his broad forehead pressed against the cold glass of the window. The freezing, empty asphalt looks like the face of an anemic woman. The sky is gray and misty, impossible to determine the distance of anything. All of the cement buildings are frozen, numb. The street, the sky, the buildings have looked the same for more than two months. There's no sign of any change in the weather.

"They all said this was the happiest thing to do, but how loathsome and ugly it was!"[1] he says to himself.

A few minutes later, he asks himself: "If it's true, what they say, that this is the happiest thing, isn't there any other happy thing?"

That afternoon, the young man commits suicide.

Translated by Shu-ning Sciban

---

1. The phrase "but how loathsome and ugly it was!" is in English in the original.

Song of the Earth

January 1961. This is the fourth of the five experimental stories written during this period. It describes a university student's frustration as well as excitement while witnessing the intimate behavior of a pair of lovers in a quiet café. Cinematic techniques, such as the use of middle distance and close shots, and unconventional syntax can be detected.

The Classical Music Teahouse is located on Hengyang Road, just left of the stylish New Park, on the second floor of an ice shop. The entrance to the ice shop is filled with ice-making machines that go *clug-clug* all day. Their lead pipes, encased in thick powdery frost, turn and twist everywhere.

Unless you're part of the in crowd, you'd never find the exact location. The small wooden staircase to the teahouse is to the left of the ice shop. It's easy to overlook. Once you make it up the small wooden stairs, a dark, secluded cavern awaits. Inside, faint music plays throughout the day. The air in the cavern is musty, the sofa covers are grimy and the records sound scratchy, but business still thrives. College kids hang out all day long, and don't want to leave at night. Whether they really like the place, who knows? Basically, it's their hangout, a place to get away from school, home and the dorm.

One Thursday in October, the Classical Music Teahouse is more or less empty and the air is cleaner than usual. In the background, Mahler's *Song of the Earth* plays. The palm trees between the seats are glossy with health. In one corner, hunched against a wall, sits a young man with broad shoulders and a flushed face. He wears a yellowish khaki uniform and is reading a Japanese novel. He is from the countryside in southern Taiwan. He has thick black hair that covers his forehead and hangs below his eyebrows. His strong, sturdy legs are clothed in tight-fitting khaki pants. He is a regular at the teahouse. He has come to write a letter to his widowed mother, explaining that he lost the six-hundred yuan she sent him in a card game with his roommate last night. Near the end of the letter, he writes that he regrets, really regrets, what he did.

The student reads a few pages of his book and raises his eyes to take a break. That's when he sees them, a couple huddled together, their hair combined in one mass. The girl's hand is in her boyfriend's hand, and their lips are pressed together. They came in half an hour ago and took a seat to his left. Facing a corner, they thought that since they were sitting at the very back of the place, with the palm trees hiding them from view, nobody in the front would be able to see them. As for the young college student, his head was buried in his book, so they indulged themselves. She is wearing a tight wool sweater, bright red, her small but firm breasts pressing out and up. He wears a gray nylon jacket and his hair is slicked back in the popular "duck tail" style. When they came in, the student felt a spasm of resentment. It's the feeling any lonely boy gets when he sees another guy walk in with a girl. The young man lets go of her hand, then holds her face, all the while kissing her. After a moment, he suddenly embraces her. She slides her arms down from his wrists, grabbing at his back, her fingers shivering. Her sharp, bright red fingernails sneak inside his jacket. His kisses drench her lips like rain. When he relaxes his arms, she seems about to faint, on the verge of losing consciousness, and falls on him, burying her face in his shoulder, her whole body shuddering. Lifting his head up, he whispers softly in her ear. A moment passes, and they remain in the same position, motionless. She lies there gently and her shuddering slowly subsides. The pair of lovers, embraced in each other's arms, fall happily into what seems like deep sleep. The young man drops his head and gently begins to kiss her piled-up hair, inhaling its aroma, nibbling her soft, supple hair. Then he starts to kiss her ear-lobe. Once more her body shivers and then she begins to tremble with sobs, her shoulders rising and falling. His hungry lips find the nape of her neck, her temples, the corners of her eyes, in a path that leads back to her lips. His right hand slides down, caresses her tender waist, then moves up, grasping her left breast. She raises her hand and hits it, but it continues to fondle her breast. Then he begins to caress her other breast. She no longer resists. His hands drop to her waist, dig deep under her red sweater, extend upward, moving about at will. But then her face becomes flustered with fear. She summons her strength and pushes him away. He withdraws his hands. She leans back toward the sofa, her face buried in her own hands, shaking even more than she had earlier. He extends an arm and wraps it around her shoulder. He quietly whispers in her ear. Afterward, he gently grasps her hands. She is docile and tender and looks at him with deep affection, her eyes glimmering with tears. She glances from the corner of her eyes and pouts. Quickly, she lifts her hands, like a pair of flying white pigeons. She arranges her hair and smoothes the creases in her red sweater. Then they stand up together, hand in hand, smile at each other, and leave.

The student lowers his head and continues to read. Before long, he closes the book, and leans his head against the back of the chair, lifting his face to stare at the ceiling. His shining eyes stare at the pale blue lake surrounded by recessed light bulbs.

He leaves, descending into the dark, warm, humid night that has inundated Taipei. Dinner at the dorm has already been served and he feels a ferocious animal hunger rising inside him like a storm—he goes down Gongyuan Road with all its noise and confusion, ready to stop at a small noodle shop to fill his belly. In the busy city's night market, red wine and yellow fruit float in the air—peerless, brilliantly illuminated fruit.

Translated by Ihor Pidhainy

Midsummer on the Prairie

May 1961. This, the fifth of Wang's experimental stories, depicts a group of soldiers on a one-day training exercise. Many paragraphs function like stanzas in a poetic work. The story also contains one of the first examples of Wang's use of an existing Chinese character to convey a new meaning. This is one of the most striking techniques in Wang's literary repertoire and is mistakenly believed to have first appeared in his first novel, Family Catastrophe. *The setting is Zhuzikeng in Taizhong, where Wang was stationed for a short period during his compulsory military training in Taiwan.*

This stretch of prairie runs north right to K City, but the city's voice is inaudible. From here, K City looks like a shallow lake, cool and refreshing. This morning, as the sun climbs up the mountain slope on the eastern side of the prairie, it gilds several small hills (they are shaped like steam buns) on the western and southern edges of the grassland, wrapping them in a bright, golden, Chinese robe. The small mountain's sweeping shadow (like a king's robe), spreads flat, hesitating, over the prairie. The sky is null, an empty land, the azure color as formless as the sky itself. The pure-fire sun will roll back and forth as it pleases across its playground; up in the sky, it cannot play the arsonist and set fires. An extremely hot day is about to begin.

On the prairie near K City, the terrain has a slightly higher elevation. Pale green sugarcane grows on top, taller than a man, but the southern side is untouched by human development. This area contains a dried up riverbed with exposed heaps of pebbles that look like white bones; also a wasteland of withered wormwood—deep brown shoots of parched grass grow on it like a heavy beard, reaching waist high. This is what comes of the sunshine's daily conspiracy, its extortion by deception, but a minuscule patch of green life continues to multiply at its feet.

The sun's rays plate all of the trees on the hillsides with golden masks. At this moment, the air still retains the freshness of early morning; the dew on the grassland has not yet disappeared. Before long, the singing of the cicadas starts. It comes from the mountain forest, confirmation that the sun's heat has penetrated the leaves of the trees. The cicadas' sensitive bodies detect the scorching heat. The crying of the cicadas is the whisper of the tree spirits.

A group of men wearing grass-green military uniforms and grass-green helmets comes through the valley between two small mountains on the eastern side, from a valley graced with a bamboo grove. The ant-like line of men, an apricot-colored army flag in the lead announcing their presence, emerges into the abrupt expanse of this vast world. Their route suddenly appears to lack any fixed direction and they fall out of step. Nervousness, a lack of confidence, spreads among the troops. A man wearing a yellow helmet, who had been standing apart from the soldiers, accompanying them independently as they forged ahead, now quickens his pace and runs to the head of the column. In a loud voice he reprimands a soldier, and the troops' forward march comes to a complete halt. The soldiers at the head of the column shift direction, resuming the advance. The march is still ambling and awkward because the ground beneath their feet is rugged and rough. The man wearing the yellow helmet stands motionless, both hands on his waist, legs spread wide and firm like two poles, looking sideways at every soldier who passes in front of him. They are all extremely young and dressed identically: a rifle on every man's right shoulder, a small wooden stool hanging from the left wrist, an extremely wide cartridge belt buckled tight around their slender waists, a bayonet on their belts hanging flat against their buttocks, its handle tapping the canteens at their waists. This tapping, the sound of the metal ring on the rifle strap, the footsteps of more than one hundred men, all combine to generate the strange sound of these troops. Nothing else can be heard, not even the voice of one man talking among them. At the tail end of the column, many other men follow along, the movement of their feet more halting, unable to keep up with the progress ahead. Each pair of these men carries a wooden box or a wooden plank bigger than a door, one man holding each side. A piece of white canvas painted with black concentric rings is stretched over the planks.

The troops make their way to the old route of the riverbed, descend the bank and walk to the river's edge. Although the riverbed usually is dry, it rained heavily last night and water has flowed down from the mountain, so there is water in the channel. It is not even knee deep but roars ferociously. Approaching the riverbed, despite their strict discipline, the troops fall out of formation. They waver back and forth, make a faint, helpless sound, the sort of noise people make when they face natural obstacles that expose the smallness of humans, their emptiness, insignificance. After a moment, some of the men find rocks that can serve as stepping stones; one after another they leap on them. Their unsteady bodies sway over the snow-white foam, like mountain goats—leaping. Many men, because they lack confidence, fall into the river as they jump.

Their senior officer, the army man wearing the yellow helmet, takes his turn jumping across. This proud man, under many pairs of eyes, anticipating, glum, jeering, raises both hands high, at times even raises a leg like a rooster—finally he too crosses the river safely. The men carrying the heavy loads take turns jumping—most of them fall into the water.

The troops begin to assemble again on the other side of the river, on the vast, bare stone beach, apparently lifeless but so ancient its age is incalculable. Order, temporarily lacking, is restored by a whistle and a reprimand: everything is under the control of one specific authority. The line of young troops, now facing an even bleaker and more desolate region, continues to forge ahead.

Green grasshoppers with dew-laden wings spring up beneath the trampling feet of these invaders on the prairie. Their beating wings emit a sound like thin pieces of metal being struck. The bodies of some of the grasshoppers are wrapped in pale brown shells. Perhaps they are older than the ones with green shells, their youthful green faded now by the sunlight. And there are many small dragonflies, flying only shoulder high, flying, stopping, but never landing. The troops finally reach their destination, that wasteland of brown wormwood—the soldier carrying the army flag runs out from the column, takes the flagpole's sharp metal end and, with two jabs, inserts it into the hard, resisting earth.

A misty layer of dust rises from the wasteland and mingles with sunlight. Concealed in the dust are disordered, running shadows, many pairs of feet trampling the earth, and the officer's short, firm, continuous shouts. The dust gradually drifts to the ground. On the wasteland, about thirty paces apart, in row after row, soldiers stand like stone columns. As soon as they hear the command, they spin their guns uniformly, then pound them to the ground. They thrust out their chests, pull in their chins and stand at attention, absolutely still. The ramrod bodies cast straight shadows. For a moment, the officer cannot make them out clearly: have these soldiers under his command actually turned to stone? Amazement mingled with dread makes him delay his decision to issue an order. Just momentarily puzzled—it is like a dream world in the dust-filled sunlight— he comes back to his senses and gives the order. Life appears to flow into the lifeless stone columns. They begin to move. Every row turns to the right, turns to the left, lifts its feet high in unison like horses being trained. After a short time, trickling sweat turns their backs black with moisture, their shirts stick to their skin, lines of sweat trickle down their chests and black spots appear under their arms . . .

The sun, like a light-hearted tune, slides in the smooth, flawless, blue sky, almost reaching the meridian. The pupil of its eye suddenly opens wide, laughing, mocking, as it looks down on this large group of men scattered on the prairie like specks just slightly bigger than ants. If it opened its pupil only a little wider, these insignificant men would groan. The sun ignites more than one hundred helmets like more than one hundred silvery bright sacrificial fires. But beneath the fire and steel is only weak, grass-green, plant-like flesh.

There is one young soldier, his face wet with perspiration from sweating so much. His complexion is as pale as lime mixed in ice water. Due to lack of sleep, the hollows of his eyes have become a pair of gloomy caverns; beneath his cheekbones are two dark shadows, like smears of black powder. He looks up, watching that blue sky bigger than the prairie. Besides the sun he sees only one small cloud, five or six degrees from the sun. If only that small cloud would cover the fierce, hot, burning sun—even if only briefly—he longs for that moment of shade. That short moment of shade would be like a drop of water lightly, gracefully moistening the lips of a starving, thirsty desert traveler. In his mind he prays silently, hoping the cloud will sail toward the bright, shining sun. He hopes the cloud can wrap up the sun like a mother's blanket. The cloud does not heed his prayer; it sails past, below the sun. The pale youth, standing at attention, bends like a blade of soft, weak, green grass.

By noon, the clouds have climbed higher. They are like mothers bearing many infants in their arms. They display their primeval strength as they rise from the horizon and expand. On such a fine summer day they take delight in bringing out their children to enjoy the fresh air and gossip leisurely with their neighbors. While some hold their round, plump children to their breasts, there also are expectant mothers with protruding pot bellies. But despite their numbers, these sky mothers are only willing to wander at the edges of the sky. They will not stray far from their homes.

The men on the prairie already have dispersed. Some sit, some stand, some lie down. It is their rest time, but they cannot find their own shadows. The sun is directly overhead, shining straight down; they are men who have lost their shadows. Their downcast eyes, seeking out a place not invaded by sunlight, cannot even find a shadow. The field ration lunches have been consumed already. The officer wearing the yellow helmet issues an order: for the time being they can take off their helmets and wipe the sweat from their faces.

They obey his order, take out their handkerchiefs, wipe their faces and the backs of their necks. The sun beats down even more fiercely on their smooth, shaved heads. Many men, unable to bear the heat, put their helmets back on. Some raise their heads, extend their necks, grasp their canteens with both hands and rest them against the roof of their mouth, letting a fine trickle of gurgling water flow over both sides of their mouths. Some of them stand up and go over to where a group of several men have gathered. They are scrambling to snatch a shining aluminum bowl—it's set on the ground and full of salt. They dig their hands into the bowl, grasp handfuls of salt and stuff it into their mouths, then mix it with water from their canteens. Already, salt has become an indispensable food in their lives. When they sweat, they sweat salt. When so much salt is lost, they weaken—it's like fainting from fatigue. So they rely on salt to revive themselves. That bowl of white salt under the glare of the burning sun reflects light rays like dazzling diamonds. That bowl of white salt is a portion of life essence, the source of their physical strength.

Rest is rest but it is short-lived. The officer stands up again from the wooden stool he has been sitting on. He puts on his helmet, adjusts it and tightens the strap under his chin. He takes a whistle from his pocket, blows it rapidly, shrilly, violently. So disturbing, this sound that passes through all the fatigued, weak bodies lying and sitting on the ground in the wasteland or perched on wooden stools. Compelled by the whistle, they stand up, their heads hanging in dejection, and go to where the rifles are stacked—stacked like bundles of dried straw. Each takes a rifle. Again they form a line, become soldiers who resemble a solid stone wall.

Just as during the morning routine, they separate into squads, each at long-range from the others. This time each squad does not form a line; they stand in circular formations. Raising their rifles, their eyes look out along the barrels of their guns, the canvas strap wrapped around their left arms. Their hands, raised in pain, are numb. Besides this drill, they also practice sitting, kneeling, lying down.

The officer wearing the yellow helmet suddenly goes over to one youth and forcefully hauls him up from the ground. The officer shouts at him in a loud voice. Standing before his commanding officer, the youth dully sticks out his chin, his two hands far from his body, his legs splayed crookedly. This is his defense before his commanding officer. The officer extends his hand, points at the crooked, thin, splayed legs, still wide apart, not correct at all. The officer springs, slaps his face. The youth is devastated. He brings his legs together slightly. But the officer is not satisfied. He wants his orders to be carried out strictly by those under his command, correctly and without error. Violently, he kicks that pair of crooked legs. The officer is wearing leather boots, hard as iron. The youth finally submits to his force, straightens his legs, aching and weakened by the kick. When the officer hit the youth with his hand and kicked him so fiercely, the drills abruptly stopped. In the sunlight, the troops watch stupidly from a distance, these two men antagonizing each other. The officer dismisses the youth's attempt to resist him—in the end, the soldier's resistance is broken by his iron will. The officer turns his head, shouts at them, orders them to continue their drills! But the spirit of resistance in the young man's breast prevents him from lowering his head. The spirit of resistance, like the head of a stubborn ox pressed down for a moment, rises again. Hostility concentrates in the young man's mind like a storm cloud, ever darker and darker. In his mind, he curses the officer with spiteful, sharp, harsh words. Separated from the others, standing far apart, he looks like a banished criminal. But there is no sense of shame or cowardice in his burning soul, no, certainly not. On the contrary, he feels proud. When the officer leaves, he neither orders him to fall in nor to continue standing at attention. That is another way of saying he must continue standing there, towering at attention.

At noon on the prairie, the sunlight forces a layer of mist to rise from the ground. The few small hills appear to be falling into the middle of a deep sleep. Far off K City, that pleasant blue lake, has turned murky. The city has degenerated, its dreams more obscene than those of the small hills. The soldiers on the prairie are lying down, sitting, squatting, too. Their water is already used up. Because they are exhausted, suffering from the scorching heat and thirst, they all squirm uncomfortably.

The proud officer does not rest with them. He sits far away on an extremely narrow wooden stool. He takes off his yellow helmet, holds it in both hands, calmly lays it on his knees. His pride makes him sit apart from his soldiers, but you also could say they repay his hostility by excluding him. He is an upright soldier, strict about his responsibilities and unemotional in his conduct. His hair, just like that of his soldiers, has been shaved, but on the crown of his head very short, stiff hair remains. His face is like a piece of chipped flint: hard, slim, red. On his face, the line of unmoving muscles conforms precisely to the discipline and order he holds strictly in his heart. He has killed men—with a bayonet, with a bullet. But, in his heart, he is not without "love." He likes the more than one hundred youths he leads, these well-disciplined, active, agile new recruits. He feels he has never led such fine troops. But they do not know he loves them. That one standing at attention as punishment, the one who tried to disobey his order, he certainly must hate him the most. That soldier, he's like a single erect pillar, apart from the rest. Both of them are alone, both outside the circle of the crowd. Seeing that his commanding officer is gazing at him, the soldier holds his head high—his resistance, like a loose belt immediately pulled tight, makes him stand even straighter, more rigid. The officer, too, knows he is now standing at attention more properly, not due to submission but rather a kind of defiance, defying pride with pride! Fine, make him stand a little longer, the officer thinks, retaliating in his heart, an ice-cold decision. His pride does not permit him to be touched by anyone's ridicule.

Not far from where the youth is standing at attention as punishment, a soldier who has fainted under the scorching sun lies face up on the ground. The officer gets up from his small wooden stool and walks toward the sick man to check his condition. Although he is clothed, he is lying fully exposed to the sun as if naked, offering himself to the sun, his eyes looking straight into it. His eyes fall shut the next moment but the sun's impression still stabs through his eyelids, a fiery, embryo-like shape penetrating them. The officer's body stands straight, both hands at his handsome slender waist, his head looking down, inquiring of the sick man whether or not he is better. The sick man has only one answer. Naturally, the officer is not convinced by the sick man's words. He raises his head, opens his mouth in a grin, the sun like golden, boiling water spilling onto his head and face. The sun—a wild, white-bright, long-whiskered, raging beast—dazzles the officer. He immediately lowers his head. In his heart, he pities the sick man but he himself is powerless. As for that youth standing at attention, all of a sudden he feels the earth spinning—the sun in the sky performs a whirling dance. Quickly, he gathers all his physical strength, strives to control himself. He is determined that on no account will he faint before the officer releases him. Through his force of will, the sun's whirling gradually slows.

A group of men goes over to the officer and explains something to him. He answers them. They form a line, one man in front, turn their backs toward those who are resting, and leave. They walk single file, their feet parting the pale brown prairie grass along the way. They discover some grass that looks like it has been sprinkled with lime, bleached white by the sunlight. Reaching a place where the grass is relatively high and dense, they make a detour behind this patch where, in unison, they pee. Afterward, they again form a line with one man leading, walk back to the officer and report for duty.

The sun has already reached the western half of the sky. The officer goes over to where the men are resting, lifts his whistle and blows it, a shrill sound, loud and clear. They stand up, adjust their clothing, pick up their guns. They—these many ant-like men—assemble again in a dense black block, the individuals indistinguishable. Following some words of exhortation, one squad moves out. Later, two more squads move out. The first one walks to the targets—those objects made of wooden frames and white cloth with black rings painted on them—each man supporting one frame. They form a column and every man bends his back under the weight of the heavy load. Lowering their heads, limping every step of the way, they hobble south toward the hills. Some of the squad members who came out second insert bamboo poles into the ground nearby. On the top of each pole a triangular red flag flutters. More men, their shoulders struggling to support a bamboo pole bound in a rolled-up red flag—it looks like the canvas-wrapped mast of a sailboat—and another long bamboo pole with a tin plate attached to its base that looks like a butterfly net, follow far behind the men carrying the targets. Another squad takes charge of the task of carrying boxes of bullets to an embankment—the embankment is as high as a man and has green grass on top. They take bullets from the boxes they carry chest-high and, like farmers sowing, scatter these golden seeds on the embankment. The ammunition is scattered this way (according to regulated quantity and prearranged position) for the convenience of the shooters.

The squad of men carrying the targets is like a fine stream of black, running water flowing through the withered yellow earth, a little green still mingled with spotted brown. Finally the flowing black water dries up, absorbed into the thirsty earth—they descend into the ditch.

The remaining troops raise their heads and look into the distance toward the ditch. Slowly, in succession, the solemn targets rise up. The men prepare to fire. They line up below the embankment in neatly arranged rows, sitting cheerfully on wooden stools. The first row of men, hearing the command, stands up. Both hands holding their guns across their chests, they keep their stance, anticipating the next command. At the second command, they step forward. They crawl up the embankment with great difficulty because they cannot use their hands to climb or keep their balance. On the embankment they form a long, long row, the muzzles of their guns pointing toward the sky. They wait for the next command—between commands there always are empty moments. On the embankment they feel the pleasantly cool breeze blowing from the gap in the western hills. That's the wind from the sea, from the dark blue Taiwan Strait. Many faces crack a smile. They can catch the breeze because they are standing on high ground. They are thirsty. The abundance and purity of wind and of water are the same. Greedily, they inhale. The order to shoot is given. They drop to their knees and fall forward. Then the exploding sound of hard, solid particles, loud and clear, brittle, steel-like, that destructive "popping" sound, engulfs the whole prairie like a shallow layer of tide water. As the sounds of this ragged burst of gunfire pass, the targets in the ditch sway until eventually they fall forward to the ground. Before long, the targets are raised again, their surfaces covered with patches. In front of every target is either a bamboo pole, grasped by unseen hands, with a fluttering red flag, or a bamboo pole with a circular plate on top, pointing at each corner of the target. After each man fires, he withdraws, ceding his place as the next man in line mounts the embankment. Burst after burst of gunfire disappears into the stillness of the universe, swallowed by stillness. Before this solemn, expressionless, silent-as-God stillness, the faint, feeble noise is like the play-acting of a child.

As in a desert basin, there is no breeze below the embankment, yet a dense fog envelops the tops of their heads. Is this because heat is rising from the ground or due to their own body heat, sweat, breathing? They don't know. Their elbows are propped on their knees, heads held in the palms of their hands, their motionless posture and switched-off minds resisting the harmful sunlight. Naively, they seem to imagine that as long as they do not make a sound and stay still, they can escape the sun's attention, like hiding from a wild animal on their trail. All of their faces are scarlet, their canteens with their small, round, pouting mouths, are abandoned at their feet.

The prairie enters the afternoon, enters the weary, still afternoon. The singing of the cicadas has already ceased, perhaps because they cried all morning and are worn out. After the first burst of gunfire and before the second, the stillness of the prairie is like a pair of wide-open eyes, watching attentively, like waiting spirits. This is a living realm no longer. Here, it is like a different, silent planet. The air inhaled is "dead." Not only is there death in the air, death also exists on the hillsides—banana trees exposed to the sunlight all morning, already withered, their leaves drooping, arms stretched out like a martyr on a cross with his head hanging down. Not just one, a whole group of dead statues stands on the hillside. And who can doubt that in the afternoon those singing cicadas, with their songs of praise, will also die a martyr's death?

In the target ditch, the workers' feet are immersed in the filthy water it holds. They take off their shirts, revealing smooth, straining, exposed bodies that go forward to raise and lower the targets. Pulleys creaking, they use both hands to raise the target or twist under it to use their shoulders to raise the frame. When they have to lower a target, they must stretch their whole bodies like apes, both hands hanging from the top of the iron frame, using the weight of their bodies to pull it down. Each pair takes turns raising and lowering the targets. When one has pulled down the target ten times, exhausted, beads of sweat covering his shoulders like pearls, his partner goes to replace him. Then, like an exhausted dog, like a flat tire, he sits paralyzed on stone steps above the water, gasping with difficulty. Because the target ditch is narrow and the men are crowded together, plus the sunshine and the fumes from the filthy water, the air is as foul as poison gas. This long, narrow gap in the earth—didn't it appear because the earth's crust cracked, exposing the reality of the world of mortals to the air? These many naked, exposed, cursed, gasping souls!

The sky, like gauze woven by cicadas, is spread in a pale, misty sheet. The clouds' posture has already changed, a child at its mother's breast, now climbing up on his mother's shoulder. The drama played out in the sky is strange and multifaceted, with actors—clouds; stage lighting—sunlight; stage scenery—the color of the sky, all apparently already fixed in the program. If God is the director of the play, the breeze would be God's stage direction, God's gestures. The puffy white clouds become ugly old maids. After a while, the bellies of the clouds turn gray. On summer afternoons, a thunderstorm, like a well-rehearsed performance, usually is re-enacted. The cheerful weather suddenly seems to weary of its existence. The sun, like a monarch, hustles out. Heavy gray curtains are pulled down. See, suddenly the many healthy clouds have just disappeared, forcing man—dumbfounded and amazed—to confront life and death (or, you might as well say, extermination). What unseen, gigantic, fearful hand, without the least compassion and with supreme cunning, has destroyed their lives?

The sky is a pool of gray ink, an expanse of gray nothingness, bottomless—what is behind it? Our souls fling themselves in, straight into it, fly without restraint. That is freedom. It makes man giddy, makes him tremble. On the prairie a wind like ice-cold water springs up, bringing a nightmarish commotion to this quiet, dead-still region. The grass bends at the waist, the trees on the mountain sway too, as if offering many pairs of outstretched hands. That martyred banana tree, waving its damaged sleeve in the ill wind, starts dancing. The dense, dark clouds above the mountain watch over the suffering of birth, like hens hatching eggs on the summit. Happiness, like a drink after a long thirst, mixes with the clutching fear and dread of the unavoidable rain, spreading among the crowd. But on the surface they appear indifferent, exhibiting no concern as the shooters continue to tower up on the embankment, without any change, following the commands, falling prostrate, opening fire like tidal waves. Even the men sitting below the embankment just look up to watch the dense clouds. They cannot leave their seats without authorization. Like wormwood grass bent by the wind, they are unconscious plants, fatalistic.

A silvery tree root reaches down to the horizon, shakes itself violently, as if to terrify mankind. Only a flash, then it disappears, returning to who knows where, to the unknown. A tediously long wait. Both plants and homo sapiens know what will follow: the longer they wait, the more surprised they will be. Finally the planet and a huge rock collide; a crashing sound, then a booming explosion, a sound different from any explosion on earth, it becomes louder and louder, one after another, with threatening power. Many huge rocks rolling endlessly on flagstone! The men on the prairie look up in unison. What is happening in the sky? Who jumped up there? The ashen color, except for the meaningless information it gives them, divulges no secrets. That part of the sky appears fundamentally unknowable, yet also knowable . . .

The rain arrives. The sick man lying on his back is the first to hear the rain's eager, rustling steps. The rain, like a young girl, walks on lithe, delicate feet. The rain, he can see, wears gauzy white robes. From the west side of the prairie, she rushes forward like a lover. The sick youth turns onto his side, his pale face wearing a sorrowful smile. He has lain on the prairie for half a day, fainted and regained consciousness, fainted and regained consciousness, without resisting the sun that has gnawed at his flesh like a wild animal. Now, he thinks, I shall give myself up to a newly arrived mistress.

The officer blows his whistle rapidly, shouts orders. The men on the embankment drop below it. All of the men grab their rifles, carrying them muzzle-down. White rain sweeps across the whole prairie. In an instant they are drowned in the rain's white ocean. Their eardrums ring with the lashing of the rain. They cannot hear each other talk, nor can they make out their companions' faces, just a vast expanse of white. In the rain every man becomes a solitary individual, unable to establish a link with his companions. The officer's whistle loses its effect, his authority washed away in the rainfall. Already, the spell cast over the confused privates is broken. Their unity crumbles, is scattered in all directions. With nowhere to go for cover, this crowd of men has to sit on wooden stools in the open country, allowing the rain to lash their bodies. They are like huddled, primeval cavemen, their entire existence controlled by nature. The tree-root lightning spreads out again and again. When the silver color turns fiery red, their eyes reveal the fear of cavemen. Their ability to understand something higher, stronger, more powerful, is no greater than that of cavemen. Humanity's posture of respect, of dread, of worship has persisted from the ancient past and will never change.

After the thunderstorm's cavalry passes by, bright lake-like puddles remain on the prairie. Tranquility spreads over the hills. In the open countryside the air is full of fresh, pure moisture. Quietly, all creation seems to be enjoying a refreshing rest. The trees on the hills look dense, damp and green in their purity and grace, just like wise women. The trees are all the same height, arranged neatly without any distinction, full of a solemn, holy beauty. The sky divides into gradations of color and brightness: near the ground is a layer of ash gray, above the gray a layer of white, and above the white a layer of transparent blue sky like water. There is no more suffering, no more brutality. The lingering sound of the thunderstorm seems far off, circling the prairie. Like all memories, it belongs to the past. Before long, even memories fade, leave no trace. The sun becomes a red face, a kindly old man, peeping down from high in the clouds, already moving to the west, approaching the horizon. The humans, still there after the thunderstorm, stand up, their entire bodies drenched, their clothing stuck to their flesh like skin. They limber up their arms and legs, cold enough that they all shiver a little. Then they face the setting sun—that red, drunken, lukewarm, setting sun. Now it brings them pleasant warmth. The rifles, baptized by rainwater, can no longer be fired. When the officer holds the guns, examining and pulling back the bolt in turn, his expression is serious, his lips pressed together. These short stubby M1s have to be disassembled, oiled with a piece of cloth, cleaned with great effort. The gun barrel must be cleared with a cleaning rod—that is the only way to remove all the rust. The troops feel happy because the only thing he can do is lead them back to the campsite to rest.

Obtaining the officer's permission, they peel off their shirts and pants, exposing their naked bodies, dressed only in their underwear. They wring out their drenched uniforms, carry them to the embankment, spread them on the still damp grass and leaves, letting the breeze up there and the warmth of the setting sun dry them. Tomorrow they will have to wear the same uniforms. The men toiling in the target ditch are lined up single file. All the men who were hidden under the targets have returned. In the radiance of the setting sun, the big targets reflect the splendid golden light. Isn't each one a sun, too? Sunlight gilds this group of men with shaved heads and naked bodies. Wearily, idly, they sit on their wooden stools waiting for the sunset. The officer's wet clothes never come off. His self-esteem and sense of superiority over his soldiers prevent him from taking off his clothes in front of them. His yellow helmet— symbol of his rank and authority—still properly covers his head!

The sun sinks. The western sky is a fiery expanse of color, like a blazing furnace. The glow of the setting sun triggers a glum mood of homesickness in the men.

The officer blows his whistle. He wants them to put their damp uniforms back on and assemble to go back. They line up in the violet dusk after dressing. Quietly, without a sound they gather together, the wooden stools suspended from their arms, their guns hanging from their shoulders, accepting the necessary order to "dress right!" and "count off!" After waiting for the troops to form an orderly line, the officer slowly walks toward that one exiled man, virtually forgotten by the other soldiers. The officer orders him to rejoin his unit. He sticks out his chest, raises his hand to salute him, turns around and proudly steps forward to return to the troops. His clothing is soaked, his dark, wet, clinging shirt revealing his broad back. The officer watches him join the ranks and then goes over to the sick man lying on the wet ground. He, his body covered in dirt and his face smeared with black mud, is clearheaded but he shivers from the cold. Facing the troops, the officer beckons. Two soldiers, big and tall, at the front of the line give their guns to the soldiers next to them and run over to the sick man. They support him with their arms under his armpits. The apricot yellow army flag is raised and the troops begin to move. The flag, saturated with rainwater, hangs heavy, motionless in the evening breeze, leading the way at the head of the troops. Propped up, the sick man follows at the rear of the troops, the officer also at the rear. Dusk on the open countryside grows ever darker, the darkness gathering like a tidal wave about to swallow them.

Like the dusk, the anger of the soldier who was punished gradually dims. Fury like burning flames no longer burns in his heart. Those flames have been extinguished, leaving behind just wisps of smoke.

They cross the river! Because of the big thunderstorm, the water level is higher and it makes rapid gasping, breathing sounds. Again they do not take off their boots, but simply lift their legs high, wading straight across the river. Then they disappear into the dark lush bamboo forest to the east.

The night prairie returns to nature. What humans did during the day, the running sweat, the cursing, the hostility, the gunfire, the groaning, even the virtues like patience, responsibility, discipline— none has left the slightest trace. The dark prairie is like a vast, soft bed. At the same time, it is also like a warm woman, her chest quietly rising and falling when she breathes. That chirping sound of insects is her opening her eyes often in the night.

Warm earth, loving earth, she is eternal. Without exception, whether beautiful or ugly, her bosom accepts all, embraces all. With her ancient wisdom (preserving eternal youth) her love is not total—although we do not doubt her love in the least—rearing we insignificant, ant-like humans, who look toward a future that is like the endless night sky.

The sky pulls open the black curtain that covers it. Infinite new and brilliant pearls flash like falling raindrops, but hang suspended in midair.

Translated by Michael Cody

Conclusion

May 1961. Fearful that his experiments would not be accepted by readers, Wang returned to a more conventional writing style after "Midsummer on the Prairie." This story about university student life and a unique friendship was the first product of his stylistic shift.

A shy smile hangs on his long, thin face. He has a head of black hair, as fine as silk, combed right to left. Usually, he does not go to class. Most of the time he is the departmental library, his face raised to scan the books on the shelves. If he happens to discover a modern author—a Thomas Mann or André Gide—like lightning his hand flashes out, pulls the volume down and ruthlessly, passionately, turns the pages. Typically, a massive book bag hangs from his right shoulder. It is a converted U.S. army gas-mask bag with a strap that he winds around his waist and attaches to a copper ring on the right side. So many things are stuffed inside: a dictionary with several loose pages, a stack of manuscript paper, a novel he has designated as "must read within a month." There are two other books, also novels, which he holds in reserve. After he has finished his current reading, maybe he will move on to them, although in practice it is not like that. When the time comes, he will covet a book he has not designated as part of his reading plan. Nevertheless, whatever the future brings, at this moment he loves these books, carries them with him and has to turn their pages every day in the tenderest, most loving manner. Besides these, the book bag contains a volume of modern American poems, among them, no doubt, several he is not very clear about, although speculating about them only adds to his delight. All these things swell the book bag like a pair of olives stuffed in someone's cheeks. In his own opinion, he is going to be a great author, which means he too will write one thick, heavy book after another, just as great as the dust-covered, worm-eaten volumes on the shelves. What's more, he even has the opportunity to realize his aspirations: every day, from morning till night, he sits hunched in the departmental library, head down, his absolute concentration just like that of a Tibetan lama crawling through a pilgrimage. The departmental library is located at the very end of the hall in the Faculty of Arts building. Someone visiting for the first time would think it is an exit, but after entering would realize there is no way out.

Not long after the start of his fourth year, he suddenly fell in love with a girl in his class. You could say this was an unfortunate event. She was a conceited girl who held herself as straight as a pencil when she walked and never looked sideways. Even in conversation with someone walking beside her, those eyes of hers retained their fixed, soldier-like, eyes-front position. Love, though, is like a miracle cure. Every morning he was up before six, in sharp contrast to his usual lazy routine of sleeping in until nine. He became a spirited, beaming child. What's more, he had his hair cut once a week, that fine silk-like hair, which he still combed from right to left. He also bought a notebook to keep a diary. Every night he waited until it was late and everyone was quiet, then took it from a locked drawer and wrote every sentence they had said that day, including "good morning" and "good-bye." He often mentioned names like Ricoeur, Kafka, Sartre and Kierkegaard to her. But misfortune arrived! One evening—it was during the intermission of a piano concert—he unexpectedly discovered her sitting together with "him." This "him"— his name was Liu Dafeng—was from a different department. Although he and "him" did not know one another that well, they did know each other's name. She was looking deeply into "his" eyes, and "he" had a kind of complacent smile on his lips. That sort of smile, it definitely was not a good sign—she was talking and laughing with "him" in a very warm manner. No further explanation was required. Everything was clear: Liu Dafeng was the winner. He did not wait for the performance by the foreign pianist—now sweating profusely, disheveled hair a clump of wild grass, arms waving, feet stomping—to end. He lifted his long legs, stepped over the knees of the other listeners and, feeling his way through the dark, walked out. He walked for many blocks, through the depths of the night, not returning home until the crescent moon had sunk in the west. He woke in the middle of the night and said to himself, "Feng Shengping, your love affair is over. You don't need to think about it anymore." Having said this, he turned over and went back to sleep. When he met her the next day, his face looked small and pale. He was extremely circumspect, nodded and smiled faintly. Since then, their love (if it could be called love) has been transformed into friendship—which means they nod to one another when they meet. That's how their love affair concluded. People actually admire this kind of conclusion to a university romance. It is considered ideal, possessing both nobility and grace. Nevertheless, when he encountered Liu Dafeng afterward, Feng Shengping hastened to avoid him, as the treatment Liu Dafeng received from her, compared with what she got in return, clearly was not very fair.

It certainly would not be hard to find someone else who met a similar fate during four years of university. Each one of his five other male classmates was a good example. Those five—they were like sworn blood brothers. They went out together, studied together, all went to see the last movie showing on Friday nights. The leader was Lü Mizhang. He wore a pair of tortoise-shell glasses with thick lenses, and was exceptionally honest and kind. Every semester he ranked first in his class—he never failed to do so. Another classmate was Zhang Zeyun, distinguished by his short stature and tendency to speak in a rush. The other three attracted less attention so it is not necessary to introduce them here. It is enough to say that these five good friends arranged their lives in an orderly way, quiet and calm. As for what they knew, they were vaguely aware of his failed romance but maintained a decorous silence. The main reason for this was that he tended not to spend that much time with them. Once, when he did happen to join them, they went out of their way to be warm, kind and, hard as it is to believe, even sympathetic. Zhang Zeyun gave him the thumbs-up and praised him: "Feng Shengping's great. We should all learn from you, even ask your advice." The rest of them unanimously agreed, saying Feng Shengping was great. Feng Shengping listened to their compliments and could not help blushing. The best student in the class, Lü Mizhang, was especially friendly. He approached him as if he were going to disclose a secret and said, "Hey, Feng Shengping don't work too hard. Relax with us! I notice you're always alone. It's great when we all get together and shoot the breeze. Let bygones be bygones, don't think about them again!" Their kindness, the warmth in their eyes that surrounded him, deserved a response but Feng Shengping, standing in their midst, was speechless.

Feng Shengping lived his life according to an ideal. He had read many books and, after his misfortune, read even more. That month, in just over two weeks, he devoured *The Sun Also Rises*, *The Great Gatsby* and *A Portrait of the Artist as a Young Man*.[1] He was no less disciplined or content than the others. He returned to his habit of rising punctually—at nine. On Saturday afternoon and all day Sunday he sat in a café next to the New Park with his legs stretched out comfortably while he savored his classical music. Apart from books, about the only thing he liked was classical music. He was happy to tell others that the composers he liked best were Barber, Wagner, Brahms and Glazunov. He may have been even happier to hear people say, "I don't understand" or "I have never heard of them." He also enjoyed Chopin, Tchaikovsky and Mozart, although he never told anyone. He had a deep love of music in his blood. The moment he heard a beautiful piece, he straightened up on the sofa and a slight smile appeared on his face, as if he wanted to find someone he knew, grab him by the hand and say: "Listen to how beautiful this piece is! How beautiful!" Nevertheless, when he left the café, he inevitably suffered a spasm of melancholy and lapsed into sadness for the rest of the evening. At times like this, he would remember his failed love affair, open the drawer and take out his diary—he had long since lost the happiness he once derived from writing to himself—to write a few lines.

---

1. The titles are given in English in the original.

One day, as the final exams approached, the afternoon sky was dark and austere. Many of the students who had been at school preparing for exams had already gone home because they could not stand the cold. At five o'clock, he walked out of the departmental library, the big, bulging book bag hanging from his shoulder. The halls were filled with a chilly, milk-white mist (adding to the Faculty of Arts' considerable charm). Using his keen sense of smell, he detected the gloom in the chilly fog. This sense is the first a writer must have. Walking outside, the two lines of thick coconut trees were like the columns of a Greek temple, their lovely trunks wrapped in a white veil. A layer of fine white wool appeared to have grown on the grass. Not a single person moved in the foggy stillness and it was so quiet you could almost hear the sound of the fog dripping onto the grass. He pushed open the wooden picket gate and went through the back of the campus, strolling over the green grass of the courtyard between Dormitories B and C.

"Feng Shengping, come quickly. Lü Mizhang has received the top scholarship and is throwing a party!" Zhang Zeyun was standing on the roof of Dormitory B, his body half visible above the cement retaining wall that ran around the edge of the building. He lowered his hands—they had formed a speaker over his mouth—turned, and was gone. Feng Shengping hesitated a moment, then accepted the invitation and walked into Dormitory C.

Lü Mizhang lived in Room 106. According to regulations, each room had to have eight occupants. A long crack split the glass in the door of Room 106 but probably no one noticed because a picture of a naked woman was taped to the inside. Already, many people were sitting inside and the table was covered with things to eat. There were piles of peanut and melon shells and torn tangerine skins. Besides the five inseparable friends, including Lü Mizhang, also present were Liu Dafeng and three native Taiwanese students. The latter lived in the same room as Lü Mizhang and were lying on their beds clutching their cotton quilts and reading. Lü Mizhang got up immediately to welcome him and offered him his own seat. Feng Shengping untied the strap around his belly and put down his heavy load. He realized Liu Dafeng's eyes were on him, so he nodded in greeting, as if they were delighted to see each other. As for the other classmates, he did not acknowledge them—it was as if they had turned into strangers. Lü Mizhang passed over a big paper bag containing fruit candy and Feng Shengping picked one out.

When two people who have had their differences are unfortunate enough to meet in the same place, they are not the only ones who pretend to be happy. Everyone else also joins in the pretence, which is exactly what Zhang Zeyun did.

"Are you ready for the exams, Feng Shengping? No? Don't lie to us! Of course, you don't need to prepare," he jeered. "You can take it easy and still score eighty or ninety percent. Feng Shengping, he's one of the stars of the Foreign Literature Department."

Everybody was looking at him.

Feng Shengping, speaking haltingly, criticized Zhang Zeyun: "Don't forget, we have a scholarship holder sitting here!"

It was fortunate that Feng Shengping's seat was some distance from Liu Dafeng, who was sitting near the window in a straight-backed wooden chair. Feng Shengping avoided eye contact, but the impression he had of him, glimpsed through the corner of his eye, was stronger than of anyone else in the room. It was like wearing glasses while drinking hot tea—the lenses steam up and everything in front of them is obscured. Although there was some distance between them, Liu Dafeng was the reason for the mild pain he felt in his heart. This unfortunate situation was relieved by the fact that Liu Dafeng was in the midst of an intense conversation with Lü Mizhang. Imperceptible to the others, Feng Shengping felt a great sense of relief at Liu Dafeng's ability to occupy himself. He even sensed a brotherly bond with him, one of sadness and concern.

Zhang Zeyun suggested they play bridge. He held a pile of cards in each hand clamped lengthwise between his thumb and index finger. With a magician-like flourish, he moved the two piles of cards closer together and, with a twist of his thumb, the cards performed a flying, rattling shuffle as if blown by the wind. Then he pushed his palms together so the cards arched up and fell into place one by one. Feng Shengping did not want to play so Zhang Zeyun went to ask somebody else. They rearranged the chairs and sat down around the table.

Oh, they're coming! Lü Mizhang and Liu Dafeng, with smiles on their faces, were walking over. "Feng Shengping, do you two know each other? This is Liu Dafeng, a fourth-year chemistry student." If two people have fallen out, find a way to reconcile them and restore their original relationship: this was Lü Mizhang's way. "We know each other, we do," Feng Shengping said, standing up and bending forward slightly. "We were in the same English class during first year." A bright, easy smile appeared on Liu Dafeng's face.

They sat down on the edge of the bed opposite him.

"Feng Shengping is an outstanding member of our class. He's done lots of literary research and often publishes articles in Hong Kong magazines. Liu Dafeng has done a lot of literary research, too. Now you two can talk to your hearts' content. I'll take advantage of the opportunity to listen for a while."

"Hey, Frank Lü, quick, come help me. This hand is falling apart," Zhang Zeyun called out. "Ah, that's disappointing." Lü Mizhang stood up, having lost his chance to listen in.

Now the two of them sat face to face.

Feng Shengping thought hard. What should he talk about? His eyes flicked restlessly over Liu Dafeng's face. Liu Dafeng's eyes shone, staring back at him with a kind of wild joy and excitement.

It was Liu Dafeng who spoke first. He leaned back against the bedpost, one leg pressed over the other, two long, slender arms hooked over his knee.

Feng Shengping felt a surge of happiness: no author is unhappy to hear praise. "Oh, that drivel! . . . Please don't flatter me . . . Which of my works have you read?" He realized his voice was not very steady because of the quivering of his heart. It was indescribable, like gratitude, also nervousness.

"I've read almost all of them. Have you written a new one?"

"Not yet, but I'm in the middle of planning one."

"What are you going to write? A novel?"

"No, this time I'm going to write an essay."

"What's it about?"

"I'm thinking it mainly will discuss Malraux's philosophy. Malraux is an important contemporary French novelist." He knew he was verging on pomposity, but his habits were as familiar to him as his fingers. Since he could not overcome them, he gave in to them! "His view of life is based on action. Do you know why? Because he believes that only by relying on action can you fill your life with meaning. Can you deny this? You can't. The prevailing views of the twentieth century are all like this, such as Ricoeur, Kafka, Sartre, Kierkegaard . . ."

Once he started, there was no stopping him. He continued to talk on about Ricoeur's philosophy, as serious and passionate as a priest. Liu Dafeng sat with his eyes wide open, attentive and focused as he leaned forward to listen. Gradually, Feng Shengping felt that he could control the rhythm of his speech. The quivering in his heart had stopped, like a loose nightgown slipping off by itself. Liu Dafeng was wearing a light blue wool pullover, the neck and cuffs edged with two red stripes. He was wearing glasses. His long face was cut by high cheek bones, a bright clear forehead matched with a pair of neat, ink-black eyebrows. His hair, although he never used hair cream, maintained its body and shape as if he did. When he smiled, he revealed two rows of strong, beautiful, white teeth. He really is a friendly, open-minded person, Feng Shengping thought. In particular, he noticed that his expression was warm and focused and that he nodded continuously. Feng Shengping felt a surge of warmth. He could not help grasping Liu Dafeng's hand and saying, "We should become good friends. Starting from today, we should be good friends."

"If I hadn't listened to you, I never would have heard about these excellent writers. I haven't done enough reading for sure. I'll definitely look for their books. Where can you buy them?"

"I have them at my place. If you want to read them, I'll lend them to you, no problem." The happiness of giving was immeasurable.

"Then thank you very much. But I'm afraid my English isn't good enough. I won't understand."

"That won't be a problem. It won't. You'll definitely understand." Now, in contrast, it was Feng Shengping who was full of confidence.

It is unavoidable: a pleasant discussion always turns to movies.

"But I don't like to watch movies."

"Why?" Liu Dafeng raised his eyebrows.

Feng Shengping formed a smile as he picked up a melon seed, placed it between his teeth and crunched down on it, but then immediately took the seed, shell and all, out of his mouth and said:

"I used to be like you, a typical fan of movies" (again, he was a little overconfident) "but later I found that movies don't measure up as art. Every movie is based on a formula. It's always a man chasing a woman, two or three scenes of them strolling together, then they end up at the altar. Is love really that simple? At least, we know that love in China is very complicated. If a man wants to capture a woman, who knows how many times he has to escort her home, how many unanswered letters he has to write, how many conversations of the 'this semester passed very quickly' type he has to engage in."

Feng Shengping blurted out these words inadvertently.

"Of course, of course." Liu Dafeng's eyebrows resumed their equilibrium.

Watching Liu Dafeng, Feng Shengping again felt just how kind he was and how superb his composure. Exhilaration churned once more in his chest. He was ready to tell him other faults of the movies when the card players finished their game and stood up. Some of them picked up their books to leave. In a short time, they had become friends and friends always regret the quick passage of time. Each following the other's lead, they stood up. Feng Shengping shouldered his book bag and secured the waist strap, just like an infantryman equipped and ready to move out.

"We'd best talk another day. Where do you live? I'll visit you," Feng Shengping said.

"Consider yourself invited. I have some records there—do you like music?"

"How could I not like music!"

"That's even better. This Saturday evening, do you have time? Come and listen to my copy of Brahms' *Fourth Symphony*, I just bought it."

"Brahms!" Feng Shengping clapped enthusiastically.

They copied their addresses in each other's date book. Her address was written on the first page of the small black one Feng

Shengping carried. Just then, everyone simultaneously exchanged goodbyes and left Room 106. They walked down the stairs, some returning to Dormitory B, some taking the wooden back gate across the campus to leave via the main gate. Liu Dafeng was going to the main gate. The two new friends—good friends—heartily shook hands, then parted. Feng Shengping walked by himself toward the bus stop for route number one.

"What a good person! What a good person!" His heart sang with praise. He could not prevent tears of emotion from welling up in his eyes. "If I were still dating her, if it were still like that, we'd unfortunately be rivals in love. It would only take a meeting with him like today's to make me automatically withdraw from the competition. I would unite the two of them. They are an ideal couple. His composure is superb, he is gentle and generous. And she is beautiful. I really would act this way. I would tell him, 'She's yours. We're good friends. Your happiness is my happiness.' " In fact, thinking in this way, his happiness was boundless, "True love is in giving, in sacrificing, in stepping aside out of empathy."

But he also was confused, "According to normal human behavior, I shouldn't become good friends with him. It was he who stole the woman I fancied. If anything, I should be jealous of him. Why am I not jealous, not at all?" He carefully examined his feelings for a while and could not find even one little particle of jealousy. "Strange, why is that?"

The fog had already thinned somewhat, but the temperature had dropped even more. Thick, moldy, green moss covered the walls around the homes on both sides of the lane like a bed of green down. The yellow bus stop was not far ahead.

"Maybe because love was already gone without a trace. Love was like a bird that had flown into the infinite twilight."

Translated by Lloyd Sciban

Two Women

September 1961. Written shortly after Wang's graduation from university, this story examines jealousy and its ability to empower and motivate a character. The heroine's gradual transformation reflects the young author's keen powers of observation and profound understanding of human nature.

That tall woman who just went by, followed by those four scampering children, is a washerwoman in our neighborhood. She has been washing clothes for about four years in this area. She holds her head high, always has a slight film of white powder on her face, always walks with a stiff, quick gait. She rarely talks to anyone. Moreover, judging from the seriousness of her demeanor, she seems to be burdened with many worries. The dirty children who trail behind her are only some of her brood—she has seven in all. Her husband, who used to be a janitor at the district office, is a lazy, unemployed braggart. He's another regular in the neighborhood—he likes to gab in the grocery stores, restaurants and barbershops, making fun of other people in a loud voice. Sometimes he quarrels and gets into noisy fights with the clerks and runs after them into the streets. While he idles away his time, his woman washes clothes at one house after another, from sunrise to sunset, working like a mule.

Although everybody thinks of her as rather cold, I know she loves her children deeply. One time I saw her lead her marching retinue into a small Taiwanese candy shop and buy each of them a piece of walnut cake. I watched her distribute the cake tenderly. In ecstasy, the little ones nibbled their pieces of cake and, tramping in their tiny clogs, chased after their mother, who walked too fast for them to keep up.

Wouldn't anyone sympathize with this woman, considering her husband is a man utterly devoid of integrity? His idleness and his dependence on her are a great shame to all men. Nevertheless, it is said in the neighborhood that this woman loves her husband fanatically, that she is only too willing to dedicate all her labors to him. There even is a rumor that it was she who intentionally engineered his corruption, that it was she who purposefully induced him not to work. A story concerning this matter has spread throughout the neighborhood.

Fifteen years ago, when Taiwan had just been liberated, she was a girl with a round face and plump arms. She was not very attractive, but did emit a healthy glow. Her father owned a store that sold cookware. In the shop, hanging from the ceiling and around the walls, were gleaming bronze pots, rush-leaf fans and roll upon roll of iron wire. If a gust of wind blew, the bronze pots, the iron wire and the pans would clash and clang. Her mother, a frail woman with her hair swept up in a knot, usually sat in the shadows at the back of the shop, yawning long and deeply. Her father sometimes stood with his hands on his hips in front of the shop, sometimes climbed a ladder into the attic to study a physiognomy text. It was the day-to-day life of a small merchant: contented, dull, desolate. She used to help her mother with the meals or move a bamboo bench to the front door so she could lie down and relax. She was eighteen that year. Because of her leisurely, idle life, her skin glowed like a red candle and her weight increased day by day. Her mother often sighed for her: "Ah Yu, if you keep gaining weight, who will marry you? Why don't you eat less?" Her daughter, about to stuff a peanut candy or several kernels of corn into her mouth, always answered slowly: "I'm so hungry all the time!"

That summer a mainlander in a black Chinese-style suit came to town. On a hot afternoon, he passed their shop and went in to buy a bronze teapot. He had not lived in the area long and he seemed, in every respect, like an alien who had just come from across the sea. After paying, he did not leave the shop at once—his hungry eyes stared at the figure of the fleshy young woman. He grabbed a bunch of nails and inquired about their price as an excuse to linger a bit longer.

The next day, the mainlander appeared again. This time, he was bold enough to talk to her in his awkward Taiwanese. From then on, he frequented the shop often, either to buy a tiny bowl or to chat with her and her mother while buying nothing. He became a regular caller.

A month later, gossip was circulating in the community. At sunset, they often strolled hand in hand along the paths between the rice fields outside the town. That was fifteen years ago. You may remember, that was the time when a huge chasm gaped between the Taiwanese and the mainlanders. The townsfolk were enraged, thinking that the reputation of the community had been defiled. The most furious among them were her parents.

"Disobedient wretch, look what you've done, you've made your mama sick," said the old man, who had been absorbed in his physiognomy book. Pale with anger, he pointed at her with trembling fingers:

"Listen, you're too young to see things correctly. You should know that those mainlanders all have wives back home. Do you want to be his concubine?"

"But he's not married, Papa."

"How do you know?"

"He showed me his papers."

"Papers? Are you so easily fooled? Isn't it possible his papers are forged? You must be out of your mind!"

"But he told me that he wants to stay in Taiwan forever. And he said he would never go back as long as he lives."

"That's easy to say. It's all very well to say so, but what if he does go back one day? What if he fetches his wife to Taiwan even if he decides not to go back?"

"It won't happen, Papa. Don't go on. It's useless anyway for you to say more. I've decided to be with him. I'll never marry anyone but him."

Her eyes blazed.

"Fine! Fine!" the old man's lips curled up. "She's so obedient! She's my good daughter! But, I'll make myself clear. I'll never permit you to marry him. I'll never bless this marriage. That scoundrel, I'm going to find some men to kill him. He came from across the sea. Let's see how he goes go back!"

She was stunned speechless by her father's final words and could not talk for a while. Her father, she knew, was like most of the strong-willed petty merchants who would do anything, no matter how vicious, to protect his rights and interests. That very night, she ran away from home. She sneaked to her lover's place, shedding tears and begging him to take her away at once. He was astonished. Finally, unable to refuse her, he eloped with her into the swarming multitudes of Taipei.

Ten years passed in a twinkling. From a fresh-faced girl, she turned into a clumsy woman. Her face swelled broad and white. Her eyes became a pair of mere slits. She always wore a dirty dress with a button missing. Her hair became a small square slab against her head, put there by the poor skills of cheap hairdressers. Her skin lost its glow, paling to grayish-white and growing coarse. She bore him three sons and experienced poverty, illness and worries she had never even thought of in her childhood. They lived in distressed circumstances from the moment they arrived in Taipei. They set up a noodle stand. They sold used clothes under the bright lights of the evening marketplace. Then, he finally got a job; he was employed by the district office as a janitor. Whenever they suffered hardship, she thought of her parents and shed secret tears. But she could not go back home. Her parents had never forgiven her for that disgraceful affair. Yet time, though cruel, also is a tender old man with a pacifying power. Those he holds in the grasp of his huge palm eventually grow exhausted and slumber in the embrace of destiny. Gradually, she no longer missed her parents. Naturally, unconsciously, she poured her whole being into her children. A new family was waiting for her to look after them and, in the process, bring her consolation.

Nonetheless, in the tenth year, before she became pregnant with her fourth child, something happened. One morning when she was searching for money in her husband's pockets before going to the market, she found a letter. With her alert female intuition, she sensed the threat from the letter, felt the dark clouds hanging over her family. She took out the amount of money she needed and stealthily slipped the letter into her clothing.

After drinking his usual three bowls of rice porridge, her husband put on his coat, got on his rusted bicycle and headed to the district office. She waited until he was far away and her children had gone to school before she took out the letter. It was as expected; the letter was addressed to her husband from Diaojingling, Hong Kong. The poor quality paper was inscribed with crooked brush writing:

Jianyi, my husband, it has been twelve years since we were parted. I have not heard a word from you. I, Dabao and Ermao miss you every day. I hope you are doing well in Taiwan. We really miss you a great deal. For twelve years I have supported the family by sewing. We have had an incredibly difficult time. Life is tougher since the Communists came. Recently it has been hard to fill one's stomach even once a day. We often have nothing to eat for the whole day. It's the same with the other villagers. No one can help each other. Fifth Uncle and Aunt have died of starvation. There were about a hundred families in the village. Now there are only ten left. There are not even any stray dogs or mice. We escaped from the mainland last month. We are now in Hong Kong. Fortunately, I happened to run into Uncle Liu yesterday. I learned from him of your good life in Taiwan. I also obtained your address. I was overjoyed. Can it be that heaven above has had pity on me and means to reunite us? Life is hard for us in Hong Kong. I hope you will send us some money right away to help with our life here. And I look forward to you fetching us to Taiwan. Hope you are well.

Respectfully yours,
Yulan

She finished reading the letter and placed it on her apron. Her face was pale, hollow. The crowing of the rooster outside, the noise made by the children playing in the sunshine, no longer reached her ears but blended into a vague humming sound. Finally, a child's cry entered her consciousness. She stood up slowly and walked toward the cradle of the whimpering baby, picked up the infant and hugged him. She loosened her blouse and suckled him. The child was less than six months old. She let his tiny mouth greedily suck her milk. Her nostrils closed and opened in labored heavy breathing. She cast a glance at a corner of the house. Having fed her baby, she wrapped the infant in a scarlet cloth and carried him on her back.

"My father was right, my father was right!" she said to herself.

She found her basket, locked the door, and went to the market with a black umbrella.

This woman who sent the letter, what kind of woman was she? This woman who also lovingly claims her husband, what did she look like?

She said she has almost nothing to eat. She said she has two children. Imagine! Those two children, like hers, were also born for him!

Lately she has seen women on the streets of Taipei dressed in blue shirts with their hair combed into smooth buns. It is said they have just fled from the mainland. The woman named Yulan, is she also dressed like that? A smooth, round, brown face, a pair of dark and lively almond eyes, a blue shirt, a round bun. She wondered where she had seen such a person in Taipei. She visualized what she looked like, her hostility concentrated on that face.

Jealousy, like numberless serpents, snapped at her heart. She was like a clutch of burning thorns; her neck, her forehead, her temples were inflamed. The woman's jealousy was like worms writhing around the core of a piece of fruit. She could almost feel the pain of being gnawed.

On returning from the market she put the basket by the door and wiped away her sweat with her sleeves. She unlocked and opened the wooden door and stood there thinking. Suddenly a strong urge overwhelmed her. She rushed into the house, took up the letter and reread it. Every word in the letter breathed that woman's delicate, tender voice. She crushed the letter in her hands. Her large bony hands squeezed the letter into a solid ball. She went to the kitchen door, pushed it open, entered and threw the ball into the burning brazier. She watched the flames languidly, painfully burn that hard-to-consume object.

At noon, her husband came home. She prepared him lunch without delay. She set the table with her eyes averted from him, looking instead at the plates and bowls. Then, turning around, she walked away. But when she passed behind his back, she glared at him. After lunch, he took off his shirt and, bare to the waist, planned to take a nap. He sat at the edge of the tatami, smoking a cigarette. He smoked only half of it and then extinguished the butt against the bed panel.

"Ah Yu, did you see a letter in my pocket?"

He had wanted to ask earlier but had put off doing so.

"What letter?"

She was scooping water in the kitchen and heard him but did not lift her head.

"A letter from Hong Kong, sent by a friend."

"I burned it."

Her eyes, like an animal's, bored into him from the edge of the water barrel.

He was startled, realizing his secret was out. Still, he intended to deny it: "How could you? It's a letter sent by my friend. Why did you destroy it?"

She stood up beside the barrel. Holding the bronze water ladle, she walked toward him. The hard, shining ladle waved back and forth in the air several times. His sallow brown arms guarded his head. He jerked to his left, then his right. The ladle, like hailstones, fell on his head, knuckles and shoulders.

"Ah Yu, if you have something to say, say it. Ah Yu, don't beat me, don't be so unreasonable. Ouch! You're hurting me, you'll kill me. Would you listen to me?"

She panted and, with one hand on her hip, lowered her voice and said: "How can you face me? You lied to me. You said you weren't married. You seduced me from my home and made me live this poor life with you. But no matter how hard this life is, I've endured it with you. I even gave you all these kids. But you, you, you have another woman back there, a damned stinking bitch, a batch of little bastards. Where is your conscience, Chen Jianyi? Are you a man or a dog?"

Having said this, she picked up the ladle, stepped forward and wanted to beat him again. Nevertheless, she abruptly threw the ladle away and, covering her face with both hands, burst into tears. She fell into a chair and released her tears and wails, like a river breaking through a dam and gushing in all directions.

Her husband hovered over her. In his gentlest voice, he explained to her, comforted her tenderly, begged her to forgive him. He said that he had wanted to tell her the full truth. He told her how impossible it was for him to betray her. He would never abandon her. He would never send for that woman. He would make this home in Taiwan his real home.

But she went on weeping bitterly. She reviled him, blamed him and threatened to kill herself. The scene lasted for a long time. The half-naked man, now stamping his foot, now adopting his most soothing voice and even putting on a smiling face, denied her charges and swore how much he loved her. At length, he was exhausted by his own performance.

After two hours, she stopped crying—perhaps she was just too tired. No matter how much sorrow remained in her, she was consoled somewhat by his promises. She reached out her plump hands, lifted a corner of her skirt and wiped her swollen eyes. She turned her face from him and said coldly, bitterly: "So, tell me what you're going to do. We might as well make up our minds. I'm all ears, Chen Jianyi, what do you want? Are you bringing her over or not?"

"Well, of course not! Is it necessary to say so? Of course not," he replied, almost ecstatic with relief.

"You might as well go fetch her. You may as well let her live here in my place. And you can drive me and my kids away and let us beg for food on the streets. But, Chen Jianyi, you listen carefully, I'm not easy to bully. If you really want to send for her, well then, the very first thing I'll do is poison her and then her sons with arsenic."

The husband glanced at her in fear and hatred, but nodded in agreement.

Then she made a decision for him. She said she would write to the woman and tell her that her husband had built a new family in Taiwan. She would suggest that it was impossible for her to come to Taiwan and would advise her not to write anymore.

The next day, the letter was written. She tossed it into the mailbox herself.

The woman in Hong Kong received the letter a week later. Indignant, she returned to the mainland with her sons. That was the autumn of 1956; a famine ravaged the mainland and death was as plentiful as flies. This was reported by Uncle Liu. From then on, nothing was ever heard of her.

So the woman in Taiwan won a complete victory; she regained a whole husband.

Nevertheless, because of her suspicion and jealousy, she could no longer trust him. In her view, since he had been able to deceive her once, he could betray her again. So, besides managing his finances, she tried every means she could to be equal with him. She was determined to make money, too, to make him respect her, to prevent him from betraying her. She started to wash clothes at one house after another, carrying a child on her back. Soon, due to her efforts, her earnings exceeded her husband's. Her position and her power were not only equal to his but exceeded them. She went a step further by suggesting he quit his job as a janitor and be supported by her. Being a lazy man anyway and hankering after an easy life, he was only too happy to accept a life that would not wring a single drop of sweat from him.

Thus it was that she possessed him so thoroughly, so entirely, that nobody could ever take him away from her again.

Translated by Li-fen Chen

Strong Wind

November 1961. A monologue of a pedicab driver during a ty-phoon, this story stands out among Wang's works as a language experiment employing a pure colloquial style.

*Whoosh—whoosh—*that wind is strong, really strong. Go ahead, blow, blow with all your might, you could blow twice as hard and not keep me from pedaling. This wind, it must be that typhoon heading toward the island. Ever since early this morning, a car, one sent out by the police, has been cruising up and down the streets and lanes broadcasting a warning that Typhoon Alice will soon hit the coast of Hualian. Just a moment ago I heard it blare that the ty-phoon should reach Taipei around midnight. It must be about elev-en o'clock now, or well past, just look, not a soul on the street. We pedicab drivers are in for it during a typhoon. When the winds pick up, it's tough just to keep moving, and if the force moves up a notch, we can forget about looking for customers. The loss of a day's wages is a big deal. Most of the time, we can pretty much tell when one of them's coming just by a change in the weather, there's no need to check the newspaper. Two days before a typhoon, clouds appear to glow, and the sky is so blue it seems saturated with water. Then as the sun sets, the sky and earth are washed in an orange hue. The next day, the sun shines amid intermittent showers, and winds be-gin to rise, causing roadside trees to sway and leaves to tumble, like coats turning inside out. By then, it's a lot harder to pedal. Nothing in heaven or on earth troubles a pedicab driver, except a strong wind. Rain? Let it pour. A coolie hat and a transparent rain cloak are all you need. We can take it. Sun? We're used to baking in it, especially in the summer, when there isn't a spot on Taiwan where you can hide from the sun. Each layer of skin that peels off is replaced by a new one, and as time passes, your skin's as tough as cowhide and as dark as black jade. Sure, it's a hard life, but livable as long as there's no wind. Shit, is that taxi driver blind? If I hadn't swerved at the last minute, I'd be lying dead in the street! The arrival of taxis in Taipei has made things really tough on us. We used to be able to earn forty or fifty yuan a day, but now we're lucky if we take in thirty. They steal our business. That bunch of turtle spawn is taking over. They sneak those motorized coffins they drive over to wherever we're staked out waiting for fares, and if we get our hands on one of them, we beat the hell out of him. Yesterday afternoon we grabbed one, thanks to sharp-eyed Old Four, who spotted him first. The guy was just sitting in that coffin of his in front of the Huatuo Herbal Pharmacy, his head sticking out the window as he called out to three young punks in gaudy shirts. "Let's get this one and beat him! Stop him! Don't let him get away!" Old Four shouted. The minute we heard his shouts, we abandoned our chess games and swarmed over. The guy was really on his toes. When he saw the murderous looks in our eyes, he quickly pulled his head in and got ready to drive away. But Ironhead Zhang, Big Tooth, Yellow Beard and I threw ourselves onto the hood of his car, with no thought for our own safety. He couldn't drive away now—four lives were at stake. Without a word of warning, we dragged him out of his car. Old Four grabbed him by the collar and screamed, "What the fuck are you parked here for?" "I, I'm doing my job. I'm not hurting you guys, I can park anywhere I please," he said. Old Four gave him a vicious slap and, with a yell, we all rushed him, slapping him, punching him in the belly, and driving our fists into his face. We drew quite a crowd. All the time we were knocking him around, he was crying and yelling for help. His khaki uniform top was quickly torn to shreds and his hat disappeared. Finally, his face turned white, he looked down at the ground and fell to his knees like a limp noodle. Old Four and Yellow Beard stepped up and jerked him back to his feet. Old Four's eyes were nearly popping out of his head and he was breathing hard as he shouted, "Keep it up! Keep hitting him! Don't stop till he's dead!" Now, if we'd stopped then, everything would have been fine, but squat little Wu Dalang,[1] who had a terrible temper, picked up a club and brought it down on the guy's head with a resounding thud. His head snapped back and he crumpled to the ground. Wu Dalang raised the club with both hands and was about to hit him again; fortunately, I grabbed his arms in time. "Don't," I said, "you'll kill him." By then everyone was staring at the puddle of sticky blood on the ground, frozen in their tracks. Some of the onlookers screamed, others backed away. We began pushing Wu Dalang through the crowd, urging him to get out of there as fast as possible. Normally a man of action, he just stood there woodenheaded. We kept trying to get him going, until his eyes froze; he climbed onto his pedicab and quickly pedaled into a nearby lane. The fellow lying in the road was in bad shape, his ashen face all bloody, as if it had been dipped in a vat of pig's blood. Lots of blood, and I knew we had to get him to a hospital for emergency treatment. So I put him in my pedicab and drove him to a neighborhood clinic. He was very young, twenty or so. He'd deserved a beating, but had we gone too far? I think so. And we all wound up at the police station. As for Wu Dalang, we knew he wouldn't get away. And he didn't. They nabbed him shortly after nine that night. They told us that when he heard the guy hadn't died, he sat down on the ground and wailed. And not just wail, but laugh and wail at the same time. This time, I figured, things were going to go badly for him. Some months earlier, he'd been arrested by vice police who broke up a game of Pai Gow, and he nearly hit one of them over the head with his stool. When they cut him loose a week later, he couldn't walk without two people holding him up. It wasn't going to be any easier this time. As the saying goes: Heat in the sky produces rain, heat in a man creates trouble.

1. Wu Dalang is a well-known character in two classical Chinese novels, *Shuihu zhuan* (The Water Margin) and *Jin Ping Mei* (Golden Lotus). The name is used here as a nickname for a short, stocky character in the story.

Whoosh—that was an even stronger gust. Listen to that wind roar. It even blew out the streetlamps. This lane's darker than a tunnel. Is this the right house? Aiya, I don't think I have any change on me. See here, not a single one-yuan note. How about giving me those extra two yuan, sir? A typhoon's coming and that was a long ride. Twenty's not too much to ask. Thank you, thank you.

That's how you've got to treat your customers. Put small change in your right pants pocket, and ten-yuan notes in the left. Then when they ask for change, reach into your left pocket and show them the big bills.

Yow, it's hot, I'm covered in sweat. Typical typhoon weather. It's stopped raining, and now there's just that hot, dry wind. The paper said this one's coming at us across the sea from the Philippines. Not much out of the ordinary at sea, but then a funnel develops up in the sky, and that's the eye. It keeps spiraling faster and faster, and pretty soon it's a typhoon, which begins to move like a spinning top. It can cross vast oceans, and all the trees, homes and living beings in its way bend in the direction of the wind, lying quietly beneath its feet. After the winds sweep across Taiwan, it continues on north, spinning its way into the vast Eastern Sea. Then all traces of it disappear in the ocean.

It ought to be about 11:30, I'd say. No sense going home now; better to fight it out here in the street. Sure, the wind makes the going tough, but there's money to be made out there, lots of it. Ha ha, go on, blow, blow that money into my pocket, like so many leaves.

Need a ride, mister? Zhonghe, that's a long way. I'll take you for nineteen yuan. Steep, you say? If you think so, mister, go ask the other drivers. Even in the daytime I have to charge sixteen from here to Zhonghe. You'll be my last fare tonight, that's why I'm not asking for more. How much, sir? Seventeen? Add one, make it eighteen. It's only one yuan. All right, all right, you say seventeen, then seventeen it is. Climb aboard.

Seventeen yuan for a ride all the way to Zhonghe isn't nearly enough. Cheating customers isn't my style. My fares are reasonable, calculated by distance, the way it should be. I never ask for more than I deserve. The night before last, at something like two in the morning, a young woman shouted for a pedicab on Yanping North Road, said she wanted a ride to Kunming Street. I told her I'd give her a break and only charge her seven yuan. She turned and walked away, so I asked her, "How much then?" She said one yuan. One yuan! Do you hear what I'm saying, mister? One yuan. Two o'clock in the morning, from Yanping North Road all the way to Kunming Street! What a joke! But I said all right, okay, climb aboard. See what I mean? My fares are really low. Believe me or not.

Want to hear about that young woman? You know, the one I just mentioned. It's worth listening to, because it's true. You don't believe I let her ride for one yuan, well that's your business. The point is, I did it for practically nothing. But what I'm going to tell you now you've got to believe.

Think about it, two in the morning, a pretty young thing, carrying a bag, out all alone. Who wouldn't be surprised? While I was pedaling along I kept wondering what it was that brought her out. What was she, a call girl? A girl from a good family? These days it's not uncommon for girls to fight with their fathers over the right to choose their own partners, and they wind up running away from home. Well, about the time we reached Taiwan Cinema I heard the muffled sound of sobbing behind me. She was crying, but she didn't want me to hear, so she'd covered her nose with a hanky. She told me to stop when we reached the far end of Kunming Street. She paid me and walked off. I watched as she headed toward the Danshui River, but I didn't see anyone waiting for her there. We pedicab drivers see just about everything on the streets of Taipei day in and day out, until nothing fazes us anymore. We can't spare the time to get to the bottom of things we see, and, besides, what would we do even if we could? Most fares are people we've never seen before, and when they get to wherever they're going, that's the last we ever see of them. Shadows and silhouettes, that's about all they are to us.

But that night something didn't seem right, so I stood off to the side of the road and smoked a cigarette, feeling kind of uneasy. I looked toward the riverbank, where a streetlamp cast a dreary, hazy light on a murky yellow mist. Just then a cop walked up, and I told him what was going on. I'm afraid something might have happened to her, I said. The cop, who was a mainlander, like me, reacted by giving me hell: "You idiot, why didn't you ask her what was going on? And why didn't you follow her? What am I supposed to do after all this time?" I don't know how he could blame me. Since when do I start up a casual conversation with a single woman? But if something actually had happened, then I . . . I started to sweat. So I left my pedicab there and walked up the riverbank with the cop. We looked across the wide river, which was socked in with a heavy fog, the water flowing under the belly of the fog, giving off occasional flashes of light, like sleepless eyes in the night. All we could see, except for the fogbank, were some round stones. "Let's start by searching the riverbank," the cop said. "Cock your ear and listen to see if you can detect any sound from the river other than the flow of water." Every once in a while, a fish broke the surface of the water with a splash, like a crashing wave. The fish must have been having nightmares. All of a sudden, I pointed and shouted: "There, see that? Isn't that her?" There was something white on the first row of stone steps, like a pile of clothes or something. When we walked up to it, we saw it was her, all right, her face buried in her skirt. She had no idea we were there in front of her. "Hey, you, what are you doing here?" the cop asked as he shook her to wake her up. She looked up, and I don't think she knew what was going on. But what was really strange was there wasn't a trace of surprise in her eyes. It was a vacant, faraway face. The cop took her over to the stationhouse and told me to come along.

She was a thirteen-year-old girl from one of the whorehouses behind the train station who'd been sold into prostitution at the age of eleven. When she couldn't stand it any longer, she ran off in the middle of the night on the pretext of buying some medicine. She couldn't stand it any longer, at the young age of thirteen. Her clients were all coarse men, that I know. If you went there, you'd see what kind of life those girls live. That night she'd planned to jump into the Danshui River to wash away the filth and shame that covered her body. The cop praised me for "having the courage to do what's right." He said that anybody who "lacks compassion isn't human," and that my actions that night showed that I was "rich in compassion." I said it was nothing, that we live on this earth to serve others, as Sun Yat-sen once said.

That's strange, the wind seems to have stopped. That's not a good sign. A monster typhoon, a real howler, is on its way. It must be midnight by now. Hey! What's that? So fast? It's coming, it's coming, the big blow's on its way! Here's the rain! Boy, it sure is coming down, like a waterfall. Let me stop and put on my rain slicker, mister. That rain's washing my face. It's warm, like Shaoxing wine. There's the bridge up ahead.

Wow, the river's really swollen! It's not a river anymore, it's an ocean! Not a soul on the bridge, the wind must be fierce up there. Hear that sound, like peals of thunder. Shit! Charge! . . . I can hardly breathe . . . the bridge looks like it's swaying, it's made of sturdy concrete . . . I don't imagine it'll . . . last year a pedicab crossing this bridge during a typhoon was swept into the river . . . said it can't be crossed, but we're halfway there . . . halfway makes me as happy as if we were already on the other side, with the first half behind us, the rest of the way should be easy . . . the first half, now the second half . . . we made it, mister!

The fare has gone now. Streets are deserted. The people, whoever they might have been, have cleared out. This corner of the world now belongs to one person only—Typhoon. He goes wherever he wants, entering that lane, taking the roof off of that house or picking that tree right out of the ground. He's like a black lion, leaping, pouncing, roiling. If I reach out, it feels like I'm touching his black muscles, sleek, powerful, tough.

I have to make it back to Taipei, but it won't be easy. How am I going to cross that bridge? There were two of us on the way over, one pulling with the other seated behind, enough weight to keep the wind from blowing us over the side. Now I'm alone. There are times when another person, even though he may be a burden, can also be a big help. The first order of business is to take down the canopy. Get some sleep, my tattered canvas, it's not worth it fighting with a killer typhoon. And this seat pad, sure it's plastic, but I'll tuck it away too. Now to take off my rain slicker, since it's useless in the face of the wind. Next my coolie hat, off it comes. And my shirt, so it won't get soaked. Heh heh heh, that leaves the one thing that can stand up to the water, the skin on my body. Permanently water-proof. Better than any raincoat ever made.

My God, this has turned into a night of storming madness, the wind is knocking me senseless, I can hardly remember where I am. Heaven and earth have fused; waves are at my feet, the sky rests on my head, and I must quietly remember. This night is like a drunkard whose supply of alcohol is limitless. As I gulp mouthfuls of wind, I float drunkenly, like an immortal. The wind, like waves on the ocean, crashes into me, one gust after another, and even at a dis-tance you can hear the waves roar. I'm pulling an empty vehicle behind me, but what a burden its emptiness creates! I'll be fucked! Is one inch too much to ask? It feels like somebody's picking up my front wheel. I can't move even when I stand on the pedals, I'm afraid the chain might break. Listen to it groan. I'll snap this spindly han-dlebar in two if I'm not careful. I think I'd be better off getting down and pushing it along. Uh-oh, it's changed direction again. Walking in the strong wind makes me feel like a grass-skimming sorcerer, simply tearing along. I've got to plant my feet firmly on the ground, like trees anchored in the earth. *Whoosh.* This wind's a real shrew. She grabs me by the hair and shakes my head, she turns me cross-eyed. The next gust's going to be even worse, I can tell from the sound . . . it's sucking my breath away . . . here comes another . . . even stronger . . . grab hold! My God, knocked me over . . . ow— ow—you fucking . . . ow . . . let me catch my breath, sit here on the ground and catch my breath . . . I thought it was going to pick me right up off the ground just then, I damn near took off flying, all that stopped me was the concrete curb. Cut my face, I'm bleeding, must be deep. Hurts like hell, like a knife gouging my face. How come I can't steady myself? The wind must be stronger than I thought. I'm gasping for air, like a bellows. My lungs feel like they're about to leap into my throat. Forty-two years old, can't do what I used to do at twenty or thirty. Then I could climb a mountain and never once have to breathe through my mouth.

What's that sound? The glass cover on that street lamp shattered. I sit here, my ears filled with the whistling of the wind, it's like a dream. There goes another cover. Ah, the crisp sound of shattering glass. Sitting here makes me feel lazy. My arms and legs have had all they can take in battling the wind. Like me, they're hoping to experience the joy of rest. Let them do what they want, there's nothing wrong with taking a rest. Except for my mind; that can never take a rest.

I can feel the blood slowly warming up in my arms and legs, giving birth to a new burst of energy. I've rested long enough. I should start out again. And this time, no thoughts of danger. Lower your head, hold your breath; without realizing it, you can mount a much better attack. My legs are stronger now, and even though the wind hasn't lessened, this time it's not going to pluck me off of the ground. My steps are now as steady as a king's or an emperor's. Go ahead, blow, you hooligan, see if you can make me wobble now.

The lamp posts are like sentries standing at attention on both sides of the bridge. Once I pass by another five or six, I'll be on the other side. They're like an honor guard, welcoming me into the palace.

The spot beneath me has turned from water to earth—thick, warm, firm earth. When a man's standing on the ground, he feels safe, free from the danger of falling. Man is tied to the earth. Look at the bridge behind me! It stands securely hidden in the darkness, all but obscured, swallowed up by the darkness. It's past midnight; there are no people, no cars, and the only person daring to cross that bridge has been a middle-aged pedicab driver.

I can't see a single light in the city of Taipei, on the other side of the dike. If I stood on this dike in broad daylight, I could see green coconut palms like blades of grass filling the spaces between the rooftops. At this moment I can see nothing, not even the shadowy outlines of trees. But I can imagine them standing all alone, bending to the force of the wind. And I'm sure that some of them give way, snapping like so many pale, wispy necks. I'll just slide down this bank. The situation in town is different from that on the bridge. Here the danger is not falling into the water, but all those fallen power lines, so I have to move slowly down the middle of the street to keep from getting electrocuted. Everywhere I look, it's like a battle-field, with crackles and sizzles all around me. Oh, there goes a bill-board! Glass shatters, the wires pucker up in loud whistles. What a raucous, uneasy dark night! What's that noise, the one hanging over all the others? Like an ocean wave, or the sound of panic during a retreat, what is it? It must be the rustling of leaves. But no, there's another sound, buried beneath all the others, there but not there. An echo maybe? One that stirs my heart. What is it? Sort of like many bass strings being strummed at the same time. Ah, maybe it's just the sound of your power, Typhoon. Maybe it's your soul, the frequency of your waves.

More water? Is there a river in town? I'm all confused. This isn't a dream, is it? Wait, that's no river, it's a sewer overflowing, sending water flooding into the street, turning it into a watery canal.

I have to make it across the street. And my pedicab? Bath time. The water isn't all that cold. Too bad, since cold water is rejuvenat-ing, while warm water makes my skin itch. When you walk through water it's like somebody's holding on to your feet to keep them down. Just a few steps and I'm splashing loudly. Damn, it keeps get-ting deeper. It's up to my waist. It damn well better not get much deeper, since I can't swim. I can float a little and dog paddle, but only a few strokes. I have to keep to the middle of the street; if I don't, I might fall into one of the roadside ditches. It's really deep right here, almost to my chest. Slow down, take tiny steps. That'll reduce the chances of falling. Now it seems to be getting shallower. Back there, the deep part was like a valley, and now the ground is rising. A street that's become a river. My pedicab has turned into a water tank. I think I'll tip it over and pour the water out of its gut. Heh-heh, what if I found a fish caught in the canopy? That'd be great. My coolie hat and rain slicker are long gone, washed away. With the going this hard, suffering no losses is out of the question. My house is up ahead a bit, I'm just about there.

Oh, quiet down, Typhoon, quiet down. I'm almost home. When I walk in the door, you can turn as wild as you want, it won't affect me. There's no wind in my house, and no rain. See there, in the midst of that pitch darkness, that little window with the candle, that's my home. Yinhua hasn't gone to bed yet, she's waiting for me. A candle in the window in the midst of pitch darkness, Yinhua, you lit that for me. Even though the candlelight is weak, no matter how hard the wind blows or how heavily the rain falls, the candle stays safely lit, as if sleeping peacefully behind a curtain in the Earth God's alcove. Open the door, Yinhua, it's me, I made it home through the typhoon.

Are you still up? Ai, next time, don't wait for me, get an early rest. Is your cough any better? Still as bad as ever. Guess how much I earned tonight. The money's right here. Oh, no, it's all mushy from soaking in the water. Here, I'll count it out for you. See there? Yinhua? Seventy-two yuan. Altogether seventy-two yuan. Almost twice as much as last night! Tomorrow you take this money and go see a doctor. Have him write you a prescription. That'll make you better. We can go to bed now, as soon as I push the pedicab in.

Whoosh—whoosh—that wind is strong, really strong. Go ahead, blow, blow as hard as you can. My fine companion, you spent the day with me. We climbed the bank together, forded the water, crossed the bridge, so now come inside with me to rest.

Translated by Howard Goldblatt

Contract Fulfilled

April 1962. This story revisits the subject of sexual awakening and the appreciation of female beauty. The original Chinese title was accompanied by the annotation "for Hsien-yung," a reference to Pai Hsien-yung, another great modern Taiwan writer and a former member of the South and North Club, the student writing group that both Wang and Pai belonged to during their university days.

In the quiet, southern part of Taipei, in a lane with flowerpots arranged along both sides, the professors of a certain university live with their wives and children. The secluded alley is much like the professors who have chosen to live there, obviously refined and elegant, but with a whiff of pedantry, a hint of senility. The striped, wooden facades of the two rows of houses have turned black, and green moss has crawled right over the roof tiles. Luxuriant beards of greenery conceal the front doors. At first glance, the two mute rows of old buildings look abandoned. That's because the residents come and go via the rear doors. Travelers who pass this way, noticing the lush, well-spaced trees or, in the rich streaming sunlight of July, hearing the intermittent song of the cicadas, often feel like they have entered a garden.

At the top of the lane, to the left of the entrance, is the home of Professor Lin's family. With just six or seven students in his history class, Professor Lin is not one of the university's distinguished scholars, but it is said he was a very fashionable intellectual twenty years ago in Beijing. If his students were interested, they could find a small volume of his works in a series published by the Commercial Press. But, as he often says, "times have changed." His students often say it, too. Sure, people always talk this way, but when he says it you can catch the sense of desolation in his words. He can't compare himself to the way he was before, when he expressed his thoughts clearly, with a firm, strong voice. Now he speaks gently, haltingly, with his eyes closed, and he smiles for no apparent reason. His students open their notebooks with guilty yawns, but he is a benign and kindly professor, especially when it comes to marks.

Professor Lin's family includes Mrs. Lin, two sons and a daughter. They have lived in this building for about fifteen years, although last fall the oldest boy left the family to study in the United States. All the kindly neighbors in the lane can remember when they first arrived. The second oldest boy, Lin Shaoquan, still waddled around in a pair of baggy pants on a tricycle that was a few inches higher than his chest. The little girl, now grown into a lovely young lady with cheeks as full and rosy as oleander blossoms, had a smile that revealed four missing front teeth. Even their parents have had to recognize that they've grown up now. Their daughter, Lin Xun, is studying at the best provincial middle school for girls. Just this summer, Lin Shaoquan graduated from a university in the south and a week ago took the exam for studying abroad (he's quite confident of success) and now is just resting at home. His year of military service in the reserves still seems far away.

This afternoon, the temperature is typical for a summer day in Taipei. There's not a trace of wind in the air. The entire city is sealed up like a small box, and the residents of the bowl-shaped basin already have fallen into a dazed sleep, covered by a thick layer of warm, soft, cottony mist. It is as though night has already fallen on the entire city. The sound of a few car horns, the tedious drone of jet engines—you can hear them all clearly. In the laneway, sunlight beats down on the houses, bushes, flowerpots. The sun's rays seem strong enough to pierce any opening. The shadows beneath the eaves look like they have been cut with a knife and then stamped like a seal deep into the yellow earth. At this moment, a musical note floats from a lake-green screen on a window in the Lin house. It is thin and fine, a golden thread of Mozart. It's Lin Shaoquan, still not sleeping, enjoying a record. He has tried to sleep but cannot.

This year Lin Shaoquan is twenty-three years old and has graduated from X University's history department. Thick glass saucers circled by wide black frames are propped on his nose. He wears spectacles for his short-sightedness. He has a pair of tangled, bushy eyebrows and beneath them a pair of cold eyes as clear as glistening lake water. His face could be described as dignified, even beautiful, except for a certain old-fogy aspect, perhaps due to his black frames and unruly, thick, black eyebrows. His mouth is the weakest part of his face, a small, delicate pair of lips not much wider than his nose. The upper lip is covered by a soft, thin, semicircular moustache. A row of pearly white teeth and a Beijing dialect as soft as cotton—it is out of this elegant little mouth that he speaks. You don't see this type of young person anymore, even in universities. His refinement reminds people of a typical Chinese intellectual. Even though he possesses a perfect physique with broad shoulders and strong limbs, Master Lin is not an athlete. He is adept at neither swimming nor basketball, which accounts for the pallor of his delicate skin.

Consistent with his speech, his skin and his mouth, his life is defined by indolence. Now, for instance, he is sitting quietly on the edge of his bed, his back against the wall, but between wall and back he has wedged a pillow that has made him as content as an emperor. He really knows how to make himself as comfortable as possible. For example, he has also found a small bamboo stool to support his feet. Naturally, a cup of tea is placed nearby. An oscillating fan wags its head vigorously like a loyal servant, the breeze covering his entire body from head to toe. His head looks like he has not had a trim in a month and a half, the hair drooping sleepily around his ears, concealing the arms of his glasses. His head looks rather like a furious hedgehog. There is an air of informality about him, something of the eccentric manner of an old-fashioned hermit intellectual. That's why his classmates call him "Old Timer."

He did not take his nap because he is concerned about something. Two days earlier, this thing disrupted his life. It is a letter that should have arrived but hasn't. They promised they would contact him. "They" are his classmates. The letter concerns his objective—when he receives it he must go immediately and fulfill his contract, the solemn pact he entered into on a winter's night with a group of young men at the university dormitory.

Four years ago, he left home and lived on a hillside in southern Taiwan. Except for Sundays, he and his classmates spent all their time in this vast highland region. The soil in the hills was as red as cinnabar. The university's buildings, small and rectangular, were situated exquisitely among the jequirity trees. In those simple, unspoiled, remote surroundings, his young life was exposed to the winds of fate. Unconsciously, slowly, alone, he took painful steps toward maturity. Yet the dullness of life in the mountains was like a strong corrosive drug, and many of his classmates, sooner or later, could not resist the temptation to bow before this goddess. They found themselves under attack by tobacco, alcohol, gambling and smuggled dirty photos. Fortunately, he did not surrender. He and a small number of students seemed to be upholding religious commandments. They did not know why they had to obey—a moral code is based only on faith—but they firmly believed it was virtuous, so they stubbornly refused to change. The group never spoke among themselves of their devotion but despite the small number of strong adherents, they formed a veritable united front, jointly accepting its authority. Before becoming adults, they wanted to protect it, like they would protect a piece of jade.

Now those years of early youth among the mountain peaks have been left behind. That mountainside, with a hundred thousand oleanders shivering in the cold wind, has been bypassed by time's river, abandoned on the sandy shores of memory. If he turns and looks back, feelings arise, a type of sadness that is difficult to describe in words. He is like a long-distance traveler turning around on the road to look back at his alpine home.

A patter of slippers on the floor outside his bedroom. From the slow rhythm he knows it is his mother. She is always the first member of the family to get up. After a moment, there is the rrr-rrr of a sewing machine. His mother often sits behind the sewing machine after her nap to sew their clothes. She always makes their underpants big enough to fit two people. Despite his protests, she never makes them smaller. "A little loose is cooler, they'll be more comfortable," she always says.

Mrs. Lin is stout, a married woman who has grown a double chin. She is, for all that, a capable homemaker, ceaselessly busy all day. When she speaks with people outside the family, her round face immediately breaks into a brilliant smile and her voice overflows with sunlit radiance. Few outsiders, though, have seen her stern side. To her family, she is a matriarch who has everything under control.

Behind the sewing machine, a pair of spectacles stretches between her two graying temples. She is not yet fifty but she needs glasses to read the paper, write a letter, sew clothes. When she wants to focus on something while wearing them, she has to lower her head briefly. The frames are interesting, the type a student would wear. In fact, they originally belonged to her younger son. Because his myopia suddenly degenerated, he got another pair (the ones he wears now). As a result, for economic reasons, she insisted that Mother get the original pair.

Mrs. Lin bends down, her lips pressed close to the sewing table. She uses her teeth to bite the thread. "You forgot to take your medicine again," she says. She tosses her head to the left, snapping the thread before turning around. She is speaking to her husband.

Professor Lin is wearing a pair of shorts, one leg kneeling on the tatami, opening the paper door with difficulty. He has just woken up from his nap; probably it was the sound of his wife's sewing machine. His two hands are pressed on the floor like an athlete preparing for a race, supporting his short, fat body. From behind her corrective lenses, she glares at him coldly. Then she turns back to the piece of clothing on the sewing machine and picks it up. She shakes it out like damp laundry, fluffs it once, turns it over and puts it down.

"Dolt, needs to be reminded every time," she mutters to the clothes beneath the needle.

Professor Lin suffers from high blood pressure. After every meal, he is supposed to swallow a pill as round as a button but he often forgets. Barefoot, he walks to the table where the tea service sits and pours a glass of cool water from a pot-bellied blue bottle. From among the teacups, he plucks a small medicine bottle and twists open the lid. A slippery pill slides into the centre of his palm. He presses his lips to his palm, sucks up the pill and works his cheeks, squeezing his thin lips together. Then he takes a drink of water, tosses his head back and the pill falls down into his stomach. Professor Lin goes toward a desk in front of the window and drops his heavy body into a round-backed wicker armchair. Thus he begins his prescribed daily routine of afternoon work.

In order to qualify for the Education Ministry's bonus of 5,000 yuan per article, he uses every morning and every afternoon of his summer vacation to work on an essay. Because he cannot come up with anything original, he just pulls together material he has read or quotes from other people's work. Nevertheless, he still works very hard. The type of work his father does angers Lin Shaoquan, who often feels he has the ability to far surpass his father. He has a certain sense of honor, believes a scholar should not be like a cow chewing on regurgitated hay. But when he sees his father bent over his work all day, he also feels pity, guilt; especially now, as he worries about that letter and hears from behind the paper door the creaking sound of his father dropping into his chair. Gazing through the green screen, the two lenses in his glasses catch rays of light from the wide-open window, scattering a fuzzy brightness. The sound of the music begins to disturb him, provoking a twitch in those sensitive eyebrows. He rises from his comfortable throne, takes a step toward the table where the record player sits and turns it off.

From a pocket in a pair of trousers hanging on the back of a chair, he takes out a paper bag. He peels back some foil and removes a bent cigarette. Holding one end of the snowy white cigarette, he sticks the other between his lips. With the cigarette dangling from his mouth, his hand returns to his pocket to grope for a pack of matches. He tears off a match, strikes it, puts the tip of the cigarette into the flame and inhales. The tip glows. The match in his right hand grows faint after he carves a circle in the air with it, while the cigarette he holds in his mouth bounces in front of his nose.

Lin Shaoquan expands his chest and inhales deeply. The smoke somersaults in his mouth and looks for an exit, leaving his nostrils in a puff. Lin Shaoquan flashes a satisfied smile. He lowers the cigarette and studies it carefully. Using his index finger, he lightly, lovingly, taps the cigarette three times. This is the second cigarette from the first pack of cigarettes he has ever smoked.

He started smoking just three days ago. He was standing in front of the window gazing at the slowly thickening evening. He thought, "In a few days, I will be completely different than before, a new person, a completely newborn person, like a pupa turning into a moth. Smoking, not smoking, what's the difference?" He went out at once to buy a pack and bring it home.

When he smoked his first cigarette, he stood under a large banyan tree at night in the garden. He exhaled silken white threads of smoke. Above his head, the sky was covered with cold stars blinking like fireflies. In the fresh, clean night air, his body felt like a fish in the dark waters of the night. He realized he had anticipated this happiness, had expected it earlier, but was not really sure. Hadn't he often stretched out his fingers, picked up a pen and sucked on the end?

He restlessly takes this second cigarette and hastily crushes it on the top of the table, one hand wiping away the ashes, the other quickly putting the butt into a drawer. Facing the closed paper door, he stands motionless, his hands resting at his sides, like an actor in a modern Chinese drama preparing to recite his lines.

"Sonny, Sonny, did you drink your green bean soup? Why don't you answer me?" It's his mother addressing him from outside the door.

"I don't want it."

"You should drink it, it's so hot outside. If you don't drink something cool, how can you manage? If you don't drink it, with this sun beating down all day, what will you do if you get sick? Aren't you afraid of sunstroke?"

"I don't want it."

"Drink a little, Sonny, even one bowl will be fine. Everyone in the family has had some. Your dad drinks six bowls a day, your little sister had some. I managed to get her to drink three bowls."

"Okay, I'll have some!"

"Sonny? You will have some? Wonderful, Mama's already poured you a bowl. Should I carry it in or will you come out?"

He makes an effort to ensure his voice is even and smooth so she will not hear the lump of smoke and saliva in his throat.

"I'm coming out!"

He pushes the door open and goes out to the dining room, which also serves as his father's study and his mother's sewing room. His mother is sitting beside the dining room table and looks at him with a slight smile. He has already swallowed the lump in his throat. The success of this experiment again fills him with happiness. Actually, it isn't that difficult. He just has to close his eyes and force himself to swallow the saliva in his mouth, and everything is perfect. She doesn't keep pestering him and he forgets instantly about being interrupted.

His mother gets him a chair, fussing to place it just so. He feels the lump rising again but shifts his gaze and manages to swallow it once more. She is overjoyed just because he has answered her. Her relationship with him now, compared to when he was a boy, or with his sister, has changed utterly. Poor Mother, he thinks, she lives every day dreading he will be the same as his brother and flee to some far-off place. She sees his bouts of impatience as a sign he will abandon her soon. She is like a neurotic woman who thinks the sound of the wind outside the window at night is the earth shaking. He realizes he has to guard against shocking her.

"Sit here, Sonny, there's sugar on the table. You can add it yourself if it is not sweet enough. You drink first, Papa will come." She turns toward Professor Lin: "You're coming, aren't you? Can't you continue later? It's always the same. When it's time to eat, he's doing this or that. Missy! Where is that girl?"

"C-o-m-i-n-g M-a!"

Lin Xun answers while coming from her room, her steps pounding on the dining room floor, but she stops when she gets to the table, her gaze averted and her hands in front of her chest, the intertwined fingers wriggling busily.

"Look!" she says.

She stretches a pink palm beneath her brother's nose. Standing on it, the size of a broad bean, is a tiny glass puppy so small it couldn't be any smaller. But it has eyes, ears and even a tiny pointed tail!

Lin Xun twists back and forth and shakes her hand beneath his nose before closing it.

"I won't give it to you."

"Oh?" Lin Shaoquan pushes back the chair and sits down, looking at his bowl. "I know who you want to give it to."

"Who? Tell me! Tell me!"

"Calm down. Don't you know what I'm going to say? I say you want to give it to—Zhang Yang!"

"Oh! Ma!" She bites her white porcelain soup spoon and shakes her mother's elbow.

"Stop shaking you damn girl! You'll spill the soup!" Mrs. Lin scolds.

Lin Xun glows, a little sister with a dimpled smile in a rosy face. Her girlish eyes sparkle like light on water, the whites so clear they seem almost blue. Her face is round, unlike her second brother's, and not as attractive. In their family, she and her oldest brother (who, wearing a scholar's cap, looks down on them from the white plaster wall) are something of a matched pair. It is also said they both resemble their father but you would be mistaken if you drew the natural conclusion, for Lin Shaoquan is not like his mother at all. In many households, a different "race" can appear. Mothers often say, "You were plucked from the dustbin."

Lin Shaoquan is extremely fond of Lin Xun. She is a prodigy who is first in her class every term. Whether it is English, Chinese or math and science, there is not one subject in which she gets less than ninety percent. Not only does she get good marks, she also participates in speaking competitions, music competitions, calligraphy competitions, long-jump competitions, and invariably wins the gold medal. He really adores her. She is wearing a black shirt that covers her chest and back with bib-shaped rectangles but reveals her neck and half of her round shoulders. The tips of her ears stick out from beneath her close-cropped, slightly curly hair. She looks exceptionally graceful, like a purebred Pekinese. He is proud to have a sister like this. He finds her all the more interesting because covering the walls of her bedroom, the back of her door and under glass on the top of her desk are pictures of famous stars. Her room is like an exhibition of celebrity photos. She is crazy for movies: Sandra Dee, George Hamilton,[1] these are new English words she will never forget. When she chats about the stars, it is as if she had met them only yesterday. While he loves her because she is a prodigy, he would not care if she were a juvenile delinquent. If his sister were a delinquent, she would be more interesting, he thinks, and he's afraid he would like her even more.

Looking at his sister, he can feel—it is *that* feeling, something he never doubts—that he already is an old man who has endured hardship. She is a young girl, but he is already an old piece of wood, rotten wood, dry and hollow. He is not exaggerating. No, when he thinks this way, he is more serious than any "old timer." When he feels this way, he immerses himself, like the wise Socrates, in deep thoughts: life is like the morning dew. She, his incomparable little sister, will not last much longer, perhaps another two years at most. Then she won't be a prodigy, won't have eyes that are tinted blue. Her face will break out, her hair will grow long and it will be permed in tight curls like a negro. She will change, become just like one of his female classmates.

Mother is scolding again:

"Look at your Papa! Do you want to drive everyone crazy! It's just what I said! He's reverting to his old habits. Put down the pen and wipe the table! Ah!" Her two index fingers are pressed into her temples.

"All right, all right," Professor Lin says evenly. "You eat first. You don't have to wait for me."

"Of course we're not waiting! But we don't want to have to keep shooing flies away from your food!" Mrs. Lin replies.

"Maybe a window is open," Professor Lin says to himself. "There's a thick layer of dust on the table. Don't you want to wipe it first . . . Ahhh."

---

1. These names are given in English in the original.

Professor Lin's words often suddenly fade away halfway through and he uses a simple "ahhh" to wrap up some complicated thought. His speaking style resembles a swimmer who appears to drown halfway across a river only to have bubbles break the surface a moment later.

"Second Brother," Lin Xun looks at her brother and says, "There's a very famous book now called *Lolita*.[2] Have you read it?"

Her eyes really are pure and innocent.

"No," Lin Shaoquan says.

Lin Xun opens her eyes wide and smiles at him, as if expecting him to continue.

"It's not a book that's right for everyone. In America, many adults won't read it," he says.

"Hmmph!" She produces a sound like a cheer of victory. "I've already finished it. Yesterday I read it all in one day!"

"What?"

"A classmate lent it to me, and it took me only one day to read." She is exceptionally self-satisfied, her eyes wide as if waiting for him to praise her.

"Someone's already translated it?"

She shakes that short Pekinese-style hair and smiles joyfully: "Don't you know? It was translated long ago, and there are lots and lots of translated editions."

Fucking translations, these fucking translators. He can imagine how they did their translations. They will have left out sentences they can't translate, preserved the shocking parts, fuck, they're a pack of monkeys. Their lives are missing something—morality. He begins to feel anxious about her. Fortunately, that pair of staring eyes is utterly innocent and unspoiled.

Because no praise is forthcoming, she says impatiently: "This week I read lots of books, including *Pride and Prejudice*, *Wuthering Heights* and *Mistress of Mellyn*."[3]

---

2. This title is given in English in the original.

3. These titles appear in Chinese in the original. *Mistress of Mellyn* is a romance by Victoria Holt.

He is greatly relieved. "Fine, you ought to read more of *Pride and Prejudice*, *Wuthering Heights*, that kind of book."

"Missy, I'm telling you, if you read these novels again, ignore your homework, I'll break your legs!" Mrs. Lin hisses.

"Ah, Ma, it's summer vacation! And you still won't let me read them?"

"It's not allowed, even if it is summer vacation! I want you to sit in the house and practice calligraphy!"

Lin Shaoquan watches his mother—he knows there really is no point in arguing with her. So many issues aren't worth arguing about, like this thing. He will just slip his sister some books.

The day already has advanced into late afternoon, even now approaches the cusp of evening. This can be sensed by the color of the sunlight, the sounds of the city. Inanimate objects reveal it, the white clouds in the sky outside the window, the coconut trees standing silently against the blue sky like shuttlecocks. It's miraculous, the countless scenes that signal the time. With his keen antennae, Lin Shaoquan is conscious the afternoon is about to pass away. He thinks suddenly that he should check the mailbox. There is a better chance now than before, because he has not gone to look for quite a while. At any rate, the letter probably will come today. Impatience rises in his heart like mercury in a thermometer. Finally he stands up and pushes back his chair. Just as he takes a step to leave the room, a voice as sharp and beautiful as an arrow calls out:

"Lin Xun—Lin Xun— "

"Liu Juan, it's Liu Juan!"

Lin Xun shoots out of her chair with the door as her target. In an eyeblink, she races in front of her brother, blocking his departure, but he turns around abruptly and rushes toward his bedroom like a startled hen. Finding the door stuck, he whips around and hurries through any door that's open.

A paper door closes behind him. He's "safe"—the word is unspoken but true. A string of jeering laughter rings in his ears. Lin Xun has stopped by the door with her head turned back toward him. That's right—this is his "weak point." What he's most afraid of are his sister's classmates. If they come home, he runs for his life. The more who come, the more frightened he is, even breaking out in a sweat. He probably has some kind of "Complex."[4] But the strange thing is, you could not say he is afraid of his own female classmates. When he is with them, he feels as natural as he does with his male friends, uses the same coarse voice to roar and shout at them, calling out their names, both given and family names. They use the same harsh tones to shout his full name back at him. But these not-yet-adults, no-longer-children, these little birds, these little butterfly girls, they strike fear into his heart, make him bashful, make him stutter.

He is a prisoner in his own room, his mind consumed with thoughts of the letter that even now could be retrieved from the mailbox. It is like a rose surrounded by flames; he cannot get at it but the heat penetrates to the core of his body. A person is like an ant—just when it is about to arrive at a morsel of cake, a child reaches out its destructive hand, grabs a leaf and pokes with it, pushing the ant farther away from the crumb. The principle really is very simple: the greater the craving, the greater the suffering. He absently drums his fingers on the tabletop. Suddenly, he raises a hand and strikes his forehead, as if the blow could stop his craving. The result, when he lowers his hand, is a wide, immaculate forehead that betrays no trace of the dark shadows of worry. With this faultless, blank forehead, he goes back to seek out his throne, gingerly protecting his emptiness like a glass of water, careful not to spill it. Two legs stretch leisurely, two arms reach out. Palms on the bed, head resting lightly on the pillow, he silently recites:

> "Vast mountains fresh with rain,
> Night ripe with fall's approach,
> Bright moonlight shining on the pines,
> Crystal water cascading on the rocks."[5]

He repeats the passage, savoring each word, his expression blank:

4. The word "Complex" appears in English in the original.
5. This is a verse from the Tang Dynasty poem *Autumn Light in the Mountains* by Wang Wei.

"Vast—mountains—fresh—with—rain,
Night—ripe—with—fall's—approach,
Bright—moonlight—shining—on—the—pines,
Crystal—water—cascading—on—the—rocks."

Babbling brooks, lustrous autumn moon, people playing the lute. You can hear the music but not see anyone. Sitting alone in a bamboo grove, strum the lute and sigh,[6] such a tasteful life. Now there is no bamboo grove, just a tiny room: Sitting alone in a tiny room, strumming the lute—no, there is no lute, just a record player—Sitting alone in a tiny room, the record player mingling with long sighs. Ah, God. Long sighs. That's impossible too. As soon as you cry out, Mama will be pounding on the door with all her might: "What is it? Sonny? What happened?"

He smiles gently. He has already forgotten what was bothering him just now. He has also forgotten why he mouthed that poem. He is not even aware that he already feels better. It is only when he is not aware he feels better that he really feels better.

"Oh, that's so weird. Oh, you don't give anyone a chance."

From the left of the paper door, a girl's voice.

"Lin Xun, she's so special, eh? A certain miserable someone wants to ask her out but she doesn't give that someone a chance. She's real bad. You know, she curses that someone, even hits him, throws him out. She wishes he were dead."

The sound of her sniggering laugh is heard.

"You're talking nonsense again," Lin Xun answers.

"Ha!" the girl replies. "Let me see! Let me see! What is it? A little puppy, it's so adorable, so cute, oh, so cute. Quick, give it to me."

"Give it to you? In your dreams!"

That girl, Liu Juan, he has met her before. A skinny young thing, her breastbone visible at her collar and large flashing, animated eyes. Her hair has a copper tint, like a warm nest of phoenix feathers, cut precisely in the current fashion for middle school girls. Of

---

6. These two phrases are from another poem by Wang Wei, *Bamboo Pavilion*. It continues: "Alone in the deep woods, only the moon shines on me."

course, when the school dean wields the scissors, these little birds turn into ugly ducklings, but with the coming of the summer vacation, every richly curled feather has grown out. This summer, Lin Xun and Liu Juan are a pair of birds who have escaped their cage.

"Bitch, okay, don't give it to me. It's nothing special anyway. Hey! What do you think? Are we going or not?"

"I can't, really! You don't know . . ."

Lin Xun lowers her voice so he can't make out the last part of what she is saying.

Some girlish secrets, he thinks. Girls always have so many secrets they can't discuss them all, although not one actually deserves being called a "secret." Even when only two girls are together, without having to worry about a third party eavesdropping, they think it is necessary to lower their voices. Lin Shaoquan begins to feel uneasy because he senses the presence of a girl beside the door. A wondrous realization dawns on him: he seems to be the object of someone's admiration. He feels quite superior. Lin Shaoquan would not be Lin Shaoquan if he did not have some kind of Complex.[7] Surging narcissism grows with unpleasant speed, reaches a peak. He stands up, walks to the table, brings his body close to the mirror. There, in the mirror, like the surface of a lake, he sees another Lin Shaoquan showing his teeth, grinning. Not a bad face, he has to admit. But it is best from a certain angle. For example, with his head facing sideways, the mouth is less obvious, mitigating the defect of its small size. There is another angle, also not bad, comparatively speaking—with the chin tucked, the eyes glancing up from those black, black eyebrows, the lips stretched wider—although it is a little like some assassin in the movies. He shrinks back from his nose, his eyes, his eyebrows, yearns to wipe away that unfortunate assassin's face. But that nose, those eyes, those eyebrows! He's so frightened by the image in the mirror he jumps. God, I'm really ugly! He arches his eyebrows again, examines them carefully. But, God, I'm very old. There are three wrinkles on my forehead! No matter how he poses, that face in the mirror always fails to please him. It keeps

7. Again, this word appears in English in the original text.

reflecting his stupidity, ugliness and anger back at him. With a spasm of disappointment, he flips the mirror over.

Like all young people, he can't tell whether he is good looking. One moment, he thinks he is Pan An,[8] the next his confidence is shattered, broken to bits. Could any girl love you now? God in heaven, no girl could love you. Muttering to himself, he crawls back to his throne.

Of course, he's just joking. Already, he no longer cares whether girls love him or not. Everyone should agree, he thinks, that love is one of life's thorns. Pluck it out and life is comfortable and free. Last year, he did not understand this truth, but now he fully recognizes it. Furthermore, he thinks he understands it better than anyone. As far as love is concerned, he detests it, not so much because of its wounding bitterness, but specifically because of the rituals and clichés involved when this boy and that girl have a conversation. Whoever they are, as long as they talk, they imitate movie dialogue, even their facial expressions are all Hollywood. Just thinking about it makes him sick. This laughable movie-ized style annihilates pure, innocent love: when a man and a woman talk, they are like actors wearing wigs and false beards. So the best thing for him to do is withdraw, just become a young hermit.

Even so, this young hermit has never forbidden himself from admiring female beauty.

(His mouth opens as wide as a goldfish's, two arms stretch left and right, his body tilts and falls onto the bed. Tears fill his eyes, he uses the back of his hand to wipe them away. Missing his afternoon nap has made him terribly tired.)

He certainly is no priest (he declares). He admires female beauty; it is just as important to him as listening to music or reading a few poems every day. He thinks, what is more beautiful than a woman's gorgeous hair? That thick, thick hair, glossy-moist, supple-soft, like black honey! If he could just untie their black hair, a water-

8. Pan An, also called Pan Yue, was an official during the Jin Dynasty (1115–1234 CE). He is said to have been so handsome in his youth that when women saw him outside the palace they threw fruit into his cart.

fall pouring down, just so, he wishes he could hide behind that waterfall and dream. What is more beautiful than a woman's eyes? They are two deep autumn lakes, and in the middle of the lake the pupils bloom like narcissi; those beautiful mysterious narcissi pose questions no man ever will be able to answer. Women, women, perhaps they are the incarnation of the wind.

No, he is definitely not a priest. Besides beautiful hair and bright eyes, he is not averse to other things as well. When he walks down a street, his eyes never overlook a woman, any exposed part of any woman's body, a pink neck, a bare arm, a flash of calf; he devours them all. His quick, sideways glance is like a net that scoops up everything worth seeing. Probably no one else can look as quickly or see more. This makes him rather cocky. Not only does he watch carefully, but the net he casts stretches across the sky. He does not want to miss even one. From a distance, he looks at the face; closer, he studies the waist; closer still, the feet. After walking past, he even evaluates the backside. With the utmost skill, this busiest of youths on the streets of Taipei gorges himself on endless beauty. So this recluse could, on the other hand, also be considered a playboy.

The most attractive part of a woman's body—he brings a fist to his mouth to stifle a yawn and then, speaking in the manner of a connoisseur, addresses the ceiling—the prettiest part of a woman, you know what it is? When it is cold outside and you are walking in the street and come across some girls with woolen sweaters draped across their shoulders, you circle around behind, focus on those woolen sweaters, see them hanging down so softly, loosely draped, relaxed and graceful at the waist, and the hem stretched evenly across the hips, glorious, full, round hips, and the hem sleeps there silently, like grass nestled by a riverbank in spring. Whether there are other people who think like him, he really doesn't know. As for another topic, the sexiest part of a woman, what is it? Is it the breasts? Or the buttocks? Based on his several years of research, he is afraid it is neither of those two. In his view, the honor is reserved for the upper arm, the part below the shoulder. This part of a woman's arm (his argument begins), with long slim lines but softly curved flesh, is completely unlike men's ridiculous biceps. Women's ivory-colored arms remain pleasantly cool even in summer. Furthermore, women show them without the slightest timidity or unhealthy psychological motivation, displaying simultaneously external beauty and inner moral virtue. Truly, this is women's undeniable pride. He, Lin Shaoquan, wants to write twenty pages to promote and develop this idea. As for the buttocks (he shakes his head several times), his investigation has never got beyond their comical aspect. He once saw a calendar with pictures of a female model. Above the waist, the model was dressed neatly, but below the waist a pair of incredibly fat buttocks faced the viewer. When he saw it, he immediately broke into waves of thunderous laughter. After that, he preferred the little white bums of babies.

Concerning breasts, what could he say? Breasts are covered—another Hollywood invention. The odd thing is that breasts originally were not secret at all, but ordinary people have been deceived by the silver screen into regarding them as a mystery. If all the female stars stuck strips of adhesive tape to their lips tomorrow, then—even though this could never happen in real life—he is sure men would press against ticket windows jostling to see the beauty of the tape (he really believes this conjecture to be correct). As a matter of fact, on the screen you never actually see a completely naked breast, but it's very easy to see them in galleries, art photos, snow-white plaster statues. Opportunities are widespread. You can freely observe scenes of breastfeeding on the side of the street. If breasts really were a danger zone, the police department would paint slips over the chests of all the female figures in oil paintings, drive nursing mothers into rooms and drape black sashes, like the kind worn on days of national mourning, across every statue.

He raises his hands to remove his glasses, stares at the layer of dust obscuring the lenses. Despite all that—he slips the ends of the frames of his spectacles back over his ears—despite all that, the nipples on the breast originally were not worth looking at. Some are wrinkled and dark, like scorched flower buds, although some he has seen are not wrinkled. They retain a pinky smoothness but are elongated like the teats of a mountain goat. The thought convulses his entire body with laughter. Trying to contain it, he shakes like a thin-hulled motor boat. He buries his face in the pillow, his two fists pounding the bed. In time the storm subsides. He again takes off his glasses, puffs on the lenses and then, using a method that hardly reflects well on him, wipes them back and forth on the bottom of his T-shirt. He talks to himself while wiping them: "So if someone is excited by nipples, he can only be described as a billy goat." This time he cannot contain his waves of laughter. He squeezes his trembling lips shut against a pillow and presses another against the back of his head to prevent the girls outside from hearing him. In fact, Liu Juan has already gone home.

After some time, he slides away the pillow that was pressing against his neck. He suddenly stops laughing, his eyes now focused and sincere, as if inspecting some scenery inside his head. Then the expression in that pair of eyes turns vague, aimlessly wanders along the foot of the wall. His lips quiver as if reciting a passage over and over. He recites faster and faster. The rocking of his head and his closed eyes reveal the repeated efforts he is making to recall the words. Slowly he turns his body and sits with quiet solemnity. Our Father, who art in heaven, hallowed be Thy name. Thy kingdom come. Thy will be done, on earth as it is in heaven. Give us this day our daily bread; and forgive us our trespasses as we forgive those who trespass against us. And lead us not into temptation, but deliver us from evil. Amen. Amen. Amen.[9] Think about something else, think of dark-green pines, think of light-green cypresses, think of temples, think of a solitary cloud. Don't press on my belly. Perhaps it's a little better this way. Can't help it, it's so meaningless. Can't help it, it's so useless. Best leave it, even though I'm about to get it, even though I'm almost there. I don't want to do anything so meaningless, I don't want to do anything! Again he lies motionless, his face looking up, staring at a water stain on the ceiling. His arms are covered with glistening beads of sweat.

"Sonny!"

---

9. The words of the Lord's Prayer are in English in the original.

Mother has come. Three of her fingers already are reaching in between the door and the frame, ready to push open the paper door.

"Don't come in!" His sudden shout is rough and angry. Immediately, he is consumed with regret (two types of regret) because he has cried out involuntarily. His mother, truly frightened by his rough voice, quickly slides shut the paper door she had pulled open a few inches.

"I'm having my nap," he explains vaguely, regretting his outburst even more. "What is it? Wait a moment. I'll open the door." But he does not get up immediately to open it for her.

"Sonny."

Another period of silence.

"Hmm."

"I have something to give you."

"What is it you want? What do you want? I'll get it for you."

"No, I want to give you something."

"—Oh!"

"Should I pass it through to you now or wait until you come out?"

"It's all right, I'll open the door for you. You can give it to me now."

Having delayed as long as he needed, he gropes for his slippers with the points of his feet and steps onto the floor. He dawdles to the paper door and opens it slowly, opens it halfway, his body blocking the opening.

"You have a letter," she says. She gives it to him, long and narrow, snow white.

Lin Shaoquan, almost like a bandit, snatches the letter from her hand, turns around immediately and bangs the door shut, leaving his mother outside.

His mother, suspicious ever since being startled by his shout, cannot refrain from lightly tapping twice on the two paper doors. She tilts her gray head forward, as if leaning over her beloved son's shoulder, until it just touches the paper door. It is unclear whether she wants to eavesdrop on what's happening in the room or is gripped by another emotion. She listens attentively for a moment before leaving the door.

This letter—it is precisely the one he has been expecting for three full days! Standing in the middle of the room, he tears open the seal with his long pale fingers. He pulls out a long folded sheet of writing paper, which rustles in his hands as he unfolds it. One after another, characters undulate across the folds of the paper like summer waves:

"Old Timer:
"We've all arrived. We're on the top floor. If we stretch out our hands, we can snatch the white clouds from the sky. We've already changed our names. No one can find us in the registry downstairs. But you, Old Timer, you'll find us of course, buddy. All right! Come quickly, immediately, as soon as you receive this letter! If you bug out now, you have no guts!
"The address: International Hotel, Fifth Floor, Number 17, Taizhong, facing the train station."
"Lost Generation,[10] 8/11"

He puts the letter back into the envelope, rushes to the chair where his pants are hanging and grabs them. He ducks his head to pull off his pajamas and slides the slender columns of his legs into Western-style trousers, closing them around his slim, boyish waist. From a side pocket, he slowly removes a fine chain, as silvery as a snake, that whistles and dances in the air. He lowers it into his hand. One end hangs beside his palm, dangling and shaking, a bunch of keys suspended like grapes. He selects a short thick one, and inserts it into a keyhole in the drawer.

From the drawer he takes out a fat, square, brown envelope. The envelope, stuffed to bursting, seems to be packed with sheets of paper. He pulls out a wad—a pile of banknotes! A thousand yuan altogether! It is his entire personal savings, tutoring fees, writing fees,

10. The words Lost Generation are in English in the original.

proofreading earnings, from last year's winter holidays. He stuffs the money back inside and folds down the flap, sealing it by running his thumb and forefinger across the opening. He stuffs the envelope into his hip pocket and turns around to pack a suitcase.

Half an hour later, Lin Shaoquan leaves the house. Walking to the city centre, he raises his head and gazes into the distance at the dusk already falling on Taipei—more than half the sky is ablaze with the dazzling light of the setting sun.

Three consecutive afternoons of torrential rain—warm, subtropical, summer rain—bring clear bright autumn weather to Taipei. The rain seems to have washed away the intense summer heat, and today the sky is high, boundless and clear, so blue it looks as though a fresh coat of fine powder has been delicately applied. The air is equally clear, more small buildings seem to be visible in the distance than before. This is the most beautiful season in Taipei. She has shaken off the unclean vapors of spring, the violent heat of summer, and looks peaceful and relaxed. Taipei at this time of year is a charming place, a clean, elegant metropolis.

In Professor Lin's lane, the bushes look vigorous and lush after the rain, as though a second spring has arrived. That's right, people seem to think spring actually has returned. The tops of the shrubs, usually as flat as tabletops, have sprouted a new layer of fresh tender leaves. From a distance, the moist, new green looks like mist rising into the air.

The immutable routines of Professor Lin's household persist through these days. Professor Lin continues to write his essay every day. Mrs. Lin's feet still shuffle quickly to her sewing machine.

Wearing a white skirt with green flecks, Lin Xun rests a cheek on hands folded on the window sill, silently scanning the quiet empty lane outside the window. The lake-green screen is open, allowing the strong breeze, so fresh and cool, to float inside. The heavy afternoon rain ended just an hour ago. Green leaves hang down like arms from the betel-palms outside the window, droplets of water falling like liquid pearls from broken bracelets. Her eyes appear lost in a dream.

Three days before, at the instigation of Liu Juan, she finally drummed up the courage to deceive her mother and go to the first dance party of her life. She borrowed Liu Juan's dancing clothes, a blouse with a wide, open collar, and a fiery red pleated skirt. She twirled like a maple leaf in the wind, dancing the fast steps of the jitterbug.[11] Although three days have passed already, the swinging, intoxicated melodies, those crazy, wild dance steps, still linger in her mind. She is like a fairy-tale princess bewitched by a spell.

With slow steps, she moves away from the window and strolls to her bed. Long, slender, coral-colored fingers curl outward, stroking her pillow, feeling the tiny cupids embroidered on its surface. With her head lowered, she caresses it for a moment and then gradually sits down on the edge of the bed. Beside the pillow is a silk handkerchief curled into the shape of a nest. Beside the handkerchief lies a puppy. What a pretty puppy, what a lovable puppy, he looks so funny now, lying with his four feet in the air. Lin Xun reaches out her fingers, picks up the puppy. She looks down on it tenderly, puckers her lips, lifts the puppy to them and kisses it lightly. The puppy again lies in her palm. She gazes at it. In a dreamlike tone, Lin Xun says: "I want to take him apart and weave him back together." She raises her eyes and looks out the window, continuing her thoughts: "I want to weave something I can wear. I want to weave a flower."

Half an hour later, Lin Shaoquan returns. Carrying his suitcase, he walks directly to his room and enters. Once inside, he closes the door.

He looks a little different than he did three days before. His hair is freshly trimmed. The fringe around his ears has been swept away, but what is most noticeable is that his formerly long locks have been cut off. What remains is as short as a sailor's. That short, thick, dry hair is as hard and stiff as the bristles of a clothes brush. His face is lean and taut, as brown as olive oil. The brownness is perfectly even, as if he had been brushed with liquid. His eyes are brighter, especially beautiful.

---

11. Jitterbug is in English in the original.

He begins to open his suitcase. His actions are slower and more deliberate than before, as if his limbs have become heavier.

The first item he removes is that brown envelope. There is a long, cruel, diagonal tear from the top right corner to the lower left. The money that was inside is gone completely. He throws the torn envelope onto the table top.

Then he removes several items in order: a soap box, a tube of toothpaste, a toothbrush.

Finally his fingers remove a small box from a compartment in the suitcase. It is an empty box of condoms, there are English words written on it. He holds it in his hand, looks at it for a moment, then tosses it onto the messy pile of clothes.

Translated by Fred Edwards and Jia Li

The Day of the Sea Goddess

March 1963. This story contemplates the theme of fate, a philosophical question that occupies a central position in several of Wang's works. It was written during his second year of military service after he graduated from university. The setting is Nanfang'ao in Hualian, on the east coast of Taiwan. Wang was impressed by the geographic setting because of its similarity to an ancient Greek theatre. Nanfang'ao also would be the setting of Wang's second novel, Backed Against the Sea.

It's about twenty days after the vernal equinox and the mountainous harbor by the sea already is as hot as the deserts of Africa. Each morning the sun rises half an hour earlier than during the winter and sets twenty minutes later in the evening. Along the east coast, in deep, deserted mountain ranges filled with sandy brown earth and gigantic rocks, no trace of spring remains. Summer has marked the place. A few black vultures cruise among huge, peony-shaped clouds, circling the mountaintop all day. What can they be doing? Searching for food? Playing? At times, a gust of wind blows in from the Pacific, stirring up sand in the fishing village tucked at the foot of the mountains. Then, like an echo, dust flies on the Suhua Highway halfway up the mountain slope, creating the illusion that a fleet of cars is passing by. But there are no cars—only two buses drive past each day along the highway, one in the morning (about nine o'clock), one in late afternoon (about the time the sun sets), traversing the sky above the fishing harbor.

It is a gray fishing harbor, gray as fossil remains, gray as wind-eroded ruins. Yet it actually has an eventful history, three-hundred years long. According to legend, three hundred years ago, the people who crossed the harbor were not of our Han race. They were naked, well-built, dark-skinned, blue-eyed giants. They came from their mountain dwellings, climbed over narrow passes, and discovered this hidden inlet. Paddling brightly patterned canoes, they were the first to struggle with the waves. It was not until the Japanese occupation of Taiwan[1] that plains-dwellers appeared with their rifles and took over the harbor. But Japanese control did not last long. Two bombs from a fleet of Allied bombers ended life in the harbor. After that, it became an abandoned ruin with no inhabitants, no boats, only a couple of huts where a few sweet potato growers lived. Black vultures invaded the harbor. Still, a harbor always is a harbor, its waters eternally deep, eternally blue. After the Restoration, a bit of reconstruction work quickly brought back the fishing boats. Now the vultures have been forced to return to their mountaintop nests, hunting for food amid the clouds, circling in the rainy mist.

Early this morning, two of them began their daily flight as usual. Like the rising sun, they start early. At times, they remain perfectly still in the sky, fixed like two black dots. Other times, they swoop down, waltzing like two dipping kites. The waves breaking at the foot of the mountains add a frill of snowy lace to the sandy beaches, while out on the vast sea nearby, resting on the serene blue cradle, float a few autumn leaves—the fishing vessels. The vultures cruise around for a while, remaining close to the high summits, as loyal as the guardian spirits of the mountains, apparently immune to the changes going on beneath them. Every day the waves are the same (the lacy frill), every day the activities on the sea also are the same (the floating autumn leaves). Then, with a graceful turn, the birds return to the dark forests on the mountaintop only to appear again a few minutes later, but no one knows if they are the same ones.

1. In 1895, after Japan won the Sino-Japanese War (1894–1895), China signed a treaty with Japan to cede Taiwan to Japan, which occupied Taiwan for fifty years, from 1895 to 1945.

In the harbor, though, obvious changes are occurring. They began a few days ago. It is the Sea Goddess Mazu's birthday, and for
the past three days the fishermen have been making preparations
for the celebration. Even now, smoke from incense curls in front of
South Gate Temple, and people are beginning to gather. Although
the sun has not yet appeared over the mountaintop, the altar in
front of the temple already is laden with offerings. Pious men and
women in new clothes burn joss sticks and bow in deference to the
gilded statue seated deep within the temple. In the lives of these
fishermen, the Sea Goddess of South Gate Temple occupies a position of utmost importance. They believe that she, Mazu, protects
their vessels from danger. Her birthday is celebrated once a year,
and on this day the villagers willingly offer all they have.

The holiday festivities, like the smell of heat slowly building in the
harbor, become more intense. The sun, bright as a silver dollar,
climbs above the mountain and bathes the harbor at the foot of the
five-hundred-meter-high mountains in its brilliance, turning the
bay's black water as silvery as mercury. The activities of the people,
up to now silently worshipful, build to a rising hum like the buzzing
of many bees. A moment later, a series of sharp staccato bursts rings
out, like popping corn, as firecrackers explode at the western end of
the harbor. These are punctuated by a final dull boom accompanied
by a flash of white light. The sea breezes carry the acrid smell of
sulfur over the water to the square in front of the temple. The people
breathe deeply.

Then, the beating of a drum is heard. The villagers begin to flock
toward the western part of the harbor. There must be some excitement over there, they think.

Fruit vendors selling brown-sugared haw, candied apples and
guavas stoop to lift their wares. The iced-drink seller begins to push
his cart, its four tiny wheels squeaking like mice. A little girl runs
along, dragging her younger brother, who is stark naked. The little
one, unable to keep up with his curiosity-driven sister, hops behind
like a small African warrior performing a war dance.

The entire village is running.

At the western end of the harbor, they find the object of their pursuit, the source of the drumbeats. Beside a heavy crane (which stands like the trunk of a solitary bare pine, pointing straight to heaven), they see a gyrating lion-head mask, its uplifted, red-painted mouth open in a wide grin, its fierce rolling eyes glaring straight into the sun.

The beating of the drum is dull yet urgent, like the pulsing of a beating heart, the rhythm of coursing arteries. Accompanying the beats are a pair of cymbals that crash in a blinding burst, as if warning that the heart finally will stop beating, the pulse finally will become still, and life finally will end. But the drumbeats continue without pause, as if in another world.

The drummer stands high above the crowd on a fish cart. He's wearing a sleeveless undershirt, sweat flowing like rivers from his smooth, round forehead, from his heavy eyelids, from his sinewy neck, from his shoulders. He is middle-aged, with disheveled black hair streaked with white—his long face is turned upward, like a totem. Immersed in his drumming, he appears oblivious to what's going on around him, even to the point of forgetting the reason for his drumming, which is to accompany the dancing lion. His sole audience is himself, his eyes fixed on the distant horizon. Isolated within the circle of drumbeats, the drummer ignores the other concentric circle, that of the dancing lion.

The lion's dancing circle is surrounded by a wall-like mass of people. A couple of muscular, red-faced young men push the children, forcing them back. "Get back there kids, you want to be stepped on? Aren't you afraid of getting killed?"

All the while the lion prances, rears, rolls its gaudy, fierce, yet comical (grinning) head like a madman. Within a radius of six steps, as if in a cage, it dances like a whirlwind, whether out of ecstasy or in an effort to get free, no one knows.

The dancer's head is hidden under the lion mask. No one can see his face, and no one knows who he is. He is wearing a pair of black tights with fringe running down each leg, and a pair of black cloth slippers tipped with two furry balls. His two long legs, muscles rippling, weave an intricate pattern on the hardened earth. Sometimes one leg bends, other times both, or one kicks out. Besides his legs, the spectators can see his torso (also clad in a sleeveless undershirt) and the arms that carry the fifty-kilogram lion's head. The arms are as thick as the circumference of a rice bowl, smooth and bronzed, like two writhing serpents. A green dragon is inscribed on his upper left arm. Many young fishermen like tattoos, but because the lion's head weighs at least fifty kilos, the villagers assume the arms must belong to a young man of extraordinary strength.

"Good," a fisherman nods now and then, his face hidden beneath the peak of his cap. "It's been six or seven years since I've seen anything like this."

He is an elderly fisherman, his face like shrunken leather, a pair of thin shoulders. His arms are crossed in front of his chest, a white plastic cigarette-holder between two fingers of his right hand. Beside him is another fisherman, shorter but no younger or heavier, who rolls his watery brown eyes, smiles and nods all the while, his smile revealing a mouthful of cavity-darkened teeth.

"Who do you reckon he is, Fuzai?" the taller man asks, taking a pull on his cigarette.

His friend shakes his head, still smiling.

"Can't tell, is it Chen Junxiong?"

"I think it looks like Lin Wengui. See how easy he does it, as if it doesn't take a bit of strength, as if the lion's head is as light as a coconut shell. He holds it so straight, even when he's turning, like he's holding a jar of clear water. Look, look at his steps. Ah, right! Step down heavily, but come up lightly, without a bit of sound. Look at that circling step, round as the full moon, like the circling vultures on the mountaintop, like the bay behind this mountain . . . this is what I call a real lion dance! Haven't seen anything like it for six or seven years. Once before, only once, I saw one as good as this. That was Cai Jinzhong, you still remember him?"

Fuzai nods, he remembers. Cai Jinzhong, with a pale, square, childlike face, a pair of round black eyes, strong square shoulders, was a powerful young fisherman. He also was the only one in this harbor to win the harpooning championship for three consecutive years. He once hit a spotted black shark that was two meters longer than his fishing boat. When they dragged the monster—as big as an island it was—back into the harbor with ropes, the water turned bright red. But he also was one of the victims when that boat capsized in the typhoon last year—there were fifteen men, and none returned alive.

"It doesn't look like Lin Wengui, no, it isn't Lin Wengui. I think it looks like Chen Junxiong now. It is Chen Junxiong!" the taller man murmurs. Beneath the long peak of his cap, his black eyes are hidden by wrinkles.

The lion stops dancing and stands still. Then it slowly squats. With two legs outstretched, it sits on the ground. The lion's head begins to gyrate, up and down, left and right, the wide mouth working continuously in a chewing motion. Then it leans back and lies on the sandy ground. Its two legs paw the air for a while. A moment later, the lion is on its knees. It stands up and stretches taller and taller until it stands tip-toe, its chest thrown out, basking in the sunlight. With a yellow silk cloth hanging down from the back of its head, the lion looks like a gilded statue beside the water. The staccato burst of a string of firecrackers overwhelms the sound of the drum commanding the lion forward.

The crowd follows the lion. Out front, the lion proceeds with a rolling gait. The two elderly men exchange glances, and then follow the excited, surging crowd.

The lion's destination is the lonely yet sturdy temple facing the harbor.

After passing through the many arches formed by ladders leaning against the prows of the fishing boats, beneath bamboo poles tied with bamboo leaves and scarlet thread, they finally reach South Gate Temple where the Sea Goddess dwells. From sunrise until now, the goddess has enjoyed five hours of offerings. A scattering of paper ash fills the air like dragonflies in the autumn wind.

In the tiny temple, coated with greenish stucco, the melancholy Mazu lies curled by the seaside as if pining for lost, distant vessels. In the evenings, when the wind rises, the temple sobs like a gigantic shell.

The temple was built with contributions from every villager, constructed from blocks of faith. Each brick, each tile carries the name of its donor, the date of the donation, and a line of prayer. The captain of the *Sea Peace*, together with his crew of fifteen, once encountered a violent storm during the night. With the fifty-year-old captain in the lead, everyone knelt on the wave-washed deck and prayed: "Oh Mazu, please lead us safely into harbor, please protect us so we may see the lights of our homes again and the faces of our loved ones." Then the storm gradually subsided and a lone star twinkled in the sky. It was their street lamp on the sea. Under its guidance, the vessel reached safe haven after a few hours' journey. So the crew of the *Sea Peace* donated a mahogany gate weighing about five hundred kilos, painted shiny black. The altar in the centre of the temple holds another prominent offering: a large gilded vase donated by the crew of the *Divine Light V*. There is another story behind the golden vase. It involves the same struggle between life and death, men's fervent prayers, faith. The wide mouth of the vase holds a bouquet of snow-white lilies in full bloom.

Facing the Sea Goddess, the lion pays its respects with three deep bows. Then, prancing energetically around the circle formed by the wall of people, it begins to dance its second round.

From his pocket, the tall, thin old man fishes out a betel nut wrapped in taro leaf. He has finished smoking his cigarette. With his eyes still on the circling lion, he takes out a pocket knife, cuts open the betel nut and stuffs it with a wad of reddish paste, then puts the whole concoction in his mouth. The blood-red juice of the betel nut trickles from the corner of his lips.

In no time his gaze becomes confused, his pupils contracting like a cat's. He sees another Chen Junxiong, standing beside the one beneath the lion's head. There are two Chen Junxiongs in front of his eyes. The old man blanches. The spectator Chen Junxiong, wearing a broad smile, is gesturing to a friend standing next to him, while the dancer Chen Junxiong, with intricate steps, still prances ecstatically in front.

Fuzai calls to him in a small voice. The gangly old man turns toward his friend, his face still as white as a sheet.

"Look, isn't that Chen Junxiong over there? It must be Lin Wengui then," Fuzai remarks. "No, no, look," he continues, "Lin Wengui is over there too. It must be someone else, only I don't know who."

Lin Wengui is standing opposite them with his hands on his hips, his curly black head leaning forward, smiling in concentration. The gangly old man smiles to himself with a sigh of relief. You're getting old, he says to himself. There aren't two Chen Junxiongs, there's only one, the spectator. It's someone else who's dancing. He lifts his arm and wipes the sweat from his forehead with the back of his hand.

"You don't know who that is?" another voice suddenly interjects. "You don't know who he is! Ha! Ha!"

"Oh, it's you Old Wang," Fuzai greets the newcomer. "Who is he?"

"It's Sa Keluo."

"Sa Keluo? The aborigine²?"

"Yes."

The gangly old man watches the dancing lion, then nods.

"Right, it is Sa Keluo."

"Ah, young people, these young people, they're all such show-offs," Old Wang remarks. "I was like him when I was young, I was even better. I once danced a lion that was at least twenty kilos heavier. I danced from dawn till dark, from the foot of the mountain to the summit, and then from there back down. I danced through the entire harbor, people remember my name even now." Old Wang's face is flushed crimson, his breath heavy with the smell of alcohol. "Don't you remember? Ah, what bad memories you have. I certainly remember."

"Of course I remember, Old Wang," Fuzai laughs.

"My friend, it's lucky that you remember. Ah, hurry up and remind me, I forget so many details. How heavy was that lion's head? How old was I then? I was ten, wasn't I?"

2. "Aborigine" refers to a native Taiwanese, someone not ethnically Chinese, but rather Polynesian.

Fuzai laughs, "But I'm recalling another occasion."

"Which occasion, my friend, which?"

"I recall that when others were dancing lions you were dancing with a bottle. Once you danced from the pier straight into the bay."

All three of them laugh. Fuzai pounds Old Wang heartily on the back, making him stagger three steps forward.

"Old Wang, you ought to know that the fast has to be kept till sundown today," Fuzai says.

Hearing this, Old Wang fidgets uneasily for a while. Then he changes the subject.

"Ah, my friend, you know why Sa Keluo, that aborigine, is doing the lion dance today? You don't know, do you? Listen, I'll tell you. That aborigine usually is a good-for-nothing loafer, you all know this. When he isn't drinking or gambling, he usually goes to sleep as soon as he gets back from a fishing trip, you all know this too. Why, last week he won five hundred yuan from me, almost taking my last fen. Damn him, he tricked the money from me while I had a drink too many, you know that. But why does he come out and dance to-day? Ah, the sun is hot, the lion's head is heavy. If it were me, I'd probably fall after taking a couple of steps. Then why does he do it? Do you know?"

His companions shake their heads.

"Because, one night in December last year, when there was a crescent moon"—the drunkard suddenly becomes sober and digni-fied, as if not intoxicated at all—"it was a night when there was a crescent moon. The boat he was on, the *Yu Li III*, was already half-filled with snakehead fish, but chasing after a school of shiny mack-erel led it further and further away from shore, so it got more and more isolated until the school of fish suddenly disappeared and they found themselves alone in the middle of the vast sea. Then the moon went in and the sea turned pitch black, dark as hell. In an instant, the boat fell into the maw of a cyclone.

"Now, falling into the maw of a cyclone is like being sucked into a fire, strong boats often are swallowed up this way, dashed to bits and destroyed within seconds, like being burned to ashes in a fire. The boat swirled like a drowning man, sinking one minute, rising the next. Its rudder was broken, the cabin was full of water, and the motor stopped. The boat was useless.

"The half load of fish made it even more difficult to keep an even keel in the storm. To lighten the load, the captain ordered his crew to cut away the fishing ladder. So one of them took an axe, climbed to the front and chopped off the ladder. But the boat was still too heavy—it was almost submerged in the water except for the prow. The captain ordered the broken rudder removed, then for all the fishing gear to be thrown into the sea, and as the boat was still sinking, he ordered them to strip off the wooden platform in front of the smokestack. But the boat kept sinking, as if a hand was pulling it down from below. So the captain climbed the prow and, sobbing, cried: 'The fish, throw the full load of fish into the sea!' This was a command he should have given much sooner.

"Without the fish, the vessel became light as a feather. But after losing the fish, the men were left with nothing. Even their clothes were torn to shreds, and they, a naked crew of twenty, bound themselves to the deck with ropes. Their strength was completely useless, all of their efforts futile. They were at the mercy of the cyclone. Perhaps the only thing they could do was pray. Ah, you should have heard their prayers.

"Some promised to fast for nineteen days as soon as they got back to the temple.

"Another said that he would place a fresh lily in the golden vase on the altar in front of the goddess every day, and fill the altar light with oil every evening.

"Another promised to build a wall, starting from the left of the temple, around the mulberry orchard in the back, all the way to the right, in place of the fence damaged by the typhoon the year before.

"Still another said he would donate a gigantic incense burner, bigger than anything the temple had before.

"But you should have heard Sa Keluo's prayer.

"At first, Sa Keluo could only woodenly repeat the sacred name of the Goddess Mazu, not daring to make any promises. Because he was ashamed. He knew that all the promises he'd made before had come to nothing. Not being able to resist temptation, he'd be sure to spend all his savings on booze again. 'Oh, I'm a very weak man, Mazu, I'm a very weak man.' Bound to the deck of the vessel, Sa Keluo murmured his confession.

"But he made up his mind that, this time, he must give something. He had confessed innumerable times before and maybe the Goddess wouldn't listen to him anymore. She'd dismiss his words as lies, although each time he had been sincere in his repentance. But isn't repentance without action also a form of lying? So Sa Keluo resolved that this time he must do something.

"Thus, he promised, 'This time, Mazu, if I reach home safely, I'll perform a lion dance for you on your birthday next year. I believe this time I'll keep my promise, Mazu. This time I will definitely not break my promise.' The goddess must have believed him, because he was smarter this time.

"He kept his word. Look, he's dancing in front of the goddess."

Sa Keluo lifts the lion's head up high, and then slowly lowers it, and then raises it up again. He repeats the ritual three times. Then he becomes still. The drumming also stops. A red-faced man emerges from the crowd holding a bundle of flaming sandalwood incense in both hands, the thick black smoke curling into the air like strands of black hair. The man walks to the huge incense burner and stands there, shaking his hands until the flames go out. He lowers his head and respectfully places the incense in the burner. The burner, molded from pure iron, has a gaping mouth like an open well. Its belly is covered with flowery carvings of phoenixes and dragons. The burner, which sits on an iron tripod as high as a man's shoulder, was donated by one of the crew of *Prosperity III*, a fisherman named Li Changchun.

"I have to go now, watching this makes me dizzy. I want to go home and sleep," the drunkard says.

"Old Wang, what you said just now, are you sure you didn't make it all up?" the gangly old man asks him.

"There was not a word of truth, all lies," Fuzai chides.

"I swear by the Goddess of Mercy, by the King of Heaven, by

the Goddess Mazu, that every word I uttered is true. Sa Keluo told me the story himself when I was having a drink with him. If I, Old Wang, have uttered a single syllable of falsehood, Old Wang then . . ."

"Okay, okay," his companions laugh.

"I'm going home now. I'm dizzy, really dizzy." He turns, about to leave, but turns back again: "Hey, remember, you'd better stand me a drink at the feast tonight, both of you."

They watch him lurch toward a shabby alley.

Sa Keluo holds up the fifty-kilo lion's head. At first it felt heavy, but now he no longer feels its weight. It has become part of his own weight. It's like he was born with it, he thinks. "If you were born with two heads, you wouldn't feel they were heavy, just as you don't feel the weight of your head, your arm, or your midsection."

After the red-faced man offers the incense to him, Sa Keluo's lion leaves the temple. He has fulfilled his promise, like casting off a burden. Hidden under the lion's head, he smiles in happiness, self-confidence, triumph. So he raises his voice to call out: "Keep the dance going! Keep it going! Don't stop!" Today is a holiday, and the holiday has just begun. His dancing has just brought the festivities to a climax. He wants to give all his remaining strength (in fact, he has just begun to tap his reserves), he wants to give the rest of the lion dance, now that he has fulfilled his promise, to the festival.

"Get back there, kids! Beat it!" The shouting of men! The thunder of the drum!

Along the garbage-filled back streets, the bright lion's head bobs up and down like a cork floating in the sea. It is like the pied piper who stole away an entire village of enchanted followers. The display of strength and beauty, the boxing-like advance and retreat, makes the eyes of the young men glow. One day they, too, will conquer the festival, just like Sa Keluo.

Sa Keluo dances across Harbor Street, across Sanmin Road, through Zhongxiao District—half-deserted streets lined with low roofs, their red tiles turned light gray by erosion from the sea wind, covered with fishing nets (like women's hair nets) spread out to dry. Sa Keluo's soft-soled shoes walk over sandy yellow paths, over flagstone roads, over the asphalt-paved dock. Frightened hens and wing-flapping pigeons scatter from behind empty gasoline drums.

At the corner of Minquan Lane and Xinsheng Road, the procession comes to a halt. A group of pipers appears before them, their wailing brass pipes raised high in the air, their cheeks puffed out. Two tottering puppets walk behind the pipers. One is the ghostly black face of Qi Ye,[3] with his tongue hanging out and standing as tall as two men put together. The other, Ba Ye, who also has his tongue hanging out, is a grotesque, madcap pigmy. Sa Keluo stands still in surprise. The two puppets then begin to advance with a sickening, ghastly, yet comical gait. Qi Ye turns his stiff neck, hangs out his tongue, and moves his stiff skeleton jerkily beneath his yellow robe. He is like a rheumatism patient. The pigmy, though, prances along waving a tattered goose-feather fan. They are right in Sa Keluo's way. But after a few seconds, Sa Keluo wakens from his trance and continues forward. Rushing toward them, he dances between the two and forces his way through. He is like a real lion. The two puppets separate, a bald head emerging from the middle of Qi Ye, gaping in astonishment. Ba Ye also stands aside, his upper half astride the bald head of another fat man. Their woebegone expressions prompt a burst of laughter from the bystanders. Sa Keluo's heroic action wins universal praise.

As the procession emerges from Minquan Lane, another wave of disturbance ripples through the crowd like a light breeze. The men turn their heads and show their teeth in a dazed grin. In front of them appears a group of pretty girls whose clothes are as colorful as butterflies. They are girls from the teahouse. They have come out to watch the performances on the street. It is said that two-thirds of the village's income is spent on them, which is why the village re-

---

3. Qi Ye and Ba Ye are messengers from hell in traditional Chinese mythology, the equivalent of the Grim Reaper.

mains poverty-stricken. As if to prove the truth of this, a few of the young men now leave the crowd in high spirits.

The appearance of the girls during the daytime means it is time for the fishing vessels to return—the girls always come to the pier to welcome their "catch," and today is no exception.

Hearing that the vessels are returning, Sa Keluo's lion, which had been heading away from the harbor, now turns and advances toward the pier. Already, the sun has climbed high, the sky is as blue as the sea, and except for the distant horizon there is not a hint of cloud. The sun, like a hoary old man, peers down into this village by the sea. Beads of perspiration trickle down everyone's face, but everyone also seems to have forgotten it is lunch time.

Sa Keluo advances toward the harbor. The brilliant, colorful lion's head, when lifted high in the air, shines and sparkles like a jewel-laden crown. The two black trouser legs under the lion's head are streaked with even darker stripes of sweat.

"Don't you want to rest for a while?" one of the men running alongside him asks.

"No," comes the answer from beneath the lion's head.

As they approach the pier, they hear the deafening throb of motors as the fishing vessels enter the harbor in formation like a naval squadron on the open sea. The crew of each vessel must have caught sight of the lion because all of them are perched on their fishing ladders like clusters of resting sea gulls. Within a few seconds, the serene surface of the water is in turmoil, as if attacked by a tornado. Vessels bump, ladders rear like horses, alarms and whistles blow, bamboo paddles wave in the air, and the water churns. The first fisherman jumps barefoot onto the pier. As he ties the thick rope he holds in his hands to a stone stump, he shouts: "Mackerel— Moonfish! Mackerel—Moonfish!" Hearing his call, the spectators on the shore cheer in unison and rush toward him like a swarm of bees. For the past three months, they have only been able to gather the rancid meat of bonito from the sea. By now, they are sick of it. This fish, because of a poisonous gland on its back, doesn't get a good price in the fish market. The appearance of mackerel and moonfish means the end of bonito season, and the village can start making money again.

The boats celebrate their harvest with firecrackers. All of their small triangular flags are raised. The young fishermen, clad in red vests, sit high up on the ladders watching the nimble dance of the lion down by the waterside. They shout, laugh and cheer, urging it to dance faster, to prance higher. The lion is obedient, its head bobbing like an engine. Then, the lion suddenly stops. Facing a vessel, it slowly retreats three steps. Studying the vessel, it retreats three more steps. Then, fast as a canon ball, it rushes forward and leaps onto the deck. Elevated above the water and the land, Sa Keluo continues rolling the lion's head as all the people on the boats and on the shore cheer.

Baskets of silvery fish are unloaded from each hold. The mackerel are like silver bottles, while the moonfish are like silver purses. The laborers carry baskets on each end of thick bamboo poles balanced on their shoulders. First they take the fish to the fish market, then load them onto trucks for transport to Taipei, and via the southbound railway even to Taizhong, Tainan and Gaoxiong.

Sa Keluo jumps down from the prow of the boat, landing in the midst of the procession of laborers. Stepping ahead, he cuts in front of them and, dancing in time to the beating drum like the band leader of a marching column, leads the way to the fish market.

The fish market is behind the harbor at the foot of the mountain. It is a huge warehouse-like building, coated with pitch and as empty as a garage. Seen from afar, its huge dark opening looks like a mysterious cave. The interior is dark and drafty; fluorescent lights shine even during the daytime. Hanging on the walls are knives, saws, picks and axes. Anyone walking near the market can smell the sickening odor of blood, while the water near the foot of the mountain is perpetually tinted red.

The procession approaching the market place proceeds with difficulty. The thick bamboo poles on their shoulders and the heavy baskets hanging on the poles make the laborers' knees bend like arches, their backs hunch like harps. In the sunlight, their flushed, perspiring faces are twisted. They can hardly endure the sun over-head and the heavy burden on their shoulders.

To reach the fish market, they first must walk up the gentle in-cline of a path that is even more deserted than the other streets in the village. It is a dusty path, twisting like a snake, covered with loose soil that is easily whipped up by the wind even when no one is walking on it. Now, with the procession marching past, yellow dust swirls like smoke about their heads.

Sa Keluo dances with each step he takes, panting heavily as he climbs along. Gradually the smell of blood fills his nostrils. At the same time, he smells the sea breeze, which is less humid and more refreshing than it was on the land below. This is a silent, barren area, where even trees refuse to grow. The only vegetation is the ferns growing by the path, drowsy in the noonday sun and coated with layers of dust. But with a slight turn of the head, the scale-like roofs of the village can be seen spread out below and, to the right, there is a glimpse of the shimmering sea beneath the sunlight. Suddenly, Sa Keluo lurches out of step. He stops. He bends over, but straightens again with an effort and continues dancing onward, his body lean-ing slightly to one side.

The procession suddenly stops, like a fleet of armored cars that has halted on the battlefield because the one in the lead has broken down. Stopping in the midday sun, their shoulders burdened with fish baskets, the laborers look at each other. Above them, two vul-tures from the mountaintop circle, lured by the strong smell of fish or drawn by the commotion below. Then a slight disturbance begins at the front of the procession and gradually spreads to the back. The laborers cast off their burdens and rush forward with other specta-tors for a look.

Sa Keluo lies in the middle of the path like a bundle of clothing. His head is still hidden by the lion's head, but his shoulders are ex-posed. One arm is curled under the lion's head, encircling a pool of blood. He lies like a lion shot by a hunter.

Sa Keluo dies on the way to the hospital. The doctor says he died of exhaustion, of heart failure. So Sa Keluo lies on the black leather couch in the hospital, his face and body covered by a white sheet, silently, as if in deep slumber. The festivities of the day—in spite of the accident that has cast a dark shadow over the hearts of the villagers, in spite of what they will never forget as a good, unfortunate, boy dying during his lion dance on this day—are still festivities, and the celebrations continue as usual.

Written in September 1962
Translated by Ch'en Chu-yun

Line of Fate

June 1963. Like "The Day of the Sea-Goddess," this story also is a meditation on the theme of fate. Specifically, it describes a boy's effort to change his fate after having his fortune told by a classmate. Wang has confessed that in his twenties he felt that humans stood helpless before fate, and the protagonist—an only child with an artistic streak—certainly shares some characteristics with the author.

The wind sprang up yesterday at dusk and continued straight through without a break until after ten this morning. The sky, typical of windy weather, is a dull, heavy gray, as if heaven itself has been blown full of gray fog. Such a dry and windy winter.

At an elementary school in the suburbs of Taipei, the wind bends the trees that serve as a wind break bordering the playground. They are cold-resistant eucalyptus, but even they, battered by the strong winter gusts, look weary and worn. The bell has just rung for the end of the period. In the playground a few students, struggling against the wind, head toward the toilets. The rest of the children huddle in the classrooms with the doors and windows shut fast for warmth. The school grounds look like an empty barracks.

Students in the Grade Five E classroom crowd around the center of the room, each child's attention directed toward the heart of the circle, and each utterly engrossed.

"Then how long do you think he can live?"

"About forty more years."

"That's short. How about me? How much longer can I live?"

"Not even forty years."

The fortune-teller sits in the middle of the ring, looking extremely bored and condescending. He is an ugly child. His eyes roll constantly, his nose is small and sharp, his lips dried and cracked, his ears round and thin. He's so repulsive that each part of his body seems to give off a bad smell. He has never been a good student—he lies frequently, cheats during exams, and is not above petty theft. But at this moment, he is transformed. Not only does he bask in the respect of his peers, his features transfigured by the light of authority, but he also feels superior to everyone around him. He has just acquired the skill of palm-reading, learned in a public park from an old fortune-teller. His classmates believe in him and instantly become devoted clients. So, in no time at all, he has been transformed into the new class hero.

"Who's next? But, mind you, I can't tell too many. My master warned me that telling too many fortunes will reduce my own luck. If what I say is good, don't rejoice. If bad, don't be annoyed. If your heart's not in it, it won't work. Who's next? Hurry up! This is your only chance to get your fortune told free. Where else can you find such a good deal? In the park they'll charge you at least ten yuan each. Give me your hand! Closer! Closer!"

He begins to divine another classmate's fortune. A burst of laughter breaks out among the vigorous, boisterous children—the child is being told he will have three wives. To young boys, this is hilarious.

Near the front of the classroom, sitting by the window with the upper half of his body in the light, the lower half in shadow, one child watches the proceedings from a distance. He is the only one still separate from the group but his isolation is not due to any lack of curiosity, or because he wants to snub the ugly fortune-teller. On the contrary, he is paying the utmost attention, his eyes as round as saucers. On his face, two conflicting emotions—whether to join his classmates or to remain seated—are obvious.

Just then, one of the children leaves the group, but only to climb higher onto a desk to get a better view of the proceedings. Chancing to glance back, he spies the outsider.

"Hey, here's another one!" he says, drawing the attention of the others to the fact.

"Hey, Gao Xiaoming, hurry! You're the only one left," his classmates yell.

Seeing he has been discovered, the child squirms uneasily.

"No, no, I don't want to," he says.

"Oh yes, yes you have to," they counter. They seem more interested in his fortune than he is himself. Two of the stronger ones already are on their way toward him. They grab at him, fight with him, tickle him, all in an effort to drag him over to the group. Finally, he yields to majority pressure.

Gao Xiaoming is a thin child, small for his age, but with a pair of shining, dark eyes. He is one of those strange, mysterious, yet exceptionally gifted children. Despite his fragile body, his soul burns with passion and a fierce will. His physical weakness forces him to take four or five sick leaves each semester. What upsets him, though, is not getting sick but having to miss class. During each bout of sickness, he fights with the doctor and struggles against his parents, and always succeeds in staggering back to school before his fever has completely subsided. Nor do the classes he misses affect his grades, which always are among the top three in the class. But he rarely makes the top two—mostly, he ranks third. This semester he was elected class vice-president, just three votes behind the president. This, again, probably could be attributed to his bad health. As was the custom, he went up to the front of the room amid applause and politely shook the president's hand in congratulations. Then he calmly walked back. Once seated, his lips pressed tight, the tears he could no longer suppress began to fall. Now as he goes toward the fortune-teller his slight body trembles a bit, betraying his inner excitement.

"More! I could die from all this work!" the prophet remarks. "Why didn't you come earlier? Hurry up!"

Gao Xiaoming sits down, looking at his classmate, and then bravely extends his left hand.

The spectators are silent as the ugly child lowers his head to study the lines on the palm before him.

"Well?" someone asks impatiently.

"One wife," the fortune-teller announces. Everyone laughs.

Gao Xiaoming blushes: "Quit joking! I only want to know the important things. I don't care how many wives or how many children. Just tell me what I will be. What's my career? Will I succeed?"

"That I can't tell. My master didn't teach me how."

Gao Xiaoming is deeply disappointed. He's always wanted to be a poet, but now the fortune-teller can't even assure him of that.

"I can tell whether you're going to be rich, though," the ugly one offers.

"Will he?" someone asks.

"Nope."

"Ah!" Sighs of sympathy from his classmates.

But Gao Xiaoming feels no disappointment. They have no idea how low an opinion he has of money. Poets are born to be destitute and, since he faces the same fate, this proves he will become a poet after all. Secretly, he feels elated.

"Okay. I know everything now," Gao Xiaoming says, withdrawing his hand.

"No, you don't," one of his classmates shouts. "You haven't heard the most important thing yet. How long will you live?"

"Right, we don't know yet whether he'll live to a ripe old age or die young!" another joins in. Everyone agrees.

"Give me your hand again," the fortune-teller orders.

"No. There's no need, because I don't want to know," Gao Xiaoming replies, covering his left hand with his right as if hiding a scar.

"What a queer one you are. Why don't you want to know? Why don't you when you can? Look, Gao Xiaoming, even if you don't want to know, your lifespan is still written right on your palm. Since it's clearly written, why not know it?"

Gao Xiaoming hesitates.

Then he extends his left hand once more.

A short moment later Gao Xiaoming asks the question himself: "What does it say?"

"If what I say is good, don't rejoice. If bad, don't be annoyed. Agreed?"

"Agreed. What does it say?"

"I hate to tell you, but you will only live to be thirty."

Gao Xiaoming stares at him.

"Only live to be thirty!" he repeats the fortune-teller's words, then asks, "How can you tell?"

"This line here. Only thirty. Look, this is called 'the life line' or 'the earth line.' From here to here, ten years; here to here, twenty years; from here to here, thirty years—that's all. Your line ends here; you will only live to be thirty."

Gao Xiaoming looks down at his palm. No doubt about it, the downward curve stops midway.

"Just take a look at mine. Look! It's twice as long as yours. Forty, fifty, sixty, seventy, eighty, ha ha! I can live to be eighty!" the ugly fortune-teller brags.

"Then you're an old turtle!" another child interrupts, sticking out the middle finger of one hand. Everyone laughs again, uproariously, because to them a turtle is not only an object of ridicule but also has obscene connotations.

Just then the wind carries the ringing clamor of the bell, signaling the beginning of the next period. The circle breaks up as each child jumps back into his seat.

Gao Xiaoming sits in the quiet classroom, his heart drenched in gloom. In the tiny garden outside, the petals of a rose bush are being stripped by the wind. At last he knows his lifespan: he has only seventeen more years to live. What a short life, not even half as long as other people's, how unfair! With such a short time limit, how will he be able to achieve his dreams? He planned to write thirty books— poetry, novels, plays, an autobiography. He already knew what he would write about: one book about his mother, one about himself, another about being sick, another about a hero, from his birth to death. His intention was to write very slowly, to polish the tip of his pen gradually. He didn't want instant fame. Once he had written an immature work, he would burn it. He'd always planned to publish his first book after he turned thirty—thirty and he'll already be dead. A surge of impotent fury wells up in him as he thinks of his hopes and unfulfilled potential ravaged so cruelly. Enraged and doomed, he sits quietly in the hushed classroom.

Outside the window, the branches of the eucalyptus trees sway gently, like two brooms sweeping away dust and sand. The glass panes rattle in the wind like the warbling of a brook. Gao Xiaoming pays no attention as his teacher explains a fraction problem. He keeps opening his left palm and gazing at it blankly.

His classmates have forgotten the game already. After class, they completely ignore the boy they worshipped as an idol just an hour ago. Once again, he is just a delinquent. But Gao Xiaoming cannot dismiss the fortune-telling. He is the only one who can't forget his fate.

During lunch, Gao Xiaoming finds his food tasteless, even his favorite, a mandarin orange, which his mother specially put in his book bag. The bitter taste on his tongue won't yield to the sweet flavor of the orange—tongue and orange remain separate, like a divorced couple. He feels ill.

After lunch a cold sweat breaks out all over his body because he thinks of the dreaded figure of Death, thinks of it being so close, as if it stands right in front of him, close enough to touch.

During the afternoon music class, they discover Gao Xiaoming is absent. He is the best singer in the class, but his sunny voice is missing on this occasion. No one knows where he is.

At the edge of the playground, by the bamboo fence, there is a weed-covered air-raid shelter. Gao Xiaoming sits curled up in the cool gloom. He has been here for more than two hours and has pondered many things he never even considered before—death above all. For example, he sees a tiny white flower at his feet. The life of a flower can be as short as three or five days, just one spring at the longest. Later, watching a sparrow searching for food at the mouth of the shelter, he reminds himself that sparrows don't live long either. He has never seen one with the feathers on its head turned gray. Where will he go after death? Is there a place to go? There must be—even at night there is someplace for us to walk. But what if there is no such place? What if death means total annihilation? Like this flower—it will mingle with the earth after fading, leaving no trace. And that sparrow, if it happens to fall from the sky and mingles with the earth, it will leave no trace. What if people die, leaving no trace? Isn't this possible?

If this really is the end, such a hopeless end—he begins to feel uncomfortable in the dim shelter—then he wants to know why people are here on earth. The only way to resist this tragic end, and compensate for it, is to live longer. But he will live only half of a normal person's lifetime. He gets up off the ground and leaves the cave.

He does not return to the classroom. Leaving his book bag behind, he escapes the school grounds on his own by climbing over a low wall. This is against the rules and getting caught would result in a serious demerit. He thinks about this before making his move, but since he has only seventeen more years to live anyway, he lifts himself up and over the wall. There's no need to care about anything now.

He spends the afternoon wandering among the rice paddies. Then he makes his way into town. People on the street see a grade school student, pale, without his book bag, walking slowly in the wind and gazing often at his left palm. At nightfall, his heart becomes heavier. Forgetting completely about his book bag, he does not return to school but heads straight home.

At school, his abandoned book bag, like the clothes discarded on the river bank by a would-be suicide, causes a stir of alarm. His home-room teacher, Miss Wang, tiny, young, bespectacled, a recent teachers' college graduate, dares not take the book bag to the school principal, nor can she bring herself to take it to the boy's parents. She just cannot face up to the responsibility. So she stays behind in the empty classroom, clutching the bag to her breast and praying fervently that Gao Xiaoming will appear.

Instead, Gao Xiaoming appears before his parents. His complexion is strange, as if he feels a pain somewhere in his body. At dinner he sits gazing at his plate without making a move. His mother is worried.

"What's the matter now, anything wrong?" she asks, a shadow over her heart. He must be back in that hateful cycle of illnesses again. She feels his forehead for signs of fever. Usually the trouble begins with that symptom. But this time there is no high temperature and his skin feels icy. She is both relieved and worried.

"How come you're so cold? Anything wrong?"

"Nothing."

"Don't eat if you don't feel like it," she says after a while. "Maybe it's your stomach again. Go to bed earlier tonight."

His mother is a pale, consumptive woman but, owing to courage and a strong will, she has managed to lead a life no different from that of the average woman. She has married, had a child, does her housework and edits a women's magazine as well.

"Xiaoming, where's your book bag?" It is after dinner and she has suddenly discovered it is missing.

"I left it at school."

"Why?'

Gao Xiaoming thinks for a moment, then answers reluctantly: "The student on duty locked it in the room after the flag-lowering ceremony. I couldn't get it."

He is not unhappy because he lied. He is just unhappy he had to lie at this particular moment.

"You really are in a muddle. Don't forget to take it with you next time, okay?"

"Yes."

"Mama," he says after a while.

"Hmm?"

"How old was Grandpa when he died?"

His mother looks at him in astonishment.

"He was fifty. Why?"

"Nothing, just curious. What about Grandma?"

"Fifty-one."

He still feels unsatisfied. He turns to his father, who is puffing away on his pipe while reading the newspapers.

"Papa, how old was Grandfather when he died?"

His father is no less surprised than his mother was. He waits a moment before removing his pipe, knocks it against the arm-rest of his chair, and replies: "Why are you asking? He died young, but re-member, Xiaoming, he made many contributions."

The child hasn't the heart to go on to ask about his paternal grandmother. He knows enough. He hoped to gather some com-forting evidence to refute the fortune-teller's words, to amass proof of his ancestors' longevity. Or perhaps he hoped to find that all his ancestors were short-lived, which actually would prove the proph-ecy to be true. The more afraid we are of something, the closer we approach it, the longer we gaze at it.

"Papa, Mama, I'm afraid I can't live much longer," he says.

"What's this?" his father asks.

"I know for sure. One of my classmates said so. He said my life line—this one here—is too short. He said I can only live to be thirty. Thirty, you hear me, thirty. I'm not going to be able to see the last half of my life. Also, Papa, Mama, you'll see your child pass away before you do."

"What nonsense! Impossible! You must stop this nonsense, Xiao-ming. That friend of yours was only joking. How can you take his words seriously? He was only kidding."

"No, he wasn't. He told everybody's fortune."

"Look, Xiaoming, if it wasn't joking, it was superstition, pure and simple. Did he have any scientific proof? If such a thing were true," his father patiently explains, "then life would not be such a mystery to so many people. We would have to rewrite history, be-cause all those heroes would no longer be worthy of admiration, and all the thieves and robbers would be innocent. History would turn out to be a solo performance by just one character—Fate. In other words, you seem to believe your friend can rewrite history." There is a sarcastic tone in his father's voice.

Gao Xiaoming's expression doesn't lighten up at all.

"Besides, take a look at my palm." His father extends his own left hand. "Come over here and take a look at my so-called life line. It isn't long either, only halfway. But I'm still living, am I not?"

He is thirty-nine.

"Hurry up, go to bed, and forget your funny ideas," he orders.

"The child thinks too much and worries too much. Otherwise, he would be much stronger."

His mother has not said a word. She looks at him with anxious eyes.

Gao Xiaoming stands up to obey his father. His expression is no brighter. He stops in the bathroom on his way to the bedroom.

His parents are silent. His father picks up his pipe, stuffs it with tobacco and lights it with a match. He resumes his smoking, but ignores the newspaper on his knees. After a while he suddenly seems to remember why he is smoking and picks up the papers again. His mother begins crocheting her tablecloth.

"Xiaoming," she calls in the direction of the bathroom, "you're not taking a bath, are you? There's no hot water tonight. Are you taking your bath in cold water? Don't, or you'll get sick. Just wash your hands and feet. You'd better hurry off to bed. You couldn't eat a thing at dinner."

The parents fall silent again.

A shout comes from the bathroom a moment later.

"Papa! Hurry!"

"What's the matter?"

"Hurry! I'm hurt!"

"What!"

His father jumps up and rushes to the bathroom entrance. But the door is locked.

"Open up! Xiaoming!"

The child does not answer. Sounds of whimpering come from within.

"Open up! What's the matter?" His father beats furiously against the door, but it does not open. He feels the horror of impending disaster. With all his strength he shakes, batters, pounds and kicks at the door. Finally, without knowing how, he opens it.

"Xiaoming!" he exclaims.

The boy is sitting on the tile floor, his right hand holding his left. Blood is gushing from his wrist. Beside him on the floor is a safety razor.

The child faints as his father lifts him up.

"Zhujun! Hurry! Get a taxi!" his father yells.

Gao Xiaoming has used a razor to extend his life line. He has slit his palm from the center where the line ended all the way to his wrist.

The hospital in the middle of the night.

"His wound is almost two inches long, from the middle of the palm all the way to the wrist. Quite deep, too. He missed the main artery by a fraction of an inch. It was a close call all right. Had he carved a tiny bit further, that would've finished him. Now? Now he's out of danger. Heavy loss of blood, though. He'll have to rest at least a week. There's no danger now, I can assure you." The young doctor sits facing the parents. He is a famous surgeon, a kindly man who understands the parents' anguish. He repeats this assurance, "No danger now, please don't worry." He watches the couple before him, a trace of unusual attention in his gaze. He is genuinely interested in people and, after working for hours, tries his hand at writing short stories now and then. "What I find strange," he continues, "is that from the look of the incision, it doesn't seem to be an accident. Can you perhaps tell me exactly what happened?" His tone is matter-of-fact.

The parents exchange glances.

"We truly don't know," they reply in unison, appearing to be entirely honest and sincere.

"Oh!" The doctor is very disappointed, but then he smiles comfortingly. "Don't worry, there's no danger now. He'll be all right in a week."

"If he's lost so much blood, won't he need a transfusion? If he does, I can give him my blood. We're both type A," the mother says, her face pale.

"No need for a transfusion." The doctor answers, getting up. "It's late now. You'd better get some rest. Come and see him again tomorrow, and don't worry. He'll be all right."

The doctor sits alone in the room. He shakes his head, smiling inscrutably. Don't think you can pull the wool over my eyes, he tells himself. You can't fool me! I didn't want to embarrass them, that's all. Times really have changed, he thinks. What only grown-ups were capable of in the past, now children are, too . . . He shakes his head. He goes so far as to speculate that it must have been on account of love. The little guy must have fallen for some girl, and his parents were opposed—he thinks of their solemn faces, their mutual glance. He's sure of it. Sitting alone in the quiet room, the doctor half shuts his eyes, shakes his head again and smiles contentedly. He is unaware that the wind outside has stopped.

A week later—Gao Xiaoming has taken his longest sick leave ever—the child is discharged from the hospital. On his left palm is an indelible scar, and it looks exactly like a life line.

Translated by Ch'en Chu-yun

Cold Front

June 1963. Written at the same time as "Line of Fate," this story shares the same interest in child psychology. It is about a boy in his early teens wrestling with feelings of guilt that arise during his sexual awakening. This is the last story Wang wrote before going to the United States to study.

I

He was only a child, a child not yet thirteen, and he looked even younger than that. Just now he had squeezed out of the dark interior of the bus but he was not going to walk along the railway tracks with his friends, those little ruffians who jostled and giggled the whole way home. He stayed by himself, loitering under the mercury lamps of the bus station. Those little ruffians would compete with each other to see who could walk the longest along one of the rails, just like Tom Sawyer. They would walk until the sky was so dark they could not see the rails clearly, with just the last glimmering, dusky glow still burning at the farthest edge of the plain. And then— the climax of this competition each day—while they were running across a steel trestle bridge, they would suddenly hear the mournful hoot of a steam whistle. That would elicit excited, nervous shrieks as they ran faster toward the far side. Once there, they all would hop off the earthen embankment like a flock of small birds. Then, watching the lamp-lit windows of the train cars flash by like the frames of a movie and gazing at the coal smoke gushing up like a fiery river, they would raise their arms to holler and throw a volley of stones. There was not a one of them who did not enjoy this game: those lamp-lit train cars, the sparks and thick smoke, the thrill of leaping down the embankment just in time—they wanted to act it all out every day after school. But, since last Tuesday, he had not joined them.

He waited for a while as the train cars rushed past on the express tracks, then dashed across when there was a break. It was March, early spring, and although there was a feeling of spring in the early afternoon, a cold front was approaching. The air cut to the bone as soon as night fell but he did not feel the cold, even though he only wore a blue school jacket made of coarse cloth and a pair of Boy Scout shorts that left his spindly legs exposed. He had forgotten the cold because he was entranced by another mysterious game. That game was waiting for him at the corner of a large street. He did not yet know that this game might be even more dangerous than jumping from in front of a train.

As he walked dumbly along the left side of the street, he wound his book bag around his wrist and then, with his palm up, slung it over his thin shoulder. Three times he stopped the bicycles riding toward him, forcing the riders to dismount and him to leap out of the way in fright. Gradually he approached the corner. It was already very dark, just like a winter night. In no time, the night had turned so dark that it was impenetrable, like a blindfold. So he opened his round, black eyes wide to look into the distance, toward the glass shop on the corner. The lamps in the glass shop shone brighter than the other shops, perhaps because of all the reflections cast by the glass and mirrors. The game was there, under that circle of dazzling, eye-catching brilliance. He hesitated for a moment, then walked over. As he passed by the shop, he quickly looked at a mirror hanging on the wall inside. His small heart pounded and his ears flushed crimson. It was a color picture of the profile of a naked woman. Her flesh was as pure and white as jade and her blonde hair hung down like a lion's mane. She held her head on an angle and had narrowed her eyes while she brazenly held her hands to her breasts. One of her thighs was drawn toward her abdomen. The boy stood outside the door gazing at her. In order to see her, he had painfully endured a whole day at school. Actually, he only had to close his eyes any time he wanted and he could remember every part of her naked body. But, even more, he wanted to see her with his own eyes every day, to see her standing before him, just as if she were his first lover.

He walked past the glass shop and hid in the unlit darkness beside the street. Not long afterward he stepped out from the darkness again and passed by the glass shop once more.

Had he not been afraid of raising the suspicions of the workers in the shop, he would have walked back and forth over and over again.

The boy walked home along this main street, a route that was twice as long as walking along the railway.

By the time the boy reached home it was already past dinnertime. He hung his head and walked into the living room where the dinner table was set. His father and mother had been waiting for him there for a long time.

"Oh, you little devil, what time is it? You came the long way home! Where did you have to go?" his mother asked him.

The boy just stood there and did not reply.

"You little devil, you little devil! You really worry your mother to death!" His fat mother patted her chest as she spoke. "The only thing I worry about is that you might be hit by a car on the road. I don't worry about anything else. Where did you go, anyway, that you took so long finding your way home? Don't try to lie to me. I know where you went. I know what you did. Tell me and let's see if you're ashamed of yourself"—the boy looked up and into his mother's eyes—"the teacher kept you in detention again, right?"

Because he had been coming home late for the last few days and could not find any more appropriate excuse, he always said that the teacher had kept him in detention.

"You don't follow the rules, you don't follow the rules. Fine, it serves you right. The teacher is right to punish you, I'm glad!" She clapped her chubby little hands to show her approval.

"All right, all right. Don't just stand there looking stunned. Come and eat," his father said. His father had a build that was the complete opposite of his mother's. He was as skinny as a stork. While he was waiting for the boy, he had helped himself to lots of cold beans from the table.

"Eat! You've explained it simply enough! The food's all cold and the fire's gone out. Who can eat now? If we have to burn another lump of coal it'll cost us another one yuan-fifty. How can we afford to cook? You go and try to cook!"

He reached out his chopsticks and ate another mouthful of cold beans, as if to say the food still had to be eaten. Yet this mother, the same as all mothers, could achieve all manner of miracles—in the blink of an eye the table was filled with piping-hot food. Not only were the dishes attractive and smelled delicious, they made her "Daddy" extremely satisfied.

The boy was the first to finish eating.

The boy sat in the bedroom that belonged to him. Ever since his brother had gone to the United States, he'd had his "own" bedroom. In the middle was a large window that opened to the south. Outside was the family's little papaya orchard. Because it was night, he could not see the rows of papayas, only blackness.

The boy sat beside his desk. He turned out the room light and turned on the desk lamp. After a moment, he got down from the chair, took out his book bag, put it on his lap and took out a large-format exercise book. Reseating himself at the desk, he picked up a pencil, spread out the exercise book and started to work in it diligently. He sprawled over the book with his head down. Later he knelt on the chair and continued to work without a break. His mother came in once and told him to go and wash his feet. His reply shocked her. It wasn't that he said, "I won't," it was the way he angrily shouted at her.

It wasn't until eleven-thirty, when the boy's eyes were blurred with fatigue, that he finally closed the exercise book. In it he had drawn countless pictures of the naked woman in the glass shop from memory, as well as countless pictures of naked women as he imagined them. The imagined ones were more vulgar than the ones drawn from memory.

The boy's bed wasn't a bed or a tatami mat, it was a closet. Probably only he could have thought of such an unorthodox way of sleeping. Before his brother left home, he had slept with his father and mother (something he was very embarrassed to let anyone else know about). This made him feel ashamed, and he was always angry with his parents. He also wet the bed often, and this made him even angrier with himself. Now that he had his own closet, it was the source of great happiness.

He turned off the desk lamp and stood in the severe cold darkness. Taking off his clothes, he prepared to get into bed. Suddenly he stopped at the entrance to the closet, his heart filled with remorse.

The remorse he felt was extreme, for what he had done that day, for going by the glass shop again, for the exercise book filled with human figures. He was filled with that "it's too late, there's no way to repair the damage, you can't go back even if you want to" kind of remorse. Moreover, he felt frightened. He had studied "Health and Physiology," and therefore knew that he should be afraid—it had already happened four nights in a row.

Thinking of the preventative method outlined in the "Health and Physiology" book, he pushed the soft, warm, red silk-covered quilt that covered his bed outside the closet where it fell in a pile on the floor. On this cold night he was going to cover himself with only a light, gosling-yellow wool blanket. He hoped it would not happen again tonight. Accompanied by the movements of his lips in silent prayer, and the violent chattering of his teeth in the cold, he entered dreamland.

In the middle of the night, the cold front blew into Taipei.

The cold air that invaded his blanket awakened him. He turned on his side and wrapped the blanket around himself more tightly. Then he was jolted from his semi-consciousness. He discovered that it had happened again. He sat up anxiously, opened his eyes and looked straight into the blackness before him. Shortly afterward, his frail little arms began to tremble slowly, and then they started to convulse up and down like a pair of little rabbits. But it was not like the shivering brought on by the cold. It was more violent than shivering. He was weeping.

After his agitation subsided, he began to assemble the remnants of his shattered self-confidence. He resolved to attempt resistance one more time, resistance that would brook no failure. This time he finally realized the vileness of that picture. For the first time, he saw her—that naked woman's—tyranny, cruelty and danger. He realized that he had to use all of his strength and all of his determination if he was to subdue her.

Standing before such an opponent, as daunting as a mountain, he tried to determine whether his thin, weak arms possessed the strength to grapple with her. Then he became aware that there were a number of things he had to do first.

His initial thought was that he would not go past the glass shop again. Never again would he see that picture, and he would forget her face or, more correctly, her body.

He would burn his exercise book.

Every five minutes he superstitiously and silently recited the prayer: "Hail Mary, full of Grace."[1] (He had learned that from a foreign nun in an English class.)

As if encouraging some other sinner, he continued, while lying there in his closet, to tell himself how he must do these three things, until a rooster in the distance announced the coming of dawn.

II

He did not wake up until the sun was shining through his window. It was a bright, clear morning but the air was terribly cold and there were no birds singing outside.

---

1. This is in English in the original, as are the subsequent references to this prayer.

"Hail Mary." The first thing he remembered was to pray.

Then he hopped resolutely down from the closet—because he had become aware of the need to avoid his bed. In the past, before getting up, he always had spent twenty or thirty minutes lying there thinking about making love to all kinds of women.

After he dressed, he walked up to the window and gazed at the frigid sunshine outside. Unconsciously, he began to pray in a low voice:

"Hail Mary, Jesus Christ, please grant me one pure day. Please grant me a day as clear as today. Please grant me a day that is just as cold. I don't mind if you freeze me, starve me, or punish me, just help me to leave that picture. I don't want to be defeated again. I don't want to walk in her dark night anymore. Oh, Hail Mary, Jesus Christ."

He prayed earnestly, and when he had finished, he repeated the prayer again. He felt less helpless, felt much better and believed the picture would not dare violate him again.

Then he got busy with the second thing: burning his exercise book.

He took the book into the kitchen, but there was no fire burning in the stove. He had forgotten that his mother never cooked breakfast. Closing the kitchen door, he searched for matches in the charcoal basket. Just then, the sound of footsteps came from outside the door. It was his father. From their sound, the footsteps were clearly headed in the direction of the toilet.

"Little Hua, what are you doing in there?" he asked from the other side of the door.

"I . . . I'm looking for a piece of paper . . . I lost a piece of paper. Probably Ma took it to start the fire with."

"Don't blame Ma," his father pushed open the door.

Fortunately, he had already thrown the exercise book into the charcoal basket.

"You still haven't gone to school! Off you go quickly, you can look when you get back!" Having spoken to him, his father continued on his way to the toilet.

He took the exercise book back to his room. He had to keep it for now. He would take care of it in the evening.

It was already almost seven-thirty. He hurriedly went about organizing his book bag and didn't bother to brush his teeth or wash his face.

His class schedule was stuck on the back of the closet door so he crawled back into the closet carrying his book bag and books. He placed his books in the bag based on the timetable: English, Physics, Geography, History, "Class," Phys. Ed., and "Curricular." "Physics" meant Physics and Chemistry, "Class" meant class assembly, and "Curricular" meant extracurricular activities—this hour was in fact used for extra lessons with extra fees. He discovered that the exercise book was still lying to one side of his book bag. He didn't want to take it along. However, on second thought, if by some chance his mother discovered it. . . So he put it in the bag.

He grabbed his little boat-shaped cap and slapped it on his head. Shouldering his book bag, he ran off quickly to find his mother. She was in front of the vanity mirror combing her hair and yawning. There was a towel around her shoulders. This was the time when she gave him his meal money. She gave him both the breakfast amount and the lunch amount. She reached into a drawer and pulled out a ten-yuan note. He took the money, then stuck out a hand and asked for another yuan. She moved her face closer to the mirror and inspected her right eye. He asked for half a yuan. She inspected her left eye. He ran out.

Walking through the fields, he filled his lungs with the cold air. It was like the air-conditioned air in the movie theatre. In the morning, he always walked to the bus station along the railway tracks. Since he could see if a train was coming from a long way off, the trip in the morning did not count as a dangerous game.

The undulating, tender green fields stretched all the way to the river. A layer of white mist rose above them like sprouting grass. He felt an unfamiliar, mysterious kind of joy. He liked the morning, hated the dusk. A new discovery drew his interest. White vapor, exactly like cigarette smoke, was streaming from his nostrils. Opening his mouth wide and round, he exhaled. An even purer white, warm vapor streamed out. He closed his lips and walked onward, storing up even more heat. Then he opened his mouth and blew out lightly, "I'm smoking a cigarette, the kind Dad is trying to quit." He blew a little harder. "I'm smoking a pipe now." He blew even harder, "I'm smoking a cigar." Then he blew harder still and a plume of thick, dense white steam emerged, just like what came out of the train's smoke stack.

The rails were still covered with crystalline dewdrops. He climbed on, extended his arms straight out from his sides and began to walk. He walked like a tightrope walker until he arrived at the steel trestle bridge. The trestle bridge was about thirty meters long and there were no railings on the sides. Beneath the bridge flowed a swift, roaring, white-water river. In the evening, they knew the time the train came and always crossed the bridge the moment before it arrived. As they dashed forward, churning their little legs, they were afraid of stepping into the gaps between the wooden ties or that they might have miscalculated the time and the train would come too soon. If that happened—they had no idea how to respond. Their only choice would be either to grab onto the front of the train or to jump into the rollicking stream. That was the point of the game. Each time was a challenge, a risk, and every day the excitement was different than the day before. He looked behind him. He did not see any train or hear the sound of wheels. He looked ahead. No column of smoke from a train in the dense forest in the distance. So he quickly ran across the bridge. By the time he got to the other side he was panting because he was out of breath. He did not know there were no trains on that line in the early morning.

Just as he arrived at the bus station, a bus drove away in a cloud of black smoke, leaving him there by himself. He stood gazing into the distance, but he was not looking toward where a bus should be arriving. Not here yet. Again, not here today. Perhaps already gone. She was a student from the First Girls' High School. She was in the second year of junior high like him—he had seen that from the badge on her collar. She was probably the best looking girl in the entire world, so he thought. Usually, when he saw her in the bus station, he was struck dumb. Once he was lined up behind her. That made him cough, swallow and scratch himself. Finally, he changed his position and stood at the end of the line. But she was as cold toward him as a chilled cucumber. It seemed she never so much as shot him a sideways glance. One evening during the summer this year, he ran into her on Nanchang Street. That really was a miraculous and exciting encounter. He had not seen her since the summer vacation began, and now he saw her holding her mother's arm (how he knew it was her mother he could not really say), walking by in front of him. He felt that she had become even more beautiful. Her black hair was combed into a ducktail and a sparkling barrette clasped the hair in the middle of her head. As she walked past, she looked at him. His heart filled immediately with warmth and gratitude, but to his dismay, she turned her face away quickly and fixed her eyes on the cosmetics arrayed on the display table. It was as though he was not worth a second look—ah, to be sacrificed to feminine arrogance at such an early age. Even more dispiriting, he noticed she had grown taller than he was. That night he felt his whole world was falling apart.

But she remained the only young love in his heart. Moreover, she had never been included in his fantasies before rising from bed, even though before he went to sleep he asked her to come and plant a goodnight kiss on his lips and tell him she loved him so much.

She had not come and the bus had already arrived. The exceptionally vicious bus conductress rushed him onto the bus and chased all of his love away without a trace.

The bus drove straight to the front of his school where he jumped off. As he approached the gate, he felt a pang of unease because it was quiet and there was nobody in front of the gate. As well, all of the windows in the main building were silent, not filled with the faces of students looking out and hooting and shouting as usual. They were already in class! This frightened him to death. Just then, three little prefects carrying a large paper folder came up to him. They wanted to take down his name. He immediately picked up his feet and fled, running through the school gate and past the exercise field toward the building at the rear. When they realized he was fleeing, they gave chase, shouting; "Hey, hey, stop! What class are you in? Student number!" They did not run as fast as him— he had already run up the stairs to his classroom. Standing outside the door, he took off his hat and shouted loudly: "Reporting!" The whole class turned toward him and laughed uproariously.

"Come in, come in, come in!"[2] the English teacher said.

His face scarlet, he hunched over with his tongue stuck out in embarrassment as he hurriedly sank into his seat. "That was close," he thought, sitting down, "I was almost captured by the prefects."

English was his favorite subject. Then, in order, there was art, music and literature. Physics and chemistry, geometry and natural science were names he hated to hear. His English grades were not too bad and he often had the honor of being called up to the blackboard to write for everyone.

From behind him, one of the most despicable creeps in the world was pushing him. He ignored the first three pushes before he turned his head.

"Don't push me, okay, Big Tooth!"

"You were late!" Big Tooth conveyed this news to him, exposing his two big yellow front teeth in an ugly leer.

"What's it to you. If you touch me again I'll tell the teacher!"

"You were late, lazy bones," Big Tooth said, continuing to giggle.

The only way to deal with people like that was to ignore them. He was not worth worrying about.

But Big Tooth was quite willing to make people who already hated him hate him even more, so he gave him a few more shoves. The boy leaned his chair forward to avoid him.

The English teacher put his book back on the desk, and then closed it. Placing both hands on the book, he cleared his throat and said:

"All right, everyone put their books into their drawers. Do it

---

2. The final "come in" is in English in the original.

gently! Be quiet,[3] there are people in class next door. It is Thursday again today, Thursday,[4] our weekly quiz day."

Oh my God, he had forgotten that today was Thursday! He forgot last night! He turned his head and looked at everyone. All of them had remembered and appeared to be very well prepared. Slowly he placed the book in his drawer. He was the last one.

The English teacher turned around, took a piece of chalk and wrote the questions on the blackboard.

He could not spell any of the vocabulary words, fill in any of the blanks, or make out any of the grammatical mistakes. He felt more ashamed than ever. He always had the highest marks in English. He really wished he had just skipped the class, never come at all. What agitated him even more was the likelihood that when the English teacher saw his "zero," he would be so astonished that his attitude toward him would change from praise to coolness—this was what depressed him the very, very most. Then the bell rang to end class. The examination papers were passed, one by one, from the back to the front. Big Tooth took the opportunity to poke him once more as he passed him the pile of exam papers. Big Tooth had answered all of the questions. The boy stealthily slid his own paper underneath Big Tooth's and, feeling mortified beyond belief, gave the papers to the teacher.

But then something happened that made him feel even more bewildered. In the physics and chemistry class that came next, there was another exam. He had forgotten about that last night as well. Of the four questions, he could not figure out even one of them, so again he hid his paper under Big Tooth's when he handed it in.

If there was one course that he did not like, but at the same time did not especially hate, a course that he could take or leave, it was geography. The geography teacher possibly was a mute. They had never heard him speak a single sentence. From the beginning of class until the end he simply wrote on the board in his small, stan-

3. English in the original.
4. English in the original.

dard handwriting, although not all of the students copied what he wrote. For example, the boy worked together with Little Black next to him, taking notes in alternate classes. When there was an exam, they studied together. Today was Little Black's turn, so he had nothing to do.

Behind him, Big Tooth was not copying either. He took out an English book and started to read English in a strange voice. Big Tooth was not a party to the co-operative effort with Little Black, but whenever there was an exam he shamelessly asked to borrow their notes anyway. Just try to borrow our notes for this month's exam; we'll let you get a big goose egg, Big Tooth, he thought cruelly, momentarily feeling very much at ease.

He had nothing to do so he took his pen and started to doodle in the margin of his book. He drew a tree, then he drew a house, and then a person. Soon he drew a woman. With a few more strokes she became a naked woman. This immediately reminded him of the exercise book in his book bag. He had a powerful, irrepressible urge to take it out. But at that same moment he remembered his prayer. He realized that—never mind five minutes—he had already forgotten to say his prayer for two or three hours. So he punished himself and said "Hail Mary, full of Grace" twenty times over. Still, in the end he took out the exercise book. He browsed through the pages of lurid human figures. Of all the things in his life, he thought that drawing these figures gave him the most pleasure. It was like being in the midst of a passionate love affair—he would walk through fire for it. This made him feel that he really did lack the resolve to keep his vows from the previous night—as a result, he no longer heard the ever vaguer and less distinct sound of his exhortations.

He remained immersed in the drawings right up until the bell rang to end class. He did not leave the classroom afterward but just waited in his seat. As soon as the next class started, he once again sank into their midst.

He concentrated on drawing. That creep behind him started to shove him again. A black cloud of hatred rose in his gut. This time, Big Tooth would reap heavy punishment. He had done it before— flicked his fountain pen in front of Big Tooth's chest and sprayed ink on him, ruining his uniform so he could never wear it again. This time, he was going to go for Big Tooth's face. He gripped his pen and turned around. Big Tooth could see the cruel expression on his face and sensed the sinister, vile intentions behind it. Big Tooth appeared confused and uncomprehending, but alert.

"I wasn't trying to hurt you . . . the teacher was looking at you . . ." That was all Big Tooth managed to get out.

He felt a large hand pressing down on his head, so he lowered the hand holding the pen and turned around. The teacher was standing in front of him.

"You haven't been listening the whole time. I noticed that a long time ago. What are you drawing?" the skinny history teacher asked, taking away his exercise book.

Strange to say, having lost his exercise book he felt a sensation of awakening, followed by a feeling of happiness. But he also felt afraid, as if he were suffering from a fever with alternating hot and cold flashes. Great waves of joy washed over him followed by huge swells of fear that drowned him. Break free! He thought: I'll never again be hurt by the guilt I impose upon myself, and that bewitching body won't curl around me like a poisonous snake. But when he remembered that the teacher was going to look at the pictures he had drawn, he broke out in a cold sweat. He thought of Big Tooth, whose goodwill had been met with such scorn. Fortunately, he hadn't flicked his fountain pen at him—fortunately, the history teacher's big hand had saved him from that.

"Go right now and ask him for it," Big Tooth told him after class. "If he gives it to the home room teacher, you're dead."

He nodded his head blankly, thinking that Big Tooth wasn't as repugnant as he used to be.

The teacher quickly walked out of the classroom. The boy followed him into the hallway. The teacher, though, had already reached the stairwell and almost flew down the stairs. The boy flew down after him, leaping two steps at a time.

"What is it?" The teacher stopped. Knowingly, he asked: "You want your thing back, right?"

"Yes."

"Yes! First let me have a look at what you were drawing."

"Notes, it was my Chinese literature notes."

The teacher opened the exercise book. Fortunately, the first page was in fact Chinese literature notes. The teacher closed the notebook, but did not give it back to him.

"Next time you're in class, are you going to pay attention to the lecture or not?"

"I'll pay attention."

"Next time you're in history class, are you going to copy out homework from other classes?"

"No."

"If you do, then next time I really will confiscate it and won't give it back."

"I won't. I won't copy things again."

"Take it then, I'll forgive you this time, but next time you're in for it." He felt no joy at getting it back, though. Instead, contrary to all reason, he never wanted to see that exercise book again. It's true. Now he had to find some way to get rid of it, destroy it, but being at school made that a technical impossibility.

How could he forsake it, the child wondered. It was impossible. By just after two in the afternoon, he was once again immersed in drawing.

He no longer cared whether the teacher caught him or not. He was like someone driven mad by love, caring about nothing else. He would accept only one thing: there would be no conflict, no struggle. Giving himself over to it absolutely and completely was a joy. He came to appreciate the joy of drug addicts, chronic gamblers and suicides.

He knew that the next class was physical education. This was a ray of light, a breath of the ocean's dawn breeze blowing through the blackness of the maritime night. Temporarily, he could get away from drawing. He looked up from his pictures and heard the clear, transcendent sound of the class bell. He hoped this bell carried with it news of his salvation. Up until now, he had been a weakling who feared physical education, but now he saw it as an ark in which he could escape the flood. The classroom burst into pandemonium. Before putting their youthful, animal life force into action, the boys anticipated the excitement of unleashing their physical energy. They shouted out loud and sang songs, roared with laugher as they took off their outer clothes. Then they raced each other out of the classroom and charged off toward the chilly, windy exercise field.

When he bolted out of the classroom, the class president grabbed him.

"Huang Guohua, today it's your turn to keep an eye on the classroom.

"What?"

"It's your turn to watch."

"Like hell!" he protested. "Who says it's my turn?"

"Fuck you," the class president said. "What's wrong with it being your turn? Look you guys, he's such a little shirker. It's his turn to watch the classroom and he still says it's not his turn!"

Even though the boys were keen on physical education, most people probably have a natural inclination to idleness, and they were even more inclined to it than most.

So the boys all started to laugh at him, calling him a "stupid ass." But he continued to stand there expressionless, steadfastly claiming that it was not his turn. Then he said he would rather trade with someone.

"So let me do it then, you little yellow dog,⁵ I'll give you my algebra exercises to copy," one boy said, pointing at himself.

"Let me do it, little yellow dog," another pointed at himself. "I'll treat you to a popsicle tomorrow." They all loved eating winter popsicles.

"Let me do it, little yellow dog," Big Tooth squeezed in and called out to him.

"You can do it," he said to Big Tooth, and then ran off after the other boys toward the broad, flat exercise field.

The physical education teacher led them in a run around the

5. The boy's surname, Huang, means "yellow."

field. They ran around it four times in a row, and then he made them keep on running. The idea was to make them warm up. They gradually ran slower and slower and the pack got more and more spread out as they all puffed and gasped for breath. The teacher ordered them to stop and walk around the grass field on their own until their breathing returned to normal. Huang Guohua felt warm all over, he felt very good. Under his sweater, his skin discharged streams of sweat that made the sweater feel prickly, as if someone with a silver needle was pricking a pattern on his body. He felt so fine, finer than he had ever felt before.

Then the phys-ed teacher took five or six balls out of a bamboo basket. He gave each of them a slap as he walked over, making it appear that he was surrounded by the balls. He wanted them to play soccer. The boys were extremely happy and immediately divided into six teams that began to play on the field. They played wildly, energetically contesting the ball. Many were injured, but they immediately rejoined the battlefield. Huang Guohua was as wild and intoxicated as the rest of them. He loved the cold, and he loved charging around burning hot, as though on fire. He loved chasing that soccer ball, which never stopped bouncing and leaping. When he stopped occasionally and raised his head to gaze off beyond the field, he could see Datun Mountain standing erect in the distance. Its round peak appeared so tall, so blue, so clear. On most days, the top of the mountain was shrouded in gray mist, but the cold front had brought clear skies and swept the mist away, exposing the pristine, azure peak. Just then, a silver airplane was descending slow and level in front of the mountain. This was when all the scenery was at its very best. He was sorry when the phys-ed class ended. He had hoped it would continue right until dark.

He was grateful to God for giving him this opportunity, an opportunity to exercise. Perhaps, he thought, there is only one thing in the world—exercise—that can lift people from the morass of lust.

But the gloomy darkness of dusk was falling. The self-confidence born of his happiness and sense of accomplishment gradually cooled. As he left the cold, thin mist of the exercise field, he thought that what he had just accomplished counted for nothing. He still felt mired in hopelessness. The gathering dusk only seemed to increase the weight and pressure of the burden weighing on him.

He also did not know why he was so forgetful. It had been such a long, tedious day, but this was the first time he had thought of the night. He had a feeling that, once again, it was going to subject him to a slow death, because during that long, tedious day he had done nothing to protect himself against it. Like a child who loves to skip class, he had forgotten everything in the midst of his enjoyment. Not until the darkness came did he remember that his father was waiting at home and the severe punishment he would receive after the school contacted him. Thinking back over the day from the morning up to then, he was astonished and annoyed to realize that of the three things he had promised himself, he had already abandoned two. And now the daytime had passed—the time to make amends had passed. He had sacrificed those two promises for nothing, and the exercise book was still in his book bag. It seemed like several centuries since he had last recited Hail Mary, full of Grace. He did not want to try to make up for that now. He was already weary of his self-deceiving consolations, and he knew that the Holy Mary would not answer his pleas again. So, no more "Hail Mary," no more "full of Grace." He wanted to find someone else to pray to, but he could not, and he was ashamed to go looking. So he prayed no more. He believed he would never pray again. No matter what, there was still the third promise, he thought. Unconsciously, he grew excited again. There was still the promise about not passing in front of the glass shop again. No matter what, no matter what, he would hold fast to that promise. He repeated over and over to himself that he would hold fast to it, and so this promise became his prayer.

His courage returned as he listened to the sound of dusk's gradually approaching footsteps. In fact, his courage grew stronger than he imagined it could. Oh, this time he would overcome the glass shop, he was going to defeat this dark night. It could never come again. There would only be a fifth night, never a sixth night. He decided then and there that after school he would go back along the railway tracks with his fellow students.

But after the flag lowering ceremony, the class president waylaid him again.

"Huang Guohua," the class president said, "Today it's your turn to sweep up, and this time there isn't anyone willing to take your place."

Once again he would be going home by himself.

III

The white mist of dusk had already begun to rise lightly over the surface of the roads. The cars and trucks with their round, wide-open, orange eyes, emitted waves of thunderous noise as they emerged, one after another, from the foggy realms. The streetlamps proposed a toast to the descending darkness, but the darkness abruptly engulfed everything, so that nothing was visible except the beautiful little eyes of countless lamps. The eyes of heaven, though, remained invisible because of the dense mist.

Alone, Huang Guohua made his way toward home. In the nocturnal darkness, it was just like he was lost in the black labyrinth of his dreams. The bus windows were closed tight and there were no lights on inside. He was wedged in among the crowd of adults wrapped in their overcoats. Rocking to and fro with the body of the bus as it passed around corners, and moving with the monotonous rhythm of its stops and starts, he almost fell asleep. Arriving at his stop, he squeezed out through the cracks between people, enduring curses from two adults, one of whom secretly gave his ear a twist, virtually wrenching it off. With great effort he managed to extricate himself and get off the bus to stand in the cold but refreshing street. The mercury lamps cast his small shadow on the ground.

The boy hesitated. He did not know which route to choose. Naturally, he absolutely would never go by the glass shop again, but the idea of going along the railway gave him pause too, because he was not familiar with the train schedule and did not know whether he would be able to get across the bridge or not. He was afraid he would be caught in the middle of the bridge with the train coming behind him, or coming from the other direction. Thinking of the danger of the railway, he could not prevent his small body from trembling in the cold air. But, in the end, the boy, his heart still pounding, pushed out his small chest and bravely strode out into the darkness toward the railway.

Compared with the darkness of the night, the plain the railway extended over had an even deeper, darker complexion as it lay sleeping under the night sky. There was not a single spark of lamp-light on that black plain, no sound either. There was no train, no chirping of insects. Not even the mournful sound of the wind blowing through the grass. Standing on the boundary of this black, silent world, his insignificant self held it in awe and veneration. He drummed up his courage and stepped onto the wooden ties, then began to race along them. He could not see the ties beneath his feet clearly, so from time to time he stumbled over them, or stepped on the sharp stones of the track bed. All he heard were the chaotic sounds of his footsteps and the heavy gasping from his mouth. Soon he heard the sound of flowing water. He had already run to the bridge.

The bridge stretched straight as an arrow toward the opposite bank with a phosphorescent glow like two hungry steel skeletons. He climbed onto the bridge. He walked slowly, careful to step on the wooden ties and mindful of the gaps between them. He was in a hurry, like someone in a nightmare, but he could not go fast. His steps were jittery. It felt as though he had already walked for a long time, but when he stopped and took a look back to check, he had come only a quarter of the way. He put his head down and contin-ued to walk. Suddenly he heard the sound of a steam whistle. He thought it was his imagination, so he stopped to listen carefully. The country all around was as still as ever. He continued walking. By then, he had walked to the middle of the bridge, so he was halfway from where he had started, and halfway to the end. The steam whis-tle sounded again and this time he knew it was not his imagination. However, he could not make out if it was coming from behind or in front of him. He got ready to bolt, but which direction should he run? He suppressed the sound of the wild pounding in his chest and concentrated all his attention in order to grasp the direction. The whistle sounded again—it seemed to be behind him. At the same time, he began to hear the accompanying sound of wheels. The train suddenly appeared. A powerful lamp on the front of the train beamed straight to where he was standing. He raced forward at once, his feet leaping one gap after another. He knew the train had already mounted the bridge and he could hear the sound of the wheels getting louder while the lamplight became brighter and brighter. The boy was running for his life before this one-eyed monster—the train passed the middle of the bridge, passed over the last quarter of the bridge, arrived at the end of the bridge, then passed over the end of the bridge and continued to rush straight onward.

The boy was curled motionless at the bottom of the embankment. He heard the train roar past above his head like spring thunder. Then he heard it move into the distance like the thunder's rumbling echo. He had leapt straight down as soon as he reached the end of the bridge.

He curled up at the foot of the embankment and did not move for a long time, not until he could no longer hear the sound of the train. Then he sat up and started to wail. He sat there alone in the wilderness, sobbing loudly until he felt he had cried enough.

He picked up his book bag—its strap was broken. Using his hands and feet, he climbed up the earthen embankment. He noticed that his hands and knees were all scraped. After he walked a short distance, he found an irrigation ditch. Scooping water from the ditch, he washed the dirt from his wounds. He also washed the dirt from his face and his lips. As he washed he thought: "I have defeated you. This time I really have defeated you!" His excitement had not yet completely subsided, and he was still upset enough to feel like crying out loud—but just as he was beginning to whimper he burst out in arrogant laughter. "I can already do it, I can already cope with it. I know it won't be hard to deal with it next time and I'll be able to defeat it again. I'll definitely be able to defeat it completely," he thought.

IV

The night was very cold and very still. The cold front had come to the night like a goddess to the forest, easier to find than during the day. People inside their houses knew the cold front had intensified.

The boy was as silent as the cold front. He kept his mouth closed tight, as if clenching some precious object that would be lost as soon as he loosened his bite. Because of the exertions of the day, his face was pale, his eyes hollow. Under his mother's suspicious eyes, he finished eating his dinner. In order to avoid her gaze, he retreated to his own room.

He took out his exercise book. He put it on the desk. This time he did not want to draw in it, he wanted to destroy it.

Once he had heard a story about Indian monks who lived in a monastery in the mountains of India. They were different from other monks because they had covered the walls and ceilings of the monastery with drawings of naked women. Every picture portrayed the most obscene position possible. That way all the monks could see them and not avoid them even if they wanted to. This was a way of making them confront images of women. Only those among them who truly were not moved could be regarded as eminent monks who had gained enlightenment. He now remembered this story.

He opened his exercise book and looked directly at the bodies of the women he had drawn. He looked at one page after another in order to look at each and every picture. The entire time, he stared at them with derision and was not seduced by them anymore. As he turned to the last page, his purity was still intact. This test made him understand that he had made another step forward.

Now he wanted to burn it.

He rolled the exercise book into a tube and walked toward the kitchen with it. His mother was bathing and his father was smoking—he knew they would not come into the kitchen. He closed the kitchen door and latched it. Then he moved the kettle sitting on top of the stove. Using a poker, he stirred up the ashes in the stove. The flames sprang up joyfully—now there was a strong, hot fire burning in the stove. He threw the exercise book in. The flames danced as if performing some wild, festive ritual. The radiance from the fire was so bright it seemed like the entire room was in flames. Countless weird black shadows cavorted across the walls. Then the flames gradually sank lower until they had shrunk back to the ashes and all that remained were a few firefly-like embers. The kitchen returned to darkness and the air immediately turned cold. He stood up from the bamboo stool beside the stove, opened the door and left the kitchen to return to his bedroom.

Sleep was about to come over him. He sat by his desk and waited for it.

The heavy curtain of night had fallen, and the sounds of the universe floated quietly back to the surface of the earth. All the people had entered sleep. His father and mother, too, had returned to their room to sleep.

"Tonight there won't be any more mistakes," he thought, "tonight that mistake will have no chance to appear. Ah, you tried to frame me, to entrap me, by making me fall into the pit of sleep and warmth. You listen to me! Tonight you won't have any opportunities. You won't get me because I won't let you come in." The night was very quiet, there were only a few dogs barking their cold barks in the distance. The wall clock in the living room struck eleven. It was time to go to bed. He got up from his chair.

First, he turned off the desk lamp. The room sank into deep darkness. Then he took off his clothes, one item after the other, until in the end he wore no underclothes at all, including no underpants. That skinny, pale body of his trembled with cold. It trembled like a long, thin, pale candle flame. He sat naked on the chair, spread out his arms and closed his eyes. He could feel the cruel cold front crawling onto his naked body and attacking him from all directions, viciously swirling around and inundating him. Every nerve in his body could feel the violent lashing of the cold front's fingers. He wanted to remain just that way until daybreak.

Soon his cheeks began to burn and his head began to split with pain. In his ears, he could make out a strange new, yet appealing music. At first he really liked it, imagining that he was hearing the sound of sap rising in the papaya trees in the cold night outside the window. But later he realized it wasn't, it was not the sound of sap rising. His head was so painful now that he could no longer lift it. Some time after that he coughed violently. It felt as though a fire was burning in his throat and his whole body was engulfed in flames. By then it was the middle of the night and the first few calls of the morning rooster could be heard. Because of the cold, the crowing was especially intense.

Translated by Terence Russell

Flaw

January 1964. After completing his two-year military service in 1963, Wang won a scholarship and entered the master's program in creative writing at the University of Iowa. "Flaw" is the first story he wrote in the United States. It represents the maturing of his writing style and is one of his rare, romantically sentimental stories. Stylistic features that would appear in his novels, such as the innovative use of characters, neologisms and unusual syntax, can be found on many pages. The setting is post-war Taipei in the 1950s and 1960s and some readers re-gard it as an elegy for old Taipei before its modernization.

I must have been eleven that year, because I had just passed the entrance exam and enrolled in the junior-high program at Normal College. At that time, we were still living on Tongan Street, our earliest home in Taipei, and had not yet moved to Tonghua Street. Later we moved again to Lianyun Street. I've always felt that the earlier the home, the better it seems to have been. Every time we moved, it was to a less attractive place. Perhaps it is just nostalgia for childhood, so strongly linked to the earliest years, that gives rise to this sort of illusion.

Tongan Street was a quiet little alley with fewer than a hundred families along its entire length. Slightly curved in the middle, the street stretched all the way to the great gray river at the end. From the vantage point of the river bank, few pedestrians were visible on the street which, with its gray-white body and meandering path, was virtually a small river itself. Such was the tranquil picture when I was eleven. Later, when small cars were allowed to pass along the street, the atmosphere of quiet seclusion was lost altogether. My present reminiscences hearken back to the era before cars arrived.

In any event, at that time on Tongan Street, cats could be seen strolling lazily along the tops of the low walls from one house to the next. The whole landscape was filled with glistening green foliage and delicately fragrant odors from the profusion of flowers and plants growing in the front yards behind those low walls: thyme, azalea, cotton rose, oleander and broomtop. Flowers especially took to Tongan Street. They bloomed in the spring and again in the fall. Most unforgettable, though, were the evenings on that tiny street, when silent street lamps illuminated the darkness of the road. Night seemed even quieter than day. The little grocery stores, unlike their counterparts on the busy streets, closed at half-past nine. Midnight began at half-past nine. Night enjoyed its deepest and longest sleep on this street. Light breezes rustled the oleander leaves while distant stars twinkled in the sky, and after a few hours, night passed and day broke. In the early morning mist, the owners of the small grocery stores, again unlike their counterparts on the busy streets, began removing the shutters from their shops.

In spring that year, a young seamstress opened a shop at the end of the street near the river. It was a time when Taipei, still untouched by affluence, was just beginning to prosper, and a number of three-storey buildings could be seen cropping up here and there. Ever since the previous winter, we children had been keenly watching the construction of this kind of building on the vacant lot opposite our houses. We felt excitement mingled with sadness, excited because, as children, all new experiences captivated us—new sights, new sounds, new objects, new undertakings—and sad because we were losing our favorite playground for after-school ball games. The building was completed in the spring, and the young woman moved in. It was divided into three units, and was three storeys tall. The woman and her family occupied the whole unit on the right side— the ground floor was the store, while the second and third floors served as family rooms. It was said she owned the entire building and we children naturally had assumed that she would occupy all the space herself, but it turned out she reserved only one unit for her own use and offered the others for rent. A week after they had been taken, she changed her mind and sold them off. The fact she was able to occupy only part of the building made us feel a little sorry for her.

I was a precocious child. I looked at least two years younger than my actual age but, like a typical undersized child, my intellectual development compensated for physical weakness by being two years beyond my chronological age. One day I discovered that I was in love with the young woman. This realization came to me during the spring vacation, right after the soft spring showers, in the blossom-filled month of April.

Being a sensitive and introverted child, I had an instinctive fear of glamorous and sophisticated women, and only took to those with kind faces (I still do, even now). The woman at the dressmaking shop was exactly the type I liked.

She was about thirty-five or so, and did not wear much make-up (this was very important). She wore neither rouge nor powder on her face and only a tiny trace of lipstick on her lips, which were often parted in a warm, white smile. Her eyes were not only beautiful but, even more important, glowed with gentle kindness. My love for her stemmed not only from approval of her looks, but was rooted in sincere admiration of the goodness of her character as well.

Love in a precocious child, like a heavy blossom atop a frail stem, is a burden too heavy to bear. Only then did I realize the consuming nature of love, how the joyous blazing flames of love burn the very fuel that makes the flames possible. I found it hard to believe that true happiness could be achieved by masochistically burning myself up. Although I had been in the world for a mere eleven short years, I had endured enough minor suffering to be able to devise a method for avoiding pain. This was: if you happened to form an emotional attachment to a certain object or a certain person, the best thing to do was to look immediately for some flaw that would enable you to withhold your affection and so lighten the burden. During the next few days, I often hid myself directly opposite her shop and scrutinized her with cold detachment in an effort to discover some ugliness in her. But the longer I watched, the more beautiful she seemed.

I realized then that love had so deeply embedded itself that there was no way of uprooting it. I would have to live with it.

It was already the last day of the spring vacation. I made up my mind to enjoy it to the full by playing outdoors for the whole day. Early in the morning, I went over to our new playground (which had been relocated to the vacant lot in front of the garbage heap beside the grocery store) to wait for the other children to show up. We started our ball game much earlier than usual that morning—it must have been before eight o'clock because our shrill cries woke an office worker living in one of the wooden buildings. Still clad in his pajamas, he opened the window and leaned out to yell at us. Our ball often hit the ragged old woman who kept a cigarette stand next to the garbage heap. She tried to chase us away with a broom but lacked the strength and energy, so she could only stand there brandishing her broom like a sentinel in front of her stand, hitting out at whoever ran near her. But all of us were careful to stay away. On top of it all, Ah Qiu's pet mongrel kept dashing madly among us. For some reason or other, it seemed to have picked me as its target, jumping on me repeatedly and making me fall several times. It was only when Ah Qiu's mother appeared and summoned him and his four brothers back to breakfast that we finally broke up the game and unwillingly dispersed. By then, the sun had splashed the entire street with gold. Thick greenery clustered over the tops of the plaster walls. Market-bound housewives were already holding summer parasols to ward off the sunlight—its rays had become so strong lately that the buds of the broomtop and oleander were bursting into flower before their time. I felt thirsty and made my way into Liu Xiaodong's yard to drink from their faucet. Water flowed over my face and neck, which I left for the sun to dry. As I passed the dressmaking shop, I saw the young woman standing in the doorway talking with another lady, now and then teasing the baby this woman held in her arms. I climbed up the incline at the end of Tongan Street, walked down the steps on the other side and headed for the river.

In the sunlight, the river was alive with undulating glitter, like a million thumbtacks rising and falling in rhythm. On the opposite bank, two ox-carts were crawling along the sandy beach. Standing under a freshly budding tree, I could smell the fragrance of the baked earth along the riverbank and feel the river breeze, which was still cool at that hour. As I walked away from the tree, I could not help raising my voice and started singing "Crossing the Sea in Summer." Keeping the beat with my hands, I went on singing all the way up the river. I walked into a bamboo grove, found a relatively flat patch of ground and lay down.

The river stretched in front of me, glimmering through the bamboo leaves. Behind me was a section of farmland as colorful as a Persian rug. The huge patches of green were rice paddies; the big blocks of rich dark brown were freshly plowed but unsowed earth; the slender strips of light green, like the thin glass squares used under microscopes, were bean tendrils, while the golden patches were rape blossoms, swaying in the spring breeze. The short dark figures of the farmers could be glimpsed working in the distance, and occasionally the faint odor of manure drifted in from the fields.

I lay quietly, thinking all sorts of whimsical things, but they all were happy thoughts as I let my imagination roam with the breeze-driven clouds in the sky. I turned over and, resting my chin on my arms, gazed at the river through the bamboo leaves. I thought of the young seamstress. There was no one in whom I could confide my love, only the river. Later, this river also was the place where I made painful efforts to learn how to swim. Today, looking back, you could say my childhood passed along that river bank. I often sneaked away from home, made my way alone to the river under the summer sun and, bracing myself against my fear of drowning, would try to teach myself the art of floating in the water. But I never did succeed. I finally gave up because I no longer had the courage to struggle.

Since the river could not respond to my confidences, I returned to my former position on my back and covered my face with a handkerchief.

I lay there until the sun had traveled directly overhead, then removed the handkerchief and sat up. Thinking that my mother would be waiting for me to come home for lunch, I stood up and headed home. All the farmers had disappeared from the fields. Probably they, too, had gone home to eat.

At home I saw our Taiwanese Oba-san.[1] She had not gone home yet and was still doing the ironing. As soon as she saw me, she asked: "Young Master, have you seen my Chunxiong?"

I replied that I hadn't.

"Weren't you playing with him outdoors?"

I said I wasn't.

"I can't think where he could've gone. I told him to come and help me mop the floors, but there hasn't been a trace of him all morning. My Chunxiong just can't compare with Young Master, Ma'am. Young Master is smart, and works hard—so young and already in junior high. He'll be in senior high next and, after that, a top official," she said, shaking out one of my father's shirts.

Our Oba-san often praised me like this, remarking that I would proceed to senior high school after finishing junior high. A college education after senior high was beyond her comprehension, so after that, I was to become a high official.

Mother answered her in broken Taiwanese: "It'll be the same with you. Chunxiong will also go to school, also earn money and support you."

"Thank you, Ma'am, thank you. But I was born to suffer, Ma'am. Chunxiong's father died early, leaving me alone to raise him. I have no other hope, only that Chunxiong will be like Young Master, work hard in school, study in junior high and afterward in senior high. No matter how hard I have to work, wash clothes all my life even, I want him to be educated."

"He won't disappoint you," my mother replied.

Oba-san only sighed.

That kind old woman. I still remember her broad tanned face, like a piece of dark bread, warm and glowing, the perfect blend of

---

1. Wang uses the Japanese term, a reflection of the 50-year Japanese occupation of Taiwan. The reference to her being "Taiwanese" means she is descended from early Chinese settlers and did not arrive in 1949 with the defeated Guomindang.

simple goodness and unpretentious love. Where she went, no one knows. As I grow older, gentle people like her are harder and harder to come by. They are not the sort of people who adapt easily to an increasingly complex society, I suppose. I also recall another minor detail about her, the result of the peculiar powers of childhood observation: I often noticed her bare feet, with ten stout toes fanning out, pattering along on the shiny floors of our house. Perhaps the reason I found this extraordinary was that we all wore slippers in the house and there were many pairs of spare slippers in the hallway reserved for guests. Oba-san probably never got used to this alien custom and so never wore any. I often wondered back then that, even if she had agreed to wear slippers like the rest of us, where would we have found a pair large enough to fit her?

That was the last day of the spring vacation. Another detail I remember was that I went out and bought a diary that afternoon. A certain fascination with the world around me, interest in my innermost thoughts, freshly sprouted love, and spring itself, urged me to imitate Liu Xiaotong's elder brother and keep a diary. All my thoughts for the day were faithfully recorded that evening in my diary's first entry.

After the spring vacation, love continued to plague me. It seemed to be urging me to take some action, to do something that would bring me closer to her, at least emotionally. I thought of taking something to her shop and asking her to mend it for me (a sorry means of courtship, I admit). But that shop of hers only took women's clothing. I could not think of anything else, so one day I finally took a Boy Scout jacket with a missing button to her shop.

Her shop was tastefully furnished. Pictures cut from Japanese fashion magazines adorned the walls, and a vase of bright red roses stood on a small table in one corner. Four girls were sitting in the room, talking and laughing among themselves as they pedaled on machines spread with pieces of brightly colored material.

"What do you want, little one?" a round-faced girl wearing a string of imitation pearls lifted her head and asked.

"I want a button sewn on," I said, turning to the seamstress, who stood at the table measuring a dress. "Can you do it?"

The woman took my jacket and said: "Ah Xiu, sew the button on for him." She handed the jacked to the round-faced girl, then turned and went on with her measuring.

I felt the sorrow of rejection.

"Which button is it?" the girl asked me.

I told her, with my eyes on the woman.

"How much?" I asked the woman.

"One yuan," replied the girl.

The woman did not seem to have heard my question, for she did not even lift her head. Grief sank roots into the depths of my heart. But after a while I saw the woman put on a pair of glasses, and curiosity took the place of sorrow. I found it strange that she wore glasses, it seemed the least probable thing in the world. I did not like the way she looked with glasses—she no longer looked like herself. Moreover, she was wearing them too low. They made her look old and gave her an owlish expression.

Suddenly aware that I had stood gazing in the shop much longer than necessary, I asked the round-faced girl: "Can I come back and get it later?"

"No, stay. It'll be ready in a minute."

I waited nervously in the shop for her to finish. I glanced again at the pictures of the Japanese women on the walls. They were all very pretty, with dazzling smiles, but strangely, they all had single-fold eyelids.[2] I looked again at the roses in the corner. They were still flaming red. Feeling that they seemed to be redder than roses usually were, I looked more closely and discovered they were plastic.

After a while, a boy came down the stairs, munching a piece of fruit. He was taller than I was, also in a Boy Scout uniform, and wore a pair of glasses. With a flash of insight, I realized this was her son. I had seen two smaller children with her but had never seen this one before. Like all newcomers to the neighborhood, he never came out to join our games. Completely disoriented, I, who was

2. Single-fold eyelids, with no crease visible in the upper eyelid, are generally considered less attractive than eyelids with a double-fold.

secretly in love with his mother, watched him go back upstairs carrying a thermos bottle.

After the button was replaced, I hurried out the door with the jacket. In the doorway I met our Oba-san coming in. Afraid that she would report me to my mother, for I had come to the shop without her knowledge, I slipped away as unobtrusively as I could.

Despite the fact that I had been received with cold indifference at her shop and had seen her son, who was much older than I was, my love did not change. The love of a child does not change easily. I still bestowed all the passion of my eleven years upon her.

Thus I loyally allowed my love to continue, without hope, without fulfillment, and without anyone else aware of it. This hopelessness, however, imbued my love with a trace of melancholy beauty. Actually, I could not tell whether this sense of futility was a source of sorrow or happiness. But I was sure of one thing: with this kind of love, I was happier than adults in one respect—I was spared any unnecessary anxiety. I did not have to worry whether one day my love would suddenly come to an end. As long as my admiration existed, my love existed. Looking back now, I would say I was quite happy then.

The trip I made to her shop, I recall, was the only time I undertook such a venture. I never found another opportunity. Besides, for some reason, I suddenly lost all courage and found myself deeply ashamed of the incident. Whenever I thought of myself going into her shop on the thin pretext of replacing a button, my shame would grow until the experience became a positive terror, causing me to sweat in anguish. Courage is a strange thing—the first plunge should never be credited as true courage until tested by subsequent attempts.

Although I was never in her shop again, I often was in front of it. There was a grocery store opposite her shop that sold all kinds of tidbits for children and where I frequently stood vigil. Munching on a cracker, I watched as she moved around in her shop. Sometimes I would see her husband, a man of thirty-something, riding a motorcycle and said to be working in a commercial bank. Strangely enough, I never felt a trace of jealousy toward this man. This showed,

I suppose, that I was still a long way from maturity. I did not seem to realize the full significance of the word "husband." I thought of him merely as another member of her household, like her brother, her uncle, or her brother-in-law. But if she talked with another man, for instance if she chatted momentarily with the barber next door, my jealous rage led me to visualize the barber lying on the ground with a dagger in his heart.

Thus the days slipped by, one after another, like the turning pages of my diary. Soon it was summer and the end of the school term approached. I began to worry about my grades. I was very weak in algebra, and was afraid I would not be able to pass the finals. My algebra teacher had already warned half-jokingly that he expected to see me again next semester. I shook with fear. Never in my life had I been forced to repeat a grade, and now the threat loomed large. Yet mingled with the anxiety was a sense of unbounded expectation, expectation for the freedom, the happiness, and the unlimited possibilities of the summer vacation. In the dark shadow of the finals, I sat for hours on end with the algebra textbook in front of me but, instead of studying, I often just gazed at it anxiously. I grew thin and pale.

Finally, the heavy, burdensome finals were over. All the students hurled themselves into the free skies of the summer vacation like birds escaping from cages. I was just one ecstatic soul among thousands. Many children, oppressed by the exams, had eagerly awaited the arrival of the summer vacation. While waiting, they believed it never would arrive, or that their joyous hopes would be snuffed out by the pain of suffering—oh, exams, oh, summer vacation!

That first morning of the vacation, I opened my eleven-year-old eyes to the riotous singing of birds and a world brilliant with sunshine. Exams were a thing of the past. No matter how badly I did on them, they were no longer on my mind. No child, perhaps, is able to worry about the past. Sitting up in bed, I could feel the truth: the summer vacation really had arrived. Certainty did not come from any indication on the calendar, but from a certain sound, a certain odor, a patch of sunlight, all distinctively characteristic. I heard the shrill buzz of the cicadas, saw the reflection of a basin of water shimmering on the ceiling, smelled the cool fragrance of mothballs as my mother took our winter clothing out of the trunks and laid it in the sun—and I knew this was it. Happiness was that child as he jumped out of bed.

Each year, with the awareness of summer came the reminder to sort out our fishing gear. We would rummage among kitchen coal bins and come out with the slender bamboo poles our mothers had put aside (and which we had painstakingly whittled ourselves), take them to the bathroom and, with great effort, try to clean them, thinking of the great catches in store this year, although for the most part we only were able to catch frogs.

I found my fishing pole that day as usual, and cleaned it up as before. But, holding it in my hands, all of a sudden I felt that it was much too primitive. It was my own handiwork, which I had once been so proud of, but now I could see its crudeness. I felt I needed a brand new fishing pole, a bona fide one, not a plain home-made one like this. I wanted one with a reel, a bell, one that was gracefully pliant, like a whip. I made up my mind to ask my father to buy me one. I had high hopes of getting it, because I had an indisputable reason: I was eleven.

I threw my fishing pole back into the coal bin.

I headed for the garbage dump to look for my friends. It had been two whole weeks since we had played our last ball game, all because of the final exams. Our mothers would not let us play.

I passed by the dressmaking shop, hoping to catch a glimpse of her, but today her shop was closed. She must be out with her family. I felt a little disheartened. I saw her every day, but the one day I did not was enough to make me feel empty.

My friends were already in the middle of the game. I hurriedly joined in and immediately became involved in the ferocious battle. We played happily until noon. The side I was on lost and they blamed me, while I blamed myself for joining the wrong side. But we all determined to fight valiantly again tomorrow and win. As I walked home, the dressmaking shop was still closed. Again I felt a sense of emptiness.

When I got home, my mother was complaining about the fact that Oba-san had failed to show up that morning to do the laundry, and that if she was too busy to come she should have sent Chunxiong over with a message. Then she turned on me and said I had disappeared all morning like a pigeon let out of its cage—not even my shadow could be found. She had wanted me to look for Oba-san but could not find me anywhere. I was cruising for certain trouble if I played like this every day, and I shouldn't spend all my time in ball games even though it *was* the summer vacation. Naturally, these words were the ones I least liked to hear.

After lunch I felt drowsy. The white-hot sunshine outside made it hard to keep my eyes open. In the room, a few flies were buzzing intermittently on the dining-room table. I couldn't help myself from dozing off for about ten minutes. Waking up, I gazed at the bright sunlight outside the window and the flies on the table in the room, and a familiar thought dawned upon me. How could I have forgotten? Summer vacations always turn out to be boring.

Just then Mrs. Liu, who lived next door, came over for her daily chat with my mother. With egg-roll-shaped hair curlers all over her head, she stepped into the doorway and asked: "Is your mother at home, little one?"

"I'm in the kitchen, Mrs. Liu," my mother called. "Find a seat and I'll be out in a minute." But Mrs. Liu had already traced the voice to the kitchen.

In a moment, they both emerged from there. My mother's hands were covered with soap suds. She found a piece of cloth and started wiping them.

"How come you're doing the wash yourself?" Mrs. Liu asked as she sat down.

"Oba-san didn't show up today. I thought I might as well."

"That's what I came to tell you," Mrs. Liu said, setting her curlers bobbing. "You know what's happened to Oba-san? She's lost all her money. Twenty thousand yuan in savings, and she lost it all. She's sick now."

"Oh? Is that so? I didn't know she had so much saved up," my mother said in surprise.

"All the money she'd earned by working day and night as a washer-woman, saved up bit by bit. She says she was saving for her son's education. Bad luck that she should lose it all. But lots of other people on our street have been hard hit, too. Mrs. Ye lost ten thousand—seems like she just put the money in a couple of days ago, and it was the money for the fuel coupons at her husband's office at that. Mrs. Wu lost three thousand. It's all that witch's fault, and now the whole family's skipped."

"Who're you talking about?"

"That woman in the dressmaking shop. You can't imagine how unscrupulous she was. One hundred and fifty thousand, gone just like that. Who'd believe she was capable of doing such a thing? Everyone saw that her business was good and trusted her, saw that she offered higher interest, of course, and never dreamed she would suddenly skip out like that. Sheer betrayal, that's what it is."

"Unbelievable," my mother said. "She seemed like such an honest person. Oh, poor Oba-san, what is she going to do . . . "

I did not stay to hear my mother finish. I ran out of the house and headed straight for the dressmaking shop.

The shop was still closed. A few women holding their arms in front of their chests were standing near the doorway chatting. I stood gazing at the shop as pieces of the nearby conversation drifted into my ears.

"They left in the middle of the night. No one knows where they are now."

"They could report her to the police, have her arrested."

"No use. All she has to do is declare herself bankrupt and she won't have a care in the world. Besides, now that she's got the money, the law can't touch her."

"It was all planned," another said. "You noticed she was in a hurry to sell most of this building as soon as she moved in."

"They say she sold that shop of hers last week, too."

A few maids were peering in through the windows on the right. I went over and looked in through a small pane of glass. The room was empty—all the sewing machines and the furniture were gone.

"Just imagine, she didn't even pay the girls their wages. How mean can you get?"

Hearing this, I suddenly felt my ears burn with anger.

Mrs. Liu had already left when I got home. Seeing me, Mother murmured: "Unbelievable, just unbelievable. People are getting worse and worse. More people get rich and more cheating goes on.

People are getting prosperous, but if their morals go bad, what's the use of all this prosperity? Luckily we aren't rich. Otherwise, who knows? We might have been duped, too."

Our family was not rich. My father was teaching in a high school then and, in Taiwan, a teacher was by no means well off. But was Oba-san well off? Why cheat her out of all her money? And those girls who had worked for nothing, why deprive them of their wages?

I took a book up to the rooftop that evening. I had decided to heed Mother and do a little studying. The sky above was a soft quiet blue. I sat on the reddish tiles and leaned my head against the railing.

I could see the dressmaking shop down across the street. The door was still closed. The chatting women had gone.

Thinking of the young woman, of her pretty yet gentle face, I found it hard to believe that she was a swindler. But she was a swindler. Every time I told myself the truth, my heart contracted in pain.

I still cherished my love for her. I wanted to keep that love. I closed my eyes and thought of her magnolia-like face—yet I was always reminded of her flaw. I saw the ugliness of that face, and the flower hung down and withered.

Dusk slowly enveloped Tongan Street. Wisps of pale smoke began to curl from the chimneys nearby. The scene in front of me turned misty, and I discovered that my eyes were filled with tears.

Oh, youth—perhaps my sadness then was due not only to a woman having disappointed me, but to the discovery that some aspect of life had deluded me, and had been deluding me for a long time. The sorrow and the anguish of the discovery disturbed me deeply.

From that day on, I understood a bit more. I learned that "flaws" are an integral part of life, and that more "flaws" were to come. From that day on, I forgot the beauty of that woman, although I never could forget the details of this incident. No wonder. That was my first love.

Translated by Ch'en Chu-yun

The Black Gown

March 1964. The second story Wang wrote in the United States is the darkest in the author's oeuvre. It describes a dinner party where a five-year-old girl is confronted by an attention-hungry intellectual. "The Black Gown" demonstrates the mature author's ability to control his language. Wang also employs rarely used forms of characters and creates new characters to convey special meanings. The setting is the former Taipei residence of Yu Guangzhong, a well-known Taiwan poet, and the prototype of the little girl is Yu's youngest daughter. Wang and Yu were old friends and Wang was a frequent visitor at the Yu home.

It was a September evening in Taipei. The calm skies reflected the end of the turbulent typhoon season and signaled the tranquility of the days to come. I was attending a banquet given by a friend of mine, a member of the literary set. The banquet was held to celebrate his son's one-month birthday. My friend had three older daughters, but there had never been a similar feast for them. It was only because the parents were exceptionally delighted at the birth of a son this time that a special celebration was called for. I arrived at my friend's house neither too early nor too late, just when all the guests were assembled in the living room exchanging pleasantries while waiting for the chef to complete his preparations.

The living room was tastefully decorated in the Japanese style, with delicate landscape patterns carved above the doorway. Cream-colored sofas lined the room. Next to it was a verandah with glass-paneled doors that had been slid to the side, allowing the room to open out into the garden. The guests, teacups in hand, were either sitting or standing, and because they were conversing leisurely among themselves, they could hear the droning of insects in the garden as well as watch the fireflies flitting back and forth.

There were many guests that evening, close to forty. I was acquainted with only a few, as most of them were relatives of the family. I lit a cigarette, joined some people I knew and leisurely exchanged remarks on the trifles of daily life. White-clad, tray-bearing waiters milled about us, as did the guests. The gentlemen frequently let out booms of laughter, while the ladies fluttered their fans lightly like so many dancing butterflies.

Just then I happened to notice among the guests a man wearing a black Chinese gown. He appeared to be quite busy, first talking with a group of people in one corner, then chatting with another cluster in a different spot. What aroused my interest was his black gown, for such outfits were by no means common in Taipei, just as bushy beards were not frequently seen. Naturally, there were some eccentric individuals fond of donning long gowns and sporting beards in the city, but only a very few. This man was comparatively young—he could not have been more than thirty, and was handsome, with a pair of black-rimmed glasses over a well-shaped nose. He also seemed to have a wide circle of acquaintances. I watched him greeting almost every guest in the room.

I had no idea who the bizarre character was, but just then I heard someone else hail him from across the room:

"Hi, Mr. Jin, it's been quite a while, where have you been lately?"

"Over at Zhongxin University. How are you, Mr. Lin?"

"Fine, fine," the man addressed as Mr. Lin replied. "Oh, by the way, I happened to come across another of your articles yesterday, the one on existentialism in *Politics Monthly*. Very profound indeed. Quite a lengthy discussion, too, I should say. Around thirty thousand words, wasn't it?"

"It was nothing, nothing at all, sir. I would appreciate your valuable comments."

It was only then that I realized who the young man was. He had emerged only recently as a figure of no small repute in academic circles. Within just three short years of graduating from the philosophy department of a certain college, he had managed to climb to the position of lecturer. The remarkable thing about him, though, was not his scholarly ability—indeed, that consisted of only a few thin volumes—but his adroitness in advancing himself. On account of his special relationship with the head of his department, he had been promoted to his present position after serving only one year as a teaching assistant. Recently he had managed to secure, via an educational organization, a scholarship to an American university and now enjoyed the unique privilege of going abroad next year without having to undergo a single test. The newspapers had made quite a fuss about all this and carried the news together with photos of him, although it was said that he had called on his reporter friends to make it into the headlines. His articles, as numerous as propaganda leaflets, appeared frequently, but were mostly plagiarized translations from works in foreign magazines. Yet society—so desperately anxious to discover a new genius—had eagerly crowned him as our authority on existentialism, the psychological novel, modern art, the works of T.S. Eliot . . . I had been hearing plenty about him for a long time, but this was my first glimpse of the man himself.

He joined another group of guests and must have heard something amusing, for he threw back his head and laughed. Then he casually placed his arm on the shoulder of another person, who was at least ten years his senior.

At that moment, our host came over to announce that dinner was ready and to escort us to our seats. The banquet was set in the two north-facing rooms with the dividing bamboo-and-paper door removed. There were three circular banquet tables covered with snow-white tablecloths and set with slender ivory chopsticks. Napkins curled like spring-rolls in the glasses, and each table had a chrysanthemum centerpiece. A screen decorated with floral and bird patterns stood behind the tables.

The guests were seated, and I settled myself at the table near the window. Just then, our host and the man in black approached the table, each politely deferring to the other to precede him. Our host pointed to another table:

"There's a seat over there, Mr. Jin, over that way please."

"There's one here too, Mr. Jin," a lady at our table volunteered.

"Fine, fine, this is fine. I'll take this one because there are more ladies here." He pointed to our table, chuckling cheerfully.

So it was that the man in the black gown joined our table.

It was only then that I noticed we were indeed outnumbered by the ladies. There were three elderly matrons, two married women, and one young lady who kept her composure as if she had not heard his words.

The man in black had barely settled in his seat before considerably enlivening the atmosphere at the table. Asked about his plans for his departure to the States, he replied gaily: "It's too early to say yet, much too early, but next July at the latest." His brows shifted rapidly as he spoke, giving his face a lively air. There was a black birthmark near the corner of his lips. His teeth were extraordinarily even and white. Again, he placed an arm on the shoulder of the gentleman sitting next to him.

A waitress came over to serve wine. The man in black glanced at her furtively before lighting a cigarette and inquired of each guest he did not know at the table: "Your name, sir?" He also asked the young lady: "Your name, Miss?"

Just then, all of the guests turned their heads as our hostess entered the room with her baby son in her arms, fresh from his nap. Behind her were her three daughters, dressed like tiny angels, holding hands and advancing shyly. Our hostess circled each table to allow the guests to admire the baby. Even though the dinner was being held in honor of the infant son, it was his five-year-old sister who attracted the most attention. Holding a furry white teddy bear in her arms, the little girl was an exceptionally pretty child. With her big, innocent, agate-like eyes, two shiny black braids and white dress, she seemed to have come straight out of a Christian religious painting. Everyone looked at her with admiring fascination.

The little girl and her older sisters approached our table with their mother. Everyone hastened to congratulate the hostess and admire the baby. Then, as the guests turned to play with the little girl, she shyly let go of her sisters' hands and hid behind her mother. A Mrs. Wu, who seemed to know the little girl well, bent down and picked her up. "Qiuqiu will sit with Auntie Wu. There's plenty of room here," Mrs. Wu said to our hostess, who smiled and left her young daughter at our table.

Qiuqiu sat between Mrs. Wu and the man in black. He had been beckoning to her all along, trying to attract her attention, and now he called her by name. Perhaps those who revel in the welcome of others also take pride in being liked by children. So the man in black picked up a piece of cold chicken from the dish of hors d'oeuvres and carefully placed it on Qiuqiu's plate.

Qiuqiu, however, typical of an attractive child, was inclined to be aloof and ignore the advances of other people. She chose to pay no attention to the man in black's repeated efforts and seemed to take only to Mrs. Wu, holding on to her dress and leaning against her. I noticed that the man in black was slightly disappointed. He kept quiet for a while, picked up his wine glass and took a drink. Then I saw vanity working on his face, vanity stirred up by his initial disappointment and fanned by his pride. Knocking his chopsticks against the edge of his bowl, he asked: "Listen, Qiuqiu, doesn't this sound nice?" But Qiuqiu still paid no attention. Her lashes were lowered as she watched the bear in her arms.

Mrs. Wu fed Qiuqiu some food, and then introduced her to each of the guests at the table. Mrs. Wu named each guest in turn for her to follow.

"This is Uncle Qin. Say hello to Uncle Qin."

"Uncle Qin," Qiuqiu repeated obediently.

"This is Auntie Gu."

"Auntie Ku."

"No, Auntie Gu."

"Auntie Gu."

"This is Grandma Wu."

"Grandma Wu."

"This is Grandpa Wu."

"Grandpa Wu."

"This is Uncle Jin."

Qiuqiu did not respond. She stared warily at the man who had been sitting beside her all along. Then fear came into her eyes. Her tiny mouth drooped and her head lowered.

"Who is this?" the man in black asked, pointing at his own nose.

"This is Uncle Jin," Mrs. Wu coaxed.

"This is Uncle Jin," the man in black repeated.

But Qiuqiu still refused to comply. She edged even further away from him by snuggling in Mrs. Wu's lap and whispered something in her ear.

"What did she say?" the man in black asked.

"Oh," Mrs. Wu smiled, "she's afraid of you. She said she doesn't like your black gown."

All the guests laughed.

"She hasn't learned to appreciate Chinese culture yet," the man in black said gravely. Then, as if to excuse himself, he continued: "She used to know me very well. I often brought her sweets, and she would greet me, and even want me to hold her. I don't know why, but she seems to have forgotten me today." After a pause, he added: "Actually, children remember and forget very quickly. All of you watch, it won't take three minutes before she will know me again. If you don't believe me, just watch.

"Look, Qiuqiu, can you tell me what this is? Would you like to have it as a gift?" The man in black removed his Rolex wristwatch.

Qiuqiu glared at him with distaste.

"Don't you want it? Come over here to Uncle Jin and this watch will be yours. I mean it, I'm not kidding you."

Qiuqiu remained immobile.

"And this, too." He undid the front of his black gown and took out his fountain pen, "I'll give you this, too."

"I don't want it," Qiuqiu pursed her lips and replied angrily. "My father has them, too. A lot more than you have."

Everyone chuckled approvingly.

The man in black, fastening his watch and slipping his pen back into his vest pocket, said: "Then you won't get a single thing."

"I don't want anything of yours. My teddy bear is better than anything you've got!" Qiuqiu retaliated.

We all laughed again. Mrs. Wu, in particular, doubled up with laughter. She bent over Qiuqiu, holding her tightly. The man in black also managed a forced grin.

"I give up. I give up. I can't beat her. She's young, but obstinate," the man in black said before lifting his cup again to take a long drink.

"Go away, I don't want you sitting next to me!" Qiuqiu suddenly shouted hysterically.

"Qiuqiu!" Mrs. Wu admonished.

"Go away! Auntie Wu, please make him go away. I don't like his black gown." Qiuqiu's face was contorted with impending tears. "Shh-shh, Qiuqiu," Mrs. Wu said, but her eyes were on the man in black.

"Mr. Jin, I think I'd better change places with you," a guest volunteered.

"There's no need," the man in black replied. "She'll get used to it."

"Go away! You go away!" Qiuqiu repeated.

The man in black was bent over his plate eating a piece of fried shrimp. He turned to her and pursed his lips: "Children should mind their manners, don't you know, and not annoy their elders."

"We will change places with you then," Mrs. Wu said to the guest who had made the offer and the person next to him.

Thus Qiuqiu ceased fretting, and the battle between the man and the little girl finally came to an end.

Huge platters of tempting delicacies appeared. There were shark fins the size of large combs, and pigeons as plump as rubber balls. The food served that evening was unforgettably delicious. Many of the guests voiced their approval and asked each other about the name of the restaurant that had produced such delicacies.

But the man in black ate very little. His plate contained only a small pile of bones. Yet alone and without a word, he had downed quite a number of drinks. The veins stood out conspicuously on his temples. I suddenly noticed while studying his profile from the angle where I sat that his face seemed extremely gaunt. Whether this was because his complexion suffered from the effects of his drinking, I could not say for sure.

Just then a waitress came with another dish, a steaming plate of meat balls coated with pearls of rice. She accidentally brushed against his hair while removing the empty plates. Fingering his hair, he raised his head and retorted sharply: "Be careful, you!"

He did not seem to relish the meat balls either. Instead, he picked up a toothpick and started picking his teeth.

Qiuqiu had been watching him surreptitiously. Probably because of the distance now between them, she felt more secure and began to study him. With every mouthful of soup, she stole a glance at him.

Their eyes met. The man in black lifted the corners of his mouth into a smile, a smile that was almost a sneer. Then the smile stopped halfway. He was thoughtful for a second, and then, to my astonishment, his eyes suddenly glared, his nostrils dilated and his lips twisted into a horrifying grimace.

Qiuqiu was stunned. He immediately relaxed his features into an ordinary smile and spoke with the guests nearby, acting as if nothing had happened. Qiuqiu edged closer to Mrs. Wu and lowered her head, not daring to take a second look.

After a brief conversation, the man in black turned again in Qiuqiu's direction. His eyes possessed a look of stealthy appraisal. Just then the frightened Qiuqiu happened to steal another glance at him, perhaps because she was scared and wanted to see whether the ghastly face was still there. The man in black immediately made a second face: the protruding eyeballs, dilated nostrils, and contorted nose and lips produced an effect even more hair-raising than the first.

Qiuqiu's face instantly went pale, her lips turned white. Her eyes, made even darker by terror, stared at him without moving. The man in black realized his success and a flush of excitement appeared on his face. Then he removed his glasses, lifted the bony shoulders encased in black, and for the third time, displayed his hideous face. In addition to the protuberant eyeballs, contorted nostrils and lips, two white rings circled his eyes and his tongue hung out more than three inches long.

Qiuqiu suddenly burst into tears, startling everyone in the room.

The guests sitting at the other two tables turned around inquiringly.

The man in black had immediately relaxed his features again and was laughing out loud as he said to the sobbing little girl: "Strike me dead, strike me dead. I didn't know you couldn't take a joke."

Another guest who had witnessed his tricks found it impossible to keep silent any longer and spoke out: "You shouldn't frighten her like that, Mr. Jin. She's still a child. Keep scaring her like that and she'll have nightmares."

"Not only nightmares, she might even get sick," added another guest who had also witnessed his antics.

"Don't be afraid, don't be afraid, Qiuqiu." Mrs. Wu held the little girl tight against her comfortingly. But she still cried hard. "Oh, her hands are ice cold!"

Qiuqiu continued to cry, letting out terrified screams now and then, likely as her memory recalled that hideous image. She seemed oblivious to her surroundings, just stared blankly into space, sometimes choked in silence, sometimes bursting into tearful shrieks that racked her whole body.

It was no wonder she was so thoroughly frightened. That hideous face would even have scared the wits out of adults, let alone a little girl. It was the ugliest face I had ever seen. I had never thought it possible for a human face to be distorted so grotesquely. Nor had I believed that it could transform itself so quickly and completely from utter ugliness back to the utmost friendliness, as the smiling face of the man in black had just demonstrated.

Qiuqiu's mother came hurrying over, inquiring anxiously: "What's the matter, Qiuqiu? What's the matter?" Her last question was directed at us.

None of us thought it proper to describe what had happened.

"She's afraid of me," the man in black volunteered. "I noticed that she didn't seem too happy tonight and thought I'd cheer her up a bit, but she started crying instead."

"It's nothing," Mrs. Wu added. "Mr. Jin likes children, and likes to play with them. But Qiuqiu probably doesn't like Mr. Jin—

doesn't like his black gown, that is, and she started to cry after a while."

"I think you'd better sit at another table, Mr. Jin. She'll still be scared of you whenever she sees you and won't stop crying if you stay here," a guest remarked.

The smile disappeared from the face of the man in black, but he immediately smiled again and said: "Okay, I'll go, I'll go—so, after all, I'm still the one to go!" His self-deprecation was surprising. Tut-tutting, he stood up.

He went over to the next table and arranged to exchange seats with another guest. Then he returned, picked up his wine cup, plate, spoon and chopsticks and whatnot and held them wrapped in his napkin. He looked at Qiuqiu, who was still crying relentlessly, and suddenly bent over dramatically to execute a deep bow. After that, he turned and went over to sit at the other table.

The scene ended with his bow, as if to inform everyone there was nothing more to expect. The guests, like an audience returning home after a show, directed their attention once more to the banquet, which was far from over, as there were still several courses to come. After a while, the room was filled again with the happy sound of clinking chinaware.

But Qiuqiu's cries never quite subsided. Her mother carried her over to her own seat and we could still hear her sobbing there. It was only after being comforted and consoled by a number of ladies sitting near her that she finally stopped her sobbing.

The banquet that evening continued merrily until well after nine o'clock. Even then, the guests did not take their leave, but returned to the living room to chat over tea. I saw the man in black busily making his rounds once more in the room, now chatting in this corner, then laughing in another. But I did not see Qiuqiu again. Qiuqiu had been carried away by a maid to be put to bed, because she was really very tired.

Translated by Chʻen Chu-yun

Nights of the Shining Moon

June 2006. Wang Wen-hsing and French writer Jacques Rou-baud were invited by Centre National de la Reacherche Scientifique (CNRS) and L'Atelier Litteraire Bipolaire (ALIBI) in February of 2006 to write stories that employed numbers as thematic material. This story was Wang's contribution. It calls attention to the vast, unknown universe and a power beyond human comprehension, a motif with profound religious overtones. Also of significance is the remodeling of a religious theme common in traditional Chinese zhiguai and biji literature. "Nights of the Shining Moon" is the most recent fiction published by Wang Wen-hsing.

"It was early in the eighth month during the nineteenth year of the reign of the Qing dynasty Emperor Jia Qing.[1] Outside the south gate of Fuzhou, the capital city of Fujian province, was a district named Nantai. The area had a sizeable population, with numerous boats docked along the riverside, many of which housed prostitutes plying their trade. One day, two young boys, both dressed in red, appeared in Nantai. Hand in hand, they walked along the lanes, chanting:

> On the night of the fifteenth day of the eighth month,
> On the night of the fifteenth day of the eighth month,
> A fire engulfs the houses along the riverside,
> Sending many a pearl maid out wailing into the streets.

"In the local dialect, 'pearl maid' meant prostitute. The two youngsters recited the lines repeatedly for three days. No one knew

---

1. Jia Qing reigned from 1796 to 1820. The year mentioned here is 1815.

who they were. Apprehensive, the inhabitants of Nantai reminded each other to be vigilant on the night of the Mid-Autumn Festival, and to take special precautions over cooking fires and burning candles. The fateful night came and went; there were no fires. In the following year, however, at midnight on the twenty-ninth day of the fourth month, a conflagration raged along the riverside. It burned steadily for two whole days and destroyed thousands of houses and the brothel boats. It was exactly eight-and-a-half months from the fifteenth day of the eighth month of the previous year, thereby bearing out the strange song chanted by the two youngsters. Maocai[2] Wang Ziruo, a friend of mine, was in Fuzhou at the time and witnessed the event."

The above account appears in a collection titled *Lü Yuan Anecdotes*, written by the Qing dynasty writer Qian Yong.[3]

The person reading the story was Liu Peiji, who came across the collection while sorting through his books. He was still in the midst of his rummaging but was standing up by the time he finished reading the story. He had experienced a considerable jolt. He planned to travel to Fuzhou in a month's time, and thus felt the coincidence was particularly significant.

Liu, an associate researcher in the Institute of Chinese Classics at the Academia Sinica in Taiwan, was going to Fuzhou to take part in a conference titled "The Life and Scholarship of Zhu Xi."[4] At the time, travel across the Taiwan Strait had just been sanctioned, and he was among the first in his institute to attend such a meeting in China.

2. The title given to someone who passed the lowest level of the civil service examination and eligible for appointment to an official position in the local government.

3. Qian Yong (1759–1844) published his *Lü Yuan conghua* (Lü Yuan anecdotes) in 1838. The anecdote quoted here is titled "Bayue shiwu bu" (The night after eight months and fifteen days) in chapter 14, "Xiangyi" (Miraculous and extraordinary).

4. Zhu Xi was an eminent Song dynasty philosopher (1130–1200) who founded a center of learning in Fuzhou.

Lü Yuan Anecdotes had been in Liu's possession for nearly twenty years, but it had been buried among other books in his office and he had never bothered to read it. Now the collection had turned up by chance while he was going through a pile of books. Opening it at random, he had come across the story, and the reading swiftly followed.

The next day, Liu went to consult a colleague who was familiar with the Fuzhou dialect. The friend enlightened him on the correct pronunciation of certain words in the song, observed that Qian Yong, the story's chronicler, might have erred in recording a word or two and offered his own substitutions to improve the song. For instance, the term "pearl maid" not only referred to a prostitute; in the Fuzhou dialect, it could just mean a young woman.

Liu himself was born in Taiwan and knew the local Taiwanese dialect. He tried reciting the verses in Taiwanese, and found the rhyme scheme of the song generally viable, requiring a change in only one character.

Since he was born and raised locally, Liu had no apparent connection with Fuzhou. But he knew that his maternal great-grandfather had for a time served as an official in the city. Liu's father was from the province of Anhui; his mother from Jiangxi. His mother's maiden name, however, was Qian, the same as the writer who recorded the story.

Liu would be in Fuzhou for nine days, although the conference itself lasted only four.

The rest of the time would be taken up with registration on the first day, a city tour on the second, and then, after the conference ended, two-and-a-half days for more visits and tours. The dates were March 10 to 18, 1987.

Upon his arrival in Fuzhou, Liu was taken by car to a small guesthouse located beside West Lake outside the city. Since most of the other conference participants were from various provinces in the country and he was the only overseas member, Liu was accorded special treatment and housed in serene lakeside accommodations. The guesthouse was an old three-storey structure, sparsely occupied. In fact, Liu seemed to be the sole occupant on the second floor. What was unique about the guesthouse was that it had a large garden. From his window he could look down on it—beyond lay the misty lake. When he first arrived, Liu stood in front of the window for a long time and noticed that outside was a wide ledge. It could be used for placing flower pots or, more likely, served as a safety device in case of fire; you could step out the window onto the ledge. Then he noticed that the window itself was divided into one large central pane flanked by smaller ones on each side that could be opened to let in the lake breeze. The central window, though fixed, was equipped with handles along the bottom and could be lifted out in its entirety. Such a precaution, together with the outer ledge, no doubt ensured the safe evacuation of the room's occupants.

When Liu entered the guesthouse, two red-clad attendants came forward to help him with his luggage. Since he traveled with only one shoulder bag, which one of the attendants took and slung over his shoulder, the other, empty-handed but trying to be helpful, carried the room key. They accompanied him to the second floor. The pair, dressed in dark red uniforms and caps, looked similar enough to be brothers. Both had dark complexions, pointed noses and chins, and bright dark eyes. Liu tried to make small talk with them but the two remained expressionless and did not respond to his remarks.

When he came downstairs after settling in, he again saw the two attendants, this time in the garden. One sat on a stone bench and the other stood behind him with one foot resting on the bench. The first was strumming a lilting tune on a *huqin*, a three-stringed violin-like instrument that he held in his arms, but neither sang. The two were very close together. As soon as they saw Liu approaching, they turned and left the garden.

That night, Liu stood at the window and saw a bright three-quarter moon high in the night sky. When he looked down into the garden, he heard the lilting sounds of the *huqin* and, upon closer scrutiny, saw two red figures sitting in a corner on a stone bench. For some unknown reason, the pair again turned around and vanished immediately.

The next day, Liu did not see the two attendants during the day but when he stood before the window he once again caught sight of them in the garden under the moonlight. They were sitting on the garden bench, one of them playing the instrument. An idea stirred in Liu. He thought of the two red-clad children in Qian Yong's story. With the moon hanging above, he tried working out the time frame, but found no connection, it being neither the eighth nor the fifth lunar month. This time, the two figures stayed longer. Liu did not recognize the tune being played but it sounded to him like a folk song.

The next day Liu had a disconcerting experience. He had returned to his room earlier than usual, at around four o'clock. When he unlocked the door he was surprised to see the two red figures sitting in his room, facing him. Moreover, they were sitting on his bed. Just as before, one played the *huqin*, while the other sat close beside him. Obviously the two had entered his room to clean it during his absence and had lingered to play music. In some embarrassment, the pair stood up. Without any apology, they picked up the *huqin* and left the room, not even tidying the bed they had rumpled.

That night, Liu did not see the twosome in the garden. The moon remained a bright presence in the sky, but the two figures did not appear. Liu, on the other hand, felt a little guilty—evidently they were keeping away from the garden out of embarrassment. In the bathroom before he retired he came across a piece of paper they obviously had left behind. It was a song sheet with a simplified score but without any lyrics. The title read "Crescent Moon over the Nine Seas."

Liu thought he would return the sheet to the pair when he saw them the next day.

But he could not find them the next day. On the first and second floors a new attendant, young and plump and wearing a white uniform, had replaced the other two. When Liu inquired as to where he could find the former attendants, he was met with this mystified reply: "There aren't two attendants—there's always been only one." When Liu specified two men in red uniforms, the other was even more puzzled. "No one wears a red uniform here. Ours are all white," he said.

Bewildered, Liu took the song sheet to ask the woman behind the reception desk. "We don't have two attendants here, only one. In red uniforms, you say? No way. There aren't any red uniforms here," was her reply.

The mystery was finally cleared up a few hours later. Upon Liu's further inquiry at the reception desk, a slightly balding man in his forties, wearing a pair of glasses low on the bridge of his nose, finally emerged from a back room. "Yes, yes, they were interns sent over by the Red Flag Hotel. They were here for only three days—and have gone back to the hotel," he replied. Liu was then told that both the woman and the white-uniformed attendant had been working the midnight shift. Since they had just been rotated back onto the day shift, they had not met the two attendants in question. Liu handed over the song sheet to the older man and asked that it be returned to the two interns. The man was a little reluctant, saying: "They won't be coming here anymore." But then, in an effort to be of service, added: "All right. If I see them—I'll hand it over."

As he returned to his room upstairs, Liu thought to himself that it looked as if the two uniformed attendants had left after appearing for exactly three days. True, they never did sing the folk song themselves. But the word "moon" appeared unequivocally in the song sheet title. And though the number eight did not show up, nine did.

That night when he stood before the window he suddenly detected a faint burning odor. Outside, all he could see was white— the moonlit garden appeared to be shrouded in white smoke. Looking more closely, he saw a small fire burning in one corner of the garden. Someone was burning trash, and even as he watched the fire gradually burned down and died. He closed the two smaller side windows to keep the smoke from drifting into the room.

The next day when Liu walked past the reception desk the middle-aged man greeted him in a friendly manner.

During the three following days, Liu pushed the incident of the attendants and the song sheet to the back of his mind. The conference had ended, and the participants were taken on various visits and tours. During the daytime, Liu's mind was occupied elsewhere, but each night, whenever he saw the shining moon growing fuller, he remembered Qian Yong's story and the two attendants.

That night a strange thing occurred. He was awakened from sleep in the middle of the night by the sound of banging on his door. He opened the door to find the hallway engulfed in flames. This was a dream. In the hallway, the two attendants, in red uniforms, were coming toward him, arm-in-arm. One was playing the *huqin*, and both were chanting loudly in the Taiwanese dialect:

"On the night of the fifteenth day of the eighth month,
On the night of the fifteenth day of the eighth month,
A fire engulfs the houses along the riverside,
Sending many a pearl maid out wailing into the streets."

People were rushing back and forth, some shouting: "The fire's from Nantai!" Others were screaming: "The fire's everywhere! The whole city's burning! Everything's on fire!" Unable to leave, he thought of retreating into the room. There was the large window from which he could make his escape. He found himself standing on the ledge outside. Now the whole garden was ablaze. Each tree became a burning bush. The place was filled with running figures, many of them women, sobbing as they scurried around. Liu thought he should run into the lake, but as far as he could make out, the entire lake was also covered in flames. How could he get away? He looked up and saw the sky was burning too. A few birds plunged to the earth, engulfed in a golden blaze.

Then he detected a disturbing sound. It came from a distance, and with each report the ground seemed to reverberate. The fire raged on. He could see nothing but flames. He was in despair. The people running around looked like burning torches. A few, he saw, sat in the midst of the flames. They held their palms together, and let their bodies burn in the fire. He seemed to make out a number of statues of Buddha in the flames. Liu felt the fire engulfing his own body. His hair was ablaze, so were his arms. But strangely enough, he felt no **pain**. In fact, he didn't even feel the heat . . .

Then, he woke up.

The dream, he felt, was so vivid, so real. He felt, in fact, that he had undergone **a trial by fire**. Whether the experience was real or not, what was the difference? He thought of the earlier calculations about the night of the fifteenth day of the eighth month. Then he realized there was a third way—counting backward instead of forward. But that would make the outcome fall sometime between the eleventh and twelfth lunar months, not the second month, as it was now, according to the lunar calendar. Gazing at the shining moon outside the window, he finally found the solution: the number "eight" meant eight moonlit nights after his arrival, and "fifteen" referred to "five out of ten," indicating the idea of "middle," and hence "midnight."[5]

After he got up the next morning, he found that all the other rooms on the floor had been filled during the night with a newly arrived group from Henan province. He discovered this after hearing the sound of doors slamming shut in the early morning. Then, outside the window, he saw these people, all together, performing their morning exercises in the garden. Soon afterward they left on their scheduled sightseeing tours.

This was Liu's final day in Fuzhou. A visit to the temples at Drum Mountain had been planned for the morning. As he waited for the car to pick him up, he went to look in the garden. Sitting down on the stone bench, he saw a piece of paper at his feet. It was the song sheet, a little scorched around the edges. It may have been left behind by the group from Henan, Liu thought to himself, or the paper could have been part of the trash burned the other day. His guide to Drum Mountain arrived and, as he walked up to Liu, politely handed over his business card. On it were the characters Wang Maocai. En route, Liu asked his guide whether he knew or had heard of a Wang Ziruo, but he received a negative answer. He then inquired in

5. The Chinese word for "fifteen" is comprised of two characters: "ten" and "five." Since five is half of ten, "ten-five" can be interpreted as "five out of ten" or "middle."

an oblique way about *Lü Yuan Anecdotes*, saying he wanted to find a copy, but also to no avail.

Liu decided he would write down this story on his return to Taipei.

Completed on February 25, 2006
Translated by Ch'en Chu-yun

PART II

NOVELLA AND PLAY

Dragon Inn

February 1966. Wang Wen-hsing's only novella was written after "The Black Gown" as a preparation for writing novels. He began it while still in the United States but completed it following his return to Taiwan after receiving his MFA degree from the University of Iowa. "Dragon Inn" is about several Guomindang officers, their dangerous journeys into exile from Shanxi province in mainland China to Taiwan, and their reunion there. In this work, Wang returned to the language style used in "Midsummer on the Prairie."

I

By noon, the commotion in the market had calmed down considerably. At this time of day, the market was like a deserted beehive in June with only two or three bees left buzzing about, the buzzing being was the voices of vendors who were trying to sell what remained of their merchandise. A hot wind flapped the canvas awnings. On the dry ground beneath the awnings lay cut-open watermelons, piles of white radish and prickly yellow-green pineapples, which attracted swarms of flies. Occasionally the wind puffed up some of the awnings, revealing now and then the grayish sky they normally concealed, as well as a few betel palm trees with their thin trunks and the tile-covered eaves of the Confucian Temple that lay to the east. If the wind blew just a little harder, a few more awnings would be turned up and an old wooden structure on the corner just opposite the market would come into view. A large black board hung in the middle of the building inscribed with gilded characters: "Dragon Inn."

A stillness began to settle over the market, the silence broken only occasionally by the sound of voices haggling over prices—the vendors were lowering them grudgingly in order to sell off what remained of the day's merchandise. Soon, even these sounds ceased, and the only people who passed through the market were pedestrians who did not even glance at the stalls.

As the awnings flapped in the wind, from time to time the words "Dragon Inn" were revealed. This "Dragon Inn," which stood in the semitropical sunlight, was a restaurant. The proprietor, who hailed from Shanxi province in China, came to Taiwan to flee the Communist takeover. He came alone and penniless. When he first arrived, he collected cigarette butts during the day and slept on the streets at night. Later, with a little help from some Shanxi friends, he put some money together and opened a streetside food stall that served a variety of lamb dishes. Who would have thought his business would boom and, within a few years, that he would amass quite a fortune. The successful entrepreneur bought this old building and opened a restaurant that served Shanxi cuisine, which attracted all kinds of patrons longing for hometown fare. There was a couplet hanging in the main hall upstairs that read, "Old friends drink wine together when far they roam; Dragon Inn is where we gather and remember our Shanxi home." This couplet, presented by a famous personage originally from Shanxi, summed up customers' feelings about the restaurant. Because business boomed and a steady stream of guests flocked to its door from morning to night, the vagrant who had built his business up from nothing had, amazingly enough, become a wealthy and successful businessman.

On the road leading to the restaurant a small jeep with a canvas top appeared. The jeep slowly drew nearer, sounding its horn several times along the way, and eventually pulled up at the Dragon Inn's door. A man in a white cotton dress shirt emerged from the jeep and stood at attention. Then a tall, thin, middle-aged man dressed in the khaki summer uniform of an army officer climbed out. This man also stepped to the side and extended an arm into the vehicle. An old man with a back bent like a bow emerged from the jeep. The two men standing on either side helped him alight. The man in uniform leaned into the vehicle and said, "Old Liu, go home and wait for my call."

The man's uniform had a gold star pinned to the left collar.

"Yes, Sir," the driver answered.

The man in uniform moved to the old man's left and, with the other man walking on the old man's right, they headed toward Dragon Inn. The jeep emitted a puff of exhaust and drove away.

With the old man walking between the other two for support, they climbed the stairs leading to the restaurant. "Take your time, Dad, remember you've got gout in your leg," the uniformed officer told the old man.

"It's much better. I'm feeling much better now," the old man responded.

The elderly man was short and spry, but his most prominent features were a short, brush-like moustache, a pure silvery white, and long white eyebrows that curled up like whiskers. He walked stiffly, due perhaps to the gout in his leg.

"That's right," added the man standing to his right. "Now that you're in Taizhong, that sore leg of yours must feel better, Sir. The climate here is much better than Taipei's." A gentle smile appeared on this man's plump, round face, which was covered with smallpox scars.

The three men walked under the sign bearing the characters "Dragon Inn," passed through the doorway, and entered the lower floor of the restaurant. The room, by no means small, was rather cool. Waiters with teapots in their hands bustled about. The man with the pockmarked face quickly parted from the father and son and walked over to a counter. He softly addressed the old cashier seated behind it, "Friend, could you please tell me how to get to Banquet Room Six?"

The old cashier looked over a pair of reading glasses that had slipped down from the bridge of his nose. A smile appeared on his face, and he said: "It's upstairs. It's upstairs. Please wait just a moment and I'll get someone to show you up. Room Six! The party for Room Six is here!" He raised his voice and shouted down a corridor, "The customers are here! Hurry up!" A voice answered from down the hallway and a tall, thin waiter dressed in a white uniform came running out. "Take the guests upstairs," the man behind the counter said. The pockmarked man thanked him profusely. The waiter smiled and bowed: "This way please. Please follow me."

The three men walked down a long corridor. On both sides were rooms with doorways covered by bamboo curtains. Some of the rooms were already occupied by customers eating and drinking. They turned a corner and started up a wooden staircase, their feet thudding on the steps as they ascended. The waiter turned around to look at them for a moment. About halfway up, they came to a landing where the staircase turned. The waiter suddenly turned around and said to the father and son:

"Commander, Young Master, do you know who I am?"

The two men did not seem to remember him.

"I'm Zhang Degong. I used to work as a driver at your residence, Sir. When you lived in Taiyuan, it was over ten years ago," the waiter said excitedly. His eyes narrowed to two small slits and his mouth, smiling in delight, opened wide to reveal not only all of his upper teeth, but the gums above them as well.

"Oh, you're Zhang Degong," the old man said. "I didn't know that you had come to Taiwan, too. How long have you been here? How did you end up working here?"

"I escaped from China thirteen years ago, Sir. I came with my unit. I retired from the army last year, and a brother-in-law of mine helped arrange for me to get this job." At this point, the waiter smiled again, narrowing his eyes and grinning broadly. He was so excited that he stood awkwardly, wringing his hands and shuffling his feet. He asked the old man: "Sir, Young Master, have the years treated you well?"

"Yes, yes, and you seem to be doing well, too," the old man replied. "Your job here is pretty good, isn't it? How's the pay? Have you made your fortune, Zhang Degong?"

"How could I make a fortune here?" the waiter laughed. "I certainly get by. Ah, I make a living, have clothes to wear and food to eat."

"That's good," the old man replied.

The man with the pockmarked face, who had been standing to one side and listening to the conversation, now joined in, adding, "Not bad, making a living is pretty good."

"Zhang Degong," the old man said, "let me introduce a friend of mine, Mr. Jiang. Like you and me, he also comes from Shanxi." The man with the pockmarked face smiled warmly and extended his hand to the waiter to shake.

Embarrassed and shy, the waiter smiled nervously as he put out his hand, his five fingers stiffly extended, and pumped the other man's arm in a series of exaggerated strokes.

"Okay, Zhang Degong, take us upstairs," the old man instructed.

They headed up to the second floor and stepped out into the main room. Because of the many windows in the front and rear of the room, it was much brighter here than downstairs. Normally the room was rented out for meetings; there was a rectangular conference table covered with a sky-blue tablecloth in the center. On the wall facing them was a picture of Sun Yat-sen flanked by a pair of Republic of China flags: white sun on a blue background in the upper left corner of a red field. Many framed or mounted paintings and works of calligraphy hung on the other walls. As they walked through the large hall, the old man spent some time strolling back and forth examining the calligraphy and paintings. He paused for several minutes before the inscription that read, "Old friends drink wine together when far they roam; Dragon Inn is where we gather and remember our Shanxi home."

"Well, take us in to the banquet."

The waiter led them out of the hall and took them to the doorway of Banquet Room Six. Standing to one side, he bowed and parted the beaded curtain that covered the doorway. The old man stepped through the curtained doorway first, followed by his son and the man with the pockmarked face.

A good number of people already filled the room. When they saw the old man enter, they softly whispered to each other, "He's here! He's here!" All eyes turned toward the doorway and everyone stood up, their faces wreathed in smiles. What was surprising about them was that all were remarkably large in stature—all, like the pockmark-faced man, were majestic in size. Like him, they also wore white cotton dress shirts. At this point, one of the men stepped forward and addressed the old man. "Commander," he said.

"General Guan," the old man replied as he hurriedly stepped forward and extended his hand. Guan clasped the hand of the old man, who asked, "How long has it been, General?"

"Thirteen years," the man replied, his eyes growing misty. He then turned to the man in uniform and said while extending his hand, "General Tian, we meet again." General Tian firmly shook the other man's hand. "Commander, there are a lot of others here today. Take a look," General Guan said.

"Commander," another man said as he came forward.

"Brigadier General Zha," the old man replied, stepping forward to shake his hand.

"You have a good memory, Sir, to still remember me. You look as healthy as ever."

"Ah, I'm old, nothing like I used to be," the old man responded with a sad sigh.

"General Tian," General Zha said to the old man's son as he reached out to shake his hand. "How are you?"

"Doing fine, and how are you, General Zha?" he asked.

"Oh, Sir, do you remember this fellow?" General Guan interrupted.

"Sir," said another man as he walked up to them.

"Colonel Qin," the old man said, shaking his hand.

As Colonel Qin greeted the old man, his voice seemed particularly resonant. He then turned and shook hands with the old man's son.

Another came up, a man with a head of snowy white hair but whose face suggested he was only middle-aged. As he arrived, he said nothing but wore a warm, innocent smile on his face.

"Staff Officer Duan," the old man called out.

Duan grinned but said nothing as he extended his arm to shake the old man's hand.

"Staff Officer Duan," the old man's son said. The white-haired man walked over, put out his hand, but said nothing.

Staff Officer Duan smiled and withdrew to one side.

"Commander," called out a large, fat, ruddy-faced man.

"Ah," the old man exclaimed, "Colonel Lu." The old man seemed particularly pleased. He continued, "I . . . I had heard that you had been . . ." He swallowed the rest of the sentence he had been about to say and warmly extended his hand, adding, "What a great pleasure to see you."

The ruddy-faced man seemed transfixed for a moment as he stared at Commander Tian's hand, and then put out his left hand and shook the back of the old man's right hand. "General Tian," Colonel Lu said addressing the old commander's son, saluting him by clasping his fists together in front of his chest, rather than shaking hands with him.

Standing somewhat further away was a man wearing glasses and another with a long scar on his cheek. Each of them softly greeted the old man with "Sir," then politely bowed to Commander Tian.

"Ah, Brigadier General Qiu and Colonel Feng," the old man replied, nodding to the two men. He said to the group, "I recently had a chance to meet Qiu and Feng. Though we all live in Taiwan, it's been a real challenge for all of us to get together."

"Well, now we've finally gotten together," Pockmark-faced Jiang, General Guan, Colonel Qin and the others responded in unison.

"General Guan, let's get everyone seated," the pockmark-faced man said.

"Everyone take a seat. Commander, please sit down. General Tian, please," Guan responded.

The men bustled about as each moved to find a seat. They respectfully urged their old commander to take the seat of honor with his son seated to his right. Then the others spent several minutes politely declining to take this seat or that, being careful not to take a place superior to their status. This was especially true for Pockmark-faced Jiang and General Guan, who agonized for some time over who should take the seat to the left of old Commander Tian. They finally decided to give the seat to Guan because he was older than Jiang. With everyone seated, the banquet could begin.

As the men were getting seated, the waiter Zhang Degong watched dumbfounded, so distracted that he forgot to serve tea to the guests. Holding the teapot in his hand, he simply stood and stared at these men. Could his eyes be deceiving him? He had never seen so many important men in one room. Actually, he had seen VIPs before, but never as many as he saw here: one there, a second there, a third. . . . They were all heroes from the Anti-Japanese War, men he had long admired, exceptional heroes whose names were known in every household of his native Shanxi, right up there with the seventy-two heroes of the famous novel *The Water Margin*. And now they were all here. It was the first time he had ever seen them. Up to then, he had known them only by reputation. Each and every one of them was here. There was General Guan, "Master Guan of the Magic Gun" of the Twelfth Cavalry Division, famous for exterminating the enemy. And that Colonel Qin was "Tiger Qin with the Big Sword," who organized the Big Sword Society that protected the countryside. Colonel Lu was known as "Executioner Lu the Third," a guerrilla leader who rested by day and traveled by night, killing the enemy like you cut down grass. Brigadier General Zha was "Steel Armor Number Two," who commanded the armored divisions that crushed enemy troops. And that Staff Officer Duan, wasn't he none other than "Duan the Fox," the traitor's invincible adversary . . . ?

Zhang Degong was in the midst of trying to identify all these famous people when he suddenly heard the old man say to the others, "This waiter was also under my command. Quite a coincidence, don't you think? He was one of the soldiers who drove for me when I lived in Taiyuan. I just ran into him at the foot of the stairs. He's doing well now, making big money, doing better than the rest of us."

Suddenly finding himself under the gaze of men he had long admired, Zhang Degong didn't know whether he should speak or not, so he simply smiled in his own, unique way—a big grin that revealed even more of his upper teeth and gums.

"All of these men are old friends, Zhang Degong. They are faithful brothers of mine who worked in my headquarters back in Shanxi during the Anti-Japanese War. All these men, Colonel Lu, Brigadier

General Zha, and Colonel Feng, worked under me . . . all of them. And that goes for the man you just met—Commander Jiang." The old man pointed to the pockmark-faced man.

Division Commander Jiang? Zhang Degong's eyes bulged so far they seemed about to fall out. Why, it was none other than Commander Jiang Chaigui, renowned at home and abroad because he had received the enemy's surrender at a famous battle and been awarded the nation's highest medal of honor. When he thought of how this high officer had just so humbly shaken his hand, he began trembling with shock. Commander Jiang continued to nod and smile at him, as if he were about to stand and shake hands again across the table. The waiter was filled with delight but excused himself by saying he had to go downstairs and check on the meal preparations. He spun around abruptly, parted the curtain and left the room. He stood in the corridor, staring dumbfounded at his right hand, which now somehow seemed different.

The table had already been set with cups, plates and utensils. General Guan stood and poured wine for all of the guests. Some tried to decline, saying "let me, let me," while grabbing for the bottle, but he just held it up high, away from his body and out of the others' reach. Commander Jiang had closed an eye and seemed to be staring at something when he reached out and snatched a fly in mid-flight. At just this moment, Zhang Degong hurried into the room with a large platter of cold appetizers on his shoulder.

General Guan stood erect, raised his cup and said, "Please stand and join me in a toast to our old commander." All voiced their agreement, stood and raised their wine glasses.

"Today is the seventieth birthday of our fellow Shanxi countryman and superior, Commander Tian," General Guan began. "This is also the first time that many of us, brothers in days gone by, have had a chance to meet with Commander Tian since coming to Taiwan. It is also the first time that those of us now living in Taizhong have gotten together. While we're happy that all of us have finally gotten together, we're even more delighted that we can all celebrate this special occasion with our old commander. May he live as long as the pine and stork and enjoy longevity without bounds."

General Guan and the men turned to the old commander and raised their glasses. He responded by raising his glass and all of them drained their drinks. "Thanks to all of you," the old commander responded. "Please sit down. Please sit down."

After everyone was seated, the old man said, "This is really too much. Since our lives are so difficult now, why bother to spend money for this birthday celebration. I'd have been just as happy if you'd saved your money and just ordered a bottle of wine and bought a bag of peanuts."

Everyone roared with laughter.

"Of course we had to do it, how could we not celebrate your birthday!" General Guan said with a chuckle. "And not just this time only. Now that you're living in Taizhong, from now on we'll celebrate with you every year. Strange as it may seem, many of us didn't know you moved here more than six months ago. We're all just too busy trying to make ends meet. It was just last week that Old Jiang sent a card saying that the sixth of this month was your birthday. He asked me to invite all of our old compatriots who live in Taizhong to get together and hold a banquet in your honor. It was only then that I realized you had moved here. I was delighted to read Jiang's letter. I'd heard that you came to Taiwan quite some time ago, Sir, and I knew you'd lived in Taipei, but I had no idea what your address was. Now you are in Taizhong and plan to live here for some time. As soon as I read the letter, I contacted Old Lu, Old Qin and Old Zha, who were just as delighted as I was when they heard the news."

As he spoke, General Guan's voice was filled with emotion. It was piercingly high, a step up in pitch above most men's. His plump cheeks normally were rather smooth. Now that he had been drinking wine and perspiring, they were even smoother and shinier than usual.

The old man spoke: "That's right. I never expected I would run into all of you in Taizhong either. I ran into Commander Jiang on the street last month, and he got in contact with General Qiu and Colonel Feng, and they each came to see me. Taizhong may not be a big city, but it was still no easy matter to arrange a time for us to meet. It took us six months to find a time when all of us could get together."

"Yes, yes, that's true. Isn't it ironic that this is the first time we've seen each other, even though some of us arrived long ago. Everyone dig in. Commander, General Tian, please help yourselves. Help yourselves, everybody!" General Guan said as he used his chopsticks to serve himself.

All the men at the table began to eat, rubbing shoulders and elbows as they consumed the food with gusto. Although General Jiang was large in stature, he seemed to be a picky eater and barely opened his lips as he ate, which made both his cheeks bulge as he chewed his food. Still every inch a hero, Colonel Qin ate like one. Unlike everyone else, Colonel Lu used his left hand to hold his chopsticks. In only a few minutes, the first platter had been picked clean and the second course was served.

The old man sipped some wine, put down his cup and said, "General Guan, I can still recall the last time we saw each other at the Guanghe Ju tavern in April of 1949. Remember?"

"How could I forget—I can even remember what day it was," General Guan responded. "It was the twelfth of April, the third day of the third lunar month, only the thinnest sliver of a new moon was visible that night. You invited me for a drink to see me off, and that night I went up to the front. Early the next morning, the encirclement campaign erupted, which is why I can still remember every detail. I also recall that Taiyuan fell less than two weeks later, on April twenty-fourth."

The old man nodded as he listened. After a few moments, staring off into the distance, he said:

"It seems like these things happened only yesterday. Can any of you believe that more than thirteen years have passed? After we parted, General Guan, I heard nothing more about you. The same goes for General Zha, Colonel Lu and Officer Duan. Three nights before Taiyuan fell you all came to my home to urge me to leave. I realized that if I stayed, an old fellow like me who'd been retired for so long would be powerless to do anything, so the next day I took your advice and left for Datong. I heard nothing more about any of your whereabouts. Except, that is, for some erroneous information on what had happened to Colonel Lu. It's been even longer since I saw Colonel Qin. I think the last time I saw you probably was in 1947. Was it the end of 1947? Yes, the end of 1947. And from then until now, I heard no news. Today, I'd like to hear each of your stories, of how you escaped and ended up here in Taiwan. I've already heard General Jiang's, Colonel Qiu's and Colonel Feng's stories, I just haven't heard from the four of you yet. Why don't each of you take a few minutes. Let's start with General Guan. How does that sound?"

General Guan took a drink of wine, rubbed his chest, and said:

"I realize that it will take more than just a few words to explain my experiences in fleeing to Taiwan. Sometimes I wonder if these things really happened. The circumstances were so extraordinary, were so much against reason and conscience, that I shudder to think they actually happened. Sometimes when I'm alone, I'll suddenly remember something and ask myself, 'Did that really happen? Am I still alive?' And then I'll hit my own hand to see if it hurts, and sit in a stupor of disbelief. Only then do I realize that I'm still alive and that I somehow escaped death. They say the past is like a dream, but the experiences I had—if they weren't a dream, what were they? Not a dream, but a nightmare."

He stared at the table for a moment, and then started to recount his story in his high, piercing voice.

"After Taiyuan fell, I led what was left of a battalion of men from the bloody battle in a retreat toward the northeast. Of all the units in my division, this battalion was the best. When I realized they were the only men I had left under my command, not even a whole battalion at that, you can probably imagine my feelings as we retreated. Before we had gone a mile, I suddenly heard shouting in the ranks ahead of me, and then the sound of shots being fired from all directions, followed by what sounded like someone yelling slogans. I knew something was wrong, so I quickly ordered my driver to drive up to see what was happening. Before I had gone very far, we found the road blocked by the deputy battalion commander and two company commanders. They took out their pistols, pointed them at me and ordered me out of my jeep. I then realized that this last, most loyal battalion was also the last to defect. I got out as ordered. I looked around for the battalion commander and the commander of the Third Company, men I had known and led for more than a decade. I hoped they would step out of the ranks and help me put down this revolt. I saw them standing behind the three who had their guns trained on me, staring sternly at me. I averted my eyes and the deputy battalion commander came forward and took my gun.

"I was quickly tied up. The major took over command of the battalion and ordered the men to turn around and return to Taiyuan.

"Outside of Taiyuan, I was handed over to the Communist forces and taken to an elementary school that had been temporarily turned into a prisoner-of-war camp. While I was detained, I could see that fires burned all over the east side of the city, Taiyuan's warehouse district, which had been torched by the retreating Nationalist forces.

"They were herding people from all over the region into this P.O.W. camp. As I watched everything collapsing around me, I almost gave way to tears. Since my troops had defected, I knew I had little hope of survival, so I felt sad, but also resigned, as I silently watched what was happening around me.

"Because I was an officer, as long as I was enroute to the camp I was escorted by two Communist soldiers, guarding me and keeping me away from the other prisoners. But after entering the prisoner-of-war camp, they regarded me as a regular prisoner, put me with everyone else and treated me just as they treated the others. I remember that not long after arriving at the camp, all of us were beaten. Several really strong guys came up and began to beat us fiercely on our backs with fists as big as bowls. Many gave in to weakness and let out pitiful wails while others were beaten unconscious. One fellow I saw vomited blood all over his chest. After I was beaten, a Communist army officer walked past me, quickly turned and asked, 'Are you an officer? Stand at attention!' I remember the ripping sound as first he pulled off my epaulets, then in quick succession he tore off the decorations on my chest, my collar insignia, and then grabbed my cap with its white sun badge. He threw the cap on the ground and trampled on it with all his might. His angry eyes glared at me and then he slapped me across the face. Originally, I had thought of responding to his unreasonable behavior with a smile, but suddenly I noticed something cold and sticky in one of my eyes and my sight clouded a bit. This came from the saliva he'd spat at me.

"Then we were taken over by a well where they shaved every hair from our heads and left us bald. Then they ordered us onto the school's athletic field where we waited to be organized into groups to be taken to other prisons. They ordered us to sit on the ground, take off our uniforms, turn them inside out and then put them on again. They ordered us to put our hands on our heads. The whips the guards carried could fly at our heads and backs at any time. Anyone who was not sitting just so or did not have their hands placed just how the guards wanted them received a whipping. Some lowered their arms when they began to ache from holding them on their heads. These men were quickly dragged off, beaten viciously and then made to kneel in another area away from us. Some were ordered to crawl from one end of the field to the other with the guards striking them on their buttocks.

"Finally, they began to divide us into groups. It was chaotic as Communist officers called out names from the gray paper folders they held. Some prisoners answered right away, but those who didn't fell victim to the whips of the guards who stood among them. This commotion continued for two or three hours. I was first put into a group of thirty-five men whom I could tell were all colonels and generals, and I knew that this group of ours would be treated differently from the others. A while later, I heard my name called out again and I was put into another group. Not long after, the Communist soldier in charge of this new group sent me away, saying that I was not his responsibility. I found myself in a third group, and it turned out that they also refused to accept me and sent me away. At this point, I realized that in the confusion, they had completely mistaken who I was. When I saw the new group I had been assigned to, I noticed that they were all captains, and I began to hope again that I might somehow survive. It no longer seemed certain that I would have to pass through the gate between life and death.

"They hurried us into trucks, but before we boarded they covered our eyes with black blindfolds. Since this seemed to be how condemned prisoners are normally treated, what little hope of survival I still possessed left me.

"With our eyes covered, we had no idea where we were headed. After half an hour, we stopped and they removed the blindfolds and led us off the trucks. We had been taken to a Buddhist temple. The doors and windows of the monks' quarters were shut tight. Not a sound could be heard, and it looked like the monks who lived there had fled. When I saw the blue ceramic pagoda on top of the tile roof of the main hall, I knew this was the Temple of Lofty Goodness in the western suburbs of the city. I used to come here each spring to burn incense. It occurred to me that it was now springtime. When I noticed that guards were stationed where the corridor turned, I knew the monastery had been turned into a prison. I understood that, for the time being, I was going to be incarcerated and not executed. It felt like a tremendous weight had been lifted from my mind, and my slim hope of survival, which had been almost extinguished, was reawakened. As I marveled over the twists of fate and recalled the many times that day I had seemed on the verge of death only to find my life spared and then threatened again, I felt that somewhere in the unknown universe some being existed who controlled my fate. I had almost certainly been put in the wrong group (at one point, when the Communist officer who led the group I was assigned to asked me what group I had first been put in, I honestly told him that I couldn't remember). When I reflected that this mistake had been caused by the officer who wanted to humiliate me by stripping me of all my badges and insignia, I was even more amazed by the karmic workings of it all. If I had stayed in the officers' group, there's no doubt I would have ended up dead.

"There was no shortage of people in our group who, like me, secretly hoped to escape death. One anxiously asked the officer in charge, 'Sir, where are you taking us? What do you plan to do with us?'

"'Hah! Better not ask. The orders from above are to execute all of you. We're going to take care of this right away.'

"After that, we asked no more questions.

"'All right, everyone in!' the Communist officer ordered. We had arrived at a doorway to one of the halls. A large plaque that hung over the door bore the inscription 'Hall of Supreme Sorrow.'

"I noticed that all of the prisoners awaiting execution had pale faces as they passed in single file under that plaque saying 'Hall of Supreme Sorrow.' When we had all entered, the door was slammed shut with a loud bang.

"This was the second of the three main halls in the Temple of Lofty Goodness. When sutra reading sessions were held, it could accommodate a hundred monks and lay believers. It was thought to be the largest hall of worship in the Taiyuan region. Now it was being used as a prison, and we found several dozen people already in the room when we arrived. All of the Buddhist statues had been toppled. The hall was dim—the only light came from a skylight. Some of the prisoners sat, some stood, but all was quiet, except for the soft moaning that came from the sick and wounded. In one corner of the skylight a silvery gray spider's web floated like a flag.

"Not long after, the door opened with a groan and several large, strong men who reeked of alcohol entered the room, followed by an officer. In their hands they carried gleaming butcher's knives. Two of them then barred the door. There were six of these knife-wielding brutes altogether. They all had low foreheads, their eyes, noses and mouths so compressed that their features looked just like lines that converged in the middle of their faces. They wore brown cotton vests that exposed their chests and arms, which were covered with hair like apes.

"The officer opened a folder and called out the names of six men. The six executioners stuck their knives into their waistbands and pulled the benches of the worship hall into a line. The officer ordered the six men whose names he had called to remove all of their clothing except for their underpants, and to fold up their clothes and place them neatly at their feet. He then announced that they would now start the executions. When they heard this, the six prisoners lost control of themselves, let out piercing screams of terror and tried to flee. But the six executioners leaped forward and caught them. They tied them up with coarse ropes and shoved them onto the benches. They took out their sharp knives, placed them on the prisoners' heads and then stood and waited. Each of the six condemned men was fat, with white skin and plump breasts and legs. One of the men had a very noticeable black mole on his left breast. Another was trembling and shed streams of tears. When the officer in charge nodded his head a couple of times to signal, the executioners took their knives and slit the throats of their prisoners. Warm blood shot out like so many fountains. The air filled with their pitiful cries and the sounds of hoarse coughing. With each cough bloody bubbles issued forth from their severed windpipes. Within a short while, all six men collapsed, their eyes rolled back into their heads, which now lay on the floor by the feet of the benches.

"The second group of six was called out. Having seen what had just happened, they fled in all directions in fear. The officer ordered them to gather several times, but they fled in terror just the same. They ran back and forth. Even though all of us were locked in the room, they still seemed to believe they could find a safe place to hide. Perhaps because they had been stimulated by the smell of blood, the six executioners showed their canine teeth and a hungry look appeared in their eyes. It was only because the officer had not issued the order to attack that they stayed still and reined in their hunger. Still, one could hear them grinding their teeth and see them anxiously shuffling their feet.

"Finally, as the second group of six men continued to try to hide, the officer turned to the executioners and must have cast some kind of conspiratorial glance, ordering them to hunt down and kill their quarry. Quick as lightning, they took up the chase, each picking a different prisoner as the object of his pursuit. In the hall, the prisoners screamed when fleeing. The executioners chased behind them with their knives held high in the air. In a short while, all six prisoners had been caught and the cries of alarm grew even more piercing as the butchers fell upon the unarmed men. One of the prisoners raised a puny arm, his hand forming a tiny fist, as if attempting to resist. A brawny executioner easily grasped it in his enormous paw and then seemed to hold his prey with almost no effort while striking him. In just a few minutes, that thin arm, like the rest of the body it was attached to, had collapsed to the ground. One of the executioners, whose face was covered with whiskers and who had hair protruding from his nostrils and ears, threw down his knife and used his own two hands to squeeze the neck of his captive. As he throttled the prisoner, he gazed into the man's eyes, eyes from which all traces of life were gradually ebbing. I thought I saw the signs of a smile appear on those lips buried deep within the piles of whiskers. The second group of six had now been killed.

"When the third group of six was called, they fled just as furiously as the second group had. As before, the executioners chased after them waving their knives in the air. One of the prisoners had an injured foot, and hobbled along, fleeing as best he could. The bandages that had wrapped his foot came loose and trailed after him like a length of twisted intestine. In just three quick steps an executioner caught up with the prisoner and sank a knife into his back. Another prisoner, who had been cornered and had nowhere to flee, clung in desperation to a statue of Buddha. He held tight to the neck of the Buddha statue, as if it were his last savior. An executioner tried to pull him down, but couldn't even after making several attempts. He then plunged his knife into the man's lower back, and the prisoner let out a long groan, released his grip and collapsed onto the floor. The killer poured out his repressed anger by quickly stabbing the statue in the abdomen. In the meantime, in another corner of the room, an executioner had caught up with a prisoner and stabbed him in the stomach, but the prisoner was still alive. The executioner stuck his hand into the gaping wound—more than six inches deep—and squeezed out the prisoner's life. Elsewhere, another executioner was dispatching a victim he had caught and pressed onto one of the benches. He had cut through the prisoner's throat and then, without any reason, cut open the man's chest and abdomen. I could hear the panting of the executioners. The struggle of killing had winded them. They started in on the fourth group of six. Because all the running around had made them hot, the executioners stripped off their vests and long pants, so they scrambled among the pillars and Buddha statues and killed without a stitch of clothes on. Each was covered in blood. The one who'd stuck his hand into the wound was red up to his wrist, like he'd stuck his hand into a vat of blood. The bearded one had blood all around his mouth. What I'd seen up to this point was more than I could stomach, so I turned and puked my guts out.

"By the time they had finished killing the fourth group of prisoners, it had grown dark and the executioners were exhausted. The officer ordered a break in the executions and said that the rest of us would be taken care of the next day. The executioners and the officer unlocked the door and left the hall one by one, relocking the door afterward.

"Not long after, darkness fell. The light coming in through the skylight faded and the Hall of Supreme Sorrow fell into darkness. Rivulets of blood flowed from the corpses that lay scattered on the floor. We waited in terror for daybreak—that is to say, we waited to die."

General Guan paused briefly and took a sip of wine as all of the men sat in utter silence, listening to him with rapt attention. He wiped his face with a handkerchief and mopped his fat, whiskerless cheeks before continuing in his high-pitched voice.

"That night, I can't remember what time it was, but I finally began to nod off while leaning against a wall. Just as I was half asleep, on the verge of dreaming, I felt someone shaking my shoulder and calling out 'General Guan! General Guan!' I opened my eyes. Through the skylight I could see stars twinkling in the sky, and by their light, which shone into the hall, I thought I saw the commander of Third Company, once my most trusted subordinate, who had betrayed me, now squatting before me and looking at me. I wondered for a moment whether this was really happening or if I was still dreaming.

"'It's me, General, Company Commander Cui,' he said as he noticed the perplexed expression on my face. Then he continued, sobbing as he spoke, 'I'm a prisoner of war, just like you. I came over to ask your forgiveness, Sir. I saw you when you first came in, but I've been hiding from you, at least until it became quiet tonight. My conscience is bothering me and I can't bear this burden of guilt any longer. I've finally summoned up the nerve to ask you to forgive me. I know I will die tomorrow, and I must have your forgiveness tonight. Please, be merciful, Sir. Excuse my moment of foolishness.' He covered his face and wept bitterly. I didn't respond. After watching him cry so bitterly, I said, 'Stop crying. Talk with me. I have some questions to ask you. Where is the battalion commander?'

"'He's dead. Not long after you left, the deputy battalion commander grew afraid the battalion commander would try to take credit for getting the men to defect, so as we were walking along, he sneaked up and shot him dead in the back. Then Commander Sun of Second Company also fell victim to him. When he saw what had happened to his fellow officer, Sun felt he had to say something, so he questioned the deputy battalion commander, who promptly took aim at Sun and shot him too. Then he pointed his gun at the two bodies lying dead on the ground and said, 'Anyone else who raises objections or complains will end up dead like these two.' Then he sent me and Company Commander Ke of First Company to a prisoner-of-war camp. I have no idea where Ke is now.'

"'I never thought I would die, but because I violated the way of heaven, heaven won't spare me. The Eighth Route Army is short of grain now, and an order came down instructing them to execute all of their prisoners to reduce food consumption. The Lord of Heaven isn't ready to let me go yet, so he arranged for me to run into you, Sir, in this place where we face certain death. Maybe he wants me to pay for my mistake and make amends for my grave transgression. Since I wronged you, General Guan, I must ask your forgiveness. I hope you can find it in your magnanimous heart to forgive me.' This said, he knelt before me and, by the light shining in through the skylight, I could see him bowing in obeisance to me. He said, 'I'm the one who betrayed you and put your life in jeopardy. I haven't the courage to ask your forgiveness for something so grave that it makes the difference between life and death. But I humbly hope that you have an understanding heart and will be as merciful as the Buddha. If you forgive me this time, I will find a way to repay you in the afterlife.'

"He prostrated himself before me and refused to get up. I remained silent. The stars were twinkling outside. We passed a quarter of an hour in silence. Finally I broke the silence and said, 'Get up. I'll forgive you—we all have sins. All of us are going to die sometime, so I figure there's every reason to forgive you.'

"'So you'll forgive me? Really?'

"'Of course. No need to worry. Why haven't you gotten up yet?'

"He bowed twice more and said, 'You are unsurpassed in your compassion. I, Cui Guoguang, cannot thank you enough. Though I may not have enough time left in this life to repay you, I will fulfill my debt to you in the next, even if I am reborn as a dog or chicken.' He kowtowed again and then finally got up.

"'I wonder what time it is?' he asked.

"'It's close to daybreak,' I answered.

"At this point Cui seemed overcome with exhaustion and half-collapsed onto the floor. He rested his back against a wall and fell into a deep sleep. As dawn approached, it became much colder. I crossed my legs and sat quietly reflecting on what had just taken place."

"Suddenly a murmur spread through the hall. 'He's dead. Don't know when he hanged himself last night,' I heard someone say. Fearing his own imminent death and unable to stand the terror any longer, a frightened prisoner had hanged himself. Thin and weak, he had used his own belt to hang himself from the neck of one of the Buddhist statues. This enormous Buddha stared down at him with a sickening smile on his face, as if affectionately embracing his sweetheart as they made love.

"Cast in the cold, gray light of dawn, this tableau left an indelible impression that both amused and nauseated me. In the early morning light I could again make out the scene in the room: the prisoners anxiously awaiting death, the toppled Buddhist statues resting at all angles, and the corpses strewn here and there. All of those awaiting death sat around the edges of the hall with their backs resting against the wall, their eyes rimmed by dark circles, each man think-ing of his own death. As I turned to look back, I noticed a man lying not far from me in a corner with another man sitting by his side. The seated one was unbuttoning his clothing, removing it and plac-ing it over the other. One look told me that the one lying down was sick and, judging by the resemblance between the two, I could tell they were brothers. I've never forgotten the impression this scene left on me. I've often wondered what made the one brother remove his clothes and cover the other, given that both of them were but a short time away from death.

"Suddenly a sharp, ear-piercing noise came from outside, wave after wave, screech, screech. We knew the executioners were sharp-ening their knives. The noise echoed in the deathly quiet of the early morning and destroyed what little composure we had left. We all began to stir uneasily. To this day, when I have nightmares, I of-ten hear those same sounds and wake up. When the sound of knife-sharpening had ceased, the doors opened and the officer and execu-tioners entered.

"The second day of slaughter began. As before, the officer called out the names of six men to be executed. Cui was in the first group. As he left the men he was standing with, he shot a glance in my di-rection, raised his hand in a gesture of farewell, and walked over to the executioners. In a few minutes they had finished him off. There were still some who fled and ran about in fear. You could tell that one of them, the man who screamed the most and ran around the most hysterically, had already lost his mind. I thought at the time: here is a man who knows he is going to die, and who like the rest of us knows he has no hope of survival. A person can have the strength to accept death, but there is something even more terrifying than death—and that is going to your death. The first group was quickly dispatched and the executioners moved on immediately to the sec-ond group. The executioners were much quicker and more agile to-day, a definite improvement in technique over the previous day's performance.

"When they reached the third group of prisoners, one of the men's legs went weak and he couldn't walk, so another took off his clothes and said, 'I'll go first. It's just like passing through a door, being transformed into another being and then coming to earth again!' Among the five others in this group were a strong, healthy man and a fellow who was very young, just eighteen or so.

"Each time they called a new group, I expected to hear my name read out, but this never happened. They got to the fourth group and my name still wasn't called. They called up the two brothers, and the brother who lay sick was helped up to the executioners by the other. The healthier brother said to the officer, 'Sir, for heaven's sake, please have mercy. Execute me, but please spare my younger brother. Our mother is over seventy and has no one to care for her. Spare my brother to care for her in her remaining years.'

"The officer, taken aback, responded: 'You really have an active imagination. If you want me to accommodate you, I'll tell you what I'll do. I'll give you two choices and you choose one of them. The first is you both die. The other is the same—you both still die.' They killed those two brothers as fast as they had killed the others.

"Now the weak-legged fellow had to come forward. Previously he'd been so weak in the legs that he wasn't able to leave the group of surviving prisoners. The other man had come forward to replace him in the last round of executions. This fellow, however, lay collapsed on the floor like a lump of dough. The executioners could not move him nor could they get him to stay put on a bench. Killing him where he lay wouldn't work because he was collapsed in a pile and there was no place to stick the knife.

"'Hey, you, get up. Look how scared you are. You're not worth killing. We'll spare you and set you free. Get a move on, you can get out through the door over there,' one of the executioners said, pointing toward the door.

"'Really? Are you sure?' the man said with delight as he got to his feet. Walking toward the door to freedom, he shouted out with joy: 'My life has been spared! My life has been spared!' His legs regained their strength. His back straightened up.

"'Recovered now, are we,' the executioner muttered to himself as he proceeded to sink his knife into the prisoner's now straightened back. The man stuck up both hands high above his head, as if he were celebrating his freedom. His knees collapsed and he fell to the floor. The executioner chuckled with satisfaction at his own ingenuity.

"I guessed that I would be next, but I was wrong again. With the killing of the next group I witnessed another unforgettable scene. A terrified prisoner ran about asking everyone to save him, but of course none of us could. As the executioner was a few steps from seizing him, he knelt down, grabbed the hand of one of the corpses and asked the corpse to save him. The corpse stared back at him with lifeless eyes. It was only then that he realized he was holding the icy cold hand of a dead prisoner, and he was more panic-stricken than ever. He scrambled up, turned and grasped the arm of a Buddhist statue, but the staring eyes of the statue had no more life in them than those of the corpse. At this point, the executioner caught up with him, and, perhaps in a moment of inspiration, stabbed his knife into the crack in the prisoner's buttocks.

"I looked around and noticed that I was in the last group of six men. The officer was about to take care of the six of us, and so he ordered us to gather together. In an instant I thought about my life, and I felt I had nothing to worry about, since I figured my wife and child might also have been killed. What's more, in just a few minutes I would be tortured and killed by the Eighth Route Army. I'd lived forty-one years, and had no regrets. I calmly walked over to where the others had gathered.

"'Fate has smiled on the six of you,' the officer began. 'Ask your ancestors which one of them earned the merit that led to your being spared execution. We want you to know that the Communist Party can be magnanimous with criminals: We kill those we choose to kill and spare those we choose to spare. Things are looking up for you dogs. You're lucky enough to be left in the last group. We're not going to execute you. We're commuting all of your sentences to castration and will take care of that now. Everyone into that room next door!'

"The executioners had already opened a small door in the side wall. Beyond it was a hidden chamber, toward which they now dragged us. We all fought against going, since each of us felt that the humiliation of castration was worse than death. What's more, no matter how much we begged and pleaded for them to kill us, they refused to do so. We fought and struggled, and I can recall that I cried out in anguish for someone to save me as I was dragged into the small room. In the darkness I could see several small stools had been set out with a small knife placed next to each stool. Then the door was shut behind me."

General Guan paused at this point as large beads of sweat dripped from his forehead. Everyone in the room held his breath and looked at Guan with pity. He picked up a washcloth from a small saucer and mopped the sweat from his hairless cheeks. He continued in his abnormally high voice, "From that time onward I've lived a life that is only half human—half of what a normal man would live. The humiliation I suffered remains with me, something I can never erase." As he spoke, tears welled up in the corners of his eyes. All of the men bowed their heads and stared at the table as they sat in silence.

"Shunqing, Shunqing," the old man softly called out Guan's name. "You've suffered so much sorrow, but you've endured it—that's a brilliant victory. You need to gather your courage and tough it out. That's right, no matter how bad it gets, you need to hold on and keep on living. Living—that's what life is all about."

"That's what I've been thinking," Guan replied in tears. "Surviving is what life is all about. After I was released in Taiyuan, I fled to Shaanxi, and from there went to Yunnan, and from there traveled as a refugee to Dao Phu Quoc in Vietnam. For four years I endured nothing but deprivation and hardship. During that period, when I suffered bouts of depression at several critical points, I often thought of taking my life. But each time I was on the verge of despair, I would suddenly realize that life is far nobler than death. Even the lowest form of life, like a cow or a horse, must be preserved. Giving up is not the answer. After spending three years in Dao Phu Quoc, I came to Taiwan and ended my days of wandering."

General Guan hung his head in silence. He wiped the perspiration from his face and head with the washcloth (and he wiped the corners of his eyes as well). He had finished telling his story. "Eat,

Commander, the food is getting cold." General Guan raised his head and pointed at the food with his chopsticks and encouraged the others to eat. "General Tian, help yourself. Everyone dig in."

Zhang Degong smiled as he stepped up behind each of the men to refill their wine cups. When he had returned to the room, General Guan was about halfway through his story. When he heard General Guan telling the story, and Zhang Degong loved stories more than anything else, he listened spellbound, not taking into account that the cook downstairs was waiting for him to help with the chopping. Then he heard the old man say to Colonel Lu, "Colonel Lu, let's hear your story. Tell us about your experiences coming to Taiwan." Another story to listen to! No doubt the chef downstairs was cursing a blue streak. Zhang grew anxious, torn between his responsibilities and pleasure. In the end, the dispirited waiter sighed and headed downstairs.

II

"My story? My story is quite different than General Guan's. I didn't fall into a Communist trap in quite the same way he did. I also was trapped, to be sure, just a different kind of trap and, looking back on it, I don't think I fared any better than he did. But first, have some wine, Sir. We were paying attention to General Guan's story and forgot to drink any wine. Let's all drink another toast to our old commander." With that, Lu laughed and, using his left hand to hold his glass, joined his comrades as they faced the old man and drained their glasses in a single gulp.

"On the day Taiyuan fell, the commander of the Sixth Regiment, Colonel Zheng Guifang, and I retreated to the Temple of Lofty Goodness. We decided that we should not waste any time fleeing to Datong. Zheng Guifang and I were sworn brothers. Because I was three years older than him, he called me older brother and I called him Sixth Brother, because he fell sixth in position in his family. Zheng was a smart guy, really capable and good-looking as well. We had grown up together in the same village and later found ourselves together at the military academy and during the Anti-Japanese War.

"On this particular day, the city's defenses were broken and our forces nearly wiped out. I still had a little more than a company of men and he had less than half that number. We stood on the steps in front of the Hall of Great Sorrow, anxiously trying to come up with a plan of retreat. I said, 'Sixth Brother, I'm giving you command of half a company. You take them east and follow Tongpu Road. I'll head west with my men and meet up with you. Take a look at this map. Gao Village is here. We should both be able to make it there by sundown. From Gao Village they should have trains to Datong.'

"Sixth Brother looked at the map and, after a short pause, asked: 'Why should we take two different routes?'

"I explained my plan to him. 'First, we should be able to move faster. Second, we can help each other out. If one of us gets surrounded, the other can rush to his aid by providing a second front to help him escape. I have two American field telephones. Take one with you. We can keep in touch as we travel. If anything goes wrong, we can count on these foreign gadgets to notify each other. What do you think? Should we divide into two groups?'

"'I think we should,' he replied.

"'Let's get going, then. The Eighth Route Army will be here in no time.'

"'Do you want me to burn down these buildings, Elder Brother?' Using his sword, he pointed at the halls that surrounded us. In battle, he often held his sword in his hand and was accustomed to following a scorched-earth policy, setting fire to everything when he retreated from an area.

"I looked at the solemn and majestic temple halls resplendent in the sunlight. I said, 'Forget it. There's no time. Let's get going.'

"I stood up, folded the map, extended my hand to him and said, 'Sixth Brother, I'll see you again. Please be careful. Hopefully by sunset tonight, if all goes well, I'll see you again.'

"'Farewell, Brother,' Sixth Brother replied. I remember that a large vein stood out on his forehead. 'Please take care.'

"I gave him the field telephone and assigned him a portion of the men. He put a hand on his sword, strode away in his tall riding boots and led his unit east onto the plains.

"I led my men along a route to the north and everything went smoothly. I estimated that at the rate we were traveling, we should be able to reach Gao Village an hour before sunset. Both sides of Tongpu Road were planted with groves of princess trees that provided perfect cover to conceal us from the enemy forces. At that time of year, the princess trees were covered with masses of white blossoms that looked like winter snow. The American field telephone rang often with reports that everything was going well for Sixth Brother and his men.

"Just after 4 p.m. we reached Changfeng Slope. We had traveled about two-thirds of the way to our destination. Suddenly I heard bursts of gunfire and the princess petals began to rain down on me. We'd found the enemy and I ordered my men to get down, secure our position and return fire. Group after group of Communist soldiers emerged from behind the trees ahead of us. I ordered the machine-gun squad to concentrate their fire and blow them away. This barrage halted their advance and they took cover behind the trees. What awful luck! How could the enemy have pushed on to Gao Village so quickly? I cursed the bastards and called for the communications man to crawl over with the field telephone.

"'Sixth Brother,' I yelled into the handset. "'I'm really having lousy luck. I ran into the enemy!'

"'What?' he asked, his voice sounded very far away.

"'The Communists,' I answered. 'They're firing at us. Listen to the shooting.'

"'Where are you?'

"'Changfeng Slope. Where are you, Sixth Brother?'

"'We're at Oxtail Camp, almost to Gao Village. How many of them are there?'

"I looked at the groups of Eighth Route Army soldiers coming toward us and replied, 'More than I can count. At least three times our number.'

"'Are you sure they're the enemy, Brother? Could they be our people?'

"'How could they be ours?' I said, laughing, having just seen a red flag come out of the forest. 'We won't be able to hold them for long, Sixth Brother. There are too many of them. Can you get over here?'

"There was no answer. 'Come in Sixth Brother!' Still no response. 'Sixth Brother? Come in Sixth Brother! Sixth Brother!?' No answer. I heard a click, and it sounded like someone had hung up the receiver. 'Come in Sixth Brother! Sixth Brother! Do you hear me? Come in Sixth Brother! What the hell is going on?' I asked myself in utter confusion.

"Soon after, a wave of enemy soldiers came toward us, so I ordered my men to fire all their weapons in order to break up the enemy assault. I tried to call Sixth Brother again, but no one answered. I thought that perhaps they were rushing to our aid, so I waited patiently and ordered my men to do everything they could to hold off the enemy. We repulsed wave after wave of attackers, but an hour went by and Sixth Brother still had not shown up. Another half-hour passed, and then another and then another hour with no sign of help.

"The sun started to set and it began to grow dark. The enemy had already surrounded us tightly on both our left and right flanks, using a pincer attack. Half of my men lay dead on the ground. I guessed that the Communist troops would use the cover of darkness to attack us and was afraid they would soon launch a night offensive. I kicked over the field telephone and shouted, 'Fix bayonets! Break through their line!'

"From their positions in the forest, the enemy opened fire on us from the front and both the right and left flanks. I ordered my men to abandon all their equipment—helmets, canteens, packs and even their injured comrades and try to break through the enemy line at a certain point on our right as quickly as they could. With a united cry, we closed ranks and charged forward.

"Torchlight gave the forest an eerie red glow and the trees' shadows rose and fell like a band of ghosts dancing in a circle. With my handgun in my left hand and my sword grasped in my right, I charged screaming into a group of enemy soldiers. All around I could see shadows of people leaping about and killing, and could hear the mournful cries of the dying as well as the shouts of those who had killed them. After I brought my sword down smack in the middle of an enemy soldier's head, I saw a long wound open on his forehead. He swayed a couple of times and fell to the ground. Another Communist soldier leveled his rifle and then jumped toward me. I took aim at his face and fired. His face looked like it was covered with tomato sauce. He dropped his weapon and shielded his face with both hands. I knew he was a goner, so I didn't bother waiting for him to collapse. I turned around and looked for another target. Just at that moment, I was surprised when a dark shadow jumped out from behind a princess tree. He came charging at me with his sword held high above his head. The sudden appearance of the attacker, who seemed to materialize before me like some sort of apparition emerging from underground, took me completely by surprise. I rushed to block his blows but when he brought his weapon down on me, I dropped my sword and quickly pulled back my hand. Then I suddenly remembered the revolver I held in my left hand, so I fired a shot into his chest and the attacker fell to the ground. I dropped my weapon as fast as I could and used my left hand to grab my aching right hand, which was squirting blood.

"'We can move on, Sir. We've killed most of them. Oh, Colonel, are you wounded?' A corporal saw me bleeding, took me by the shoulder and led me to an open field where it would be easier to hide in the darkness. As we walked along, my injured hand continued to drip blood. Along the way, I stopped at an earth god shrine and tore some clothing into strips to bind up the wound on my hand. When I finally felt I had regained my composure, I counted the number of men still with me and discovered that only three had survived.

"Late that night I rushed into Gao Village, only to discover that Zheng Guifang had long since arrived and headed on to Datong by train. When I reached Datong, word had already spread that I had been killed, a rumor circulated by Zheng Guifang no doubt. By then, Zheng, who always was faster off the mark than anyone else, had secured a seat on a plane and flown to Qingdao.

"The more than one hundred and ten men I had commanded had died in vain, thanks to my sworn brother and friend of thirty years. And because of him, I, well, just look at this!"

He held up his right hand, but only four fingers were visible. Between his thumb and middle finger, where his index finger should have been, was a cavity that looked like the notched battlement of a city wall. He put his hand down and the guests quietly sighed, expressing their sympathy over his injury and the unfairness of the suffering he had endured.

"Where is this Zheng Guifang person now?" asked General Zha.

"I've heard he's in Taiwan," Lu replied. "He has some clerk job in a district government office in Taipei. I have not seen him again—have no interest in seeing him in fact." Colonel Lu paused for a moment and then continued. "No matter what I've been through, I'm happy to be gathered here with all of you today for this celebration."

Everyone joined in voicing their agreement and raised their glasses to toast Colonel Lu and congratulate him on his good fortune. Lu raised his glass in response, with his left hand.

"Now let's hear from Colonel Qin. Colonel, it's your turn," the old man called out.

The waiter Zhang Degong had just bustled into the room carrying a steaming hot platter of spicy roast lamb. He had been waiting impatiently downstairs and rushed up as fast as he could to hear more stories. Unfortunately, he had missed all of Colonel Lu's story, but the fact he had made it back in time to hear the next one made him so happy that he had to restrain himself. He withdrew to a corner of the room and focused his attention on Colonel Qin so he could savor every word he was about to hear.

III

Colonel Qin lifted his bowl to his mouth, lowered his head to take a sip of soup, raised his head, and asked, "My turn?" Quickly, he lowered his head again and drained his bowl. He had an unusually large head, and because it had just been shaved with a razor, it had a greenish shine to it. He let out a resounding belch, more than five seconds long, and then told his story in his thunderous voice.

"When Taiyuan fell, I was not in the city. I was in Qingcheng County. In March of 1948, I became county magistrate in Qingcheng and served until May of 1949. Qingcheng was the last stronghold in Shanxi province to fall to the enemy, and I have no regrets of conscience in spite of it. My third younger brother, who has now gone on to his eternal reward, had no regrets either.

"When I first became magistrate of Qingcheng County, the situation was getting bad. Students from everywhere were protesting and Communist activists were infiltrating every level of society. I invited my third younger brother to come and help me rule Qingcheng, and assigned him to serve under me as the secretary of the county government. We were more than just biological brothers. We'd been together since our youth, from our days of stealing fruit as children to running away and joining the army when we were older. So when it came to working together, we were just like old friends and got along great. Actually, he was the number two son in our family because my parents had only two sons. Originally there were supposed to be three of us, it just happened that our second brother died in a miscarriage. Since our unborn brother still had to be counted as part of the family, we referred to my younger brother as Third Brother.

"When I first arrived in Qingcheng, things were a real mess. The city itself was in chaos, there was no fighting spirit, and thieves and bandits were everywhere, giving Communist spies every opportunity to pursue their activities. But within three months, and mind you I don't mean to boast, I turned Qingcheng into the best county in Shanxi. It goes without saying that I restored order and, when I got through, the county I ruled didn't have a single Communist spy in it. Some say I governed too harshly, but in times of disaster extraordinary measures are called for. First I rounded up all of the Communist spies who were operating in the area, hauled them to the city market in trucks and had them shot. Then I imprisoned all of those people whose backgrounds seemed even remotely in doubt, including rounding up the three closest friends of each Communist spy. I shot a lot of them, too. I closed the two secondary schools in the county seat and locked up all of the teaching staff. I had most of these teachers, many of whom were women, killed. Naturally, there were some innocent people, but I would rather have killed ten innocent people than let one enemy spy go free. I was just as strict in my treatment of those who stole. No matter what was stolen, I had them shot. In three months I turned Qingcheng County into a place where your grandmother would be safe walking alone at night. Then I organized all of the men from sixteen to sixty into security teams. I even trained the women to handle guns and grouped them into women's security teams. This was my younger brother's idea. He said, 'Older Brother, I think the women could help us fight. After all, in ancient times there was Hua Mulan, so why not get the women involved?'

"In March of 1949, the Communists went on the offensive in Shanxi. Places not far to the east of us, including Heshun, Pingding and Xiyang, were all surrounded by the enemy. I issued an order to close the city gates and cut off communications with the outside world in order to prepare for battle. It came as no surprise that a few days later the Communists sent a battalion to take Qingcheng. They had no idea how strong our forces were and, within two hours, heavy fire from the city had forced them to break off their attack and flee. They retreated to a mountain ridge just outside the city. A few days later, they sent a battalion reinforced with another company of troops to attack us again. We kept our heads and they fled in defeat. On the third attempt, they dispatched a regiment of men and after the better part of a day of fierce combat, our artillery drove them away. As a result, the Communists knew that Qingcheng was no easy target. They pulled out their forces and targeted other counties in the region.

"Several days after the enemy retreated, while I was inspecting our defenses on the city wall, my younger brother came running up to me and gave me an exaggerated salute, his hand held up beside the rusty Japanese helmet he always wore. 'Beg to report, Sir, that a group of people are approaching us. I'm not sure if they're Communists or not.'

"Indeed, as soon as I looked, I could see a cloud of dust rolling along the yellow earth as a band of people dressed in black walked toward us. Third Brother had already climbed into the gunner's seat of one of our artillery pieces, closed one eye to judge the distance to their position and then aimed the big gun at them.

"'Halt!' I cupped my hands and shouted. 'Stay where you are. Move any closer and we'll open fire. Where are you coming from?'

"The group of people stopped and a short one came forward, cupped his hands and shouted back, 'We're from Taiyuan.'

"'What are you coming here for?'

"'Taiyuan has fallen!'

"'Taiyuan has fallen,' I repeated to my brother.

"'Really?' he responded with alarm.

"'Who are you?' I called out. 'You don't look like soldiers or civilians either.'

"'We're monks.'

"'They're monks,' I told Third Brother.

"'Merciful Buddha, monks!' he said. 'But are they real monks, or just soldiers from the Eighth Route Army in disguise. Hey brother, better talk with them to check them out.'

"'You bastards, you're not monks, you're nothing more than Eighth Route Army soldiers in disguise. I'm going to open fire,' I said.

"'Hold your fire, hold your fire!' the short one blurted out. The others shook with fear but stayed where they were. They didn't flee like enemy soldiers whose ruse had been found out.

"'What monastery did you say you came from?'

"'The Temple of Lofty Goodness.'

"'Fake monks, no doubt about it. What would monks have to fear from the Eighth Route Army?'

"'They want to kill monks!' the short one replied. "Last month all of the monks at Guangji Temple in Xugou were killed by the

Eighth Route Army. This month, all the monks at Hongan Temple in Qingyuan were thrown into wells.'

"'Huh!' I said, scratching my head, and thought to myself, 'they seem like real monks.'

"Finally I said, 'Alright, alright, whether you're real monks or not, we have no use for you here. We have too few people to fight and far too many mouths to feed.'

"'We'll help you fight.'

"'What?'

"'We can help you fight the Communists.'

"'Did you hear that? Did you hear that?' I said to Third Brother. 'Here we have monks that kill.'

"'Fake monks!' I replied. 'You just gave yourselves away—real monks don't kill people. I'm opening fire!'

"'Wait! Wait!' he called out. They again trembled in fear. 'We're real monks—when have you ever heard of fake monks! It was only because the Communist troops wanted to kill us first that we decided we would kill them.' As before, it seemed that none of them wanted to flee.

"At this point Third Brother thought of a plan. He said, 'Let me go down and check on things. I'll have a look at their heads. Real monks have scars on their scalps where burning incense was placed when they took their vows. If they have them, then they're real monks and we can let them in.' This seemed like a good idea so I let him take a team of men out with him. We opened the gate and he headed over to where they were waiting.

"I watched my brother as he inspected the head of each monk. Finally he raised his head, waved his arms at me and called out, 'They're real monks.'

"We welcomed this group of monks into the city. The short one who had acted as spokesman was an old man of about seventy. He had been the abbot of the Temple of Lofty Goodness. 'You just about killed us,' he told me.

"'Yep. If you had taken so much as a single step back, I would have had you blown to dust,' I answered.

"The sudden arrival of the monks created quite a stir in Qingcheng. Because their heads were really shiny from being shaved, wherever they went they were followed by a bunch of people interested in seeing what was going on. My brother looked at them with a smile on his face. The monks, however, wore serious expressions.

"After a short time, the old abbot became a bit uncomfortable and he asked me for guns so that he and his monks could help with the defenses on the city wall. I asked, 'Do you really want to fight?'

"'Absolutely!' he answered.

"'All right then,' I said with a chuckle, and then turned to a sentry and ordered: 'Give your gun to the old monk.' The old monk took the gun with a smile, but the way he handled it gave me some concern. 'Do you know how to fire a gun?' I asked.

"The old monk thought for a moment and then responded, 'We can learn.'

"'Enough, enough!' I grabbed the gun from him, let out a laugh and said, 'This isn't going to work. Why don't you just do laundry, prepare meals or do some other work.'

"That day my brother and I really teased the old monk. I asked him, 'Old monk, why did you leave home to take up holy orders?'

"'He had a fight with his wife,' my brother piped up.

"'If you're already a good person, why go and be a monk?'

"'Everyone who takes up holy orders has their own reasons, and we don't talk about them. Ordinary people wouldn't understand,' the old monk answered.

"On another occasion I asked, 'Old monk, do you really believe that there are bodhisattvas?'

"'Yes, there are five hundred bodhisattvas and arhats in the western paradise.'

"'Why didn't they protect you? How come you ended up being driven out by the Eighth Route Army?'

The old monk remained silent and sighed. My bother and I guffawed with laughter.

"Not long after, I found him again and said, 'Let me test you. I'll ask you a question and let's see if you are able to answer it. If you can, you're a good monk. You monks always say that the Four Noble

Truths are empty. Which Four Noble Truths do you mean?' The old monk's eyes widened, but he didn't answer. Our sides were aching from laughter.

"In the evening we invited the monks to join us for dinner. I told them not to stand on ceremony and to feel at home and eat whatever they liked. I had already eaten several bites of food when I realized they had yet to begin eating. They sat silently with grave expressions on their faces. I swallowed what I was eating, turned to my brother and asked, 'What's the matter? Why aren't they eating?'

"My brother shrugged his shoulders and turned up his hands to show that he didn't know, and then smiled.'

"'What's the matter,' I growled unhappily and put down my chopsticks. 'Is there something wrong with the food?'

"'I wouldn't dare to deceive you, Sir,' the old monk began, speaking for all of his brothers, 'but we monks cannot eat meat.'

"I burst into laughter. I had forgotten that monks are vegetarians, and I had forgotten to let the cooks know this. Not a single dish on the table was vegetarian, and the more I looked at the food, the more amusing I thought the situation was. I roared with laughter, and found that in my mirth, I couldn't help giving the old monk several hearty slaps on the back. I told him that I had forgotten and was to blame for the oversight, but I also added, 'The food is all prepared, and why don't we compromise a little. As far as eating vegetarian goes, it seems to me that such dietary restrictions are useless. Why don't we just forget about them? You've already given up your vow not to kill, what's the point of keeping your vow to be a vegetarian?'

"'We can suspend the vow to refrain from taking life, but we must keep our vow to be vegetarians. You don't understand our ways,' the old monk responded. There was some nervousness in his voice.

"'Actually, most monks would like to eat meat if given the chance,' my brother commented with a rude smile.

"'Those who want to eat meat don't have what it takes to be a monk,' the old fool replied.

"'Actually, monks eat meat on the sly,' my brother added.

"'Stop with your insinuations. Give me some proof. Those who lie will be burned in a cauldron of oil in the afterlife.'

"'Old monk!' I called out. 'Eat this piece of meat,' and with that I used my chopsticks to put some meat in his bowl.

"He used his chopsticks to return the meat to me and said, 'Eat it yourself!'

"'Sure you don't want any? Have some wine then.' I extended my arm and poured wine into his bowl.

"'We make no distinction between meat and wine,' he responded as he emptied his bowl.

"'Hey, this is different. I served you wine and invited you to drink it.'

"'I dare not accept. The sacrifice you are asking me to make is far too great.'

"'Drink it!'

"'You call this inviting someone to drink wine?'

"'If he doesn't want to drink, forget it,' Third Brother said. Then he laughed: 'Monks are afraid to eat meat, to drink wine and to sleep with women.'

"The old monk bowed his head and placed his palms together. All of the monks bowed their heads and placed their palms together.

"'You monks are afraid of sleeping with women, that's why you fled the Eighth Route Army,' I said. 'Listen to me, old monk, if you are captured by the Communists, they will arrange a marriage for you and match you up with an old nun.'

"'And if you get captured by the Eighth Route Army, they'll cut your head off,' the old monk responded.

"I jumped up with my pistol in my hand. My brother quickly grabbed my arm. 'You dog, I'll give you three seconds to drink this bowl of wine!' I shouted in anger.

"'Hah, I speak the truth, but you just don't want to hear it,' the old monk stood up and said. The rest of the monks stood up as well. 'Everyone in the province has heard the news that the Eighth Route Army General Wu Sanxiang is offering a reward for anyone who can bring him your heads—both you and your brother's heads. The Communists kill people, you kill people. Now you want to take my life, but since my head is worth no more than a few strings of coins, what makes me worth killing?'

"Suddenly a handsome young monk jumped up and said, 'Don't be angry, Sir.' He stepped in front of the old monk and continued, 'You want us monks to drink wine, but we dare not follow your order. Please allow me to break my vows rather than make our old abbot violate his.' So saying, he knit his brows, took the bowl of wine in both hands, raised it to his forehead and put the bowl to his lips. My fist flew out and struck wine bowl, shattering it and splattering wine on the floor.

"'Sit down all of you, sit down!' I ordered waving my hand. 'Keep your stupid vows, but tonight there's nothing for you to eat. If you want to eat vegetarian, I'm sorry but you'll have to wait till tomorrow . . . and tomorrow each of you will be given a gun.' I sat down. The old monk turned and looked at the other monks and they all smiled and all sat down with their hands placed together in an expression of reverent thanks.

"'Old monk,' I said, taking a drink of wine, 'you just mentioned something about someone wanting to cut off my head. What's all this about?'

"The old monk raised his eyebrows, a warm smile on his face, and replied, 'Let me explain. Wu Sanxiang hates you and your fine city to the core because he sent several contingents to attack you and all failed. So he decided on this plan of putting a price on your head so that whoever kills you and brings Wu your head, whether soldier or civilian, will receive a reward of a hundred taels of gold. He doesn't care whether you're brought in dead or alive as long as he gets your head. That's what it said on a Communist propaganda flyer we found on our way here.'

"'Uh-huh, so now my head's a trophy.'

"'Your brother's head also has a price on it.'

"'How much is my head worth?' Third Brother asked.

"'Just a bit less, ninety-five taels. But that's quite a lot,' the old monk said, as if trying to console him.

"'Hah-hah, Third Brother,' I said, roaring with laughter and pounding my brother on the back. 'We've struck it rich—we're wealthy now. Together, the two of us are worth almost two hundred taels of gold. Why didn't we find out about this sooner? But I'm richer than you are—five taels richer!'

"'Beg to report, Sir, but there's nothing strange about that—your head is bigger than mine.' Everyone laughed.

"'Hey, mess sergeant, more wine. No, change this banquet to a vegetarian feast,' I said.

"'I'd like to see the Eighth Route Army try and get hold of my head,' Third Brother added."

At this point, Colonel Qin stopped, belched loudly and tipped the wine bottle into his cup. The waiter Zhang Degong let out a long, happy sigh. Completely absorbed in the story, he smiled and said to himself, "This is great, what a great story to listen to."

"Well, we're out of wine," Qin said as he shook the empty wine bottle. "Waiter, go down and get more wine."

"Zhang Degong, go downstairs and bring us more wine," the old man repeated.

"Yes, Sir," the waiter replied feebly and left dejected.

Qin resumed his story, "The next day the enemy sent an entire division against us when they attacked Qingcheng for the fourth time. After half a day of bloody fighting, the Communists still had made no headway, and in the afternoon they stopped their attack but remained outside the city and gave no sign of leaving. This time, all of the monks joined us in the fight and distinguished themselves in battle, even though many of their shots missed their targets. I noticed that every time they shot an enemy soldier, they bowed their heads and mumbled a few lines from a sutra. I wasn't sure if this was to facilitate their own repentance or to expiate the sins of the dead and help their spirits reach heaven.

"Unfortunately, I was wounded in the head in this battle. A bullet grazed my scalp, another inch closer and I would have been reporting at the palace of Yama, the King of Hell. Fortunately it wasn't my turn to die, and I survived.

"As medicine was being applied to my wound, Third Brother laughed and teased me when he said, 'You really need to take care of that head of yours. Not only is everyone fighting over your prized noggin, even the bullets are fighting—to claim that large target.'

"'Take it easy. Put on more mercurochrome,' I told the army doctor. He wrapped my head with six big rolls of gauze. I looked a bit like one of those turbaned truck drivers, but there was nothing I could do.

"'Now they're really going to cut the price they're offering for that noggin of yours. With a hole in it, it's only eighty percent new. They should cut the price five taels,' Third Brother added.

"I didn't respond for a while. I thought for a minute, and then I said, pointing to my head, 'No discount. Now it's bigger than ever.' After that, everyone seemed to notice my head. I realized that the bandages made them think of the price on it. Even the old monk looked like he was about to laugh when he saw me. 'What are you staring at? There's nothing to look at!' I yelled at him. 'Wounded it may be, but don't think for a minute that anyone will get hold of it. It means more to me than it does to the Eighth Route Army: to them it's worth only one hundred taels of gold, but to me it's a priceless treasure. Even with a hole in it and wrapped in bandages, it's still priceless to me. Wouldn't you agree?'

"The old monk bent forward and rushed off. I noticed Third Brother was still standing nearby and squinting at me. 'Still laughing!' I said angrily. 'Have you forgotten you have a price on your head, too? Don't worry about my situation, I'd take care of myself if I were you!'

"He laughed uproariously. 'I'm concerned about your head because it's more important—it's worth more than mine.' He changed his tone: 'Even if the Communists hadn't put a price on it, I still think your head is much more important than mine.' Then he returned to his former, lighthearted tone and said, 'Besides I'm not worried—they'll never get my head. My luck has always been good. I've always been lucky and enjoyed good fortune. Think about it. So far, have I broken any bones? Have I burned so much as a single hair on my body?' he asked with a wink.

"Just after five o'clock, the enemy resumed their attack. Now another division of reinforcements had joined the first, and they had Qingcheng surrounded. This time they had more mortars, and shells were falling on the city from all directions.

"Circumstances changed for the worse as we found ourselves outnumbered and outgunned. Soon enemy shelling killed several men on the city wall, damaged two of our guns and blew up three sections of the wall. In a haze of gunpowder smoke I saw several black-clad monks carrying something. When I went over to see what it was, I discovered it was the old monk, who had been shot and killed. 'If this old fellow had listened to me and just stuck to washing clothes and cooking food, this never would have happened,' I said to the monks' retreating backs. 'He had bad luck,' added Third Brother.

"As night fell, Qingcheng was on the verge of collapse, so I tele-graphed neighboring places like Shouyang, Pingding and Yu counties to ask for support. Since the responses I received were all in some indecipherable code, it seemed clear that all three areas had fallen to the enemy. And since they had taken control of all three counties, they could concentrate their forces and surround Qingcheng. If those three counties had followed our example and strengthened their defenses, Qingcheng would not have been left to fight alone and bear the brunt of the enemy's full power. If we were to survive, heaven would have to will it so. I decided to abandon the city.

"I chose thirty men, twenty-three officers and the seven monks who had survived, and put together a plan to leave the city and try to escape that night. There was a heavily forested hill about a thou-sand yards to the rear of the city. If we could break through the en-emy lines that surrounded us and make it to the hill, we could use the forest as cover and travel by narrow paths to reach the Taihang Mountains. From Taihang, we could enter Henan and from there, cross the mountains in western Henan and enter the Hubei Central Area.

"Because I decided that we would climb down the city wall and then break through enemy lines, I ordered everyone to pack light. Only one man would carry a submachine gun.

"I told them: 'This man will start firing as soon as the Commu-nists discover we have broken their line. That will make them think we have more soldiers and greater firepower than we really do. It will create a diversion and block the enemy from coming after us so the rest can make for the safety of the hill. After he has delayed the enemy long enough for us to escape, he will abandon the gun and set off alone after us. We will wait for him at Seventh Master Shen's tomb, located beside White River Village, part way up the hill. This is a very dangerous mission, and I don't know who to assign it to. The man assigned must have courage, ingenuity and a quick mind, because the fate of all thirty of us will be on his shoulders, not just his own safety.'

"'I'll do it,' Third Brother responded.

"I was silent. As I looked over at him, I wanted to say, 'Let someone else do it.' But I held my tongue and asked, 'Do you think you can do it?'

"'No problem. I know the route and can operate the gun. I also know how to get out of a tough situation. I'm the only one here who can protect all of you. Don't say no, just let me do it.'

"'Alright, it's settled,' I answered.

"We started out early in the morning, around two a.m. All was still, not a hint of sound. We put our packs on our backs, shouldered our rifles, strapped on our swords and let ourselves down from the top of the city wall with ropes. Third Brother was the only man without a rifle, and he shouldered the submachine gun. After everyone had gone down, only my brother and I were left. I was to go down first and he was to follow. As I put my leg over the wall, I turned and shook his hand. 'Keep an eye on those hundred taels of gold,' he said to me. 'Always the joker,' I sighed.

"After I hit the ground, my brother's feet came sailing down toward me. Our team of thirty-one men crawled toward the Communist position. When we had gone only about a hundred yards, a voice called out, 'Halt! Who is it? Guangdong!'

"'Quick, run!' my brother whispered as he took the machine gun in his arms and fell to the ground.

"'Guangdong!'

"'Guangxi,' Third Brother answered back.

"'What? What did you say?'

"An explosion of machine-gun fire followed and bursts of light like a swarm of red fireflies. Third Brother opened fire. We ran as fast as we could to the hill when suddenly the machine-gun fire stopped. I could hear Third Brother call out, 'I surrender! I surrender!'

"'What?' someone near me asked softly.

"'Hurry! Run! That traitor,' someone else said with a hate-filled voice.

"'How many of you are there?' a voice called out from the enemy's location.

"'Thirty-one.'

"'Are Qin Liezong and his Third Brother with you?'

"'Yep. I'm Third Brother.'

"I almost couldn't believe my ears.

"'Don't move. We're coming to get your weapons.'

"Someone grabbed me and we began to run. After going about a hundred yards, the machine-gun fire began again. We finally understood what he was up to—he was tricking the enemy!

"We continued to run as the sharp bursts of the submachine gun continued. As we reached a knoll, the firing stopped. Only Third Brother could have pulled off something like this. He bought us time and drew the enemy closer so he could kill them more easily.

Seventh Master Shen's tomb lay beneath a stand of white poplars. We removed our gear and waited quietly by the tomb. A few minutes later, a man's shadow appeared climbing up the hillside. As it drew nearer, I could see that it was Third Brother, and from his gait he appeared to be limping.

"'You really pulled that one off, Third Brother,' I said as I rushed over to help him.

"He suddenly collapsed and fell to the ground. I scrambled over to him and cradled his head in my arms. 'Are you hurt, Third Brother? Did you get hit?'

"'Did I do all right? I almost . . . got all of them!' he said, his head resting on my arm. 'Too bad I got hit as I was retreating . . . not so lucky. There's no way to save me, Brother.'

"'Don't say that. Where's the wound? Let me take a look and put a dressing on it.'

"'There's no use . . . on a hole this big!' He turned over. In the dim light, I saw a large black crater in his back. He turned back over. 'May heaven kill the one who shot me . . .,' he said, coughing.

"'I'll bandage it for you. Then, I'll carry you,' I said.

"'Enough . . . at most I have . . . another hour . . . carrying me . . . just . . . slow you down . . .'

"'What a bastard I was. I should never have let you do it.'

"'Who says? Only I could . . . pull it off,' his voice rose higher with pride and satisfaction. 'No need to feel sad, Brother, I'm really happy now . . . I'm happy . . . to see you . . . and all the others . . . are all safe . . . you'd better get going, leave me here, don't worry about me . . . but before you go, Brother . . . could you . . . do something for me?'

"'Whatever you want, I'll do it for you.'

"'Don't let those Communist bandits get my head . . . if they cut off my head before I'm dead . . . I couldn't bear the humiliation . . . if they cut my head off after I am dead . . . I couldn't endure the embarrassment . . . so, please Brother . . . cut my head off.' Then with a piercing laugh, he said, 'When I joked about your head I never thought that . . . that now mine would be in trouble . . . Hurry Brother, it's getting light, the enemy will be coming to search for us!'

"I stood up, turned and walked over to the tomb. I hung my rifle, pack and sword on the tombstone. I took the sword from its sheath and walked back to where Third Brother lay. With a single stroke, I cut off his head. A soft, rustling sound came from the tops of the poplars as a cold wind blew and shook the tips of the branches. The others stood quietly surrounding us, as motionless as statues. I grabbed the severed head, walked over to where I had left my things, and placed it in my pack. I ordered everyone to put on his gear and get ready to move out. We all put on our packs and swords and then set off along a hillside path. My pack was somewhat heavier because my Third Brother's head was inside. Wearing this pack on my back, I crossed one mountain after another. Soon the light of dawn broke and the sun began to rise.

"As it approached noon, we climbed up to the Taihang Range. I was exhausted, my mind a blank. The sun's warmth made my forehead perspire and my eyes filled with sweat.

"'. . . Sir!' one of the men shouted beside me as he tapped my elbow lightly. I became aware that he had been calling to me for some time.

"'What is it?' I turned my head and asked.

"'There's blood leaking from your pack.'

"'Huh?'

"'Blood is leaking from your pack. It's been dripping for about half an hour.'

"I looked down and noticed that blood was dripping onto the ground behind me. I took off the pack and sadly addressed my brother's head: 'Are you angry, Third Brother? Would you like me to avenge you? If so, rest assured that I swear to spend the rest of my life seeing that the Communists are destroyed. If you're not angry, could it be that you're unhappy going too far from home or from your body? If so, then I'll bury you here.'

"At the time, we happened to be on top of a mountain. Just a few steps to one side a tall, straight pine tree stood off by itself. I chose a spot beneath this tree to bury my bother's head. The other men used their swords to help me dig the hole. When it was ready, I removed the head from my pack. I held Third Brother's head in both hands and carefully placed it in the hole. I pushed in the dirt we had excavated, filled the hole and tamped it smooth. A young monk stood to one side, bowed his head and recited sutras.

"I led the others forward as we continued on our journey. Part way down the mountain path, I turned back to look at that lone pine. Before I started up the next mountain, I turned back again to look but the tree was no longer visible. I could, however, see a vast expanse of white cloud covering the mountaintop."

After two minutes of silence, Qin reached out to grab the wine bottle and everyone knew that he had concluded his story. He bowed that enormous, shiny head of his and drank wine as if it were water. Everyone in the room sighed in response to Qin's tale.

When the story was almost over, the waiter Zhang Degong brought more wine up from downstairs. When Zhang heard Colonel Qin explain how he had put Third Brother's head in the hole, he had to clench his teeth to keep from throwing up.

Colonel Qin ate and drank heartily from the food and wine before him, as if the idea of "eating" was the most important thing in his life. He raised his shiny head and belched loudly.

"What happened to your brother's headless corpse? Did you ever find out?" Commander Jiang asked.

Qin shook his shiny head, thought about saying he didn't know, but was cut off when he suppressed a series of burps.

IV

"We ought to hear from Brigadier General Zha now," the old man said.

All eyes focused on Zha. He had a dark complexion, a bony face with a square jaw and a pair of warm, friendly eyes. He took a long drink from his wine cup, put it down, sighed and began to speak:

"When Taiyuan fell, most of our tanks had been hit and burned by artillery shells. Headquarters issued an order to disband my unit, which meant it would be every man for himself. Since there was no hope of reorganizing the unit, I just stopped my army truck and jumped down.

"'Commander Zha, come here, quick.' A jeep suddenly pulled up beside me and the commanding officer, who was standing in it, called out to me. 'We're heading for the airport. Word is there's still one last plane bound for Datong. Hop aboard!'

"'No,' I replied.

"'What? Are you thinking of defecting?'

"'Nope, I'm going home.'

"The commander was silent, but then said after a moment's pause, 'If you're going to head home, how will you get out?'

"'If I don't go back, who's going to help my wife and children escape?'

"'I won't detain you. I hope to see you again. Best of luck, General Zha.'

"'Farewell, Sir.'

"After his jeep had turned and driven off, I headed into the fields. I found the corpse of a peasant who had been hauling munitions for the army. I stripped off my uniform, put on his clothes and donned his conical bamboo hat. I stuck my pistol inside my clothes. Dressed this way, I headed for Maolü. The village lay to the southwest of Taiyuan and was on the west bank of the Fen River, about a day's journey away. I took the less-traveled paths through the forests in order to conceal myself from enemy forces. I knew that nothing good would result if I ran into anyone and was questioned.

"As I journeyed home, I thought about how worried my wife and children must have been for the past several days. My wife no doubt had gone to offer prayers at the local temple. My oldest daughter, Shuyi, who was quiet and calm by nature, would be helping her mother take care of things at home . . . My second child, our son Guobin, had turned seventeen, and was already in his first year of high school . . . Our third child and second son, Guoqiang, was just fifteen and was in his third year of middle school. The two boys were good students. Before the Battle of Shengyuan, I told them to leave the county school where they were boarding and return home to stay with their mother and sister. Then I gave them instructions about what they should do afterward. Just thinking about these things made me wish that I could see them all the sooner.

"When it grew dark, I came to the bank of the Fen River. I looked for a ferry, but none was in sight. I immediately realized that I was stuck there. I stood on the bank uncertain about what I should do. When I'd first set off, I hadn't considered the possibility that with all the chaos caused by the collapse of the Nationalist forces, there might not be any boats on the river. Suddenly the shadow of a boat floated downstream toward me. I was so happy that I almost rushed forward to call out to the boatman, but I restrained myself, since I didn't know if this was a Communist army reconnaissance boat or a ferry. There were several willow trees behind me, so I climbed one of them. When the boat sailed in front of me, I called out, 'Boatman, hey boatman, can you take me across the river?'

"The boatman heard my shout and stopped paddling. 'I'll take you across,' came the boatman's reply as he pulled his craft up to the riverbank. 'Where are you?' I remained silent.

"'Where are you?' he called again.

"When I heard his voice, saw that he was alone in the boat and could tell by the shadow cast by his head that he seemed to be wearing a farmer's hat, I made the decision and jumped down from the tree. 'I'm over here,' I said, standing right in front of him.

"'Oh!' he seemed to be startled.

"'Can you ferry me across the river?' I asked again.

"'Hop aboard,' he replied.

"I clambered aboard his narrow boat and crouched down in the stern. He stood in the middle of the boat, just slightly toward the bow. A few minutes passed, but the boat didn't move.

"'Why haven't we set off?' I asked. No reply. After a moment, I heard him begin to laugh ominously. 'Why were you hiding?' he asked. He laughed that miserable laugh again. I sensed something awful was about to happen and was on the point of jumping back on shore, but he squatted down and with a push of his long bamboo oar the boat glided away from shore and out into the river.

"I got nervous and regretted that I had been so rash to board the boat so hastily. I had no idea who the boatman was. He wasn't a Communist soldier, but was he a real boatman? Why was he the only boatman out on the river? Doubts began to multiply, but I couldn't very well ask him to return to shore. The long oar he grasped groaned in the oarlock as the boat rocked back and forth with his sculling.

"We sailed along in silence for more than ten minutes. My hand grasped the handle of the revolver I had concealed in my clothing. Suddenly the boat stopped in the middle of the river. The boatman pulled his oar from the water and placed it on the deck. 'What are we stopping for?' I asked with alarm.

"'Eh?' He laughed a little. 'No need to rush, let's take our time. I just want to take a break and have a cigarette.' There was nothing I could say, since I couldn't stop him from smoking.

"'Where are you heading after we cross the river?' he asked casually.

"I hesitated for a moment and answered, 'Home.' I thought this answer wouldn't cause any trouble. My voice was cold, avoiding any conversation with him.

"'So you're heading home. Where's home?'

"After a moment of silence, I responded, 'Yanming Village.' He responded with a burst of laughter.

"'I live in Wuyun, the neighboring village,' he said. He struck a match and a blossom of flame lit up his face, an old man's face lined with wrinkles. He suddenly brought the match closer to me, casting light on my face. Fearing that I would be discovered, I quickly lowered my head and allowed the broad brim of my farmer's hat to conceal my face. 'Have a smoke,' he said as he moved the match over and handed me a cigarette.

"'I . . . I don't smoke,' I stammered. When the match went out, my anxiety eased.

"'What, someone who doesn't smoke?' he replied with a mocking laugh. I was hoping he would pick up his long oar right away and resume paddling. 'Where'd you just come from?' he asked.

"After a few moments' pause, I said, 'I was visiting relatives.' He didn't press me further.

"'You a farmer?' he asked a moment later.

"'Yep, why do you ask so many questions?' I answered angrily.

"I waited for him to answer, but he made no reply. He remained silent for a while and dipped his oar in the water, paddling forward again.

"The rocking motion made me nervous, because now he seemed to be sculling much faster than before. To me, the quickened rhythm of his motions suggested some sort of determination on his part. I was worried about where exactly he was heading. Who was he? Was he a real boatman? Why was he the only boatman on the river? All of these questions came suddenly to mind. I couldn't restrain myself from asking, 'Boatman, why are you the only one out ferrying customers?'

"He continued to propel the boat forward without even the slightest reduction in speed. He replied:

"'Because all of the young people have been pressed into hauling munitions for the army!'

"I said no more, but he asked another question.

"'How is it the army hasn't pressed you into service?'

"'I'm sick,' I responded. 'They have no interest in the old or the sick.'

"'Ha, ha, ha,' he laughed, paddling the boat as quickly as before.

"'We're here,' he said as he put down his oar and took out a bamboo pole. He used the pole to push the boat to shore. I finally breathed a sigh of relief.

"'When I saw how anxious you were to get to shore, I decided to paddle as fast as I could. You have to admit this old boatman is more than a match for those young ones.'

"I stood up, let go of the handle of the revolver and reached inside my pocket to pull out a large bill to pay him.

"'Sir!' he exclaimed.

"'No need to give me change,' I replied, in a hurry to get away from that boat.

"'But Sir . . .'

"'Don't bother with the change,' I said as I prepared to jump ashore. Suddenly a hand reached out and grabbed my shoulder from behind and pulled me back.

"'What are you doing?'

"'Sir, don't you know that this money is no good?' I let out a sigh of surprise. 'No matter, next time you can pay me for both trips.' He handed the money back to me and relaxed his grip on my shoulder. 'No need to worry about you getting away without paying. Everyone who takes my boat to cross the river ends up taking it at least once more to cross again. At least that has been my experience since becoming a boatman here,' he laughed.

"As I jumped ashore, I felt as if a tremendous weight had been lifted from me. I hurried in the darkness to find the road and rush to Maolü Village.'

"Ten minutes into my journey I encountered the enemy. There were three of them, about seven or eight paces ahead of me. I quickly fell to the ground and concealed myself in a patch of grass. Had I not noticed them before they noticed me, there would have been no time to hide.

"'What's that up ahead? Looks like someone's over there,' one of the Communist bandits called out as he noticed the movement.

"A bullet whistled past the bamboo hat I was wearing. Without thinking, I lowered my head. Now other bullets were fired at me, some brushing my neck and back and others flying past my arms and legs. I crawled to the right to escape, but as I did so, one of the bandits called out, 'He's over there. I heard the grass move. Quick, kill him!'

"A hail of bullets rained down on me. In a few minutes, I thought, I'll be dead, and in the anxiety of the moment, I came up with a plan. I tightened my throat and cried out in a weak voice, 'Meow. Meow. Meow.'

"The sound of shooting immediately stopped. 'So it was nothing but a cat—bah!'

"'Shit, all that firing for nothing. Let's get out of here.'

"They had gone only a few steps when one of them called out, 'Wait a minute. Cats are good. It's been three months since we've been rationed so much as a cube of horsemeat in our platoon. If we could bring back a cat, we could all have a treat.'

"'You've got a point. Where did you think it was hiding?'

"'Over there, if I remember right.'

"Bullets again began to fly toward my hiding place. As they fired, they laughed and said, 'This cat's time is up. We've got it trapped in a storm of bullets.'

"'Too bad it ran into three starving guys like us,' another responded. They all guffawed loudly.

"'A cat should know better than to challenge the Eighth Route Army.' They again burst into loud laughter. Quietly and with great care I crawled away from the intense hail of bullets toward a safer spot.

"'Listen! The animal is on the move. Aim over to the right!' The bullets again began to fly in my direction and showered down upon me.

"'Stop firing,' someone suddenly called out. 'Let me listen for a second. Was it a cat? If so, why hasn't it cried out again.' The three of them stopped firing their guns and listened intently.

"At that moment I thought about meowing again, but I was afraid that the sound would make it easier for them to guess my position. I also feared that by responding to their comments I might give myself away. Frightened and not sure what to do, I was relieved to hear one of them say, 'Maybe we've killed it already.'

"'No, if we'd killed it, it would have really let out a yelp. We couldn't have missed hearing that.'

"'Maybe it got away.'

"'Yeah, maybe it got away. Let's get going. So we didn't kill a lousy cat—forget it. Let's go.'

"The three of them went off grumbling and griping. When they'd gone a good distance, I climbed out of the clump of grass where I had been hiding and continued on my way to Maolü.

"When I could see the village, the moon was already sinking toward the west. A soldier holding a lantern was on guard at the bridge leading into Maolü. I thought for a while and figured that it would be impossible to enter via the bridge. The village was surrounded on all sides by a river and normally was reached by bridges, so there was no way to get in except by swimming, but I didn't know how. I remembered there was a section of the river on the right side of Maolü that was shallow enough to ford, so I headed that way."

"When I found the place to cross, I removed my clothes. A bright star shone a cold light in the sky, and thick frost covered the ground. I endured the chill all over my naked body. As I walked into the icy cold river, my body felt as if it were on fire. Holding my hat and clothes high above my head, I entered the river, moving from shallow to increasingly deeper water. The water reached first to my waist, then to my chest and then almost to my neck. I realized the water was deeper than I had remembered. Then I recalled that it was the time of the spring thaw, and I had visions of myself drowning. But when I thought of the faces of my wife and children, and I knew they were close by, I steeled myself and continued onward. As the water covered my head, and my feet struggled to touch something, I feared for a moment that I was done for. After struggling with all my might for a few minutes, my feet again touched bottom and my head popped above the surface of the water. I had just crossed the deepest part of the stream. Not long after, I climbed onto the bank. I had finally made it home.

"After entering the village, I crept along the walls for fear of running into a night patrol of Communist troops. When I saw the empty lanes bathed in the dim light of the moon, now sinking in the west, it seemed like I was in a deserted village. When I arrived at my home, I stood before a small window and my heart started to pound as I struggled to control my excitement and joy. First, I softly knocked twice on the window and called out my wife's name. No answer. I knocked softly several more times, but still no response. I figured she was sound asleep. I walked to the front door and considered ringing the doorbell, but when I reached the door, I stopped dead. The door stood open and the inside was dark and deserted.

"I headed to my neighbors and knocked on their door. Only after several minutes had passed did someone answer, 'Who is it?'

"'Father Ai, it's me, Zha Number Two.'

"'Who?'

"'Your neighbor, the second child of the Zha family.'

For a minute there was no response. Then came the sound of the door bolt being drawn back.

"'Come in,' he ordered in a whisper. 'You're Little Whistle, Zha Number Two?' The half-blind old man looked me over.

"'That's me. Where have my wife and children gone?'

"'Little Whistle, you'd better sit down.'

"'Where have they gone? Tell me now!'

"'The truth is they're all dead.'

"'What?'

"'Your daughter was raped first, and then shot. Your sons also fell victim to the enemy and your wife committed suicide. I'll tell you about this pitiful tragedy, that is if I can prevent sorrow from strangling my voice. All this took place three days ago. A group of Liberation Army soldiers broke down the door to your home. They cleaned out your closets and trunks and then took your daughter into the rear courtyard to rape her. Your wife begged them to stop as only a mother could beg for her daughter, even to the point of kneeling on the ground and pleading for mercy. They didn't just ignore her—they beat her fiercely. Your wife was a brave woman. She ignored all danger and struggled to plead for your daughter's sake, but blows rained down upon her and she collapsed on the ground. Oh, those two sons of yours, you should be proud of them. They upheld your family honor, for when they saw their mother and sister being attacked, they ran into the house and took down the two swords you had hanging on the wall. Quick as lightning, one rushed to save your wife, while the other rushed to aid his sister. Being young, they lacked the strength to use the heavy swords properly, but they did everything they could to protect their mother and sister. Before long, however, the enemy soldiers had shot both of them dead with their revolvers. After your daughter was raped, it turned out the bandits had more abuse in store for her, for the Liberation Army soldiers wanted to take her with them to be a comfort woman for their troops. When she cried bitterly and refused to go with them, they grabbed her by the hair and dragged her. As she struggled to resist, she bit the hand of one of the men who was dragging her. Blood began to drip from his hand. Crazy with anger, the man pulled out his revolver and pumped three shots into her. She ended up dead like her brothers. When your wife saw all three of her children lying dead on the ground, she lost the will to live, went back inside and hanged herself from a beam. This is the account of the murders that took place in your home. Because my vision is so poor, I did not see these events happen with my own eyes, but I heard everything from start to finish with my own ears. Since this bloodbath occurred in the bright light of day, lots of people saw what took place. Strange to say, but I felt lucky to be blind then. How could I have stood to witness such a bloody tragedy?' When he finished recounting the events of the murders, I rested my face in my hands.

"'It's too bad that you came all the way back—there's nothing you can do, it's too late. Did you have to take a lot of dangerous risks to get here?'

"'Countless dangers, mile upon mile of road,' I said. Suddenly I felt like a city whose defenses had been overwhelmed and I began to cry in huge, loud wails.

"'Hold your grief, Number Two,' said Old Father Ai, growing nervous. 'I hear someone coming, Number Two, I can hear it very clearly. They're just six yards away, now five yards. Probably a troop on patrol—they're coming this way—they're running over—they've heard you! Number Two, be quiet!'

"I quickly stifled my sobs and held my breath in order to force the sobs of grief into my chest. 'Bam! Bam! Bam!' Someone pounded thunderously on the door. The patrol stood outside.

"'You'd better run, Number Two. Head out the back door and get out of the village as quick as you can.'

"'Bam! Bam! Bam!' There was a second round of pounding on the door as someone shouted from outside, 'Open the door! Who's making a racket in the middle of the night?' I rushed out the back door and left.

"I wandered about in the dark, empty fields with no particular destination in mind. I sneaked out of the village by hiding aboard a hay wagon and concealing myself under the pile of straw. Not really conscious of what I was doing, I walked around in the wilderness for who knows how long. In the end, I found I had returned to the banks of the Fen River.

"Eventually that long, painful, dark night ended as the pale glow of daybreak appeared on the horizon. The Fen River was still flowing; I remember the rushing sound.

A small boat floated out of the early morning mist and headed rapidly downstream with the current. I walked on with no particular destination in mind. If I reached the water, then my journey would end at the river. If I happened upon a boat, then I would continue on my way by boat. When I raised my hand to hail the boat, it stopped and headed in my direction. As the boat reached shore, I heard a laugh, and then the words, 'Those who cross the river in my boat will end up taking it again to cross the river. A pleasure to see you again, Sir.' I realized this was the same boat I had taken the night before.

"'Don't go,' he said as he grabbed me by the arm, stopping me as I was about to jump back ashore. 'You can't leave, you owe me a fare. You owe me.'

"'It doesn't matter if you try to detain me, I still don't have any money to pay you.'

"'That's fine, the more you owe me the better,' he said, his grin revealing his teeth.

"'I already owe too many debts in this lifetime,' I muttered as I looked at the circular wake the boat had left on the surface of the water. The boatman's long oar creaked in the oarlock.

"'When you work on the river, there's nothing more interesting than observing people. Many passengers are just like you. They cross the river and cross back not long after—what was the use of crossing in the first place? Where do you want me to take you this time?'

"'You don't care if I don't have the fare?'

"'Do you think I'm hurting for money? How do you know I won't ask for some other kind of payment?' he said with a laugh.

"'I have no idea what kind of payment you want or whether I can pay it, but I do know that no matter who I may be, if you ferry me across the river, you're certain to be compensated some day.'

"'We've reached the center of the river. Where to?'

"'The Temple of Lofty Goodness,' I replied. I planned to spend the rest of my life taking refuge in the temple. I'd come to this decision at dawn that morning. My family was gone and since Nanjing had fallen to the Communists three days earlier, the Republic was lost as well. The Temple of Lofty Goodness was my last place of refuge.

"'Why do you want to go there?' the boatman asked.

"'I'm going to . . . look at that!' Two corpses floated past the bow of the boat and I took the opportunity to change the subject so I could avoid having to make up any more excuses.

"'Washed down from one of yesterday's battles,' he said. As we got closer, I could make out an Eighth Route Army uniform and a Nationalist Army uniform, the two corpses floating not even a yard apart. They eventually floated out of my field of vision.

"'What's the matter? Don't want to talk?' he asked.

"'What?'

"'I asked you something and I want you to answer. Why are you going to the Temple of Lofty Goodness?' he demanded.

"'Is this interrogation of yours part of the debt I owe you—is it the repayment you were referring to?'

"'Oh, that's a riot,' he laughed. 'You're just as testy as when you crossed the river last night, maybe even testier.' At this point he started to paddle the boat in circles as if playing some kind of game with me.

"'Where did you just come from?' he asked me again.

"Angry with impatience, I nearly blurted out 'Maolü Village,' but fortunately I caught myself in time and said, 'I've already told you, Yanming Village. Why do you keep questioning me?'

"'No reason,' he chuckled. 'No special reason,' he said knowingly. 'Just asking, because you might happen to have gone somewhere else, come from somewhere like Maolü for example.'

"'So you think I'm from Maolü, is that it?'

"'Oh, when did I say that?' His eyes narrowed as he smiled and spoke to me. 'I forgot to have you give my regards to your family, your family in Yanming—your wife, your sons and your daughter. No doubt they've been waiting a long time for you to return. When they saw you, they must've been thrilled to welcome you home. With the war going on for so long, how could they have expected you, the noble head of the house, to return so suddenly? No doubt you have partaken of the joy of being reunited with your family? How come you're alone? What about that happy family of yours?'

"'You've taken far too much pleasure with your questions,' I said, grinding my teeth. 'I'll tell you what happened—they were all murdered!'

He looked at me with his mouth agape. The sly look suddenly vanished from his face and was replaced with a solemn expression. 'I'm sorry, I'm very sorry,' he said softly. He didn't open his mouth again. The boat stopped circling and continued on its way.

"Suddenly the air was filled with snowflakes. They fell thickly, a sheet of heavy snow. 'This doesn't happen very often,' the boatman said. 'It's the end of April and we're still getting snow.' The hills and plains on both banks were soon covered in white powder.

"'Wait a minute, stop, where are you taking me?' I discovered that the boat was now traveling with the current. I had no idea when he had turned around. Probably after he stopped circling, I guessed.

"He stopped the boat and pulled in his long oar. 'We're here. This is the Temple of Lofty Goodness.'

"'Where is it?' I asked, as I looked in all directions and saw no sign of a temple.

"'Alright, it's not here.'

"'What did you say?'

"'It's not here, General,' he said, the sly smile reappearing on his face. Suddenly I put my hand inside my clothes and grabbed the handle of the gun. 'General Zha,' he called out with a smile.

"'Who are you? How do you know who I am?' I released the safety catch on my pistol.

"'Sixteen years ago, I was a subordinate of yours, but you've long since forgotten me. Sixteen years ago you ordered me to be beaten with sixty blows of the disciplinary rod and had me demoted from sergeant to corporal. That night I fled in anger. I have you to thank for the fact that I'm now a boatman. If I hadn't been demoted, today I'd be a major or lieutenant-colonel at least. All thanks to you! But I have no reason to be jealous of you. You're no longer a brigadier general. What are you now? A farmer!' He laughed. 'You know, I recognized you right away, when I tried to light your cigarette. I got a kick out of watching you try to hide your identity. I decided to have a little fun at your expense, give you a hard time. That's over, you have no need to worry any further.' He laughed again. 'Fooled you, didn't I?' he said, laughing. '... You noticed this isn't the Temple of Lofty Goodness. The temple was taken by the Communists, and has been turned into a big temporary prison camp. If you went there, you'd be putting yourself in certain danger. That's why I didn't take you there. Becoming a monk isn't a solution, even if it were possible now, which it isn't, General Zha.'

"'How did you find out the Temple of Lofty Goodness has been taken over by the Communists?'

"'Yesterday, about nightfall, a young monk took my boat across the river. He had just fled from the temple. All the other monks had already left, and the abbot had left him to keep an eye on things. Since he was young, the abbot figured the Eighth Route Army wouldn't give him a hard time. When the enemy arrived, he hid in the eaves of one of the buildings. He saw with his own eyes all their guns and cannons lined up in the courtyard. He got so frightened that he began to tremble. The more he saw, the more his fears grew. In the end, he disobeyed the abbot's orders, left the monastery and fled. He was the one who told me about the takeover. This paper should prove what I say. Take a look.' He handed me an official notice printed on a large sheet of paper. I took it and read:

An Official Notice to all People Living in the Taiyuan Liberated Area

To all residents living in Taiyuan City: The Chinese People's Liberation Army has successfully liberated the city of Taiyuan. All administrative and public security functions in the city are under the control of the Shanxi Regional Command of the People's Liberation Army. This proclamation declares that martial law has been imposed in accordance with the following regulations. All residents of the city are expected to abide by the regulations.

(1) All Nationalist spies will be executed on the spot; those who hide them or fail to report them will be executed.

(2) All heads of household must go to their appropriate neighborhood registration office before 12 o'clock noon on April 26 to register their families, property and real estate holdings, the titles of books they hold, and any firearms or weapons (including all knives longer than three inches) in their possession.

(3) All buildings belonging to government offices, schools

*and temples will be given over to the People's Liberation Army
for housing troops.*

*(4) All monks and nuns must register at public security offices be-
fore 12 o'clock noon on April 26 and will at the time of registration be
ordered to resume secular life . . .*

"I returned the paper to him, cast a sidelong glance at the water's
surface and asked, 'So there isn't a single monastery left?'

"'Master Zha, your day of reckoning has come!' With that, he
suddenly jumped up and with both hands raised his oar skyward
and prepared to bring it down. 'Communist spy!' I thought to myself, and I quickly pulled out my revolver. But just as I did this, the
boat rocked violently. As I panicked and grabbed anxiously for the
side of the boat in order to keep from falling into the water, my gun
fell overboard and sank to the bottom of the river. He still held the
long oar high over his head, and I realized that he had rocked the
boat with his foot. I thought he would bring the oar down on me in
the next second."

"'Ha, ha, ha, ha!' he guffawed, throwing the oar at his feet. 'Good!
Come to your senses, have you? Don't want to kill yourself anymore, do you? Thinking of jumping in the river, right?'

"'He knew what I was thinking!' I said to myself. 'How could
that be?'

"'I wanted you to see that you really didn't want to commit suicide. Your real desire is to live. Look how fast you pulled out your
gun! Don't be deceived by a moment's sorrow, you should follow
your true ambition and keep on living. Give it some thought. De-
vote the rest of your life to the noble work of fighting communism
and avenging the defeat of the Republic. There aren't too many enemy soldiers in this area. If you climb ashore here, go into that grove
of willows and head due west, you can reach the Nationalist-held
East Shaanxi region in just half a day. From there you can fly to Taiwan, an offshore island that can be built up and developed. Perhaps
some day you can restore Republican rule here. There's no reason to
be upset over our temporary defeat. Just think, in ten or twenty years
you can stage a comeback. Here, this is the place to go ashore.'

"I was deeply moved by his words. 'And what about you?' I suddenly asked.

"'An anti-Communist force is needed in China's heartland as well as overseas. We'll meet again in the not too distant future. Just don't wait too long—ten or fifteen years tops. Get going!'

"I climbed ashore and watched the boat sail off. I suddenly cupped my hands and called out, 'Hey, Boatman, I forgot to ask your name.'

"'I am a man facing adversity—no name,' he called back.

"With the snowflakes blowing around him, he grasped his long oar and, with a bend of his legs, he propelled the boat upstream.

"This is the story of how I fled to Taiwan."

V

"Let's hear the last story. Staff Officer Duan, it's your turn," the old man said, taking a sip of wine.

Duan, his hair as white as frost, gave the same smile he always gave, and stared at the old man. From the start of the gathering up to now, he had not said a single word, yet he had never ceased to smile. After several seconds, he stood up, smiled, faced everyone and then sat down and nodded with a grin.

"Commander," Colonel Lu called softly from the opposite side of the table, pointing to his temple with an index finger.

"He spent three years in Communist prisons," Commander Jiang whispered into the old man's ear in explanation. Duan nodded with a smile on his face.

VI

Four stories had been told. The atmosphere in the room now was not what it had been while the stories were recounted. Now, the joy and ease that had been present at the start of the banquet returned. Fat General Guan's hairless cheeks were shining as he picked his teeth with his eyes closed, a satisfied, happy expression on his smiling face, the same kind of expression you make when you clean your ears. Colonel Lu's face was flushed an even deeper shade of red from the effects of the wine; he lit a cigarette and held it in his left hand. The wine had the opposite effect on Colonel Qin, whose face became paler the more he drank. He was trying to get the waiter to serve more wine. Only General Zha was different. His eyes stared straight ahead as if focusing on something in the distance. Staff Officer Duan sat to one side, observing all that went on with a smile.

Brigadier General Qiu and Colonel Feng stood before their former superior:

"Sir," they said in unison, "we would like to propose a toast to you."

General Tian gently grabbed his father's arm and said, "Dad, slow down on your drinking. Don't forget your blood pressure."

Commander Jiang glanced at the table and quietly asked the waiter, "Hey, is there any more food coming?"

"No."

"No?"

"There were a lot of other men attached to our command that I've lost touch with. Why don't I ask to see if any of you happen to have news of their whereabouts. One of you is bound to know something about them. How about Liu Fangzun? Who can tell me what happened to him?" the old man asked.

"He's dead, a casualty at the Battle of Xubang," General Guan responded.

"What about Ma Junmou, the leader of the Third Division?"

"He lives in Taiwan, right in Fengyuan. Since coming here he's become an alcoholic. He's living with a Taiwanese woman. He has no regular job and makes a living by gambling. I sent him a letter last week and told him about our party for you, but he never responded," Commander Jiang explained.

The old man shook his head and asked, "How about the commander of the Second Division, Tang Zhuanghai. What happened to him?"

"Tang Zhuanghai came to Taiwan when we retreated. He brought some gold with him. After he arrived here, he invested his gold in a venture with some Shanghai businessmen. I guess fate dictates everyone's time. Those wheeler-dealers plotted together and had him killed."

"About five years ago his case created quite a stir in the south," Colonel Lu added.

"What's happened to Gongsun Tinglin, the youngest of us and the one who earned the most medals?" the old man asked.

"He was living in Taiwan ten years ago," Lu replied.

"And where did he go after that?"

"He went back to the mainland, behind enemy lines."

"There's no doubt he was a courageous soldier," the old man replied with a smile.

"He was the youngest, always reckless," commented General Guan.

Brigadier General Qiu whispered something into Colonel Feng's ear.

"Ha, ha," the old man happily pointed at them, "you don't need to tell me. I know what you said. A game of mahjong after lunch, right?"

"Sir, I beg to report, a friend of mine in Taipei who works in the Intelligence Office informed me last month that Gongsun Tinglin died while fighting for the cause."

"Is that so?" the old man responded after a moment's pause.

"To die serving his country somehow seems appropriate for him," stated General Guan.

"I'd also like to hear what all of you are up to here in Taiwan. Tell me what kind of work you are doing since retiring from the army. General Guan, why don't you start?"

"Oh, Commander," replied Guan. "I just have a small business that gives me enough to get by, nothing worth talking about. Colonel Lu and I run a breakfast stall at the train station and make our money from the student crowd going to school in the mornings. It's just the two of us. I make the soybean milk and Lu works at the stove frying oil-sticks. They just moved up the train schedules, so we have to get up around four o'clock in the morning. It's hard work, to be sure, but not challenging."

The old man nodded his head and continued asking, "What do you do, Brigadier General Zha?"

"Since coming to Taiwan I've raised chickens for a living. Right now I've got three hundred Leghorns and one hundred Rhode Island Reds. This year I'm trying my hand at raising a litter of piglets. Next year I'm thinking of planting a crop of chrysanthemums. If I plant a thousand plants, when autumn comes I should have several thousand blossoms. These days you can get as much as one yuan per flower. Things are working out for me."

The old man nodded and then asked, "Colonel Qin, what about you?"

Qin looked askance at the waiter Zhang Degong and then stammered, "I . . . I . . . don't want to talk about it . . ."

"What's so embarrassing about it?" General Guan interjected, looking at Zhang Degong. "As long as you're honest and above board, and make a living by hard work, any job is honorable. You have no need to feel embarrassed. All jobs are the same—rank and income make no difference. That job of yours is perfectly respectable. What do you have to hide from the Commander?"

"Let me explain things for him," Colonel Lu said. "He acts as a doorman at an American minister's church. What's so embarrassing about that?"

"Working as a doorman is proper work. Why are you so self-conscious about it?" the old man asked.

"It's actually a good job, Old Qin is paid in U.S. dollars," Colonel Lu said.

Colonel Qin elbowed Lu in anger. "I'll give you U.S. dollars!" he said. "I get three hundred dollars a month—three hundred *Taiwan* dollars!"

"That's not bad. The minister pays for your clothing, food and lodging," Lu added.

"What about Staff Officer Duan? Does he work?" the old man quietly asked General Guan.

"He doesn't have a job, he can't work."

"How does he get by?"

"He has his military pension, and sometimes we all chip in a little to help him out."

"He has few needs," Colonel Feng added.

Now that the old man knew what the others did for a living, and with everyone having sat for a long while and the room grown hot, he asked the waiter to pull back the beaded curtain that covered the doorway.

With the room now much brighter than before, the waiter observed that all the men had wisps of white hair growing on the backs of their necks. With the exception of General Tian, all of their backs were curved, like the old man's. General Jiang reached for a kidney bean with his chopsticks but after several attempts still had failed to grasp the slippery object. He put down his chopsticks to use his hand, but as he reached for the bean, he knocked one of the chopsticks onto the floor. He slowly bent over to pick it up, but could not reach it. He panted for a while and then sat up. He bent over again, but still failed to grab the chopstick. Zhang Degong went over and picked it up for him.

The banquet room, which had been filled with chatter and clamor now suddenly became quiet. They stared awkwardly at each other and for a few seconds all that could be heard was the chirping of the cicadas outside the window. All of a sudden, General Guan, like a schoolchild in a classroom that had grown quiet, broke forth with a high, piercing whistle, "Tuh—weet!"

"Tuh-weet! Tuh-weet!" the others joyfully responded like a bunch of students. "Why doesn't someone say something? Why isn't anyone talking? Ha, ha, ha. Ha, ha, ha."

"It's too quiet with everyone so silent. Let's have General Guan sing a song," Brigadier General Zha said laughing.

"I think we should have Brigadier General Zha sing," General Guan replied.

"General Guan! General Guan!" They all responded as they applauded.

Guan then began to sing with his high, piercing voice:

"Your father went and joined the army, but no word came from him.

Ever since, you have hunted geese to support your mother.

I gave the bow and fishing floats to my son to take with him,

Son, don't wait until sunset, you must return as soon as you can . . .

How excited my son was to make the journey this time,

Heedless of the seventeen years I spent raising him,

I lift the hem of my gown to enter our ramshackle cave dwelling,

My son has traveled only half a day, but his mother is worried about him already . . ."

"Bravo! . . . Bravo! . . ."

Zhang Degong's eyes filled with tears. The song was called "Fen River Bay," an old tune from the Shanxi region. Zhang wanted to leave the room to dry his eyes and had taken only a single step when he stopped.

A man wearing a white silk shirt and holding a birdcage in his hand appeared at the doorway.

"Fourth Master, why have you come so late today?" someone asked outside the doorway.

"Right! After letting my birds take some air, I went to Miracle Hall and played a game of chess with Master Hongyi, the monk. After that he brewed a pot of tea and we chatted. That's the reason I'm late."

The canary in the cage sang a sparkling song as the man at the doorway quickly passed out of view.

Zhang Degong looked at the men seated around the table. The others stared at each other, blinking their eyes as if they had passed from a brightly lit space to a darkened room.

"Who was that?" Colonel Feng quietly asked the waiter.

"I don't know. I've never seen him before. A new customer, I guess," Zhang replied.

The clamor returned as Colonel Qin came over and challenged Colonel Lu to a drinking game. Not wanting to decline, Lu asked Commander Jiang to act as referee. Lu extended his left hand and grabbed Qin's hand.

"One, two, three, good fortune and longevity, good fortune and longevity!"

"Two make a match, two make a match."

"Eight Immortals crossing the sea, Eight Immortals crossing the sea!" . . .

As the room grew warmer, some of the men opened or removed their shirts and fanned themselves with their handkerchiefs. Colonels Lu and Qin grew hot from their competition, and each stood and removed his shirt. Lu wore a gauze undershirt riddled with so many holes that it looked like a fishing net. Qin had nothing—not even an undershirt—beneath his shirt, leaving him naked from the waist up.

Several hours of conversation, intense heat, wine and food had left the old man sleepy. At first he widened his eyes to try to keep himself awake, but before he knew it, he had nodded off, his head resting on his chest. From time to time he would awaken with a jolt, but sooner or later his head would droop and he would fall back to sleep.

A man wearing a dirty old blue shirt stood in the doorway. He had a tired, dark face and held a package of candles in his hand.

"Ma Junmou!" Commander Jiang cried out. The old man woke up. "I thought you weren't coming," Jiang added.

Ma walked over to the old man. "Commander . . . it's been a long time . . . I'm late. I brought these candles to help you celebrate your birthday." His voice was so soft that it was barely audible.

"Sit down, Ma Junmou," the old man said. "Zhang Degong, bring another stool over."

After Ma sat down, he didn't say a word. He simply put his birthday gift on the table.

The old man looked down at him sympathetically, smiled and asked, "Is it hot outside?"

Ma responded to the question by bowing slightly to indicate his agreement.

The old man dozed off again. A few minutes later, he seemed to hear his son say, "Dad's gone to sleep . . . He didn't get his afternoon nap . . . I think we should be getting home . . ."

"I'll go downstairs . . . telephone . . . and have Driver Liu pick us up." It was Commander Jiang's voice. Someone has gone downstairs, the old man thought. After a while, it seemed like someone else had left his seat.

"Dad," he felt a hand shaking his shoulder.

"Hmm?" he responded.

"Captain Ma is about to leave."

"Commander—I must be going."

"See you later, Captain Ma. Thank you for coming." The old man shook Ma's hand. The phlegm rising in his throat made him hoarse, and his misty eyes sparkled as they filled with tired tears.

After Captain Ma left, the old man nodded off again. He propped his head up with his forearms and gradually became confused and could not remember where he was. At Dragon Inn, he remembered that much. But what had everyone said just now? Everything blurred. He tried to force himself to remember. What had they said? What had they said?

"Grandpa!" an innocent voice called out. A cute, well-dressed young boy stood before him.

"Little An'an! What are you doing here? Who did you come with?"

"Driver Liu brought me," the smiling boy spoke up happily.

"This is my youngest grandson," the old man said smiling at everyone.

"Oh, come over here, come over here. How old are you this year, little one?" General Guan asked while bending down.

"He's six," the old man replied.

"He's quite handsome. Look at those sparkling eyes."

"Grandpa," the boy said, "let's go home."

"We will, we will, in just a short while."

"Has he started school yet?"

"I'm in the first grade at Faith Primary School," the boy stated.

"Oh, so you're in first grade at Faith Primary School. That's great!" General Guan responded. "What do you want to be when you grow up?"

The little boy immediately stood straight up, and raised his arm to give a salute.

"He wants to be a soldier, just like his father and grandfather," the old man answered with a big smile and a hearty laugh.

"Little scamp," said Commander Tian.

All of the men had put on their shirts and some also had donned sun hats. The old man stood up and took little An'an by the hand.

"Thank you all so much," he said.

"No need to mention it," they replied as they left their seats and walked toward the door.

At this moment Zhang Degong, the waiter, rushed up behind Colonel Qin and bowed. "Colonel Qin, I beg your pardon, Sir, but I wondered if I could trouble you with a question. Perhaps you know what happened to Li Qianduan. *Qian* is the character used in the name of Tao Qian, the poet, and *duan* is the character used in the word for 'upright.' He's from Qingcheng County. He was my sergeant and was very good to me. I really hope I can find him."

"Li Qianduan? Right, right," Qin responded. "He's in Taipei. Not only am I sure of that, I happen to have his address, but not on me. Give me your address. When I return, I'll send it to you in a letter."

"He's in Taipei?" Zhang Degong cried out ecstatically. His smile was so wide that his teeth and gums were fully exposed. "Thank you so much for your help. Let me write down my address." He pulled out pen and paper and handed the address to Qin as soon as he finished writing it.

They left the room and headed down the corridor with Zhang Degong and Liu, General Tian's driver, who had been waiting outside the room, following behind them. As they reached the end of the hallway, they entered the reception room with its blue cloth-covered table. A picture of Sun Yat-sen, two national flags and the couplet "Old friends drink wine together when far they roam, Dragon Inn is the place to gather and remember our Shanxi home" hung in the room. As they left the room, they descended the stairs one step at a time. Before long they exited through the main door and stood beneath the plaque that bore the words "Dragon Inn."

The old man discovered that Brigadier General Qiu and Colonel Feng, as well as Staff Officer Duan, were heading in the same direction he was, and he insisted that they ride in his jeep. "We're not crowded in the least. No problem, we can fit everyone in," the old man said, and they all climbed aboard.

"Goodbye, Commander, see you again," the others called out as they waved farewell to those in the jeep.

The jeep headed off down the road.

After watching the jeep drive off, Qin, Guan, Zha and Lu, all wearing straw hats, set off on foot in a different direction.

Zhang Degong stood before Dragon Inn waving first to the left and then to the right, finally standing still and gazing off into the distance for a little while before going back inside the restaurant.

A short while later, the sun sank behind Dragon Inn and the entire face of the building receded into the darkness.

May 1964–November 1965
Iowa City, Washington D.C., Taipei
Translated by Steven L. Riep

M and W

May 1987. Wang's only play is a satiric comedy, mocking romantic love and materialism. Its central themes—illusion and reality, life and death—contain a strong religious flavor. The text also is notable for its use of complex punctuation and bold-faced text, features of Wang's novels. "M and W" was performed publicly at the Tainan People's Theater in August 1988 shortly after it was published. This translation, along with a stage reading of the translation of "Flaw" contained in this volume, was performed at Reeve Theatre, University of Calgary, in February 2009.

M, naturally, is a man. He is thirty-eight-years old, wears dark glasses, a black Western-style suit, black tie and black shoes, and carries a black briefcase.

W, naturally, is a woman. She is twenty-eight-years old, wears a long, red, Western-style dress and red shoes. A red purse hangs from her shoulder.

The curtain opens on a bare stage. Light shines down from the ceiling, creating a rectangle the size of an elevator car. Two people stand in the light.

W standing with her back to the audience, hitting the door. There are sound effects of pounding: Open up! Open up!

M: Don't shout, it's useless. If the elevator's broken, it's broken. Except for the light, everything's broken. At least there's still air conditioning. That's lucky. It's so late, no matter how loud you shout, no one will hear. The super's gone. Every Thursday he leaves to play mahjong. Plays all night. It's impossible to get out until he comes to work tomorrow morning.

W *looks at him*: Don't come any closer. Stand back a bit. Separate areas for men and women, —understand?

M: Oh, really? —But how do I know you **really** are a woman, eh? —Ha ha ha ha! These days, men and women come in real and fake versions, it's hard to tell which is which.

W *turns around*: Open up! Open up!

M: Stop shouting! Stop shouting! It's almost midnight. There'll be no one out there this late. And suppose someone does show up. There are two elevators. This one's broken but the other one's okay, so anyone who comes along won't discover us. Just relax, wait until the morning before calling out again. *Laughs.* He he he. "**Open up! Open up!** . . . " Shouting is useless. Save your breath.

W: You want money. —Money, here you are! *She takes money from her purse.* One thousand, seven hundred and eighty-two yuan! I'll keep fifty for the taxi. This watch is fake! The ring's also fake! My necklace is jade, it's real but I **just can't** give it to you because my grandmother told me that if I lost it I'd have bad luck. Okay, whatever I've got, if you want it, take it. It's up to you, just don't bother me anymore.

M: You think I want your money? What good would that do? After I take it, can I fly out of here? Even a fly can't fly out of here. Furthermore, Miss, perhaps you don't know this, but I have lots of money. Look, take a look. This big briefcase, it's full of money. Money's not what I need. I have too much to know what to do with.

W: Then what do you want? You don't want to do anything criminal. I'm telling you, my husband is with the Taipei police, my father is a prosecutor, my older brother is an agent with the Bureau of Intelligence. You touch one hair and you'll see.

M: My wife is a policewoman, so you'd better look out as well. If you do anything illegal, she'll lock you up.

W: Well, if you're a police officer's husband, I guess you'll behave.

M: Ahhh, Miss, we have a long night ahead of us. I think we should be polite, friendly, speak nicely. Let me begin by humbly introducing myself. Very pleased to meet you Miss. *He reaches out his hand. She rebuffs him.* This is my card. My compliments, my sincerest compliments. *He holds out the card but she rejects it.*

W: There's no point in looking for opportunities to talk to me. I won't talk to you.

M: Ahhh, there's at least another eight hours. Standing that long is intolerable. I think the first thing we should do is sit down. —Ahhh! My old bones! *He sits at W's feet and looks up at her.*

W: What are you doing?

M: Ahhh, wouldn't it be better if you sat down? Please, oh, please, please do sit down. *He gestures with his hands.*

W: You don't even have a chair. Please sit! Okay, sit! *M is on the right, W on the left, their backs to the rear wall. They are facing the audience with their legs stretched out in front. W exaggeratedly covers her knees with her dress.* I'm telling you: There's a line on the floor, exactly in the middle. We'll use it as a border. Neither of us will cross it. Okay, don't try to speak to me. If you do, I'll ignore you.

M and W are silent for a moment.

M: Mind if I smoke?

W: Smoke? You want me to choke to death? Can't you see there's not even a window in here?

M: Oh, sorry, sorry. Yeah, yeah . . . I forgot, there's no window. *He takes a newspaper from his briefcase.* Want to see the paper? It's today's evening paper.

W ignores him.

M: Shangguan Feifei Injured During Movie Shoot. Falls From Height. Breaks Left Thigh. Huh! *Short pause.* Residents Strip Naked in Central Region Village. Dance Wildly. Health Bureau Suspects Drinking Water Poisoned. Hmmm! *Rather long pause.* Midnight Terror. Woman Encounters Thief in Elevator. Robbed and Raped. Police Have No Leads. It's all bad news. If it's news, it must be bad news, it seems. The Times should be called The Bad Times. Financial Bad Times. Star Island Bad Times, Yomiuri Bad Times. —I'm a little hungry. Aren't you? Should eat something, a midnight snack. *He takes a half-eaten hamburger out of his briefcase.* Have a bite, come on! *He turns toward W, sits up on his knees and tucks a paper napkin under his chin. He picks up the hamburger with both hands and licks around the edge with his tongue. He takes a ravenous bite, swallows, takes another bite, swallows.*

W: You eat like Ah-hua, our dog, although Ah-hua has better manners.

M *continues to eat*: Woof! Woof woof! Woof woof!

W: At least clean up the floor a little or we'll attract every rat in the building.

M: Don't worry. We can be sure the cats will be right behind them. Ha ha ha ha! *He tidies up.* After a midnight snack I feel drowsy. *Yawns.* Good night![1] *Using the briefcase as a pillow, he lies down, feet toward the audience. He covers his body with the newspaper. His back is to W. He snores. Twice he reaches out with his arms to hug something but just grabs empty space. He raises his left leg, raises it high, then lowers it. Raises it, drops it, two times altogether. Suddenly he rolls up into a sitting position and crows like a rooster, yawns, spreads his arms. The light goes out for a moment. Using a finger, he brushes his teeth. He jumps up. W also jumps up. M begins running on the spot, encroaching on the boundary.*

W: You keep out!

M retreats, pumping his legs faster before slowing down. Suddenly he takes a whistle from his pocket and blows, one-two, one-two, one-two. W is mesmerized by this performance. She kneels on the floor and then sits holding her knees, transfixed. M gradually slows down and stops. He shades his eyes with his hands as if looking into the distance with binoculars.

M: Miss, ah, today is a new start, it's a new day. We, both sides, should call a temporary ceasefire for one day, okay? We'll return our POWs, we'll exchange diplomatic visits and learn from each other, okay?

W: Don't cross the line!

M: I won't cross, I won't cross. *He stands beside the line, lifts one leg and stands on the other like a rooster. Humming "The March to the Scaffold" from Berlioz's "Symphonie Fantastique," he stretches a*

---

1. English in the original.

leg over the line and then withdraws it. He does this twice before losing his balance. His foot comes down inside W's territory, while the other foot remains on his side. He hops back. Again he lifts his leg and stretches it across the boundary. He sings. He lowers his leg lightly but intentionally in W's territory before hurriedly withdrawing it. Ha ha ha ha! M sits down. W sits back reflexively. M stares at W, flashes a toothy grin and giggles. He laughs louder and turns a somersault. He springs up into a sitting position opposite W. He again pulls out the silver whistle and blows it without pausing, one strong tone, one light, one strong, one light.

W *covers her ears*: Stop blowing, okay? Looking at you is bad enough. Do I have to put up with this whistling, too? After we get out, I'll accuse you of mental cruelty. —What, what are you doing?

M *takes off his jacket, revealing a white shirt. The chest, shoulders and arms are covered with the image of a skeleton*: Me, I feel hot.

W: What are those clothes?

M: It's the year's most fashionable design, ahhh.

W: Oh my God, you're ghoulish, like some kind of vampire. Put your clothes back on. I have a weak heart. Don't frighten me. Please, please. *She pats her chest.* Put your jacket back on, quickly, quickly. *She covers her face.*

M *puts on the jacket*: Okay, okay. You—you think this shirt isn't too attractive, eh? It's true, taste is a personal matter. *He takes a Chinese chess set out of a pocket.* There's still quite a long time to go. How about a game of chess? To kill time? *W turns her back and ignores him. M arranges the chess pieces on the floor.* I've taken your chariot.

W: What did you say? What are you doing? You are just one person. —And you're playing chess?

M *nods his head*: What's more, I'm playing an unfinished game. *He shouts angrily.* Where can you run? Look, where are you going to escape? Ha! You have no way out! No escape route! Check! Checkmate! Death to you! You've had it now! Defeated utterly! The slaughter is so great not even a scrap of armor remains. Admit defeat? You give up this time, eh? Beating him in this game really was a difficult task. *He turns toward W.* Me and him have been playing for five years and I've beaten him just three times, but that's because he usually cheats. *Pause.* Now he doesn't dare play with me anymore. Good. Still, conquerors should be benevolent. Okay, next game I'll spot you one cannon, but I dare you to beat me. Until next time. *He gathers up the pieces.*

W: You're a weird one. I've never seen chess played like that.

M: Now you have.

W: How come you're always doing half of something? When you play chess, you play one half of the game and play the other half later. Then there was the hamburger. First you ate one half, the leftover half you ate later. Where in the world did you pick up behavior like that?

M: Ah, this matter, hmmm, it's a modern social phenomenon of course, it's because I'm so busy. Not only do I play chess this way and eat this way, I even sleep this way. First I get one half of my sleep, then, when I have some free time, I get the other half.

W: You mean you really were sleeping just now?

M: You really don't get it? Sorry, you still don't understand? *He takes a deck of cards from a pocket.* Let's play a game. *He shuffles the cards and shapes them into a fan.* Pick a card.

W: Gambling! You are! Well, I'm not. I won't touch them. Your stinking habits, I won't.

M: It's just a game. How can it be gambling? You don't have to pick a card. I'll help you by picking one, it's all the same to me. *He picks the card and shuffles the deck. He spreads the cards on the floor and then turns over one card.* Do you know what this card says?

W: What?

M: It says you run two travel agencies. Your income from business last month was one hundred and ten thousand yuan. *The light goes out for a moment.*

W: God—oh. How did it know that?

M turns over another card.

W: This card, what does it say?

M: You have a hobby, it's singing Chinese opera. You excel in the senior male roles, for instance, Zhuge Kongming in "Pray for the East Wind."[2]

W *is delighted and smiles faintly*: Right, that's right.

M *turns over another card*: Your favorite dish is: —stewed dog meat.

W *is silent*.

M: One night, after midnight, in the rain, you were driving home alone. You hit and killed an old woman. You ran away, didn't stop, didn't report the accident.

W: This, this, . . . I . . .

M: The man you married is thirty-five years older than you. He barely finished junior high. You coveted his family's money. Married as a concubine, but you figured his wife's health wasn't too good, so sooner or later you'd be elevated to formal wife.

W *scowls but is silent*.

M: In your first year of university, you cheated during the final exam in one of your courses. A teaching assistant found out and asked you to leave the classroom. You got a mark of zero and had to repeat the course the following year . . .

W: Nonsense! Complete nonsense! Not one word of what you said is true. My favorite dish, I'll tell you, isn't stewed dog meat, it's pickled pig's feet. And although I like singing the part of Zhuge Liang, I prefer the young maiden roles. *In a sharp voice she sings anxiously*: "Su San li le Hongtong Xian, Jiang shen lai zai dajie qian, wei ceng . . ."[3]

M: Yes, yes, yes, that's right. What I said just now was just a game, nothing more. It's not necessarily correct. But, I must say, among people's private affairs, who doesn't have a few things that aren't fit to see the light of day? I, take me for example, have very many my-

---

2. An opera based on a story from "The Romance of the Three Kingdoms." Zhuge Kongming is another name for Zhuge Liang (181–234 CE), military counsellor of the state of Shu.

3. "Su San has left Hongtong County, The road stretches before her, Never before . . ." This is a verse from "The Story of Su San."

---

self. I, once embezzled a friend's money, swindled three billion yuan. My friend, because of this, committed suicide, jumped to his death, and I took his property, too. Now I live in his luxurious Western-style house. It's in Tianmu, you could call it a villa. It occupies more than 3,500 square feet. I, once, with, a woman I didn't love in the least, got married, —because I coveted her family's great financial power. I, furthermore, am an underground dealer in counterfeit drugs. The most effective medicine I make, has killed, already, one-hundred thousand, two-hundred thousand, almost. Does my conscience bother me? —I don't have a guilty conscience, because, I feel, if big hospitals won't buy my medicine themselves, how will I get it into the mouths of sick people? To this day I continue in the counterfeit medicine business. I don't have the slightest intention of stopping—it's all because, that—*sighs*—the summer of 1982, —Let me tell you, Miss, I, really am a very bad person, for all eternity I have no hope of returning to the correct path, —It's all because of that summer of 1982 . . .

W: Hey, hey, what's the point of this nonsense? Such drivel, what are you talking about?

M: Sorry, sorry. *Pause.* Sorry. *He gathers up the cards.*

W: If you want to tell stories, they should be moving, beautiful, good, that's it. *Pause.* This sort of filth, this kind of ugliness, complete, unadulterated garbage, get rid of it. How can it be regarded as a **story**? You still need some training in how to tell a story.

M: Pardon, forgive me, my public speaking requires more— much more—practice.

W: Now, I want to ask you something!

M: What—what is it?

W: It's about your deck of cards. Now, this time, I want to see if your cards really are magic, —or not. Give you another chance to prove it.

M: Be my guest.

W: It's something related to my business. First let me ask you, why did I come here so late at night, and use the elevator? Why did I come here, and why did I take the elevator to come down?

M: Ah, such a difficult question.

W: You don't want to use your cards? Hmm?

M: Ah, I won't use them this time, —this way is even quicker. *He touches his head with his hands.* Why come here . . . why . . . why . . . because . . . So you could make a phone call. In order to hurry home and make a phone call, in order to find a Hong Kong phone number. You left this phone number in your office, so first you had to go to the office to get it. After you got it, you hurried down and were rushing home to make the international call.

W: You really do have talent, it seems. I, want to make this call, it's very important.

M and W *speaking at the same time*: It concerns a very profitable deal. It's related to one of the travel agencies. *Pause, they look at each other.* If successful, it could lead to a profit of about one hundred thousand yuan. A very lucrative deal.

W *is astonished and there is a long silence.*

M: Anything else? You want to ask—what is it, go ahead.

W: Tonight, this delay on the elevator, not being able to make the phone call, do you think it will affect this deal? Now, can you tell me, this—the whole one hundred thousand yuan, —can you see, is it **possible**, an **opportunity,** to get my hands on it. If your prediction is right, and I make one hundred thousand yuan, I'll **give you five hundred**! I sure will!

M: You'll get it, **minus** the five hundred!

W *stands up, M follows*: **Really**? Really? Good, one hundred thousand yuan, one hundred thousand yuan, I made a one hundred thousand yuan profit, I made one hundred thousand yuan net profit, **one hundred thousand yuan! One hundred thousand yuan!** *She claps her hands and jumps up and down.* You, hmmm, —really not bad. I forgot to ask you, yes, tonight, so late, why did you take this elevator down? —You **live** in this building? —or, —you said, —you live in Tianmu?

M: I, . . . I, . . . I, don't live here. Miss, actually, the question you asked really isn't the one you want to. In your heart you have another, an even bigger one, the question you want to ask.

W: What question?

M: I'd better not say it. You may not be happy when I say what's on your mind.

W: Speak up, feel free to talk. —Come on, speak up, you've got to tell me!

M: Ah, hmmm, it's this way, these past two months, you, you've always been this way, suspicious, because you discovered your husband is having an affair. You worry your chance to become senior wife could be taken by this woman. For two months you've slept badly. Every night you have to swallow more than twenty sleeping pills, only that's enough to put you to sleep.

W *suddenly is choked with sobs, covers her face.*

M: What, what is it?

W: What you said, that's really the way it is. How I hate, hate that shameless little fox. I think I've tried everything, want to get rid of her, there's nothing I haven't tried, prayer, sorcery, feng-shui, Esoteric Buddhism, . . . even foot massage, but, completely ineffective, —what I want, actually, really isn't much, I ask, only that this little fox, gain ten kilos, have half her hair fall out, that's enough, who knows, even this, two really really small requests, no matter what sort of god, none has helped me succeed. I see, I now, oh, regarding, —now this twentieth century, —I've **lost** all confidence, everything. You, . . . you, you must **grant** me this wish. I, —now, —am not asking for two wishes, okay, —allow me to **mention** just one, —I, yes, I won't ask anything else, I just want to turn her into a man, that's enough, you certainly can do that—beg you definitely, absolutely absolutely grant me this wish, okay, I now, here, from this moment, will follow you as my master—! *W suddenly kneels with a thud.*

M: Get up, get up now.

W *stubbornly does not rise.*

M: You wouldn't know this, but I'm really not into the master-pupil relationship.

W: You must take me as a student. If you don't, I'll keep kneeling here and won't get up.

M: Okay, okay, I'll take you as a student, —my apprentice, —you can stand.

W *stands*: Master! —Master, —Great master, you'll certainly help me get rid of this little fox, little witch.

M: Actually, it's, let me tell you, —there's one, a better way, than what you asked for. This approach—not only can it solve your problem, it'll root out everything—everything, —insomnia, poor appetite, that's bothering you. I can—right now—give you a good piece of news—listen.

W: What is it? —Come on, tell me!

M: Okay, it's this, you will leave this husband. You, very quickly, you'll meet someone who's very rich, a very dignified man. *M raises his head, sticks out his chest.* You'll meet your: —Prince Charming. He will take you far, far away, to a distant place, **fly you** there, fly there, to America. That little fox will **stay behind** with your husband. —What do you say, isn't this brilliant?

W *dreamlike*: Really? . . . really?

M: Of course it's true, I, —have I—you know, as God is my witness, —have I told you a word of a lie? Have I? *M approaches closer—steps over the boundary line.*

W: Really? What you said, —it's all true? That would be good—from the beginning I've wanted to leave him, —this is good, —from now on I don't have to, every day, every day, put up with his stinking breath.

M: But, recently, —encounters with the stinking breath have been less frequent. Your Excellency, on the contrary, has been anxious, begun to worry.

W: —What are you saying?

M: Nothing, nothing.

W: Yes, this way, it's actually good. When I leave, I ah, I also want what's in his safe, all of it, deeds, gold, U.S. dollars, jewelry, sweep it clean. I also want, that old man's, Korean ginseng, it's worth hundreds of thousands. Sweep all of it up at once and go, not leave even one whisker of ginseng behind for him.

M: . . . Miss, . . . Miss, do you know, who your Prince Charming is?

W *sings*: "Spring flowers smell sweeter, the autumn moon shines brighter," . . . You guess, can you guess who I think this person is?

Whoever it is, he, must be rich, extremely rich, right? *Sings again*: "When I was young, I was so happy, I don't know what happened to you pretty girl," . . . Master, master, later we'll meet often, you'll instruct me more, give me much more advice. *W takes the initiative in reaching out her hand and M grasps it passionately. M suddenly, impulsively takes the hand and puts it into his large, wide-open mouth, and holds it there.*

W: You, —what are you doing, you are? What are you doing?

M: Sorry, sorry. *M releases the jade-like hand.*

W: You, you probably didn't have good eating habits in your youth, that's why things turned out this way.

M *with a deep, deep sigh*: Ahhh! . . . In my heart, there is one wish, as yet unrealized, . . .You know this Prince Charming, in the end, —this Prince Charming, —who it is?

W: Who? You tell me.

M: You, you look at me, don't you recognize me?

W: No.

M *removes his dark glasses*: —I am, —M ah*!! —He puts the dark glasses back on immediately.*

The light goes out for a moment.

W *shrieks*: You're, **M**? !! Didn't you die on that road in California. And Xiao Wen, died there too. *Screaming*: Open up, open up, —Open up! *Sound effects of hitting the door.*

M: Don't be nervous. Listen to me. I'm not dead. That traffic accident. I was just seriously injured. I didn't actually die. The summer of 1982, that traffic accident, after my injury, I survived.

W: You're really a human being, or a ghost? You, must, don't scare me, I have a weak heart.

M: I'm not deceiving you, really. That traffic accident, Xiao Wen died, I lived. W dear, you should be happy for me.

W: Uh, *pats her chest*, you almost scared me to death. But, why do you look completely different? Before you were very handsome, why are you so weird-looking now?

M: Ahhh! . . . It's time ahhh . . . Age ahhh, . . .But the main reason is, after my accident, I had major plastic surgery.

W: Plastic surgery? I hear, in America, the plastic surgery is super.

M: True. . . . But, you know, . . . my face after the accident, . . . very difficult to repair. Also, most important, —I had two operations altogether, —so I'm changed beyond recognition.

W: Twice? Was it that difficult?

M: Not at all, it's that, the first time, the Western doctor messed it up, he **fixed** me with green eyes, blond hair and a long nose like a foreigner.

W *laughs uncontrollably.*

M: The second time, the doctor used a photo, mine, published with the newspaper report on the accident, used this photo for the operation. Because it had been printed in the paper, it was blurry, —so the operation turned out this way.

W: If you've been alive all along, you, —why, —didn't you let me know until now?

M: This, this, . . . because, . . . because the time wasn't right, . . . and, —you know, —I'm quite a shy person.

W: Since the accident, what sort of work have you been doing? —You started making your counterfeit medicine?

M: After the accident, I lost my memory for half a year. Later, very strange, I discovered something very strange. I found, without exception, I wasn't interested in anything, —I just **desperately**, blindly pursued profit. I take no pleasure in it, but it's essential, must do it, possessed, —behavior. It's, a type, just greed, but without desire, a psychological phenomenon. At that time, Taiwan really was the place to make money. I quit working for an American company, returned to Taiwan, plunged into this great money-making market.

W: You, in the end, altogether, profit, completely, how much, have you really made?

M: Up to now, profit, altogether, how much, I really don't know. All I know, money, pours pours, flows continuously, gushes endlessly, money, a lot, like bulk packs of cheap toilet paper, I collect money as easily as toilet paper, —You see, there's no pleasure in it. Actually, it's extremely troublesome, —yes, you know there are peo-

ple who say things like: "Making money, very difficult, very difficult," that kind of talk. But, from my point of view, making money,
actually, is too easy, too, too, too easy. Possibly, probably, making
illegal profits, on the whole, is too easy, too easy, making money
from the sweat of your brow, is **too** difficult, **very** difficult. But, W
dear, I, don't know if you know this, but since my disaster in 1982,
I've, always, had one, unfulfilled secret wish in my heart.

W: What is it?

M: Do you remember, a dance in the summer of 1981? That
dance, to **this day**, I can still remember: —You, wore a sheer white
outfit, —a blue satin bow in your hair, —you in the swirling colors,
like an image in a dream, under the lights, dancing, —oh, it really
was, very pretty, very pretty. When they played "The Tennessee
Waltz,"[4] I wanted so much to ask you for a dance, —but I didn't dare,
I didn't go over, because, Xiao Wen, was sitting beside me. But, you
know, in fact I really didn't love Xiao Wen, I was just after her property, that's why I was going to marry her. All these years since, I still
haven't fulfilled my secret wish: —hope, to be able, in the same setting, at, the same, under the multicolored lights, the same "Tennessee Waltz," dance with you, don't know, if there is, —now, —is that
possible?

W: Waltz? I **really** like dancing too. But instead of "The Tennessee Waltz," I prefer "Love Me Tender, Love Me True."[5] If you want to
dance, can you change the song?

M: Oh W, can I say: Shall we dance?

W: Now? Here? *Laughs roughly.* You're joking. There'll be plenty
of opportunities later, no? *Invitingly* —There will be plenty of opportunities later, —Wouldn't you agree? It's not necessary, —right
now, —to do this?

M: But W, I've already waited too long. I have no choice, —this
way, —wait longer, I can't stand to wait any longer. Please, whatever
else, . . . What I want isn't much, actually I don't really want to dance
with you, —in fact, —just want, —to lift you up, carry you on my

4. The title is given in English in the original.
5. Again, the title is in English in the original text.

shoulder, and together, sing "The Tennessee Waltz" softly, right here, spinning, circling slowly, —like this, —that's enough, —you must let me dance with you like this, must, must, I beg you, —I beg you! *M suddenly kneels and begs with his hands held in front of him. The light flickers once.*

W: You what, —kind of game, —what is it!? You—are you—nuts, aren't you? I knew, —you are, —you are, —a sex maniac! You're the same kind of dirty man I've met before, not different at all, —not at all. You're just a bunch of deluded toads, ugly monsters, who want to feast on swan's flesh, get **away** from me, get—**get away**! *Kicks him, —M falls back and rolls over, doesn't get up for a long, long time.*

M *crawls to his feet*: Motherfucker! You, this, little slut, little whore, cheap trash, —stinking trull. You think you can turn down this offer? Okay, now, let me tell you one thing. I, —I'm telling you, —I am, —I am M's, —ghost, —I'm not alive. You must, with me, dance this dance, I, can get, whatever, I want to get, —there's nothing I can't do.

W: Look at the big ghost! First you say you're a real person, the next moment you say you're **dead**, —as far as I'm concerned: **You**, are, one of those, not **dead or alive**; —you are not dead, and not alive. You're a nut case.

M: You, —why don't you believe I'm a spirit?

W: If you're a dead person, why just now, you, why did you, also say: you are alive?

M: That's because, I was afraid, you, —I was afraid you would: fear me. I, of course, hope you don't, I hope you don't: You would fear me. —I, ah, I—in fact, —like you, we are the same, we really aren't two different types: I am the same, what I hope for is: feeling. We spirits, don't like to resort to **force**, —coercive methods, —that's right, in the end, what, —let me ask, —yes, let me ask, —what's it mean? —I don't want, really don't want, —to resort to force. —Yet, but, you hurt me, hurt me too much, made me lose hope, —now, I, —I'm risking everything, —I, must have one dance with you!

W: Don't you come any closer, not any closer, if you come closer I'll give you another kick.

M: Aiii-eee! I don't believe I can't find a way to make you believe I'm a **ghost**. Yes, —a moment ago, did you notice that here, this place, the light flickered off and on? Didn't you? I can see you believe a little. Okay, I'll make this light flicker three times in a row, —Don't you believe me? If you don't, **watch**! . . . One. *The light flickers . . .* Two! *The light flickers. . . .* Three! *The light flickers.*

W *screams.*

M: You, now, do you believe? Keep watching, here, this briefcase, —you know what's inside, don't you? I told you earlier, —**cash**! —But, now, take a look, this briefcase, inside, it's full of—what? *He pulls out bundle after bundle of blank white bills from the briefcase.* —It's all **blank paper**, all **blank paper**, —**ah**—! *M scatters the blank paper all over the stage.* —Ah, —ha ha ha ha ha, —you, now, may I have this dance?

W *fearful*: Don't come closer, —don't come closer, I have a weak heart!

M stretches his body across the boundary, dancing alone toward her. He opens his jacket, revealing a black skeleton, alternates humming "The Tennessee Waltz" and "The March to the Scaffold" from Berlioz's "Symphonie Fantastique," forces W to run in circles to escape, —the light suddenly goes out and stays off for a long time. When the light comes back on, W is alone on the stage, M having vanished without a trace.

W *is jumping up and down, screaming.*

The light goes out again. The screaming continues. When the light comes on, W also is gone from the stage. All that's left is M's briefcase and W's red purse. The sound of W's screams gradually weakens, and the stage is empty and silent. The curtain falls.

March 10–May 5, 1987[6]
Translated by Fred Edwards and Jia Li

---

6. Wang Wen-hsing made this notation at the end of the original Chinese version: "The original script was proofread by the author; each word was used intentionally by the author."

PART III

ESSAYS

Preface to *New Stone Statue*

November 1968. New Stone Statue is a short story anthology that contains works originally published in Modern Literature *from 1965 to 1968, when Wang served as an editor after returning from the United States in 1965. In his preface, Wang for the first time reveals his strong interest in classical Chinese literature and also speaks about the importance of precision, one of his key concepts about literary language, and advocates a style with "no wasted words."*

Strictly speaking, China has yet to produce many works worthy of being called "short stories." The main reason for this is that we have not yet understood the meaning of "precision." In a short story, no matter the topic, it is essential to reduce words, characters, events, structure and plot to the minimum required. For a short story writer, "precision" virtually is a moral quality. If it is lacking, you can forget everything else.

The degeneration of language probably is the most serious shortcoming of today's writers. Precision in the portrayal of characters, in the depiction of events, in structure and plot, even if not achieved, is something our writers generally pay attention to. But the precision of language has never merited attention. Like a careless young girl, our writers have lost their virginity.

Words have to be like mathematical symbols, each one having its own function. One word too few, and the piece falls apart. One word too many, and the piece buckles under its own weight. We do not know how we could have allowed our literary language to degenerate to the present state. Our ancestors were the most frugal of writers when it came to using words. Just look at the verses of Tang[1] poems! If we want to revitalize today's prose, we only have to look to poetry for guidance. Poetry is the aristocracy of writing, the honored blood essence we most need in prose.

Words determine a work's success or failure. Marcel Proust said, "A writer's style and also a painter's are matters not of technique but of vision."[2] Words control tone, atmosphere and viewpoint. Redundant words sully an entire work. Writers should treat language like a goldfish bowl, wiping away any oily stains to make it crystal clear in order to see the living fish within.

Our writers have so many things to study—precision is just one, albeit the most important. To reach an acceptable standard, our writers will from now on have to look to the West, studying both thought and technique. I once heard someone say, "We have ideas; it's just that we need to learn some techniques from foreign works." That just proved he had no ideas at all.

Most of these works [in *New Stone Statue*] have been selected from those published during the past three years in *Modern Literature*.[3] While they do not quite reach the ideal standard of writing excellence, they are at the very least headed in the right direction. This volume is by no means a milestone in contemporary Chinese literature (what volume is?), but I sincerely believe it is a starting point.

Translated by Martin Sulev

1. Tang dynasty, 618–907 CE.

2. Proust, Marcel. *Remembrance of Things Past*, Vol. 2. Trans. C.K. Scott Moncrieff and Stephen Hudson. Ware: Wordworth Editions. 2006, page 1169.

3. *Modern Literature* (Xiandai wenxue) was established in 1960 by a group of students who majored in Western literature at National Taiwan University in Taipei. They included Wang Wen-hsing, Bai Xianyong, Ouyang Zi, Chen Ruixi and others.

A Brief Discussion of
Modern Literature (Abridged)

1981. Written on invitation from Lianhe bao (United daily) for the thirtieth anniversary of its literary supplement, this article stresses the poetization of prose in modern literature, which is helpful in understanding Wang's own writing. This is one of two articles in which Wang discusses his views about modern literature.

Art in any and all periods can be referred to as the "modern art" of the times. This is because the art of any era must, without exception, reflect the social life, thought, ethical standards, political climate and so forth of that era. Nevertheless, out of the overabundance of "modern art" in any period, it seems that only a few select works endure while the majority slip into the black hole of history. The small number that do endure are the genuine "modern works of art" of the times. Shortly thereafter, they become "classic art," "canonical works"—praise for them eventually comes to accentuate their venerable age. Regardless of the term used, however, the most important thing about them is that they unquestionably epitomize the art of their times. It is regrettable that only a few contemporary individuals are willing to admit that these representative works do indeed reflect the popular will. In fact, some even go so far as to suggest that such works are at odds with the times—"a little too abstruse, a little too abstruse. Far surpasses the present era, ha ha!" Ha, ha! Thus, these "modern works of art"—these genuinely "modern works of art"—at the time might be referred to more appropriately as "the art of the future" or, to use a more fashionable term, "avant-garde art." In short, the modern art of every age, the genuinely modern art, should be renamed "the art of the future."

All right then, how do these rare works of "the art of the future" differ from their myriad contemporaries? "The art of the future" certainly must exhibit some new experimental aesthetic, but the novelty of these works consists in the way they engender something contrary to the previous generation's aesthetic attitude without diverging from tradition. On the contrary, they carry on tradition and at the same time embody tradition. Their resistance is focused on the previous generation, just as the previous generation resisted the generation before it. This is not simply an example of the phenomenon psychologists call "the Oedipus complex," but rather the kindred spirit between grandparent and grandchild united against the father. In other words, "the art of the future"—let's just call it "modern art"—is linked with tradition. It is a complete reform, a molting that occurs with renewal on a daily basis and not a radical restructuring. And since it is nothing more than a molting, it clearly does not reject the value of the previous generation but simply greets it with a yawn in the hope that the art of the previous generation will come to an immediate halt. All good things when viewed at length will cause one to yawn. For example, if you live at Sun Moon Lake and don't leave for ten days, you will begin to yearn for Taipei. You would not say this is because the scenery at Sun Moon Lake is unattractive. You would say it is for no other reason than that you desire a change of scenery. Thus the emergence of "modern art" does not diminish the value of the previous generation's art. The history of human art is like a long train with each car painted a different color. When a car is added, there is no need to jettison the previous car: all the cars may proceed along the same track.

What precisely is the unique quality of "modern literature" produced by this generation of ours? That is, what aesthetic experiment constitutes the "modern literature" of our generation? (Below, we'll simply call it "modern literature" and eliminate the overly burdensome "our generation.") I believe the most concise answer is this:

prose written in the form of poetry and poetry written in the form of prose. How is this so? It is simply due to the yawn. Far too many literary histories attribute the evolution of literature to the influence of Darwin, the Industrial Revolution, world wars, and so on. In fact, these theories do no more than touch on the most superficial of causes. The primary and foremost cause of literary change is the yawn. Not until the yawn is there motivation for change. Only afterward, when times have changed, does the influence of Darwin, the Industrial Revolution or world wars assert itself. "Prose written in the form of poetry and poetry written in the form of prose" has been around since ancient times and in considerable volume. In the case of China, the *fu* form of narrative poetry emerged from classical prose; the *ci* lyric evolved from the *shi* poetic form; the vernacular style arose from literary Chinese, and so on down the line. In Western literature, fiction evolved from the historical poem; prose drama proceeded from the lyric drama, and so on. Thus, the present moment in literature is nothing more than a recurrence of this phenomenon. Yet we should further examine the true nature of this transformation—"prose written in the form of poetry and poetry written in the form of prose"—because although we have already hit upon its distinguishing characteristic, we should probe further to ascertain its deeper features. Further examination will enable us to clarify what this transformation really is.

The poetry we mentioned in the preceding paragraph referred to lyric poetry and not to long forms of poetry, such as narrative or dramatic forms. There have always been certain preferences for one thing over another in lyric poetry: structure (such as repetition, neat divisions) is preferred over character development; the repetition of language (density, multiple images, syntactic innovation) is preferred over plot development. The poeticization of fiction has followed from the appropriation of these lyrical qualities. From the inception of fiction, constant attention has been paid to the norms of plot and characterization. But the modern novel has overturned these two norms. Fiction has always been concerned with structure as well, but structure has always been subsumed within the plot. In other words, the structure of fiction has always been the structure of the plot. The detective novel, for example, begins with investigation and ends with discovery, like a jigsaw puzzle. However, the structure of the modern novel does not reside in the plot (since there seldom is a plot, and a thing cannot exist without a basis); it resides in the essence of the fiction itself. A certain structural design is found in narrative writing. The language of modern fiction, without exception, meticulously follows the language of poetry. And so it is that we arrive at the importance of language and tone in fiction. It seems that all writers of modern fiction have a mission: they must also be literary stylists. Nevertheless, it seems that in the midst of this transformation, the change in language is not as important as the change in structure itself. A cursory examination of both short stories and novels from the past twenty years will reveal that not a one has been able to avoid the general influence of structure.

Prose literature naturally includes drama, but drama basically is not that different than fiction. Both are narrative arts, so drama has evolved in the same manner as fiction. The only difference is that drama has not been quite as innovative in its use of poetry as fiction has.

"Poetry written in the form of prose": this major transformation has occurred in the realm of language. From Walt Whitman on down, modern poetry has invested much effort in vitiating strict prosodic rules. The literary form of poetry has approached that of prose, moving along the path toward free form. In terms of subject matter, poetry has gone in the direction of confessional literature, which originally belonged to the domain of autobiography but nowadays has been appropriated by poetry as a means of exploring the writer's inner self. His soul, sense of guilt, despondency, desire; all are fertile material for poetry. T.S. Eliot, Robert Lowell, Sylvia Plath are all representatives of the confessional school of poetry. That confessional literature now surpasses fictional works is sufficient to demonstrate that the boundary between modern fiction and modern poetry is dwindling with each passing day. It is also possible that eventually they will merge, reaching the same goal by different means.

Translated by Christopher Lupke

The Challenge and Primitiveness of Modernism

August 15, 1986. Written after the publication of the first volume of Backed Against the Sea, *Wang's second article on modern literature argues that "fragmentation" and "simplicity" are integral to the spirit of modern art. He maintains that the breakdown in the traditional sequence of time and space is an important feature of modern literature—a characteristic of Wang's own writing.*

If we probe deeply into the underlying spiritual quality of modernism, we find there are as many different responses as there are respondents. So when the editor of *Human World*[1] asked me this question, I thought about it for more than a month before coming to the rough conclusion that the spiritual quality of modernism lies in both its challenge and its primitiveness.

Challenge and primitiveness derive mostly from the influence of Nietzsche and Freud.[2] There is no doubt that Nietzsche's negation of the power of traditional values spurred on the challenge of modernism. His advocacy of the concept of the superman also greatly supported modernism's worship of the primitive. Freud, through his research into psychology, destroyed the extrinsic order of the

1. *Human World* (Ren jian) is the literary supplement of Taiwan's *China Times* (Zhongguo shibao).

2. Sigmund Freud (1856–1939), the father of psychoanalysis. Friedrich Nietzsche (1844–1900), German philosopher.

world, while his recognition of the libido is linked closely to modernism's worship of the primitive.

As for the spirit of challenge in modernism, we are able to find various examples in the modern arts. Literature: in Kafka's novels it is seen in the individual's confrontation with the power of religion and the politics of the despotic state.[3] In Samuel Beckett's plays and novels it is in the individual's confrontation with fate.[4] In Saul Bellow's novels it is the intellectual's confrontation with culture and society.[5] In the fine arts: Picasso challenged traditional art with cubism and abstraction;[6] Jackson Pollock took this confrontation even further.[7] In the world of music: Schoenberg,[8] Hindemith[9] and others used dissonance to challenge traditional music. The examples are too numerous to list—suffice it to say that all of the important modernists would be included in such a list.

The spirit of primitivism in literature can be seen in D.H. Lawrence's worship of animals and, in his novels, the return to North American Indian culture;[10] in the frankness of Alan Ginsberg's poetry[11] and in the supermen of Knut Hamsun's novels.[12] In the fine arts, there is the elemental form of Henry Moore's sculpture[13] and the confusion of flesh and blood in Francis Bacon's painting—art

---

3. Franz Kafka (1883–1924), Czech novelist, author of *The Metamorphosis* and *The Castle*.

4. Samuel Beckett (1906–1984), Irish novelist and playwright.

5. Saul Bellow (1915–2005), American novelist who won the Nobel Prize for Literature in 1976.

6. Pablo Picasso (1881–1973), Spanish artist.

7. Jackson Pollock (1912–1956), American abstract expressionist painter.

8. Arnold Schoenberg (1874–1951), Austrian composer.

9. Paul Hindemith (1895–1963), German composer.

10. D.H. Lawrence (1885–1930), English novelist and poet who traveled the world in search of a primitive, perfect society.

11. Allen Ginsberg (1926–1997), American beatnik poet, famous for his work *Howl*.

12. Knut Hamsun (1859–1952), Norwegian novelist, won the Nobel Prize for Literature in 1920.

13. Henry Moore (1898–1986), English sculptor.

which is too horrible to look at.[14] In music, Stravinsky's deafening *The Rite of Spring*[15]—indeed one can go back as far as Wagner's powerful operas.[16] In architecture: Le Corbusier's return to Old Testament style in the Church of Notre Dame du Haut at Ronchamp.[17]

While modern art certainly was influenced by Nietzsche and Freud, some practitioners of modernism predated them, such as Dostoyevsky,[18] Whitman,[19] Dickens[20] and, as mentioned above, Wagner. Moreover, many modernists were contemporaries of Nietzsche and Freud and were not necessarily influenced by them. Therefore, we must look further—and if we search deeper into the roots of modern art we find that they exist in history itself. What we can say is that modern art evolved and came into being, that it took shape naturally. This also answers another even more basic question: how did Nietzsche and Freud themselves come about? They also were products of history—they did not suddenly leap out, self-generated. To many modern artists who came after them, their influence was similar to adding fuel to a fire or serving a great repast to a gourmand. Nevertheless, the strength of their influence derived from the natural evolution of history.

The new spirit of modern art naturally brought about a transformation in form as dissatisfaction with traditional forms gave rise to what we might call "fragmentation." What is more, the primitivist

14. Francis Bacon (1909–1992), English painter.

15. Igor Stravinsky (1882–1971), Russian composer whose most famous work, *The Rite of Spring* (Le Sacre du Printemps), was composed and first performed in 1913 in Paris.

16. Richard Wagner (1813–1883), German composer best known for his opera cycle *The Ring of the Nibelungs.*

17. Le Corbusier is the pseudonym of French architect Charles-Edouard Jeanneret (1887–1965). His chapel at Ronchamp built in the 1950s is considered one of the classic works of the modern period.

18. Fyodor Dostoyevsky (1821–1881), Russian novelist, whose works include *Crime and Punishment* and *The Brothers Karamazov.*

19. Walt Whitman (1819–1892), American poet.

20. Charles Dickens (1812–1870), English novelist, whose works include *David Copperfield, Great Expectations* and *Hard Times.*

striving for a return to mankind's original nature brought with it a child-like simplicity.

Aspects of fragmentation: in literature, first there is Joyce's *Ulysses*, which broke down the traditional sequence of time and space in narrative.[21] The poet T.S. Eliot's *The Waste Land* carried this process further.[22] Even the movie director Alain Resnais in *Last Year at Marienbad* took a similar route.[23] The most famous practitioner of fragmentation in painting was Picasso, who broke down everything in his cubist art. Jackson Pollock took this smashing up a step further—we could go so far as to call this breaking of the whole into parts "destruction" or "annihilation."

Regarding simplicity, first we should note the motto of the architect Ludwig Mies van der Rohe: "Less is more."[24] This is the slogan of simplification in all modern art. We see it in Modigliani's spectrum-like paintings. We see it in the sparse brushwork of Miro's child-like work.[25] In literature, we read it in Hemingway's bare-bones writing.[26] Samuel Beckett minimized the number of characters to two in his play *Waiting for Godot*, then to one in later works before omitting words altogether in *Breath*. In music, we hear it in the immaculate and serious modern compositions of Bartok.[27]

Besides fragmentation and simplicity, modern art has other aspects: for example, the complexity of neo-gothicism (literature) and the return to neo-classicism (architecture). However, the most

---

21. James Joyce (1881–1941), Irish novelist, whose novel *Ulysses* was published in 1920 in France, but was banned in the United States until 1934 because of its perceived obscenity.

22. T.S. Eliot (1888–1965), American writer whose poem *The Waste Land* was published in 1922.

23. Alain Resnais (1922–), French film director. *Last Year at Marienbad* was released in 1961.

24. Ludwig Mies van der Rohe (1886–1969), German architect who was part of the Bauhaus movement.

25. Joan Miro (1893–1983), Spanish painter.

26. Ernest Hemingway (1899–1961), American writer, famous for his pared down style of writing.

27. Bela Bartok (1881–1945), Hungarian composer.

importanttransformationinformwasthatwroughtbyfragmentation and simplicity.

Over the past ten years, our fellow countrymen have become accustomed to the term "modernism," but the products of modern art are still regarded as too deep to be understood; we flinch from them on sight and dare not approach them too closely. In truth, our fear or loathing of these works is based on a misunderstanding. Modern art is extremely easy to understand, far more so than our ability to understand romanticism, the baroque or classicism because, although perhaps we have not realized it, we become familiar with modern art early on—for we live modern lives. Invisibly and unconsciously, we absorb it through our senses on a daily basis. The television commercials we see daily, the advertisements in newspapers, everyday products in the home, fashions in the street, all the popular music we hear, all of the movies and photographs we see— not a one of them is not informed by modernism. Truly, any fashion-conscious teenage girl already understands modernism. Once we eradicate the paranoia concerning modernism, it will not be difficult to gain a thorough understanding and comprehension of it. In conclusion, I believe that grasping modern art is far simpler than understanding the poetry of the Tang,[28] the lyrics of the Song,[29] Chu songs from the Warring States Period[30] or the prose-poetry of the Han.[31] Modernism is the easiest of all types of art and should become the most important focus of research in art. And after we understand modern art, then we will be able to understand the art that preceded it.

Translated by Ihor Pidhainy

28. Tang, 618–907 CE.
29. Song, 960–1279 CE.
30. Warring States Period, 475–221 BCE.
31. Han, 206 BCE–220 CE.

Endless War

January 1987. In the 1980s, Wang Wen-hsing began to publish articles about his own writing. In this autobiographical account, he describes the revolutionary moment at age twenty when he realized he had to change his writing style. Wang also reveals his admiration for the work of Hemingway.

"Endless war" refers to the war over my writing. That is not to say I am holding a forum so others can voice their objections about my work. Rather, I am talking about the tedious personal war that takes place between me and my writing. This war has gone on for thirty years already and I am much the worse for wear, but it is obvious it will continue with no end in sight.

At the start of this war, when I was about twenty, I suddenly discovered some problems had developed in the way I habitually expressed myself. First of all, my writing lacked originality. Second, it was just a jumble of words, without any steady rhythm. At that time, I was reading Flaubert, Maupassant and Tolstoy. In their language I could hear a really pleasant sound, low and gently flowing, just like a cello. I immediately vowed to abandon my original writing style because I felt that its immaturity and confusion were unforgivably shameful. With my new understanding, I attempted a few stories, including "Mother," "Song of the Earth" and "Midsummer on the Prairie." Although I could see the direction I should be going, I realized that in these few stories I remained a vast distance from my goal. Each sentence still fell short of the desired effect.

When I was twenty-two, I read Hemingway. From then on, I became even more deeply engaged in the war over my writing. Since then, I have waged a bloody battle against my writing every day in a fight to the death. It's true: Hemingway was the one who dragged me into this war, who put me through hell and made me taste extreme bitterness, but it is a hardship I endure gladly. Hemingway sets such a shining example! He not only incorporates the same low, gentle flow of sounds as Flaubert, Maupassant and Tolstoy, but he goes one step further, concise to the point of vividness, full of the color and flavor of life. After reading him, in tribute I immediately set this as my goal in life.

To write like Hemingway is no simple thing. I could write only a few words a day at most. At the same time, to avoid writing too much or too fast, I also had to write my sentences from left to right.[1] Furthermore, I still had to write a first draft (a first draft is the easiest thing in the world), and then correct it word-by-word ten times while revising it into a final version. If one sentence was unsatisfactory, I could not just continue on to the next one. If I discovered I had written a word incorrectly, I would have to throw out the entire sentence and write it again from scratch. As long as I could follow Hemingway's model, though, I didn't mind.

I remember when a friend asked me two years ago to name the author I yearned most to be like. I answered: "Hemingway." He stared at me, hardly able to believe his ears. The distance between what he saw in my writing and Hemingway's was just too great. I explained that, in terms of spirit, we were remarkably similar, even if there were some superficial differences. Yes, it's true: no matter how many unique symbols appear in my writing, no matter how I manipulate sentences, none of it represents a departure from Hemingway but rather is part of a great effort to get close to the mark Hemingway set. Explaining it this way is not a matter of false reasoning or trying to justify myself, because this "similar in spirit yet

1. Chinese traditionally was written in vertical columns, a practice that continues in Taiwan. Wang wrote horizontally from left to right in the Western style in order to write more slowly and deliberately.

different in form" phenomenon actually does exist. For example, compare Conrad and Hemingway and it is even more obvious: in spirit, they both come from the same mold, even if at first glance they seem to have nothing in common. What I mean is that it seems like Hemingway imitated Conrad, the master. Although critics have never advanced this idea, I am presumptuous enough to say that I, at least, firmly believe Hemingway's writing most resembles Conrad's.

Could my judgment be wrong? Is there a problem with my ability to distinguish different styles? Not long ago, I found the answer, which both excited me and finally put my doubts to rest. From the beginning, of all the new American writers, I most admired the work of Joan Didion.[2] I don't skip a single word of what she writes. Even when I am standing in a bookstore, I try to snatch a look at one or two lines. I believe she is extremely similar to Hemingway. She possesses many of Hemingway's strengths, even that ideal writing style I have been questing after. What excited me was that, one day a month ago, I read something about her: "The writer she admires most is Hemingway. Since she was eighteen, she often has lovingly copied out Hemingway's short stories. She loves every word, every sentence, every paragraph, even every punctuation mark." I can say that this was the most exciting moment of my life. By understanding Didion, I knew I was qualified to identify Hemingway's style. From Didion, I knew that by putting Conrad and Hemingway together, I was pretty close to the mark.

Although there have not been many exciting—and secret—moments in my life like that, there are a few others. I remember another revelation that left me feeling rather pleased with myself. It had to do with Beethoven's *Symphony No. 3*, the "Eroica." In my opinion, it is a symphonic achievement of the greatest magnitude. Not only is it the best of Beethoven's symphonies, but also the most profound of all symphonies. But because my knowledge of music is incomplete (I can't even read music), this was a secret I kept to myself. I did not dare let other people know how much I admired the

2. Joan Didion (b. 1934) writes both fiction and non-fiction. Among her novels are *Play It As It Lays* (1970) and *A Book of Common Prayer* (1977).

"Eroica." But recently in *Time* magazine I read a music review with the triumphant title: "Wagner Most Admired Beethoven's Third." You cannot imagine the joy I felt at that moment—heavenly.

Let me return to language. A friend asked me if I planned to change my writing style yet again. Perhaps my friend's query was well intentioned—he probably did not want me to remain stuck forever in a situation where none of my readers could understand me. It could be that his question arose out of curiosity, wanting to know whether I am satisfied with "marching to a different beat" or would return to "the right path" in the future. My answer is this: my present writing style will definitely continue; there is no reason for my bloody daily battle not to continue. In other words, this is a battle about being honest in the use of language. If you cannot be honest with the words you write, what kind of literature is that? What kind of pleasure could come from writing without honesty? The uniqueness, the superiority, of Hemingway's prose is the result of nothing more than the honesty in the way he used words. There will be no break in my bloody war with my writing but one day, with heaven's blessing—and I hope there will be such a day—I will be able to prevail without a single drop of blood being shed and will win each daily battle with ease. In the same way that a child dreams of owning a candy store, in the same way that a person dreams of winning the lottery, I hope that in time I will be able to write a thousand words a day as if it were nothing. Nevertheless, I know this is an illusion. It is a crazy dream because even Hemingway could not achieve it. I will still bury myself in my life-and-death war, not thinking of anything else.

Translated by Martin Sulev

Zhongyuan: An Appreciation

August 22, 1993. This is Wang's nostalgic recollection of Zhongyuan, a pseudonym Wang created for Min Zongshu, and his influence in shaping Wang's interest in Chinese and Western art. This article, written after "M and W" and before the second volume of Backed Against the Sea, *is crucial to our understanding of Wang's artistic temperament, especially his enthusiasm for traditional Chinese forms.*

If you asked me who had the greatest influence on my pursuit of literature, I would have to say it was Zhongyuan. Zhongyuan is not his real name. As I do not have his consent and he may not want me to reveal his identity, for the present I will give him this pseudonym. When I met Zhongyuan, I had just enrolled in grade six; he was already in grade nine. In terms of age, he might have been four years older than me, even five—it was a chaotic time and the school-entrance age was not standardized. All that matters is that Zhongyuan was a great friend of mine. He was tall, taller than any of his classmates, and slim. Standing beside him, I did not even reach his shoulders. Like his shadow, I followed him all day long, very much like Don Quixote and his short companion, Sancho Panza. That Zhongyuan would accept this small friend was due entirely to his friendliness, understanding and patience. We lived in the same compound—my house was about one hundred meters away from his. This made us neighbors and that's how we met. Zhongyuan had started his schooling in mainland China. After moving to Taiwan, he joined a class in a junior high, the best in Taiwan at the time. His father was well versed in classical literature and was working as a secretary in a provincial government office. All of the family's friends were noted classical scholars. Zhongyuan's Japanese-style house was furnished and decorated simply but the paper doors— not the walls—were covered completely with sheets of calligraphy and artwork these friends had produced, the unmounted pieces just stuck to the door frames with thumbtacks. Growing up in that atmosphere, it is no surprise that Zhongyuan learned a great deal about traditional Chinese calligraphy and painting. Zhongyuan's family had just four members: his parents, a younger brother and himself. When his brother was small, before he could play with us, he liked to fool around in the compound courtyard until dark, even forgetting to go home. I often heard Zhongyuan calling him in his hometown dialect: "Lian'er! Come on! Lian'er! Come on!"

Zhongyuan and I were together for about four years. During most of that time, he was just a high school student, although an extraordinary one. His interest in the arts and literature and his understanding far exceeded that of run-of-the-mill high school students, possibly even his teachers. Zhongyuan had wide-ranging artistic interests: he liked poetry, Western fiction, Western painting, Chinese painting, inscriptions on metal and stone tablets, film and music. He tried his hand at classical poetry, fiction, Western-style painting, traditional Chinese painting and seal cutting. I, usually standing amazed in front of his desk, would listen as he spoke with great excitement about these topics. Although I did not necessarily understand what he was talking about, I believe I was strongly influenced by him, especially in regards to reading. When Zhongyuan came across a particularly good passage, he would move his arms and legs about excitedly as if he were dancing and want to tell me all about it. As long as I showed enough interest while I listened and asked to borrow the book—wanting, like him, to know how wonderful it was—he would always lend it to me. Even if he had borrowed the book himself, he would not hesitate to keep it a few more days for my sake. Zhongyuan's favorite book at that time was *Jean-*

Christophe.[1] When he finished the first volume, his excitement really made him dance around. Naturally, I felt the same—I borrowed it and read it passionately from cover to cover without stopping. My "excitement" might have been a bit less intense than his, but it was pretty close. In any case, Zhongyuan was satisfied by my level of "excitement," and so was I. Besides *Jean-Christophe*, Zhongyuan's other favorite was *Gone with the Wind*.[2] I also read and liked it, but of all the books Zhongyuan lent me, my real favorite was *Little Women*.[3] I read every single word of that book, unlike others that I just skimmed. *Little Women* almost made me forget about eating and sleeping; my enthusiasm probably even surprised Zhongyuan. He, for a change, had to listen to my endless words of praise about a book. In this way, together we read *Arch of Triumph*,[4] *A Farewell to Arms*,[5] *La Dame aux camellias*,[6] *Immensee*,[7] *Le Pecheur d'Islande*,[8] *The True Story of Ah-Q*,[9] and *Family*, *Spring* and *Autumn*[10] . . . I recall expressing many "feelings" about *Le Pecheur d'Islande*. Zhongyuan had an enthusiastic response to it as well. He also read *Dream of the Red Chamber*,[11] and I would say he was quite fond of it. I borrowed it and scanned a few pages but, perhaps because I noticed they were covered with dense rows of text, the dialogue not broken out into separate paragraphs, I soon returned it to him.

When Zhongyuan found a good book, he would—motivated by his extreme respect and excitement—draw a portrait of the author. After reading *Jean-Christophe*, he used the small photo of Rolland

1. By Romain Rolland.
2. By Margaret Mitchell.
3. By Louisa May Alcott.
4. By Erich Maria Remarque.
5. By Ernest Hemingway.
6. By Alexandre Dumas, *fils*.
7. By Theodor Storm.
8. By Pierre Loti.
9. By Lu Xun.
10. All by Ba Jin.
11. By Cao Xueqin.

on the jacket as a model to draw a pencil portrait. It was one of the best pencil drawings I have ever seen. Even recalling it today, I still feel the same, although I realize I am influenced by my youthful judgment. It was an excellent likeness, the use of light and shade magnificent, as if executed by an experienced hand. Later, after reading *The True Story of Ah-Q*, he made a pencil drawing of Lu Xun. Upon finishing *Gone with the Wind*, he drew a small portrait of the actor Clark Gable.

Zhongyuan also could paint in the traditional Chinese manner—probably he had taken lessons after school. I remember he worked diligently on plum blossoms. He produced some in black ink and, later, red ones. He explained to me that when painting plum branches, they should be made to look old in order to avoid an impression of vulgarity. He also used examples from stone and metal inscription to teach me how to distinguish what is vulgar from what is not. During that time, he industriously carved seals— likely he had taken a seal-carving lesson as well. He said that if the print a seal made was even and exact, it could be considered vulgar, while a seal that displayed irregular knife cuts or a broken edge was elegant. Zhongyuan also tried to teach me about rocks, but the information was so specialized that I could not take in what he said. One day, he told me he would make a seal for me if I could find a seal stone. I said there was an old seal of my father's that he did not use anymore—I had no other stones. Zhongyuan said it would do because he could grind off the old inscription and carve a new one. That was the first time I had heard that seal stones could be ground down and recycled to make new ones. So I ended up with a seal of my own, my first.

Zhongyuan not only knew how to paint and inscribe stones, he also wrote classical poetry, especially in the *ci* format.[12] I read many of his classical *ci* "casual writings" but I lacked the ability to appreciate them. Faced with the neat metrical formation and harmonious

12. *Ci* poetry is composed with strict tonal patterns and line schemes with fixed numbers of words and lines. The style originated during the Tang Dynasty (618–907 CE) and was fully developed in the Song Dynasty (960–1279 CE).

sounds of his poetry, I just felt sorry for myself, regretting that I would never compose that kind of work. In addition to poetry, Zhongyuan also wrote a piece of short fiction that was published in a journal at his school. He spent one or two weeks writing and revising, revising and rewriting. Of all his creative endeavors, this might have been the one where he made his greatest effort. In this story, he portrayed an artist meeting an intelligent young woman. In the end, she goes away, leaving the artist disconsolate. Employing a fluent writing style, he evoked a plaintive atmosphere that truly moved the reader. The mood woven into the story, as in all of his creative writing, was influenced by countless classical *ci* poems: I remember those poems—they made his fiction even more vivid.

Probably because of Romain Rolland, Zhongyuan developed an interest in Western classical music. In Taiwan at that time, contact with classical music was rare but Zhongyuan might have heard classical recordings in school or at some friend's home. He told me a number of times how moving and magnificent Beethoven's *Symphony No. 5* and *Symphony No. 9* were. He often took out a songbook and sang the "Ode to Joy" from *Symphony No. 9*, repeating it over and over beneath the light of his desk lamp. I learned many songs from him. In addition to the "Ode to Joy," there were Steven Foster's folk songs and Schubert's and Schumann's lieder, all heard beneath the soft, greenish light of his desk lamp.

Zhongyuan also led me into the splendid world of cinema. At the time, he would have been just beginning to understand films, but he had a basic grasp of film categories and could distinguish between low-brow and art films and, given his knowledge of the other arts, between good and bad films. At that time, the Chinese Film Production Company, located at the Botanical Gardens, showed pretty good movies every weekend. He always took me with him to see them. I particularly remember Hitchcock's films, Billy Wilder's courtroom movies and *For Whom the Bell Tolls*. Zhongyuan thought *For Whom the Bell Tolls* probably was the best movie he had even seen. It was the same for me. Regardless of whether it really was any good or not, I vividly remember every detail. In addition to the movies I saw at the Botanical Gardens, I remember there was another one that made a deep impression. One day, Zhongyuan got two tickets for a movie to be shown at the Taiwan Normal University auditorium. The title was *How Green Was My Valley*. We both were very impressed and carried it around with us for a long time. Just a few days ago, I rented it to watch it again. Although it had been thirty-some years, my overall impression remained unchanged. This proves that lyrical beauty arouses exactly the same feelings in children as it does in adults. The acting skills and the complexity of the love relationship in *How Green Was My Valley* can be understood only by adults, but my feelings about the lyrical aesthetics of the film are the same as when I was young. Our emotional nature is innate, already developed when we are children.

The friendship or, I should say, the guidance Zhongyuan gave me lasted four years. When I started high school, I suddenly heard that his family was going to leave Taipei. This was shocking news. One Sunday, his family rented a big truck and left. After seeing him off, I returned home and looked at my surroundings, feeling that life from then on would be extremely dull. I hid in my room, locked the door. Free from prying eyes, a stream of warm tears rolled down my face. Later, whenever I passed his house and saw all of the doors and windows closed, I imagined that, maybe, one day, they would open once again and Zhongyuan and his family would move back. I had played this fantasy over and over in my mind many times before the day when the doors and windows did actually open again—but a new family had moved in.

I have not seen Zhongyuan since then. Many reasons prevent people from seeing each other, but I have never forgotten the boy who gave me friendship, led me into the world of art and literature, and exerted such a deep influence on my whole life.

Translated by Shu-ning Sciban

A Chronology of
Wang Wen-hsing's Life

❖

Until recently, "Wang Wen-hsing dashi ji" (Record of major events in the life of Wang Wen-hsing) has been the only published chronology of Wang Wen-hsing's life. It first appeared in *Zhongguo shibao* (China times), November 18–20, 1999; then was published a second time in 2000, with Professor Ke Qingming's supplement, on the official website of "Wang Wen-hsing's Manuscript Exhibition" by Taiwan University Library. A third publication occurred in 2007 in *Xiaoyao* (Les loisirs) magazine, with an addition by Wang concerning events after 2000. Based on these records and with some information collected by Shu-ning Sciban, the chronology detailed here is meant to serve as a brief introduction to Wang's life and important events in his writing career.

1939 Born on November 4, in Fuzhou, China.
1942 Moves to Xiamen with his parents at the age of three.
1945 Moves back to Fuzhou with his parents after the Sino-Japanese war.
1946 Moves with his parents to Donggang, Taiwan; enters Donggang Elementary School.
1948 Moves to Taipei with his parents; enters a grade three class at the renowned Taipei Mandarin Experimental Elementary School.
1951 Graduates from elementary school.
1954 Graduates from junior high and enters high school.

1957 Graduates from high school and passes the university entrance exam to study in the Department of Foreign Languages and Literatures, National Taiwan University.

1958 Publishes his first short story, "Shou ye" (The lingering night). In the following two years, he publishes other stories in *Daxue shenghuo* (University life) and *Wenxue zazhi* (Literary review).

1960 Establishes *Xiandai wenxue* (Modern literature) with a number of friends.

1961 Graduates from university and begins compulsory military service.

1963 Enters the creative writing program at the University of Iowa and subsequently receives his MFA degree.

1965 Returns to Taiwan; teaches courses on English fiction as an instructor in the Department of Foreign Languages and Literatures at National Taiwan University. Serves as chief editor of *Modern Literature* until November 1968.

1966 Begins to write his first novel *Jia bian* (Family catastrophe).

1967 Publishes his first short story collection, titled *Longtian lou* (Dragon inn).

1969 Marries Ch'en Chu-yun, and spends a year as a research fellow at State University of New York at Buffalo.

1970 Publishes his second collection of short stories, titled *Wanju shouqiang* (The toy revolver).

1972 *Family Catastrophe* is completed, serialized and published in *Chung Wai Literary Monthly*.

1973 *Family Catastrophe* is published in book form by Hongfan Bookstore.

1974 Begins to write his second novel, *Bei hai de ren* (Backed against the sea).

1976 Exchange scholar at the University of Florida at Jacksonville.

1979 Promoted to professor at National Taiwan University. *Backed Against the Sea*, vol. 1 is completed.

1981 His father dies. *Backed Against the Sea*, vol. 1, is published by Hongfan Bookstore. He also publishes his third collection of short stories, titled *Shiwu pian xiaoshuo* (Fifteen short stories).

1985 Baptized into the Catholic Church.

1988 First essay collection, *Shu he ying* (Books and films), is published by Hongfan Bookstore. First play, *M and W*, is published and performed in Tainan by the Tainan People's Theater in August.

1989 His mother dies.

1997 *Backed Against the Sea*, vol. 2, is completed.

1999 *Backed Against the Sea*, vol. 2, is serialized and published in *Lianhe wenxue* (Unitas), and published in book form by Hongfan Bookstore in September. *Family Catastrophe* is selected as one of the best 100 Chinese literary works published in the twentieth century by *Yazhou zhoukan* magazine in Hong Kong, and one of the best 30 literary works published in the second half of the twentieth century in Taiwan by the Council for Cultural Affairs in Taiwan.

2000 Donates manuscripts of *Family Catastrophe*, *Backed Against the Sea*, an assorted compilation of notes and a collection of letters to friends to National Taiwan University Library. The library holds an exhibition of Wang's manuscripts on November 15 to December 31.

2002 His second essay collection, *Xiaoshuo mo yu* (Beyond fiction), is published.

2003 The third essay collection, *Xing yu lou sui xiang* (Random thoughts from a star-rain tower), is published.

2005 Retires from National Taiwan University at the same time as his wife, Professor Ch'en Chu-yun. Begins to write his third novel, a religious story.

2006 Publishes the short story "Ming yue ye" (Nights of the shining moon).

2007 Gives six lectures on the writing of *Family Catastrophe* in May and June at National Central University in Zhongli, Taiwan. Receives an honorary doctoral degree from the National Taiwan University in November.

2008 Gives two lectures on *Family Catastrophe* and "Mingyun de jixian" (Line of fate) on March 10–11 at Raffles Junior College, Singapore.

2009 Gives a lecture on "Reading and Writing" at the "Art of Chinese Narrative Language: International Workshop on Wang Wen-hsing's Life and Works" held at the University of Calgary, Canada, February 19–21. Also delivers an English-Chinese bilingual address prior to a performance of *M and W* and short-story dramatizations at the Reeve Theatre, University of Calgary, on February 21. Receives the 2009 Taiwan National Award for Arts (Literature Category) in October. Publishes *"Jia bian" liu jiang* (Six lectures on *Family Catastrophe*), a collection of the six lectures on *Family Catastrophe* that he gave in 2007.

2010 Participates in a forum on *Backed Against the Sea* and a film on his life at an international conference titled "Enacting Modernism: Wang Wen-hsing's Works in Performance and Translation," held at National Central University in Zhongli, Taiwan, June 4–6. Publishes *Wang Wen-hsing shougao ji: Jia bian, Bei hai de ren* (Wang Wen-hsing's manuscripts: *Family Catastrophe, Backed Against the Sea*), compiled by Yi Peng (Taipei: Xingren chubanshe). This publication includes Wang's records of both his novels.

Bibliography of
Wang Wen-hsing's Works

1958

- "Shou ye" (The lingering night). *Daxue shenghuo* (University life) April 1958: 53–56.
- "Yitiao chuisi de gou" (A dying dog). *Wenxue zazhi* (Literary review) 4.6 (1958): 58–60.

1959

- "Yige gongwuyuan de jiehun" (The marriage of a civil servant). *Wenxue zazhi* (Literary review) 5.6 (1959): 41–51.
- "Can ju" (Withered chrysanthemums). *Wenxue zazhi* (Literary review) 6.2 (1959): 56–67.
- "Bi" (Paralysis). By Tong Ma (Wang Wen-hsing). *Wenxue zazhi* (Literary review) 6.4 (1959): 69–74.
- "Xiawu" (Afternoon). *Wenxue zazhi* (Literary review) 6.6 (1959): 66–77.

1960

- Pound, Ezra. "Akesa de gumu" (The Tomb at Akr Caar). Trans. Jin Sheng (Wang Wen-hsing). *Xiandai wenxue* (Modern literature) 1 (1960): 85–86.
- "Sha Gang xing shuai" (The rise and fall of Françoise Sagan). *Wenxue zazhi* (Literary review) 8.3 (1960): 16–21.
- Eliot, T.S. "Si shou xuqu" (Four quartets). Trans. Tong Ma (Wang Wen-hsing). *Xiandai wenxue* (Modern literature) 3 (1960): 98–100.
- "Wanju shouqiang" (The toy revolver). *Xiandai wenxue* (Modern literature) 1 (1960): 55–71.

- "Muqin" (Mother). *Xiandai wenxue* (Modern literature) 2 (1960): 67–70.
- "Rili" (Calendar). *Xiandai wenxue* (Modern literature) 4 (1960): 76–77.
- "Zui kuaile de shi" (The happiest thing). *Xiandai wenxue* (Modern literature) 5 (1960): 91.

1961

- "Dadi zhi ge" (Song of the earth). *Xiandai wenxue* (Modern literature) 6 (1961): 83–84.
- "Caoyuan di shengxia: huainian wo yishi yiban de qingnian shidai" (Midsummer on the prairie: Missing the lost half of my youth). *Xiandai wenxue* (Modern literature) 8 (1961): 102–14.
- "Jieshu" (Conclusion). *Daxue shenghuo* (University life) May 1961: 45–50.
- "Liuyue de ge" (June song). *Xiandai wenxue* (Modern literature) 9 (1961): 114–16.
- "Liang furen" (Two women). *Xiandai wenxue* (Modern literature) 10 (1961): 53–59.
- "Da feng" (Strong wind). *Xiandai wenxue* (Modern literature) 11 (1961): 66–72.

1962

- "Bing fei yanlei" (By no means tears). *Xiandai wenxue* (Modern literature) 12 (1962): 62.
- "Jian yue—gei Hsien-yung, for Friendship" (Contract fulfilled—to Hsien-yung, for Friendship). *Xiandai wenxue* (Modern literature) 13 (1962): 95–112.
- *Xiandai xiaoshuo xuan* (Selected modern fiction). Edited by Wang Wen-hsing and Pai Hsien-yung. Taipei: Xiandai wenxue zazhishe.
- "Xiari bangwan huijia de qingnian" (The youth who returns home in the dusk). *Wenxing zazhi* (Wenxing magazine).

1963

- "Haibin shengmu jie" (The day of the sea-goddess). *Xiandai wenxue* (Modern literature) 16 (1963): 22–35.
- "Mingyun de jixian" (Line of fate). *Xiandai wenxue* (Modern literature) 17 (1963): 31–41.

- "Han liu" (Cold front). *Xiandai wenxue* (Modern literature) 17 (1963): 64–80.

1964
- "Qianque" (Flaw). *Xiandai wenxue* (Modern literature) 19 (1964): 20–30.
- "Hei yi" (The black gown). *Xiandai wenxue* (Modern literature) 20 (1964): 58–66.

1966
- "Longtian lou" (Dragon inn). *Xiandai wenxue* (Modern literature) 27 (1966): 177–232.

1967
- *Longtian lou* (Dragon inn). Taipei: Wenxing shudian.

1968
- "*Xin ke de shi xiang* xu" (Preface to *New stone statue*). *Xiandai wenxue* (Modern literature) 35 (1968): 218–19.
- *Xin ke de shi xiang* (New stone statue). Edited by Wang Wen-hsing. Taipei: Xianrenzhang, 1968.
- "Shafukelisi zhu *Yileiketela* zhong de duibi yu chongtu" (Contrast and conflict in Sophocles' *Electra*). *Xiandai wenxue* (Modern literature) 34 (1968): 65–73.
- "An Analytical Approach to D.H. Lawrence's *Sons and Lovers*." *Tamkang Review* 7 (1968): 247–62.

1970
- *Wanju shouqiang* (The toy revolver). Taipei: Zhiwen chubanshe.
- "*Wanju shouqiang* xu" (Preface to *The toy revolver*). In *Wanju shouqiang* (*The toy revolver*), 1–2. Taipei: Zhiwen chubanshe.
- "Dier bufen: shouji (Disan yanjiushi shouji)" (Part two: The journal [Journal of the third research room]). In *Wanju shouqiang* (The toy revolver), 117–68. Taipei: Zhiwen chubanshe.

1971

- "Luolita de zhen mianmu—ping *Lolita*" (The real face of Lolita—comments on *Lolita*). *Meiguo yanjiu* (American studies) 1 (1971): 51–56.

1972
- "Wo kan *Yige xiao shimin de xinsheng*" (I read *Wishes of a common citizen of the city*). *Daxue zazhi* (University magazine) 58 (1972): 33–35.
- "*Jia bian* (1)" ("Family catastrophe" [1]). *Zhong wai wenxue* (Chung wai literary monthly) 1.4 (1972): 140–73.
- "*Jia bian* (2)" ("Family catastrophe" [2]). *Zhong wai wenxue* (Chung wai literary monthly) 1.5 (1972): 150–84.
- "*Jia bian* (3)" ("Family catastrophe" [3]). *Zhong wai wenxue* (Chung wai literary monthly) 1.6 (1972): 133–62.
- "*Jia bian* (4)" ("Family catastrophe" [4]). *Zhong wai wenxue* (Chung wai literary monthly) 1.7 (1972): 152–88.

1973
- "*Jia bian* (5)" ("Family catastrophe" [5]). *Zhong wai wenxue* (Chung wai literary monthly) 1.8 (1973): 124–53.
- "*Jia bian* (6)" ("Family catastrophe" [6]). Zhong wai wenxue (Chung wai literary monthly) 1.9 (1973): 143–76.
- *Jia bian* (Family catastrophe). Taipei: Huanyu chubanshe.
- "Fazhan wenxue de jiejing" (Shortcut to developing literature). *Zhongyang yue kan* (Central monthly magazine) 5.11 (1973): 47–48.
- "Lun Taiwan duanpian xiaoshuo" (Discussing Taiwanese short stories). *Zhongguo wenxuan* (Anthology of Chinese literature) 80 (1973): 85–91.

1974
- "*Liao zhai* zhong de Dai'aonixi'an xiaoshuo 'Hu meng'" ('Dreaming of fox,' a story of Dionysian style in *Strange tales from a make-do studio*). *Youshi wenyi* (Youshi literary arts) 39.4 (1974): 106–21.

1976
- "Gudian caizi Wang Wen-hsing tan xiandai nüquan" (Gifted classical scholar Wang Wen-hsing discusses modern women's rights). *Funü zazhi* (Women magazine) 3 (1976): 72–75.

1978

- *Jia bian* (Family catastrophe). Reprint. Taipei: Hongfan shudian.
- "Xiangtu wenxue de gong yu guo ji qi jingji guan yu wenhua guan" (The accomplishments and improprieties of *xiangtu wenxue* and its economic and cultural point of view). *Xia chao* (Summer tide) 4.2 (1978): 64–74.
- "Du Yang Mu de shi" (Reading the poetry of Yang Mu). *Lianhe bao* (United daily) 5 March 1978: 12.

1979
- *Treatment of the Opposing Political Stand: a Discussion of "Brave New World" and three other Political Novels*. Taipei: Shuangye shuju.
- *Shiwu pian xiaoshuo* (Fifteen stories). Taipei: Hongfan shudian.
- "Chuangzao wenyan, baihua, ouhua de lixiang wenti" (To create an ideal literary style by blending classical, vernacular, and Europeanized Chinese). *Lianhe bao* (United daily) 5 May 1979: 12.

1981
- *Bei hai de ren* (Backed against the sea). Taipei: Hongfan shudian.
- "Qian lun xiandai wenxue" (A brief discussion of modern literature). *Lian fu sanshi nian wenxue daxi: pinglun juan 3* (Literary supplement of *United daily* thirty years of literature series: Criticism Vol. 3). Taipei: Lianhe bao chubanshe. Reprinted in *Shu he ying* (Books and films), 187–93. Taipei: Lianhe wenxue, 1988.

1982
- *Longtian lou* (Dragon inn). Reprint. Taipei: Dalin chubanshe, 1983.
- "Suixiang si ti" (Random thoughts on four questions). *Lianhe bao* (United daily) 6 July 1983: 8.

1984
- "Dianying jiushi wenxue" (Cinema is literature). *Lianhe bao* (United daily) 12 May 1984: 8.
- "Dianying haishi wenxue" (Cinema still is literature). *Lianhe bao* (United daily) 6 June 1984: 8.
- "Heqi de ren: huai Zhang Zhihong shenfu" (Amiable person: Cher-

ishing Father Zhang Zhihong). *Lianhe bao* (United daily) 23 December 1984: 8.

1985
- "Shouji xian chao" (Leisure copy of the journal). *Lianhe wenxue* (Unitas) 1.4 (1985): 18–24.
- "Shouji xu chao" (Continuing copy of the journal). *Lianhe wenxue* (Unitas) 2.1 (1985): 98–107.

1986
- "Wo weishenme yao xiezuo" (Why I want to write). *Lianhe bao* (United daily) 18 February.
- "Xiandai zhuyi de zhiyi he yuanshi" (The challenge and primitiveness of modernism). *Zhongguo shibao* (China times daily) 15 August 1986: 8.
- "Guren yu jiu zuo" (An old friend and his past work). *Dangdai* (Contemporary magazine) 5 (1986): 92–94.

1987
- "Wu xiuzhi de zhanzheng" (Endless war). *Wenxing* (Literary star) 103 (1987): 104–05.
- "Shi wei zhijizhe si de wenxue: Wang Wen-hsing yanjiang ci" (Bosom buddy literature: A lecture by Wang Wen-hsing). *Wenxue yu zongjiao: Di yi jie guoji wenxue yu zongjiao huiyi lunwenji.* (Literature and religion: The collected papers of the first international conference on literature and religion), 463–74. Taipei: Shibao wenhua. 463–74.
- "M he W" (M and W). *Lianhe wenxue* (Unitas) 4.5 (1987): 80–89.

1988
- *Shu he ying* (Books and films). Taipei: Lianhe wenxue.
- "Yanjiu shi shouji—zongjiao ji qita (1)" (Journal from the research room—religion and other things [1]). *Lianhe bao* (United daily) 16 September 1988: 21.
- "Yanjiu shi shouji—zongjiao ji qita (2)" (Journal from the research room—religion and other things [2]). *Lianhe bao* (United daily) 17 September 1988: 21.
- "Yanjiu shi shouji—zongjiao ji qita (3)" (Journal from the research

room—religion and other things [3]). *Lianhe bao* (United daily) 18 September 1988: 21.

1989

- "Liti yu pingmian: ping Wang Xiangqi 'Huangshi gong miao'" (Three dimensions and two dimensions: a discussion of Wang Xiangqi's 'Temple of the god of yellow stone'). *Lianhe wenxue* (Unitas) 5.10 (1989): 80–81.

1990

- "Yanjiu shi shouji—zongjiao ji qita" (Journal from the research room—religion and other things). Reprinted in *Wang Wen-hsing de xinling shijie* (Wang Wen-hsing's spiritual world). Edited by Kang Laixin, 105–14. Taipei: Yage chubanshe.
- "M he W" (M and W). Reprinted in *Wang Wen-hsing de xinling shijie* (Wang Wen-hsing's spiritual world). Edited by Kang Laixin, 160–75. Taipei: Yage chubanshe.
- "Wu sheng yinxiang (shang)" (Impressions of five provinces [Part 1]). *Lianhe wenxue* (Unitas) 6.4 (1990): 35–47.
- "Wu sheng yinxiang (xia)" (Impressions of five provinces [Part 2]). *Lianhe wenxue* (Unitas) 6.5 (1990): 21–31.
- "Zui kuaile de shi" (The happiest thing). Reprinted in *Wang Wen-hsing de xinling shijie* (Wang Wen-hsing's spiritual world). Edited by Kang Laixin, 115. Taipei: Yage chubanshe.
- "Rili" (Calendar). Reprinted in *Wang Wen-hsing de xinling shijie* (Wang Wen-hsing's spiritual world). Edited by Kang Laixin, 116–17. Taipei: Yage chubanshe.
- "Shenhua ji" (Discourses on the spiritual). *Wang Wen-hsing de xinling shijie* (Wang Wen-hsing's spiritual world). Edited by Kang Laixin, 98–104. Taipei: Yage chubanshe.
- "Weihe xiezuo" (Why write?). Reprint of "Wo weishenme yao xiezuo" (Why I want to write) in *Wang Wen-hsing de xinling shijie* (Wang Wen-hsing's spiritual world). Edited by Kang Laixin, 48. Taipei: Yage chubanshe.
- "Wu xiuzhi de zhanzheng" (Endless war). Reprinted in *Wang Wen-hsing de xinling shijie* (Wang Wen-hsing's spiritual world). Edited by Kang Laixin, 49–52. Taipei: Yage chubanshe.

- "Heqi de ren: huai Zhang Zhihong shenfu" (Amiable person: Cherishing Father Zhang Zhihong). Reprinted in *Wang Wen-hsing de xinling shijie* (Wang Wen-hsing's spiritual world). Edited by Kang Laixin, 118–19. Taipei: Yage chubanshe.
- "Zhang Xiaofeng de yishu: ping *Wo zai*" (Zhang Xiaofeng's art: A review of *I am*). *Wang Wen-hsing de xinling shijie* (Wang Wen-hsing's spiritual world). Edited by Kang Laixin, 120–24. Taipei: Yage chubanshe.
- "Yixiang ren: cunzaizhuyi wenxue de tese" (The stranger: The characteristics of existentialist literature). *Wang Wen-hsing de xinling shijie* (Wang Wen-hsing's spiritual world). Edited by Kang Laixin, 125-32. Taipei: Yage chubanshe.
- "*Kalamazuofu xiongdimen* zhong de xie'e biaoxian" (The manifestation of evil in *The Brothers Karamazov*). *Wang Wen-hsing de xinling shijie* (Wang Wen-hsing's spiritual world). Edited by Kang Laixin 133–41. Taipei: Yage chubanshe.
- "Tan fumo zhe" (The possessed). *Wang Wen-hsing de xinling shijie* (Wang Wen-hsing's spiritual world). Edited by Kang Laixin, 142–46. Taipei: Yage chubanshe.
- "Delaiye de 'Fuhuo'" (Carl T. Dreyer's 'Ordet'). *Wang Wen-hsing de xinling shijie* (Wang Wen-hsing's spiritual world). Edited by Kang Laixin, 147–49. Taipei: Yage chubanshe.
- "Buniu'er he Houmo de yishu: ping Weilidianna, 'mude zhi ye,' 'wu hou zhi lian'" (The art of Buñuel and Rohmer: A review of Viridiana, "Ma nuit chez Maud," "L'Amour l'apres-midi"). *Wang Wen-hsing de xinling shijie* (Wang Wen-hsing's spiritual world). Edited by Kang Laixin, 150–59. Taipei: Yage chubanshe.
- "'Duoluo tianshi,' 'Pashou' he 'Bulong senlin de guifu'" ("Les anges du péché," "Pickpocket," and "Les dames du Bois de Boulogne"). *Wang Wen-hsing de xinling shijie* (Wang Wen-hsing's spiritual world). Edited by Kang Laixin, 156–59. Taipei: Yage chubanshe.

1991
- "Shan he lüeying (shang)" (A glimpse of the land [Part 1]). *Lianhe wenxue* (Unitas) 7.4 (1991): 10–23.
- "Shan he lüeying (xia)" (A glimpse of the land [Part 2]). *Lianhe wenxue* (Unitas) 7.5 (1991): 114–21.

- "Houqi yinxiang guan" (Viewed from later impressions). *Lianhe wenxue* (Unitas) 7.5 (1991): 122–23.
- "Lü ji sanze" (Three travel diaries). *Lianhe bao* (United daily) (Taizhong ed.) 6 May 1991: 41.
- "Shinü tu—guan Zeng Manyun nüshi huazuo" (Paintings of beauties—an appreciation of Madam Zeng Manyun's paintings). *Xiongshi meishu* (Lion arts) 244 (1991): 212–13.
- "Shijue zhi shang: Hei Zeming de gaibian" (Superior vision: The change in Kurosawa). *Lianhe bao* (United daily) 25 July 1991: 15.
- "*Xian wen* yi jiu" (Remembering the past about *Modern literature*). "*Xiandai" yinyuan* (Relationship with *Modern literature*), 66–69. Taipei: Xianwen chubanshe.
- "Gei Ouyang Tzu de xin" (A letter to Ouyang Tzu). "*Xiandai" yinyuan* (Relationship with *Modern literature*), 210–13. Taipei: Xianwen chubanshe.

1992
- "Ji'an shi zhumian *Xian wen* zhubian" (Professor T.A. Hsia's congratulations and encouragement to *Modern literature*'s editors). *Lianhe wenxue* (Unitas) 8.7 (1992): 54–60.
- "Xi bei dong nan (shang)" (East west north south [Part 1]). *Lianhe wenxue* (Unitas) 8.11 (1992): 124–37.
- "Xi bei dong nan (xia)" (East west north south [Part 2]). *Lianhe wenxue* (Unitas) 8.1 (1992): 116–28.

1993
- "Chong you xiao ji" (Brief notes of places revisited). *Lianhe bao* (United daily) 6 April 1993: 37.
- "Wang Wen-hsing lüetan wenxue jia yi" (Wang Wen-hsing's brief discussion on fine translations of literature). *Yishujia* (Artist) 37.5 (1993): 352.
- "Huai Zhongyuan" (Zhongyuan: an appreciation). *Zhongguo shibao* (China times daily) 22 August.

1996
- "Bodelai'er lizan" (Paying tribute to Baudelaire). *Zhongguo shibao* (China times daily) 12 August (1996): 19.

- "*Kalamazhufu xiongdi* yishu zhong de zongjiao guan" (The conception of religion in *The Brothers Karamazov*). *Lianhe wenxue* (Unitas) 13.2 (1996): 70–77.

1997
- "Xing yun liu shui, bifeng youmo: *Shan ju suiyue* guanhougan" (Floating clouds and running water, razor-sharp humor: A reading of *The years of living in the mountains*). *Zhongguo shibao* (China times daily) 8 January 1997: 31.
- "Bali dao" (Bali). *Zhong wai wenxue* (Chung wai literary monthly) 26.6 (1997): 83–88.

1998
- "Bodelai'er fangyi qi shou ji xu" (The imitation of translations of seven poems by Baudelaire with an introduction). *Zhong wai wenxue* (Chung wai literary monthly) 27.2 (1998): 96–105.

1999
- "*Bei hai de ren* (xia)(1)" (*Backed against the sea* [Part 2][1]). *Lianhe wenxue* (Unitas) 15.3 (1999): 12–35.
- "*Bei hai de ren* (xia)(2)" (*Backed against the sea* [Part 2][2]). *Lianhe wenxue* (Unitas) 15.4 (1999): 10–35.
- "*Bei hai de ren* (xia)(3)" (*Backed against the sea* [Part 2][3]). *Lianhe wenxue* (Unitas) 15.5 (1999): 18–40.
- "*Bei hai de ren* (xia)(4)" (*Backed against the sea* [Part 2][4]). *Lianhe wenxue* (Unitas) 15.6 (1999): 158–77.
- "*Bei hai de ren* (xia)(5)" (*Backed against the sea* [Part 2][5]). *Lianhe wenxue* (Unitas) 15.7 (1999): 128–56.
- "*Bei hai de ren* (xia)(6)" (*Backed against the sea* [Part 2][6]). *Lianhe wenxue* (Unitas) 15.8 (1999): 144–66.
- *Bei hai de ren* (xia) (*Backed against the sea* [Vol. 2]). Taipei: Hongfan shudian, 1999.
- "Wang Wen-hsing—ershisi nian yichang 'Bei hai' meng" (Wang Wen-hsing—a twenty-four year "*Bei hai*" dream). In *Shu yu shengming de duihua* (Conversations on books and life), 5–65. Tianxia yuanjian chuban gufen youxian gongsi.

- "Jian yue" (Contract fulfilled). *Zhongguo shibao* (China times daily) 18 November 1999: 37.
- "Jinri mei yu (shang)" (Contemporary language aesthetics [Part 1]). *Zhongguo shibao* (China times daily) 18 Nov. 1999: 37.
- "Dashi ji 1" (Record of major events 1). *Zhongguo shibao* (China times daily) 18 November 1999: 37.
- "Zui kuaile de shi" (The happiest thing). *Zhongguo shibao* (China times daily) 19 November 1999: 37.
- "Jinri mei yu (xia)" (Contemporary language aesthetics [Part 2]). *Zhongguo shibao* (China times daily) 19 November 1999: 37.
- "Dashi ji 2" (Record of major events 2). *Zhongguo shibao* (China times daily) 19 November 1999: 37.
- "*Jia bian*" (Family catastrophe). *Zhongguo shibao* (China times daily) 20 November 1999: 37.
- "Dashi ji 3" (Record of major events 3). *Zhongguo shibao* (China times daily) 20 November 1999: 37.

2000

- "Bodelai'er yinxiang" (Impressions of Baudelaire). *Lianhe wenxue* (Unitas) 16.6 (2000): 59–62.
- *Jia bian (Family catastrophe)*. 2000 Edition. Taipei: Hongfan shudian.

2001

- "Su Zizhan Huangzhou Chibi san gou he du" (Reading Su Zizhan's three poems on Chibi of Huangzhou). *Zhong wai wenxue* (Chung wai literary monthly) 30.6 (2001): 262–74.
- With Ke Qingming. "Wang Wen-hsing dashi ji" (Record of major events in the life of Wang Wen-hsing), *Zhong wai wenxue* (Chung wai literary monthly) 30.6 (Nov. 2001): 396–99.

2002

- *Xiaoshuo mo yu* (Beyond fiction). Taipei: Hongfan shudian.

2003

- *Xing yu lou sui xiang* (Random thoughts from star-rain tower). Taipei: Hongfan shudian.

2005

- "Jingdian juzuode zhenshi chengxian: *Yuwang jieche* guanhougan" (Realistic presentation of a classic play: a review of *A Streetcar Named Desire*). *Lianhe wenxue* (Unitas) 21.5 (March 2005): 150–54.

2006

- "Ming yue ye" (Nights of the shining moon). *Lianhe bao* (United daily) 30 June.
- *Shu he ying* (Books and films). 2nd edition. Taipei: Lianhe wenxue (With additional works)

2007

- "Yuanyuan bujuede quzhe" (Endless twists and turns). *Yinke wenxue shenghuo zhi* (Records of literary life) 3.9 (May 2007): 70–71.
- "*Xingyu lou suixiang xuwen* xu" (Preface of *Random thoughts from star-rain tower*). *Xiaoyao* (Les losirs) 15 (September 2007): 82–83.
- "Sancheng jianwen" (Observations of three cities). *Xiaoyao* (Les losirs) 15 (September 2007): 84–105.
- "Bali wuri" (Five days in Paris). *Xiaoyao* (Les losirs) 15 (September 2007): 106–110.
- "Wang Wen-hsing dashi ji" (Record of major events in the life of Wang Wen-hsing). *Xiaoyao* (Les losirs) 15 (September 2007): 111–113.
- *Wo ruhe xie xiaoshuo* (How I write fiction) (Text and DVD). Taipei: National Taiwan University Press.

2009

- "*Jia bian*" liu jiang (Six lectures on *Family Catastrophe*). Taipei: Maitian chubanshe.

2010

- *Wang Wen-hsing shougao ji: Jia bian, Bei hai de ren* (Wang Wen-hsing's manuscripts: *Family Catastrophe, Backed Against the Sea*). Compiled by Yi Peng. Taipei: Xingren chubanshe.

Bibliography compiled by Shu-ning Sciban
with the assistance of Anita Lin, Emily Wen and Roma Ilnyckyj

About the Translators

Ch'en Chu-yun comes from a family with roots in Guangdong province, China. Due to her father's career in the diplomatic service, she spent part of her childhood and adolescence in Sydney, Seoul, Bangkok and Nicosia. After obtaining a Master's degree in foreign languages and literature from National Taiwan University, she began teaching in the Foreign Languages Department of the same institution in 1970, a job she held until her retirement in 2005. She is married to Wang Wen-hsing.

Li-fen Chen received her BA (Foreign Languages and Literature) from National Taiwan University, MA (English) from Wake Forest University, and PhD (Comparative Literature) from the University of Washington. She is currently Associate Professor in Humanities at the Hong Kong University of Science and Technology.

Michael Cody has a BA in Film Studies from York University and an MA in Chinese Studies from the University of Toronto. He contributed to *Dragonflies*, Shu-ning Sciban and Fred Edwards's previous anthology of short stories published by the Cornell East Asia Series, and he continues to pursue his interest in Asian languages and cultures.

Fred Edwards is a member of the editorial board of the *Toronto Star*. He has a degree in Chinese Studies from the University of Toronto and also studied at Harbin Normal University. With Shu-ning Sciban, he was coeditor of *Dragonflies: Fiction by Chinese Women in the Twentieth Century* (Cornell East Asia Series, 2003).

Howard Goldblatt, PhD, Indiana University (1974), is Research Professor of Chinese at the Department of East Asian Languages and Literatures, University of Notre Dame. Goldblatt has taught modern Chinese literature and culture for more than a quarter of a century. The foremost translator of modern and contemporary Chinese literature in the West, he has published English translations of more than thirty novels and story collections by writers from China, Taiwan and Hong Kong. His translation (with Sylvia Li-chun Lin) of *Notes of a Desolate Man* by the Taiwanese novelist Chu T'ien-wen won the 1999 "Translation of the Year" award given by the American Translators Association. He has also authored and edited half a dozen books on Chinese literature. The founding editor of the scholarly journal *Modern Chinese Literature*, he serves on the editorial and advisory boards of many scholarly and literary magazines, and has contributed essays and articles to *The Washington Post*, *The Times of London*, *Time Magazine*, *World Literature Today* and *The Los Angeles Times*, as well as scholarly books and journals.

Jia Li is a postdoctoral fellow at Queen's University, Kingston, Ontario. She received her PhD and master's degrees in second language education from the University of Toronto. She was born in Sichuan, China. During her undergraduate studies, she majored in Chinese language and literature at Chengdu University, Sichuan. In addition to her research in language and literacy development among bilinguals and second language learners, she is interested in the translation of contemporary Chinese and English literature.

Christopher Lupke is associate professor of Chinese language and culture at Washington State University where he coordinates Asian languages. He has published extensively on Wang Wen-hsing and other writers from Taiwan and recently finished a translation of Ye Shitao's *A History of Taiwan Literature*. His other publications include an edited volume from the University of Hawaii Press titled *The Magnitude of Ming: Command, Allotment and Fate in Chinese Culture*, a guest-edited volume of the scholarly journal *Asian Cinema*, and *The Cinema of Hou Hsiao-hsien*, forthcoming from the University of Illinois Press.

Ihor Pidhainy is interested in Chinese culture, literature and history. His research focuses on travel writing, biographical writings, and the intellectual tradition in China, with a strong emphasis on the later imperial period (1400–1900). He is Assistant Professor at Marietta College in Ohio.

Steven L. Riep teaches modern and contemporary Chinese literature, film and culture at Brigham Young University. After completing his dissertation on contemporary Chinese literature from Taiwan and receiving his PhD from UCLA in 2001, he spent two years as a postdoctoral fellow at the University of California, Davis. He currently is working on literature and visual culture in Nationalist Taiwan (1949–1999), religion and woman's emancipation in the short fiction of Xu Dishan, environmental themes in the essays of Yang Mu, and the function of disability in transnational Chinese cinema.

Terence Russell is Associate Professor of Chinese in the Asian Studies Centre at the University of Manitoba. He received his PhD in classical Chinese from Australian National University and has lived, studied and taught in Taiwan, the People's Republic of China, and Japan. After devoting many years to research on classical Chinese religious literature, he has recently turned his attention to modern Chinese literature, especially the literature of Taiwan's indigenous peoples. He has translated the writing of several important Taiwanese writers and recently completed a translation of the Shandong writer Zhang Wei's novels *September Fable* (Jiuyue yuyan) and *Seven Kinds of Mushrooms* (Mogu qizhong). At present he is working on a book-length translation and critical study of the writings of Syaman Rapongan, an indigenous writer from the Taos nation of Lanyu Island.

Lloyd Sciban received his PhD in Chinese philosophy from the University of Toronto and currently teaches in the Faculty of Communication and Culture at the University of Calgary. His interests include Confucian ethics and the influence of East Asian culture in Canada. Recent publications include "Concept of Human Weakness: A Brief Comparison of Christian and Confucian Thinking" (in *Wisdom in*

China and the West, The Council for Research in Values and Philosophy), "Chinese Language Media Across the West" (in *Challenging Frontiers*, University of Calgary), and "Zhu Xi's Critique of Buddhism and his Theory of Personal Cultivation" (in *Ruxuede qilun yu gongfulun* [Confucian theories of qi and personal cultivation], Guoli Taiwan daxue Dongya wenming yanjiu zhongxin).

Rowan Sciban graduated from the University of Calgary in 2009 with a Bachelor of Arts in psychology. He is currently pursuing a graduate degree in social psychology at the University of Calgary.

Shu-ning Sciban received her PhD in Chinese literature from the University of Toronto, and currently teaches at the University of Calgary. Her research interests include modern and contemporary Chinese fiction, writing by Chinese women, Chinese diaspora literature, Chinese language and computer-assisted Chinese language learning. She co-authored *Fayin: Mandarin Pronunciation* (CD-ROM) (University of Calgary Press, 2002), *Shizi: Chinese Characters* (CD-ROM) (University of Calgary Press, 2003), and also coedited *Dragonflies: Fiction by Chinese Women in the Twentieth Century* (Cornell East Asia Series, 2003).

Martin Sulev graduated from the University of Toronto in 1998 with a degree in palaeontology. He has taught English in China and is interested in Chinese films and traditional Chinese performing arts.

Jane Parish Yang received her PhD in Chinese from the University of Wisconsin-Madison and at present is Associate Professor of Chinese in the Department of Chinese and Japanese at Lawrence University in Appleton, Wisc. She served on the executive board of the Chinese Language Teachers Association, 1999–2001, and has presented papers at MLA and ACTFL/CLTA conferences and chaired two panels at AAS annual meetings. As co-chair of the Freeman Foundation grant to Lawrence University (2001–2005), she helped led small topic-specific student/faculty and larger faculty-only study tours to China, Japan and Vietnam. More than 150 students from a variety of majors and 90 faculty members drawn from various disciplines have had the opportunity to travel to Asia on these study tours. She translated Nieh Hua-ling's post-modern novel *Mulberry and Peach*, which won an American Book Award in 1990.

Acknowledgment of Copyright

Mr. Wang Wen-hsing has kindly granted copyright permission for all twenty-nine works collected in this anthology.

"Flaw" (Qainque), translated by Ch'en Chu-yun, was first published in *The Chinese PEN*, August 1973. Copyright permission for reprint granted by Taipei Chinese Center, International P.E.N.

"The Two Women" (Liang furen), translated by Li-fen Chen, was first published in *The Chinese PEN*, Summer 1978. Copyright permission for reprint granted by Taipei Chinese Center, International P.E.N.

"The Toy Revolver" (Wanju shouqiang), translated by Jane Parish Yang, was first published in *The Chinese PEN*, Spring 1982. Copyright permission for reprint granted by Taipei Chinese Center, International P.E.N.

"The Day of the Sea-Goddess" (Haibin shengmu jie), translated by Ch'en Chu-yun, was first published in *The Chinese PEN*, Spring 1986. Copyright permission for reprint granted by Taipei Chinese Center, International P.E.N.

"Line of Fate" (Mingyun de jixian), translated by Ch'en Chu-yun, was first published in *An Anthology of Contemporary Chinese Literature: Taiwan 1949-1970*. Ed. Chi Pang-yuan. Taipei: National Institute for Compilation and Translation, 1975. Copyright permission for reprint granted by National Institute for Compilation and Translation in Taiwan.

"The Black Gown" (Hei yi), translated by Ch'en Chu-yun, was first published in *An Anthology of Contemporary Chinese Literature: Taiwan 1949-1970*. Ed. Chi Pang-yuan. Taipei: National Institute for Compilation and Translation, 1975. Copyright permission for reprint granted by National Institute for Compilation and Translation in Taiwan.

Wang Wen-hsing with his parents

Wang in his university days

Wang at work

In front of the Faculty of Humanities, National Taiwan University

Professor Wang Wen-hsing and his wife, Professor Ch'en Chu-yun

CORNELL EAST ASIA SERIES

CPSIA information can be obtained
at www.ICGtesting.com
Printed in the USA
LVHW090708301219
641963LV00015B/20/P